*Prince von Metternich*

# CONSTANTIN DE GRUNWALD

# METTERNICH

*translated from the French
by Dorothy Todd*

*LONDON*
THE FALCON PRESS

First published in English in 1953
by the Falcon Press (London) Limited
6 & 7 Crown Passage, Pall Mall
London SW1
Printed in Great Britain
by the Ditchling Press
Hassocks, Sussex
Copyright 1953
by Dorothy Todd

# CONTENTS

PREFACE                                        *page*  1

   I. ROSENKAVALIER                           7

  II. THE WEDDING AT AUSTERLITZ             17

 III. CAREER                                28

 IV. HAPPY AUSTRIA                           48

   V. THE MARRIAGE OF MARIE–LOUISE          63

 VI. AT THE MARCOLINI PALACE                91

 VII. THE CONGRESS DANCES                  118

VIII. PORTRAIT BY LAWRENCE                142

 IX. THE SYSTEM                            174

  X. THE CARBONARI                        203

 XI. 'VIENNA, CAPUA OF THE MIND'          229

 XII. HIS STAR BEGINS TO WANE             250

XIII. THE MASSES AWAKE TO SPRING         274

   EPILOGUE                               292

   BIBLIOGRAPHY                           308

   INDEX                                  313

# PREFACE

THE life of Metternich, rich in glamorous performance, in dramatic incident and amorous adventure, unfolds against an impressive background of wars, high-junketing, of congresses and revolutions. It would be hard to find a more attractive theme for those who love to evoke the ghosts of history. A variety of entertaining gossip will cheer the reader's lighter moments, but stimulation for more serious thought is inherent in the ideological nature of the problems involved.

Here was a great statesman, 'Adonis' of the drawing-rooms, 'god of boundaries' for the diplomats; respected by sovereigns, adored by women, admired by colleagues and subordinates, but who throughout his life was subject to bitter criticism, to savage and enduring hatreds. Napoleon called him the biggest liar of the century; Princess Lieven (at one time his mistress) later in life described him as the world's outstanding hypocrite; Sealsfeld, Austro-American polemist, saw him as 'the most hated man in Europe'.

But Metternich never gave a fig for contemporary critics. 'In the last analysis', he said, 'posterity alone is competent to judge the men who have helped to make history. And posterity must judge us. That is the only tribunal whose verdict matters to me; the only one, of course, that I shall never know.'

Posterity, however, never quite managed to extract a clear estimate from the tangle of party prejudice, and tradition has handed us a somewhat ridiculous stock figure: a Metternich not far removed from the villains of melodrama; a boot-licking courtier—sycophant (of the type familiar to readers of romantic thrillers). Even well-known writers have gone off the rails: the popular Rostand, in *l'Aiglon*; the great Stendhal himself in *La Chartreuse de Parme* (we know that Metternich was the model for Count Mosca).

1

The cinema, today, has also helped to spread an impression of Metternich which bears little relation to fact. We even find recognised historians and journalists of impeccable reputation seriously underestimating the great statesman. And for no better reason than that he found his favourite climate in the *salons* of the day; that he was only really 'at home' in Courts and Embassies; that he was—and to the end of his life remained—an inveterate enemy of revolution.

Thus Albert Sorel saw nothing in him but a super-diplomat of the old school and a fop to boot. The Grand Duke Nicolas Michailovitch, distinguished Russian historian, did not hesitate to describe his much-vaunted political strategy as little more than 'a natural facility for making dupes'. He added that Metternich's strength lay exclusively in bluff and an outstanding ability for making use of women.

The Chancellor has been described in turn as: 'the man who betrayed Napoleon', 'traitor to Germany', 'the man who dug the grave of the Austrian Empire', and so *ad libitum*, according to taste.

But when we come to think of it, were his methods, his character, his outlook really so reprehensible? Did he ever betray the only causes to which he was seriously committed: the prestige of the House of Habsburg, the maintenance of a balance of power in Europe? Was it unpardonable to stand as the guardian of law and order and to be known as the ruthless enemy of sedition at a time when our continent, just emerging from revolutionary upheavals, was above all craving stability and peace...?

It is conceivable that our disillusioned epoch might bring a more impartial judgment not only to the man but also—and more important—to his achievement. The 'stupid nineteenth century' believed in progress; it was natural in such a period that the famous 'system' of Metternich should be consigned to perdition together with its illustrious sponsor. But opinions have changed: we no longer confuse material progress with the evolution of more spiritual values. We have learnt, in the political field, to appreciate those intervals—however short—which hold up the headlong scuttle of the human race towards some unknown

2

objective. 'Whereas I must appreciate a desire for and the hope of human progress as laudable sentiments, I am by no means convinced that the latter is borne out by the facts. . . . There is neither steady progress nor an automatic and consistent improvement in human affairs. . . . For beneath the general flux which misleads and excites us, lies some majestic and profound law of stability.'[1]

The Austrian Chancellor would certainly have agreed with the contemporary French thinker. He had been born, he used to say, a century too early—or too late.

In any event, the scope of our research has fortunately widened during the last few years. For half a century the Chancellor's biographers drew their most valuable documentation from the eight thick volumes of *Mémoires et Documents*, published in 1880 by Prince Richard von Metternich, edited by A. de Klinkowstroem. But Prince Richard whose chief aim was not unnaturally to clear his father's reputation as against the combined attacks of the Left Wing and the Pan-Germans, had neither available means nor in fact any marked desire to publish all that his illustrious progenitor had written through the years. Indeed, the Chancellor himself had done a bit of editing to start with, hoping to hand down a fully authenticated justification of his political procedure. At the moment of publication, a member of the Austrian royal family further took upon himself the thankless task of censor. It was of course inevitable that the Memoirs should show *lacunae*, that certain awkward facts should be ignored, certain compromising statements simply suppressed.

Since then, the collapse of the Austro-Hungarian Empire has made available secrets once jealously guarded in the archives of Court and State at Vienna. Rich material was garnered from the forty thousand dossiers connected with the Prince's ministerial and diplomatic career. A number of biographies of Metternich appeared after the war, in Austria, Germany and England; foremost, a monumental work by Professor Heinrich von Srbik (two large volumes, thirteen hundred pages of text proper, one hundred and sixty pages of bibliographical notes). This work reconstructs and explains the Chancellor's life and work with consummate

1. Charles Maurras: *Mes idées politiques*, 1937.

3

ability. Its wide historical significance and remarkable integrity have combined to make a document which no other biographer can afford to ignore.

France has produced nothing similar. Since the days of Charles de Mazade (*A Chancellor of the old school*, published in 1888), and since Albert Sorel's brilliant contribution, no original work has appeared. There was room for something new.[1]

Anchored firmly in established facts and authentic documents, conforming to the recognised discipline of historical method, the author has here sought to bring to life a great historical figure within the natural framework of his country and his times. He has tried to make Metternich human; to enable the reader to understand him.

Research in the archives of the Foreign Office, at Paris; in the secret archives of Court and State, at Vienna; in the secret royal archives of Prussia at Berlin-Dahlem, have enabled him to supply almost entirely unpublished material in several chapters of this book.

In attempting a highly controversial and difficult subject, the author has found a certain advantage in his own position as a Russian emigré. It has allowed him to consider the Metternich question objectively, immune from the influence of national bias in any direction. During his frequent visits to Central Europe, he was able to get in touch with local sources of information, had free access to original documents, breathed the very air of towns and countries where his hero had lived.

Furthermore, his own youth passed at Saint Petersburg before the war, in the same atmosphere of *ancien régime*, enables him to recollect a few of the older aristocrats and statesmen, survivals of a type which no longer exists—or at least no longer plays an active part in the affairs of state. These old-time dignitaries, German or Russian, sponsors of an enlightened autocracy, were still speaking the language of Metternich; they help us to understand him.

1. Professor Bibl's book (Ed. Payot) did no more than recapitulate this author's German works. A study by M. André Robert—an interesting account of the principles of the new Austrian school—appeared in the *Hommes d'Etat* series (Ed. Desclée de Brouwer).

Enriched by a plethora of contemporary evidence, a portrait of Prince Metternich began to take shape; his human weaknesses, his doctrinaire opinions, his frivolity, love of women and pleasure, but also his incomparable qualities.

We might compare Metternich with certain famous characters of Marcel Proust: the affected and pedantic nature of his telegrams and sometimes of his more intimate letters anticipates M. de Norpois; the shrill, piercing voice is that of M. de Charlus; his social arrogance, his egotistical indifference to the sufferings or even death of others, suggests the Duc de Guermantes.

And yet, from a wider view, such literary analogies tend to understate the case. For the Prince was something more than a mere snob. He was the most important diplomat of modern times; he was also—whatever his enemies might say—a very great statesman. To posterity, he stands an embodiment of the best qualities of Austria, his adopted country. He strikes us also as a thinker whose prophetic instinct enabled him to see the dangers which threaten European civilisation in our time.

The political theories of a man who liked to describe himself as 'a rock against which the waves of disorder beat in vain', are not to everyone's liking; they are nevertheless worth consideration. Metternich's tragic mistake lay not so much in defending his own social concept and that of his class, as in attempting to make politics (essentially relative) into an absolute. But this is a fault of which he by no means enjoys the monopoly.

And was he wrong, too, in trying to maintain intact the age-old dynasty of the Habsburgs?

'Repercussions of the fall of that colossus, the Austrian Empire, could scarcely fail to rock the rest of Europe', said Metternich's contemporary the Archduke Charles. The disappearance of Austro-Hungary from the map has created a void which will not be easy to fill. Central Europe has been *Balkanised* thereby creating new centres of disturbance and discontent. Oppressed nations have recovered their independence, but the shadow of Metternich, advocate of supra-national unity, floats over the Danubian basin, still evoking memories and regrets. . . .

5

# Preface

This book was written in close collaboration with Madame Jean de Savonnières to whom the author wishes to convey his warmest thanks.

Among many other distinguished helpers, the author wishes gratefully to mention: Metternich's grand-daughter, H.S.H. Princess von Oettingen-Spielberg. This venerable octogenarian, in her lovely palace of the Fasanengasse, evoked for him in an unforgettable interview (and in French learnt at the Court of Napoleon III) the far-off years when as a child she was dandled on the knee of her illustrious ancestor. Acknowledgment is also due to the famous biographer Herr Heinrich Ritter von Srbik, who was kind enough to offer much good counsel.

Herren Bittner and Gross, curators of the archives of Court and State, at Vienna, are amongst his benefactors, as also the authorities of the Prussian secret royal archives, at Berlin-Dahlem and the authorities of the Quai d'Orsay, at Paris. All these greatly facilitated a difficult research in their several institutions.

## TRANSLATOR'S NOTE

I. When the Emperor first appears in this book, he was still Francis II of the Holy Roman Empire. Later (most authorities give the date as 1804) he resigned that title and became Francis I of Austria, only.
II. Count Lieven was only created Prince in 1826.

# I

# ROSENKAVALIER

*I was born a Cabinet minister.*—METTERNICH

IN July 1792, the free imperial city of Frankfort was in gala
mood. For the second time in two years, Electors, Princes and
the great German aristocracy had assembled for the crowning of
an Emperor with all the pomp befitting such an occasion. Francis II
of Habsburg-Lorraine, grandson of Maria Theresa and nephew
of Marie-Antoinette, Queen of France, had just succeeded after
the very brief reign of his father, Leopold. Every house and inn
was full to overflowing; the wives of French diplomats bewailed
the general lack of comfort and the indigestible, stodgy nature of
German food.[1] In magnificent weather, Francis entered the city.
His procession consisted of more than a hundred golden coaches.

The following day, countless thousands acclaimed the young
Emperor proceeding to his coronation simply robed in a dalmatic.
In the afternoon, the general festivities began: in the atmosphere
of a mediaeval fair. That evening, Count Esterhazy, electoral
ambassador from the satellite Kingdom of Bohemia, entertained
his sovereign at a sumptuous banquet followed by a ball. In this
welter of gold and diamonds, *rococo* was the rule: that Louis XV
or bastard Louis XVI style which with its silks and gildings and
*rocaille* had captivated every Court in Europe. When the young
Emperor had been installed upon his throne, under an immense
white satin baldachin, the hautbois, flutes and violins started up
with a dance and in a space which had been cleared for that purpose, a graceful young couple advanced shyly to open the ball.
The twenty-year-old Master of Ceremonies of 'The Catholic

1. Mémoires du Comte de Bray.

7

bench of the College of the Counts of Westphalia' was dressed in pale green satin with silver buttons and a lace cravat and wore a rose; his partner wore a dress of pink satin embroidered with wreaths of flowers inlaid with white muslin. Both strikingly handsome and essentially German, blond, with twinkling blue eyes: two pieces of Dresden china. Clement von Metternich, with the young Princess of Mecklenburg (future Queen Louise of Prussia) on his arm, was making his first bow to history. These two young people were to stand out, gigantic silhouettes against the whole background of the nineteenth century and almost down to our own time. The little princess who became the mother of William I, and educated the future Emperor of Germany, died in 1888. Her dancing partner, the future Chancellor, towards the end of his life was still giving lessons in political *savoir faire* to that Franz-Josef, Emperor of Austria who unleashed the war of 1914, and thus was almost our contemporary.

Invisible chains link the present with the past, and a pattern of events which still influences us today was in process of weaving during those dazzling festivities when the last 'Roman' Emperor of German nationality was crowned.

Clement-Wenceslaus-Lothaire von Metternich spent his life 'on parade'. It seems quite natural that he should make his *début* in such a setting, amidst the pomp and splendour of an imperial coronation, surrounded by an aristocracy *en fête*. Before he turned twenty, he was already on terms of familiarity with 'the great', already initiated into the arts of love. Scarcely more than adolescent, he had won the heart of a young woman of brilliant lineage and great beauty. Marie-Constance de Caumont la-Force was French; daughter of Lamoignon, Keeper of the Seals, she had been married in 1788, at the age of sixteen, to a brother of the famous Comtesse de Balbi, favourite of the King's brother, the Comte de Provence.

Just after the Revolution, the storm-tossed couple came together again at Mainz and it was there that Constance got to know her young Knight of the Rose.

If we are to judge by contemporary opinion, Constance at that time must have been a wholly delightful woman. 'She dazzled', said the Marquis de Bouillé in his memoirs; 'the first flush and brilliance of youth combined with the seductive qualities of a supremely beautiful woman. Her features were distinguished, delicate, agreeable, rather than strictly regular; they overpowered her admirers by their gracious tranquillity, becoming more beautiful in animation, yet virginal, almost child-like. She was tall and slight, moved lightly with a sinuous ease. No painter could have wished a better model for Hebe or a Psyche. Such qualities were fated to conquer all comers; how indeed could a man resist them when added to all this the lady was a bit of a coquette—the more effective in that she operated under a guise of ingenuousness, one might almost say of innocence.'

'I loved her as a young man loves', Metternich wrote later to the Countess Lieven;[1] 'she loved me with all the fervour of an innocent heart. We both desired what in fact we never sought: I only lived for her and for my studies. She had nothing to do all day except to love me: her nights were passed with her husband, but I fancy that she was thinking more of me than of him.' The young Marquis de Bouillé also seems to have been of the party: 'I could ill defend myself', he confessed, 'from a seduction which flattering pride and natural inclination became the more pungent by the very fact that I was not the sole recipient of the lady's favours. And this obligation to share her solicitude, this twin distinction, far from putting any painful rivalry between myself and Metternich had established a kind of intimacy between us, almost a friendship. The coincidence of our affections appears to have drawn us together rather than the reverse and our hearts overflowed in agreeable communication on our frequent walks (invariably together), towards Madame de Caumont's house in that lovely *alley of the Rhine*.'

We are well in the note, here, of *liaisons dangereuses*. What a training in frivolity, cynicism and dissimulation for the future diplomat! Had Bouillé, perhaps, already seen in Metternich 'duplicity, that inhuman niggardly spirit, that cold calculation which later were by no means negligible aids to the achievement of fortune and high rank'? One must have been blind not to spot in

1. December 1st, 1818.

·9

the young master of ceremonies an immoderate and unscrupulous ambition which was his later characteristic; to spot too that vanity which impelled him to combine the lightness and elegance of the French tradition (its fatuity, also) with the inflexibility, not to say dullness, natural to Germans.[1]

For Constance's young admirer, ex-dancing partner of Louise von Mecklenburg, might reasonably have considered himself as destined from birth to the highest honours. He came of a powerful noble line. His family tree went back beyond the reach of memory. In the early Middle Ages, it had been whispered to the Emperor Henry I, the bird-charmer (or might it perhaps have been to Charlemagne, himself?), that a Knight of his Court, the Chevalier Metter, was about to betray him. 'I will never believe that', cried the sovereign. 'Metter?—no—Metter nicht', and the suffix remained attached to a name already famous. Through several centuries, the family supplied the Empire with eminent champions, including three Elector-Princes of Mainz. It was to them that the Metternichs owed those rich territories of Winneburg, Beilstein and Königswart, in Bohemia, which had been added to their ancestral domain, a château near Coblenz.

Young Clement's father was himself a high dignitary of the Imperial Court, he had been hereditary Chamberlain to the Archbishop of Mainz, and had held since 1791 the important post of Governor of the Low Countries.

In the setting of the Frankfurt coronation, that gigantic comic-opera performed before the eyes of certain cynical observers, Clement von Metternich played the role of *jeune premier*. His father was the leading *comique*, heavy, sententious, solemn and swollen with pride under his overpowering wig. The Comte de Bray detected 'a certain affected ease accompanied by a fundamental pretentiousness which peeped out quite often'. Treilhard, the *conventionnel*, who was later to meet him at the Congress of Rastadt, described him as 'cold, arrogant, impertinent on

---

1. Marquis de Bouillé, 1769-1812: *Souvenirs et fragments pour servir aux Mémoires de ma vie et de mon temps,* published by P. L. de Kermaingant. Paris 1908. Bouillé was the son of that General Marquis de Bouillé, who prepared the flight of Varennes; the General and his son had emigrated.

occasion, a stickler for convention, endowed with little under-standing, and consequently obstinate as a mule'.[1]

Jean Debry and Roberjot, two other Jacobin delegates to the same congress, formed this impression of the minister: 'starchy, over-ceremonious, unintelligent and obstinate'.

The emissaries of revolutionary France had no use for all this nonsense devised by etiquette to cover the shortcomings of insig-nificant men elevated only by their stilts. For hadn't Francis George von Metternich actually proposed to receive them sitting under a dais, 'as if encased in a shrine', and had only compromised after their protest by 'evacuating this position in favour of a full length portrait of the Emperor with an armchair turned about in such a way that no man could turn his behind to-wards it'?[2]

He was really quite a good fellow, that pompous old Franz-Georg von Metternich-Winneburg zu Beilstein, worldly and a bit of a philosopher, supremely cynical about the political up-heavals of his time. 'This business will work out one way or another, like everything else', was his favourite maxim. He was never in a hurry: the Archduchess Marie-Christine begged her brother not to send her letters care of Franz-Georg von Metter-nich because the Count only opened his mail when he was so inclined. The Emperor Francis however appreciated the loyalty and probity of that phlegmatic individual who was at least sport-ing enough to ruin himself in order to cut a good figure at the coronation and on other public occasions, and who did in fact dazzle the gaping crowd by the gorgeousness and brilliance of his liveries 'scarlet velvet, trimmed with heavy gold braid'.[3]

But this elderly statesman enjoyed above all the supreme ad-vantage of having a remarkable wife. The Countess Beatrice von Metternich (*née* von Kagenegg), in youth a protégée of the Empress Maria Theresa, was generally much admired until late

1. Letter from Treilhard to Talleyrand, December 18th, 1797.
2. Jean Debry: *Discours préliminaire et historique sur le congrès de Rastadt,* under date of Thermidor 20th, in the year VIII.
3. 'Count Metternich liked to cut a terrific figure', wrote the Comte de Bray, on the occasion of a former coronation in 1790; 'he paid ten thousand florins for liveries which Prince Salm had bought for 28,000, but had been forbidden to use ... his retinue was the most brilliant at the Court of Austria.'

in life. Innumerable old miniatures reveal her finely chiselled features, the oval face shows certain signs of strength, expressive mouth and eloquent eyes; as one looks, one can well understand the influence that this intelligent woman, ambitious and scheming, must have exercised among her aristocratic coterie.

A mother's heart did not take long to be convinced that neither her second son, 'that good Pépé', lazy and obstinate, nor Pauline, gawk of a girl, possessing not one shred of personality or charm, would ever make history. Nothing would be added to the family reputation by either. Thus all her ambition centred on Clement, 'the ewe lamb of his good old mother', on that charming youth who was already drawing all hearts, spoilt child of destiny cut out for an accomplished courtier, and, who knows? cut out, too, perhaps for a great statesman. Unquestionably gifted with a sense of humour, indulgent as much to the failings of others as to her own, the Countess Beatrice for years had set herself to develop in her son the art of pleasing and the gift of *savoir faire*. 'In Germany, you must admire German music', she wrote, 'and French music when in France, and the same applies to most things.' And stout papa, piling Ossa upon Pelion: 'Comport yourself seemly, be helpful to all men and never underestimate old women whose gossip can make or unmake a young man's career more than you might suppose [*sic*]. Be flexible, be obliging, that's the most important.' At seventeen, Clement was to hear his mother describe him as 'the most successful messenger I know'.

But his more serious studies were not on that account neglected; he was given the best teachers; sent to the best schools. At fifteen, Clement matriculated at the same time as his brother Joseph, at the University of Strasbourg.

He was distinguished from the other students, however, in that his fees were charged to the chapter of the Bishopric of Mainz, a subsidy awarded to such great families of the Empire as possessed over sixteen quarterings. Prince Maximilian von Zwei-Brücke, colonel and owner of the Royal Alsatian regiment (later first King of Bavaria) received the young men into his home at Strasbourg and kept a fatherly eye upon them. Clement lived consistently in such impressive and luxurious surroundings; and his more modest fellow students described him as 'refined, a liar and a braggart'.

He certainly attended his university lectures, but he also spent much time in physical exercise, he rode and swam and fenced. He was later to claim that his fencing master, a certain M. Justet, had at one time been the teacher of Napoleon.

After Strasbourg, he went to Mainz to study law. The peaceful little Rhenish city had then all the look of a small Versailles. Since July 1791, the Comte de Provence and the Comte d'Artois had held court there. And it was in that attractive, if somewhat dissolute society of the French *émigrés*, that the young Count Clement became friendly with his delightful Marie-Constance.

At Strasbourg, he appears to have sat under Professor Koch, famous trainer of diplomatists: Talleyrand and Benjamin Constant had both been his students. At Mainz, he attended the lectures of Nicholas Vogt, official historian of the German Empire, those of Johannes von Müller, historian and well known as a journalist; he also studied with George Forster, a scholarly companion of the famous navigator, James Cook. Clement thus acquired the rudiments of political and natural science dividing a somewhat dilettante interest between them. The young Metternichs were never completely alone nor left to their own devices; two tutors accompanied them wherever they went. For, stressing his tolerance as a freemason, the old Count chose both a Catholic and a protestant to be his sons' preceptors: the abbé Bertrand and the Rousseauist, Simon; they were in fact both imbued with large-hearted and somewhat revolutionary ideas. Simon is the kindest man on earth; 'he weeps in ecstasy; his affections, his philanthropy embrace the whole world'.[1] Later, this paragon was to become the most sanguinary of Jacobins, a disciple of Marat; on the eve of the tenth of August, he was to help Santerre prepare the attack on the Tuileries; he also became a Commissar of the administration and finished his life quietly as professor of German in the college of Louis le Grand. Bertrand and Simon might well be pleased with their pupil: a true son of his age, he faced the world with a sceptical smile, he accepted the new enlightenment

1. Metternich: *Mémoires.*

13

just enough to avoid losing his religious faith; he was able to talk about anything with ease, always supposing that no particular depth would be required; in short they made him a 'gentleman' par excellence, a *rosenkavalier*.

But into what sphere was life about to carry this young aristocrat, spoilt child of fate? Late in the night, the fireworks of the coronation petered out, the music of the dance was heard no more. A few days and all this brilliant host would have departed and Frankfurt would regain her accustomed calm. The Court would move to Mainz where the King of Prussia was to meet the Emperor. The Elector of Mainz made it a point of honour to put up a good show. All Germany rushed at his bidding, some fifty Princes, about a hundred Earls and Barons constituted an almost feudal court for the sovereigns of Austria and of Prussia. The strictest etiquette prevailed. Some French officers of the bodyguard, invited to a ball, having permitted themselves quite casually to ask the Empress to dance: 'such impertinence, such lack of respect, such disregard for convention' caused a scandal: 'Frenchmen will never again be invited.'[1]

Levees and royal receptions, banquets, reviews, trooping of the colours, and meetings of statesmen went on from day to day. And what was the object of this coming together? To prepare a crusade against revolutionary France.

The coronation of Francis II of Germany was the final gesture of an era about to close; over the water on the other side of father Rhine, a new day was dawning. At Frankfurt and Mainz, we have seen a panorama of old-world splendour, golden coaches, bedizened court functionaries, footmen in wigs at glamorous social functions, the usual scramble for precedence among arrogant courtiers. At Paris, anarchy reigned: the brilliant Court of Versailles was scattered to the four winds, the nobility tramped the roads to exile, hatreds, long smouldering grudges and repressed desires were now given full rein. The royal house in imminent danger were expecting the worst.

That same July, month in which Francis II made his state entry into Frankfurt, had seen the last King of the old régime

1. Comte de Bray: *Mémoires.*

14

in France swearing allegiance to the Constitution, on the Champs de Mars, during the feast of the Federation.

From his lips, such an oath was little less than an abdication. At Frankfurt, processions, illuminations, magnificent *fiesta*; at the Tuileries, agony of mind, humiliation and despair. The Queen, Marie-Antoinette, attended the ceremony of the Federation, 'her eyes swollen by tears'; the good Germans of Frankfurt were also weeping, but theirs were sentimental tears as they saw their new Emperor looking 'so young, so kind, so innocent' (the words are those of George Forster, the future founder of the republic of Mainz). At Frankfurt, we see the endorsement of an age-old form of government. In France, all established form of government had fallen. One month later, that tragic tenth of August, the crowd unleashed was to invade the Tuileries (they had been there before on the twentieth of June), to invade and give the knock-out blow to the monarchy of France. Stupendous conflagration which rapidly spread: by April, France had declared war on the House of Habsburg, invaded Belgium and was preparing to invade the whole of our ancient Europe with a view to its regeneration.

Appalled, his eyes literally starting out of his head, young Clement von Metternich saw a spectre of social upheaval menacing all that he held dear: privilege, money, his social standing, his most cherished convictions, his whole conception of life.

And from that moment, during all those impressive ceremonies which were taking part but a few steps removed from the convulsions of France, he began to feel predestined as 'a guardian of that social order' now so sorely menaced.

But the spectre of revolution pursued him. In 1789 he witnessed the pillage of the Strasbourg Town Hall, 'an act of vandalism committed by a populace out of its mind'. He was soon to see the *sans-culottes* invading Mainz, Coblenz, even his birthplace the village of Metternich where the over-optimistic Prussian army was quartered at the beginning of the campaign—an army which would never see victory. Later still, Brussels was 'overflowed by the Jacobin lava', his father was driven from his posts of Imperial Ambassador and Governor and lost all his possessions

15

on the left bank of the Rhine: three and a half square German miles of land, 6,200 'vassals', 50,000 florins of income. The upheaval of Europe thus assumed for young Clement the aspect of a family catastrophe, a personal drama.

Two years after the Frankfurt coronation, in August 1794, the foppish dancing partner of Louise von Mecklenburg was to publish an anonymous tract 'on the necessity of arming all populations adjoining the French frontiers'.

'The French Revolution', he said, 'has reached a pitch whence it menaces the whole of Europe . . . the current war is following much the same pattern as all primitive tribal migration . . . destruction of historic monuments and of works of art, nations reduced to slavery; a striking analogy with the behaviour of barbaric hordes from the North in the Vth and VIth centuries. . . . The object of these modern barbarians is to break with all social convention, to destroy accepted principles and confiscate property. . . . Princes and people, linked by close reciprocal ties, days of grave unrest are upon you, you can only expect a few moments of your present peace. . . . Use the same methods which your enemies have found so effective. . . . Unite, the brigand hordes will flee before your face; reputable men of all nations will flock to your banners. Europe will owe to you her preservation and future generations their peace.'

The Chancellor-to-be, the life-long and relentless enemy of revolution, the future inventor of the Metternich 'system' was raising his voice for the first time.

16

# II
# THE WEDDING
# AT AUSTERLITZ

O  N the twenty-seventh of September, 1795, the brilliant sun
   shone over a quiet Moravian village preparing to celebrate a
   family occasion—it was the sun of Austerlitz. The daughter
of the local *Châtelain*, Princess Eléonore, heiress of the great name
of Kaunitz (only grand-daughter of Maria Theresa's famous Chancellor), was about to marry Count Clement von Metternich. An
attractive young person, small, twenty years old, two years
younger than her handsome fiancé, suitors from the greatest
families of Austria had sought her hand: a Liechtenstein, a Palffy,
a Colloredo. But Metternich appeared upon the scene, and immediately the girl lost her heart. 'The type of young man most
likely to appeal to a debutante's fancy', wrote Eléonore's aunt,
Princess Liechtenstein; 'he is modest and enterprising by turns.'
Without even waiting for her father's consent—every effort had
been made to impress Prince Kaunitz by comparing Clement von
Metternich with the young Pitt—Eléonore had secretly assured
him of her own.

The fiancé's feelings were considerably less romantic. 'One
marries', he used to say later, 'to have children and not to indulge
one's inclinations.' It seems he 'married with regret'. He had not
forgotten the beautiful French emigrée, Marie Constance de
Caumont. But circumstances made his marriage opportune: his
family had been ruined, dispossessed; their prosperity and his own
stood in desperate need of renewal.

Not that he had been obliged to fritter his time away in un-
suitable surroundings like so many others of his rank during that

17

unsettled period which followed the coronation. The young Metternich had travelled in England, 'in very favourable circumstances'; he had met the most important men of that outstanding era: Pitt, Fox, Burke, Sheridan, all had received him 'with great affability'. The Prince of Wales, 'first gentleman of Europe', had taken the young visitor into his own immediate circle, into that privileged society of great ladies and beautiful courtesans for whom Beau Brummell set the fashion. From the admiral's flagship he watched a review of the Grand Fleet, just off the Isle of Wight. Four hundred sailing vessels, 'no more beautiful sight could ever meet the eye'. On his return journey, he had come under fire from the English cannon, in Dunkerque Harbour.

After that, he accompanied his father to Vienna. At the age of twenty-three, he first made acquaintance with that capital where he was later to play the leading part for many decades.

The Metternichs were received politely but with a certain coldness. They meant little to haughty Austrian aristocrats and eminent ministers of the Hof burg. Who were these 'foreigners', scions of a Rhenish family, scarcely known even on the Danube: the stodgy father to some extent discredited on account of an unsuccessful mission to Belgium (furthermore dispossessed of all his lands), the son, pretentious, flippant, rather too handsome, rather too 'French'! Doors scarcely opened had shut again in their faces. They had to take stock of the situation.

Countess Beatrix, called in turn to the capital, had remembered just at the right moment a friend of her childhood, Princess von Oettingen-Spielberg, who had since married a Kaunitz and who had a marriageable daughter. The prestige of the name of Kaunitz stood high: that friend, *confidante*, and faithful counsellor of the Empress Maria Theresa (the greatest diplomat of the eighteenth century; instigator of the Franco-Austrian alliance) had conferred upon it his own inimitable lustre. All doors would be open to the man who married Eléonore: riches, power, court favour, and a brilliant career would be his.

Clement arriving in haste from Bohemia cut a gallant figure in the joust. And the bells of a modest village church were now pealing to celebrate the weddings of Austerlitz: the marriage of

Clement and Eléonore, and of six young peasant couples. The ceremony was followed by banquets, a pheasant shoot, by games of lotto and country dances.

Metternich had now achieved his ambition. He had married a considerable heiress, member of a family with a great political tradition, an outstanding figure in the Austrian scene. What advantage would he take of his new position? He always claimed he 'had no natural aptitude for intrigue', that he 'detested Courts and everything to do with them'. 'With me, all that goes against the grain. I don't like standing. . . . I dislike fixed hours. . . . I was never made for my present profession. . . .' On the other hand, he claimed a 'marked taste for the natural sciences, for medicine'. 'I managed to surmount all squeamishness and spent much time in hospitals and the anatomy theatre. I should much have preferred not to enter public life, to spend my time in pursuit of science. I only abandoned those studies for want of leisure. Had I been a Capo d'Istria, I might have stayed where I was and become a doctor.'

We need not take such words too seriously. Child of that eighteenth century then drawing to a close, Metternich, alert and curious, very naturally took an interest in the natural sciences as in every other type of human knowledge. But when it comes to being a scholar, much more a doctor, we can only regard that as a joke. The son of an ex-Governor, Master of Ceremonies so well in his role at Frankfurt, could he ever seriously have hesitated in the choice of a career? And now that he had also by marriage become the grandson of Kaunitz, whose political mantle had to some extent descended upon him, young Metternich had taken on new duties which he was not free to shelve. He received his first training in political matters as intermittent private secretary to his father during the latter's term of office in the Low Countries.

Shortly after Clement's marriage, the old Count had been reinstated in his sovereign's favour, and sent to represent the Emperor at the Congress of Rastadt. Clement went in his suite as delegate of the Westphalian Counts— 'there is nothing duller under the dome of Heaven than a ball at Rastadt', he wrote to his young wife. There were about a hundred men, almost all ministers or *députés* and about eight or ten women, half of them over fifty. But his wife, of course, was not told about those little suppers with actresses in private rooms, or the gambling with which he tried to divert his boredom. [1]

In that old Imperial city, he met, for the first time, representatives of revolutionary France and was surprised to find them 'very polite, acquainted with etiquette, calling everyone by his right name and title'. But he never could stomach them. 'I seem to see just a squad of guillotiners, Septembrist hooligans, and I am revolted.' The Republicans' clothes seemed more than anything else to shock this young 'gentleman of the old school': 'the masters wear middle-class garments, frock coat with trousers and look as one would hesitate to look in the early morning; their servants look like burglars. One would die of fright, I imagine, meeting even the best of them in a lonely wood.'

He had some negotiations with Treilhard and obtained an indemnity for the landowners he represented in respect of their property on the right bank of the Rhine. He drew pessimistic conclusions about the situation in general. 'The Empire has gone to blazes. Heaven knows how far this fire will spread. But certainly there is every reason to suppose that the rest of Europe will be shaken to its foundations by the dynamic pressure of forty million men all with the same objective.'

The only man with whom he seemed to have anything in common was . . . an aide-de-camp of General Bonaparte. [2]

At Rastadt, as indeed wherever he appeared, Clement von Metternich did not pass unnoticed. French newspapers began to speak of him and they supply us with the first detailed portrait we possess: 'Count Metternich', wrote *Le Publiciste*, 'is very young. But one can already detect his potentialities. Some day he may follow in the footsteps of his father; he might do so more quickly were he less infatuated by that personal charm which he seems to have inherited from his mother. He might also profitably realize that having been born with a silver spoon in

1. *Le Publiciste*, 5th of Vendemaire, in the year VIII.
2. L. Pingaud et Montarlot: *Le Congrès de Rastadt*, 1912.

his mouth will no longer be a substitute in the Europe of tomorrow for more solid attainments. And these are not acquired
in gambling dens . . . or even in less reputable places. But in spite
of weaknesses understandable in one so young, we find an unusually mellow personality, wit and capacities which might well
some day bring him into prominence. He should not however
mistake haughtiness for dignity, and since he himself consorts
with low company he should refrain from treating certain better
men disdainfully . . . wherein he shows himself irresponsible, to
say the least.'

After the Congress of Rastadt, Metternich retired for several
years from public life and lived in idleness; in summer as a
country squire, in winter at the capital, assiduous in aristocratic
drawing-rooms and among certain esoteric groups of scholars.
But he was only waiting for the propitious moment to reappear.
And it was merely bluff to show so little enthusiasm when at last
Francis II offered him the post of Plenipotentiary at Dresden.[1] To
which Metternich replied: 'Your Majesty desires me to assume
duties for which I feel myself little qualified; I submit, Sire, to
your commands: May Your Majesty never question my
goodwill—only my competence. I will do my best but Your
Majesty, I hope, will permit me to retire from the foreign service
should I ever feel inadequate to my appointed task.' Francis II
was not to live long enough to see that day; it was his son and
successor who, forty-seven years later, accepted Metternich's
resignation.

The road now lay open before him—a long sequence of hon-
ours and great responsibilities. At twenty-nine, Minister at
Dresden, representing the Emperor at one of the most important
German Courts.

At that time, Dresden was enjoying a calm which contrasted
strongly with the general anxiety of Europe; a real oasis in the
desert. 'Were one to judge things by the aspect of this Court the
world might have come to a standstill', Matternich remarked.

---

1. Before he died, the old Chancellor Kaunitz had recommended his grand-
daughter's husband to the Emperor as 'an attractive young man, agreeable and
witty, and worthy of some high diplomatic post'.

'Indeed if etiquette and sartorial convention, combined with rigorous and automatic procedure were enough to supply a solid basis to the State, Saxony would be politically on sure ground. The rotation of its gala days; its customs, nothing had changed since the middle of the eighteenth century.' Bonaparte had already been appointed Pro-Consul, and the ladies of the Saxon Court were wearing crinolines.

Some distinguished diplomats were to be found in this baroque little Court; Elliott, for instance, the English Minister, a mild eccentric who in the course of a mission to Copenhagen had not hesitated on his own responsibility to declare war on Denmark. He always, even amidst the calm of that Dresden backwater, managed to find enough material to enable him to send two long reports, every week, to London. 'If I come to hear of anything which might interest my Government, I inform them; if I have nothing, I invent my news and cancel it by the following mail.'

And then there were chance visitors: young Nesselrode, future Russian Chancellor, who quickly recognised in Metternich a man of parts. 'He certainly does not lack wit,' Nesselrode said a few years later, 'indeed he seems to have more of that quality than almost all the other Viennese pundits put together; moreover, he is agreeable enough when he wishes, good looking, invariably in love, but absent-minded, a characteristic even more dangerous in diplomacy than in pursuit of passion.'[1]

A rapidly sketched portrait, but everything of importance is there. Since the days of Augustus of Saxony and Aurore von Koenigsmark, Dresden had been a privileged centre of amorous intrigue. The young and attractive diplomatist lost no opportunity. It was in Saxony that he fell victim for the first time to irresistible Russian charms. Princess Katherine Bagration, *née* Countess Skavoronski, suddenly appeared in the salons of Dresden. Only just turned twenty, she had recently married a general, the future hero of Borodino. 'Picture a young face white as alabaster, with cheeks of palest pink, fine features, a sweet but by no means vacuous expression, conveying sensibility. A

1. Nesselrode to his father, April 25th, 1806: *Archives de Comte Nesselrode*, Vol. III, page 131.

tendency to short-sight gives her an air of timidity, something vaguely tentative, she is small but with a perfect figure, has a touch of Oriental languor added to something like Andalusian charm.'[1]

Metternich immediately fell violently in love. His own insipid consort was soon forgotten. A liaison began; nine months later, a daughter was born whom Katherine had the effrontery to have baptised as Clementine in order to leave no doubt as to the child's paternity. She was already showing that contempt for public opinion which later, at the time of the Congress of Vienna, earned her the nickname of 'naked angel', on account of her *décolletages* which went as far as—or beyond—propriety.

And yet, she was little more than a child—engaging, amusing, a child of somewhat easy virtue—which stands out if one compares her with that other type of Russian womanhood, Wilhelmine de Biron de Courlande (future Duchesse de Sagan), who walked simultaneously onto the stage at Dresden, and into the life of Metternich. Wilhelmine was also very young; she, too, had recently married a soldier, Prince de Rohan Guémenée, an *émigré* general, then serving with the Austrian army. But she already had all the makings of a *femme fatale*; she had rather prominent features and dark expressive eyes, was exotic and seductive, serious, slender and very tall. Wrists and ankles were small and bony, she had golden ringlets, by temperament was restless and unstable. 'A volcano belching ice. She is past-mistress in that characteristic of northern women, combining a most disorderly life with all the outward signs of respectability.'[2] She has been called the most immoral woman of her times. Metternich credited her with much wit, considerable understanding and good judgment. For the first time in his life he had met a woman who 'always desired what she didn't do, and always did what her judgment disapproved', 'she staggers from one folly to the next, breaks the seventh commandment seven times a day, gives little more importance to love than to a good dinner', and all this without moving a hair.

Even an experienced roué might have fallen into the trap. But

1. De la Garde: *Souvenirs du Congrès de Vienne.*
2. *Mémoires de Madame de Boigne,* Vol. I, page 228.

from the first the young ambassador was up against an impossible task: the task of inducing this elusive woman to act according to reason. It was the beginning of a long and painful adventure, which continued through all the vicissitudes of Metternich's diplomatic career, to say nothing of the vicissitudes of Wilhelmina's amorous career, up to the time of the Congress of Vienna. Metternich persisted obstinately, suffered and was made a fool of by younger and insignificant rivals, but he still went back. Twenty years later, he wrote: 'I gave up in much the same spirit as a mathematician might give up an attempt to square the circle. I have been as mad as that, attempting something by its very nature impossible.'

Amidst all these amorous adventures, how did Metternich find time to attend to affairs of State? Can one indeed successfully do everything at once? Luckily for him, Dresden was little more than an observation post, a school for diplomatists where official business was by no means overwhelming. Before leaving Vienna, Metternich had traced a detailed agenda and had it countersigned by the Foreign Minister; he intended to adhere to it strictly. In it, he set out even more categorically than in his anonymous brochure of 1794, his opinions about the state of Europe in general. 'The present situation', he declared, 'which is the result of the French Revolution and the wars that followed in its train, has completely superseded any upheavals which might have arisen from the three great wars of the last century: War of the Spanish Succession, War of the North, the Seven Years' War. . . . It is our duty to create new and useful alliances. We must maintain peace at home, and ensure for ourselves a maximum of freedom, (within the necessary limitations of circumstances which we cannot now foresee) so that we may play a part in keeping with the obligations of a great power.'

How could they achieve that end? At Dresden, a second line Embassy, the possibilities of action were restricted but food for reflection was not. Ought they to urge Prussia back into that anti-French coalition which she had abandoned after the treaty of Basle? Should they attempt to add the immense resources of Russia to the riches of England and the power of the Austrian

Empire, the surest means of re-establishing a European balance of power which the military genius and unruly appetites of Napoleon had endangered? These were the lines along which the young Minister's thoughts were moving at Dresden; theories which he would later attempt to implement from his new post when he went to represent his Emperor at the Court of Frederick-Wilhelm III of Hohenzollern.

The capital of Prussia was a strange sight in that autumn of 1804, when Metternich arrived there. No such frivolity as had charmed the young diplomatist at Dresden: long-faced, solemn men and harsh, uncompromising women, completely devoid of charm. He made up for it in the company of foreigners passing through: he enjoyed the favours, among others, of the beautiful Princess Dolgorouki, wife of the aide-de-camp to the Tsar.[1] He was an *habitué* of the salon of Madame de Staël. Germaine 'impresses but does not charm him'. Her wit was uncongenial, he shrank from her rough amazonian gestures; she pursued him energetically but to no effect. 'I find this masculine woman overpowering.'[2] But if the social life of the Prussian capital was unattractive, its political aspect was all-absorbing. Berlin was still the 'high command' of a vast camp.[3] But the spirit of the great Frederick has departed; this 'command' is obsessed with the fear of Napoleon. 'The King, too, seems to think of little else, and everything in his surroundings has played up to it for a long time.' The Queen, Louise von Mecklenburg, his dancing partner of the Frankfurt ball, received him as an old friend. She was placid and sentimental; she had not yet seen the light, not yet discovered her patriotic vocation. Graf von Haugwitz, the Foreign Minister, was 'completely devoted to the interests of France (practically a salaried official of the state!), no longer open to bribes since the French have seen to it that nobody can outbid them'.

And yet it did not take the perspicacious Metternich long to divine a rosy future. 'Surely never', he wrote to Colloredo, 'were two formerly antagonistic monarchies, more obviously designed

---

1. *Archives du Comte de Nesselrode*, Vol. III, page 31.
2. *Lettres à la Comtesse de Lieven*, page 186.
3. Metternich to Colloredo, September 24th, 1804. (*Mémoires.*)

C

to come together. For what could be more conspicuously and closely linked than the immediate interests of Austria and Prussia today . . .? The same dangers confront them, their views must inevitably coincide.'[1]

But convincing the white-livered King was another matter.

In this struggle for the maintenance of order in Europe, how could he be drawn to Austria's side? The answer was to hand: 'only via Saint Petersburg can we achieve our aims', the Prussian Court is terrified to do anything which might compromise their relations with France. Russia alone might bring the required pressure to bear and force the King to act, if necessary, even against his will.

For fifteen months the Emperor's youthful representative worked to consummate the Grand Alliance. At the start, he received little encouragement from his own government and Berlin turned a deaf ear to all his blandishments, as also to the threats of Russia.

But finally, the combined eloquence of Metternich and Tsar Alexander shook and converted the King of Prussia despite the opinions and advice of his 'perfidious and corrupt Counsellors'.[2]

They dangled the annexation of Hanover before Prussian eyes, and on November 4th, 1805, to everybody's surprise an alliance between Russia and Prussia was concluded at Potsdam, an alliance to which Austria immediately became a third party. For three days and three nights Metternich had been preparing a document which he begged his sovereign to consider the *ne plus ultra* in the circumstances.

His first diplomatic victory; it turned out to be purely formal and had no practical future. The German signatory indeed received the order of St Stephen but Austria was cruelly let down. The ill-will of Haugwitz had been flagrant throughout the negotiations. He had sought 'with ill-disguised determination every imaginable loop-hole'. Under pretext that there was an implied insult to his King, he had refused to add a secret clause to the treaty stipulating immediate military intervention by Prussia

1. Metternich to Colloredo, September 24th, 1804. (*Mémoires.*)
2. Metternich to Colloredo, October 29th and November 4th, 1805: *Mémoires.*

should the allied armies suffer defeat and the Austrian capital be threatened by Bonaparte. And worse than that, as soon as the treaty was signed, he had shown it to M. de Laforest, the French Ambassador. 'Please assure the Emperor', Haugwitz added, 'that all this has little or no significance, that we are and shall remain the best of friends with France.'

And so, the outcome will not surprise us: Haugwitz, sent to the French headquarters with an ultimatum for Napoleon, never delivered it, and allowed the combined Russo-Austrian forces to be crushed by the conquering Frenchman in his unbroken advance.

On the evening of December 2nd, 1805, an unusual stir was apparent at the Château of Austerlitz. Every window was lit up. Aides-de-camp and despatch-riders galloped madly through the village which ten years before had celebrated the marriage of Eléonore von Kaunitz and Clement von Metternich with appropriate pastoral festivities. The young people had now inherited the family estate. The master of the Château was away, on his diplomatic mission. At Berlin, he was making a last desperate effort—in the face of concerted opposition—to enlist the practical help of the Prussian armed forces. But an unexpected guest was lodging under the roof of the late Prince von Kaunitz, actually in Metternich's own room: Bonaparte, in person. 'A continuous stream poured in of the *colours* of fallen Austrian and Russian regiments. There were messages from Archdukes, messages from the Emperor of Austria himself and from prisoners bearing all the greatest names of the Empire.'[1] Seated in an armchair, by the fireside, Napoleon watched these glorious trophies spreading out at his feet and basked, triumphant Caesar, in the bloody aftermath of Austerlitz.

1. *Mémoires du Prince de Talleyrand.*

## III

# CAREER

Diplomacy, like the army, has always been considered a prerogative of the privileged classes. Essentially an aristocratic occupation, it develops mainly in the realm of mind. At home, in the service of his country, politician or civil servant is invariably concerned with particular interests, individual or collective: with defence of civil rights, tempering the winds of financial duress to some special class, abolishing injustice or anomaly. The diplomatist alone, like the head of the state, is concerned with his country's total welfare. He must in this resemble the philosopher: the more capable he shows himself of rising above contingency, of a capacity to distinguish the broader lines of historical evolution, the better chance he has that his work will last. For the diplomatic career is riddled with teasers. A diplomatist is sent to some foreign capital not only to take stock of conditions there but also to protect the interests of his country, and peace, in general. Should he have the misfortune, however, to become—even slightly—heated in pursuit of his patriotic duties, should he cause an atom of friction, become involved in any *malentendus*, he immediately gets a reputation for want of tact. 'Above all, no rows!' has been the maxim of the diplomatic corps from time immemorial. But if some really serious conflict arise, should war break out on the pattern which he foresaw —a good ambassador, of course, does foresee all eventualities—or better still some act of treachery against his country, a mob at his gates, the enemy in occupation, then without much more ado your diplomat becomes a great man.

And that is what happened to Metternich after Austerlitz. Berlin was no longer bearable: the treachery of the Prussian cabinet made any collaboration impossible. Tsar Alexander wished him to be nominated to Saint Petersburg. But Napoleon, who seemed fatally drawn to placing his future enemies in strategic positions,[1] suggested as ambassador to his own court: 'a member of that goodly Austrian family of Kaunitz'. And so to Paris he went, there to represent his country under the eye of the greatest man of the century. An unhoped-for opportunity to refurbish— by diplomatic means—some of that lustre which the Austrian military pundits had so sorely tarnished; at last the chance to play a leading part in shaping the destinies of Europe.

He arrived at Paris, the second of August, 1806, and soon real- ised that his task would be more difficult than he had imagined. His first conversations with members of the staff at the Austrian Embassy (Vincent and Floret) were enough to convince him that 'if the position had always been such as to cause grave alarm to any serious diplomatist, no other period had offered less favour- able opportunity to representatives of our master, the Emperor' than that of his own advent.[2]

The following day, Metternich went to Saint-Cloud and made a short speech before Napoleon and the high dignitaries of his Court. He stressed his Emperor's desire to 'revive a mutual con- fidence and friendly relationship which was not only his own sincere and constant wish but doubtless was also to the advantage of the two Empires'.[3]

That first audience was followed by a second in which Napoleon fairly dazzled the young ambassador with flashes of his genius. A rather stormy sitting closed on a Sibylline utterance which Metternich was not slow to interpret: for the moment Napoleon did not particularly want to exasperate Austria because he was preparing a new attack on Prussia.

From now on for several weeks all his reports to his chiefs would be concerned with military preparations and the beginning of the glorious campaign. 'The glove has been thrown down and

1. A year later, Napoleon was to favour the appointment of the great nationalist- reformer, von Stein, to the post of Prime Minister of Prussia.
2. See C. de Grünwald: 'Les débuts diplomatiques de Metternich à Paris' (*Revue de Paris*, le premier août, 1936).
3. In his *Mémoires*, Metternich denied having made any speech.

picked up by either side', he wrote on October 9th, 1806. 'Only the future can tell whether the power of Napoleon is to know no bounds or whether, perhaps, this new venture will itself prove a deterrent. . . . The present war is undoubtedly a life-and-death struggle. For a long time, there have been only two camps that count: Napoleon and the rest of Europe. A total collapse of the existing order in any of those countries which still preserve their independence must inevitably follow a Napoleonic victory.'

As soon as he arrived at Paris, Metternich felt justified in stating that after Prussia, Austria would be the next potential victim. 'The insidious advance engineered by the Saint-Cloud Cabinet knows no other rival than Austria; they do not seem satisfied with having weakened or intimidated her—they are aiming higher. . . . Napoleon fears our political principles in general and the Emperor's own integrity, but unfortunately has no longer any regard for our armed strength. We are certainly first on the list of victims that he feels must be immolated to his mad ambition, to his *ridiculous* system of universal domination. We are unquestionably in his way.'[1]

During the years that followed Metternich's opinion in this respect was to be constantly confirmed. Not that his personal relations with the Emperor of the French lacked cordiality. Napoleon showered favours upon him and even indulged in long friendly conversations—on one occasion leaving his luncheon standing for two hours. He appreciated the young ambassador's dignity, his balanced judgment, his witty retorts. One day when the Emperor jocularly remarked that he was very young to represent the oldest monarchy in Europe, Metternich had very aptly replied: 'I am exactly as old, Sire, as Your Majesty was at Austerlitz!' 'I am talking to you as a man for whom I have considerable regard', Napoleon assured him, in 1808. 'You have been very successful with me and are popular with people here', he remarked on another occasion.

But neither the Emperor's special amiability nor the importance he occasionally attached to trifles could disguise the nature and scope of his ambitions, his always aggressive, warlike intentions.

1. Metternich to Stadion, August 11th, 1806. (Vienna, Secret Archives.)

'It would seem that nothing now can hold up the realization of the Emperor's gigantic schemes', wrote Metternich as early as November 17th, 1806.[1] Napoleon's designs upon Eastern Europe filled him with foreboding. 'There is little doubt', he wrote on October 23rd, 'that he will present himself as a liberator to the Polish Christians and as a Messiah to Poland's enormous Jewish population.'[2] 'The interview at Tilsitt and the ensuing Russo-French alliance raise new problems. Given the Tsar's instability, as against the undeviating course of the Emperor of the French, everything will tend to draw them apart in the immediate future. Napoleon will never work in harness.'[3]

A careful study of the objectives of the Confederation of the Rhine brought Metternich to the conclusion that Napoleon intended to enforce over the whole territory concerned a uniform judicial code, universal conscription, a general system of posts and customs. All the more important functions of an independent government would now devolve upon Paris. So-called sovereigns in the future will thus in fact become little more than prefects and administrators on behalf of the Great Empire. 'With Napoleon, impossible to be merely on friendly terms or neutral; friendship and neutrality are words he simply does not understand.'

Metternich was soon able to discover that Napoleon had no intention of treating Austria any differently from his other vassal states. During August 1807, Talleyrand was replaced by Champagny, a submissive instrument of imperial policies, and who possessed neither the quick mind nor the subtlety, nor the lack of scruple of his predecessor. The atmosphere was becoming more tense: Metternich informed his government of the current rumours of an imminent falling out between the two courts. 'Such rumours', he wrote, 'are so firmly established at this moment, so ingrained among all classes, that I can't take a step in any direction without being asked by my colleagues or leading members of Society how soon I expect to leave.'[4]

In this unpropitious atmosphere discussions were proceeding

1. Vienna, Secret Archives.
2. Ibid.
3. Metternich to Stadion, August 11th, 1807. (Vienna, Secret Archives.)
4. Metternich to Stadion, September 23rd, 1807. (Vienna, Secret Archives.)

about the modification of frontier boundaries foreseen by the treaty of Presburg. A line drawn on the map by the Emperor's own hand was the obstacle against which Metternich strove in vain: there was less than nothing of negotiation about these proceedings. 'Three times', he wrote, 'I have allowed discussions to be broken off (having signed the Treaty of Fontainebleau on October 10th, 1807), retaining only the thinnest of pretexts for opening them again.' Under a threat to annex the whole territory bordering the Isonzo river, and even Trieste itself, Metternich accepted the conditions imposed upon him; as a species of consolation, he informed his government that 'there is now nothing more that Napoleon can demand. For the first time, Austria's position with regard to France is at least crystal clear.'

A poor consolation, however, for although Austria's situation was certainly 'clear', the frontier lines now fixed, that was not to prevent new demands arising and they shortly did. Metternich himself wrote about that time: 'It is a fact that Napoleon's methods appear recently to have undergone a complete change; he seems to have arrived at the stage where he considers any moderation gratuitous. More than ever it is imperative to be continually alert.'

Shortly after the signing of the Treaty of Fontainebleau a new pack of troubles cropped up. The complications were of an international order but the interests, the dignity, the principles of Austria were all directly menaced. Champagny handed Metternich a summary demand that Austria should break off diplomatic relations with England. At the beginning of 1808, Metternich was told by Talleyrand of two new projects: an expedition to East India and the partition of Turkey. 'One belongs to the realm of romantic fiction', added the erstwhile Bishop of Autun, 'the other has a more realistic basis. . . .' Austria had to make up her mind: should she frankly oppose these ambitious designs, or alternatively content herself with a share of the swag: the banks of the Danube, Bosnia, Bulgaria? 'There are difficulties', wrote Metternich, 'in carving up a great Empire. At Paris, any negotiator not willing to toe the line will waste his time in pursuit of truth and principle. He will fall dead on the way, for want of breath long before he catches up with his enemies.'

On the thirtieth of March, 1808, he informed his government of the catastrophe which having long menaced had now fallen upon the throne of Spain. 'There are ways of life which are mutually incompatible. The actual power in France cannot exist side by side with any other in Europe. For none would dare to describe as potentates that rabble of crowned prefects who— having recently become indebted to France for their very exis- tence—now pay for this doubtful and precarious privilege with the blood and money of their subjects.' 'The fall of one of the greatest thrones of Europe means no more to Napoleon than a simple insertion in the official gazette.'[1]

After the Bourbons had been deposed in Spain, Metternich reached this final conclusion: 'there is no means of coming to terms with a revolutionary system'. 'Robespierre declaring war against the nobility in perpetuity, or Napoleon against the Euro- pean powers, it is always the same tyranny, the danger has merely spread.' 'Napoleon', he wrote on June 23rd, 1808, 'is planning to wipe us out. This is his design because our continued existence (our principles and the scope of our territory) is incompatible with his type of Continental supremacy.' In his next telegram, Metternich returned to the same issue. 'Napoleon's persistent aim', he wrote, 'is the widest possible measure of domination on the continent of Europe. . . . There is no lull in his activities, no respite for this Monarch. . . . no sooner is one job finished than he rushes into another. One has only to look at the map to guess where the next blow will fall. Decidedly there is no coming to terms for long with a government which takes us back to the style, to the very words of 1793, which turns everything upside down: all principles, behaviour, the whole tradition of history. . . '

The inevitability of a new flare-up between France and Austria being taken for granted, the ambassador then had one predomin- ant desire: to hold off the war as long as possible and insure a maximum of preparedness for his own country. 'Everything depends', he wrote, the day after his arrival at Paris, 'on gaining time; consolidating all the nation's resources, overhauling the

1. Metternich to Stadion, May 17th, 1808. (Vienna, Secret Archives.)

army, proving if needs be to France (which is now synonymous with Europe) that although the Austrian Empire might be willing to give way on points of pure formality (if such there be) it can nevertheless still defend its vital integrity, its unity, the age-old link which binds so many different nations together under one paternal sway.... In short, we must now depend upon ourselves alone, upon our political system, out military capacity and above all on the flexibility of both of these....'[1]

'Our position has become considerably worse', he remarked, 'since Tilsitt. But the Monarchy still holds, indeed it seems to have filled out. The present state of affairs in Europe carries the germ of its own destruction and the comparative wisdom of our own Government might well hasten the day when 300,000 resolute men, directed by a single controlling mind and with a common objective will play the leading part in Europe. Of such moments, history affords a precedent, and they tend to follow on the heels of usurpers, wiping out all their ill-gotten victories'.[2]

But are Napoleon and France any longer, in fact, synonymous? That, for Metternich, was the question. 'Can the fate, the continuity of an Empire depend upon one man?' He now knew the Master, he realised Napoleon's genius as well as the scope of his insatiable appetite. But did he really know the country?

In the years of 1806 and 1807, years of splendour and misery, while the French army fought on the snow-clad plains of Prussia, Metternich himself had conquered Paris. The doors of the great world flew open: M. de Metternich became one of the outstanding personalities of the day, courted on all sides, at first as a man of rank and fashion but later for himself alone. His aristocratic bearing stood out among that rather mixed society of the Empire, he was young and witty and understood the art of pleasing in a marked degree. He enjoyed prestige as Ambassador from a great and ancient court, the only one, in fact, with which France was still at peace. (Mazade.) 'He had a remarkably handsome face', said one of his female admirers. 'Candid and tranquil, the eyes were as

1. Metternich to Stadion.
2. This prophetic forecast of the events of 1813 is found in Metternich's telegram of June 26th, 1807.

eloquent as an invariably good-tempered conversation, they inspired confidence. His demeanour was consistent with that gracious smile—half serious—and entirely in keeping with the personality of a man to whom had been confided the interests of a very great empire.'

At the court of the Tuileries where etiquette was partly military and extremely stilted a really well-bred man stood out; 'he enjoyed an unquestioned superiority; a certain social ease (which is the product of his background and familiarity with the ways of the aristocratic world) stood him in good stead'. (Capefigue.) He stood out by 'his lordly spending, the extreme elegance of his equipages and horses'. 'And this thirty-four-year-old dandy, with his great blue eyes and curly blonde hair', 'a piece of Dresden china', had none of the characteristics of a stodgy German. His French was excellent, scarcely a tinge of accent. He knew how to talk to women; he had forgotten nothing of those early lessons learnt on the borders of the Rhine from a Parisienne, the first great passion of his adolescent years. As soon as he got to Paris, he immediately tried to get in touch with the beautiful emigrée who had also returned to France.[1] But Mme. de Caumont was living far from the capital on her country estate and the passing years had transformed her youthful passion into an affectionate friendship. Metternich now needed new conquests. Caroline Murat, Napoleon's own sister, was to be the first.

Existing portraits of the princess give a poor impression of her charm. Is it perhaps that tastes in such matters have altered? For in the miniatures by Isabey, the drawings of the Musée de Besançon or the large picture of the Musée Marmottan, we see a rather heavy, thick-set woman, frankly a little vulgar. But it was not so that she struck her contemporaries. 'When I saw her for the first time', wrote Mademoiselle Avrillon, first lady-in-waiting to the Empress, 'I was chiefly struck by the dazzling whiteness of her skin. She had a very handsome head, radiated good health, she was not very tall and early took on a certain *embonpoint*; court life seemed to destroy all her charm and she

1. This episode was told for the first time by the Duc de la Force in a remarkable study in the *Revue des Deux Mondes*. (October 15th, 1936.)

looked very much better *en negligée* than when dressed for formal occasions.'

In his usual witty manner, Talleyrand has perhaps described her better than anyone else: 'Cromwell's head stuck on the shoulders of a pretty woman'. 'She set out to be amiable to all she met; she was by no means devoid of gaiety and a sense of humour and was quite capable of adopting an air of good-natured familiarity', Mme. de Remusat tells us. 'She lived luxuriously, kept a sump-tuous table. She was always served on golden plate in which she went beyond the practice of the Emperor himself.' She got on reasonably well with her husband, 'at least on the surface' (Mademoiselle Avrillon). And yet her liaison with Junot had already been the subject of open comment. We know nothing of the circumstances leading up to her affair with Metternich. At first sight, she disliked him. 'Baby-face', Caroline had said, being accustomed in Murat to something more rugged, more male. It has been suggested that Napoleon himself had advised her to 'amuse this nincompoop', adding 'we need him at the moment'. The Emperor, however, had certainly not intended that things should go so far: he was well aware of his sister's inordinate ambition. 'Such was her own desire to reign that she never ceased begging the Emperor to give some crown to her husband', Mademoiselle Avrillon also tells us. Promoted Grand Duchess of Berg, she wished to become Queen of Spain; before that, she had coveted the crown of Poland and had all the Polish ladies then living in Paris presented to her.[1] When Jerome had been given Westphalia, she did not attempt to hide her 'resentment that her husband Murat should not have received the royal title in recom-pense for all he had endured in war'.[2] 'Listening to you,' Napoleon once remarked to his younger sister, 'one might almost think I had done you out of the inheritance of the late King, our father!'

Was it only ambition that brought about Caroline's liaison with Metternich? The historian Arthur-Lévy claims that Madame Murat's aims went beyond any mere royal crown; that she dreamed of becoming Empress should death on the battlefield

1. Metternich to Stadion, November 17th, 1806. (Vienna, Secret Archives.)
2. Metternich to Stadion, July 26th, 1807. (Vienna, Secret Archives.)

suddenly claim her brother; that it was with this in mind that she seduced Junot. He further suggests that she had not repelled the homage of Metternich because of her preoccupation with 'the attitude of foreign powers' should her plan ever materialise. [1]

But hasn't the eminent historian of the Napoleonic era gone a bit far in these suppositions? Why should one not just conclude that two young people, frivolous, good-looking, devoid of all scruple might meet and fall in love? Why shouldn't mere *coquetterie* on the lady's part, have influenced the situation as much as any thoughts of ambitious scheming?

We can, however, concede that amorous dalliance was by no means the couple's sole preoccupation at their clandestine meetings. Political matters not infrequently predominated in the minds of the Princess and the Ambassador.

But let the lover himself speak: 'Caroline combined a charming face with unusual intelligence', he wrote in his Memoirs. . . . 'She had considerable influence with her brother and it was she who cemented all the family ties. She hoped to make her own and her family's interests as much as possible independent of Napoleon, to safeguard them in the event of his possible reverses of fortune. . . . She had studied her brother and had no illusions about him, she knew his faults and the risks he ran on account of his exaggerated ambition and arrogant desire for domination.'

That is the truth. If it is not quite clear in what way Metternich, ambassador of a foreign power, could at the moment advance the interests of the future Queen of Naples, it is more than obvious that in the Emperor's sister (since she had become his mistress) the diplomat had secured an unrivalled source of information. No detail of the happenings at Court could now escape him. He knew before anyone else that the Empress Josephine was privately ordering clothes in view of some future coronation (!); [2] he was already able on July 26th, 1806, to announce rumours of Napoleon's probable repudiation of the Empress. [3] He soon noted that even in the bosom of his family, the Emperor was surrounded by enemies.

1. A. Lévy: *Les dissentiments de la famille impériale.* (Ed. Calmann-Lévy.)
2. Report dated November 17th, 1806.
3. Vienna, Secret Archives.

As for the advice he received, well, the Ambassador had only to listen to the grievances of Talleyrand and Fouché whom he now met frequently thanks to the support of his good-looking mistress.

Metternich was not long faithful to Caroline: a new rival was soon to supplant her: the seductive Madame Junot, future Duchesse d'Abrantes, endowed with an affable, sparkling smile, and gentle, humorous eyes. 'With an obvious desire to please and outstanding good looks, she combined a sprightly and agreeable mind,[1] at times perhaps a trifle acid—but a good heart, a delightful disposition.'

Those who enjoy maudlin, sentimental stories will find all they want, and in detail in the *Mémoires* of Laure Junot. Her account of her amours with the handsome Austrian ambassador is probably to some extent imaginary: nothing has been left out, the romantic setting ('Folie Saint-James' at Neuilly), mute declarations, ('Never had he said so much, yet hardly a word was spoken'), faintings and tears ('I could only sob and sob. He was on his knees before me. . . . He got up to support me, his lips met mine. . . . I do not know what happened but he carried me into the grotto, a few steps away, and when I came to myself again, I had committed a sin I was to expiate with tears of blood.') If one is to believe the later confession of the beautiful Magdalene, Metternich—in pursuit of this affair—seems to have wasted a great deal of precious time. 'Every evening, at ten o'clock, a cab deposits the ambassador, unarmed, near the Neuilly bridge: he goes in by the grotto gate—and leaves again at three o'clock in the morning. From there he goes to a house where another cab is waiting in charge of a man-servant he had pretended to dismiss. . . .' But when matters of importance were afoot, Metternich never missed a rendezvous with Caroline Murat. Fickle as he was in love, his political line never deviated. Caroline maintained secret contacts with Fouché; she did her best to be on terms with Talleyrand[2] and the Austrian ambassador was the *confidante* of all three.

1. *Journal de la princesse Mélanie de Metternich*, December 19th, 1837. (*Mémoires et Documents*, Vol. V, page 115.)
2. Madame de Rémusat: *Mémoires*.

Metternich was well aware of Talleyrand's exceptional intelligence and appreciated their consistently pleasant social relations. He was also aware, however, of the corrupt nature of many of the French statesman's dealings; there is no more explicit proof of this than a dispatch sent by Metternich to his government at the time when Talleyrand resigned from his post as Foreign Secretary.[1] 'Men like Talleyrand', he remarked on another occasion, 'are as dangerous as a two-edged sword.' 'Nothing, actually, is more to be feared than knavery and humbug masquerading under a cover of frankness and good will.' He thought no less of Talleyrand's friendship—deep wounds call for stringent remedies. In any event, the Ambassador adds, 'my means for checking up on him are legion; I have so many lines out, so many counter-checks—I take no risks, and take no man into my confidence—that I feel able to make these assertions with full assurance'.[2]

Towards the end of his period as Ambassador, Metternich was to discover the surest means of winning Talleyrand over to the Austrian cause: On behalf of the Austrian government he gave him the by no means negligible sum of one hundred thousand francs, after which there was no secret—diplomatic, military or whatever—that Talleyrand was not prepared to whisper into the ears of his benefactors.[3] 'Talleyrand', wrote Metternich on January 31st, 1809, 'has taken off all masks as far as we are concerned. He now considers the Austrian cause so much his own that he seems willing to enter into all kinds of negotiations which he once refused.'

1. 'The smaller courts of Europe for a long time now have been loading the French Foreign Office with gratuities. All who had contact—close or even remote—with M. de Talleyrand, have become rich. One finds immense riches among the inner circle of his liege-men, and the number of medium fortunes—all flowing from the same source—can scarcely be counted. . . the collapse, indeed, could scarcely be more overwhelming than it is now, among the satellites. . . Foreign agents are regretting their liberalities and are already trying to calculate what the new Minister will cost them.' (Metternich to Stadion, August 9th, 1807. Vienna, Secret Archives.)

2. Metternich to Stadion, September 24th, 1808.

3. The correspondence between Metternich and the Chancellor's department at Vienna concerning this strange episode was first published by M. Dard in the *Revue des Deux Mondes* and subsequently in his admirably documented book: *Napoléon et Talleyrand*, Paris 1936.

Metternich had no illusions either about Fouché. He knew well that this man of action, this practical fellow who had 'no use for theories' had also no moral scruples, and would ride rough-shod over obstacles. But he also knew that the all-powerful chief of police was whole-heartedly and by conviction opposed to Napoleon's new schemes of war—and that, for him, was enough.

Metternich drew valuable conclusions from his long conversations with these two men. Five years before the march to Moscow, it was Fouché who remarked, 'as soon as he has made war on you there will only remain Russia and China'. On another occasion it was Talleyrand who said: 'Whatever you do, you will never be able to stem the torrent.' It was also Talleyrand who reported after Erfurt the plea he had made to the Tsar: 'What are you doing here, Sire? It is your task to save Europe.... The French people are civilised, their sovereign is not; the Russian sovereign is civilised, his people are not: the Russian sovereign must therefore become an ally of the French people.'

Two French statesmen who hated each other and only met to conspire against the state. Metternich compared them to passengers who, seeing the helm in the hands of a mad pilot about to take the ship on the rocks, are preparing to seize it themselves. 'We have now reached a point', he wrote, 'where allies are available within the Empire itself. And these are no mere petty schemers, but men who are fully representative of the whole nation.'

A conviction was steadily growing in the mind of the Ambassador that 'the cause of Napoleon is no longer the cause of France'. And however widely he extended the scope of his research, the conclusion remained the same. Bonaparte's companions in arms: Berthier, Davoust, Masséna, Augereau, dowered with public millions, gorged with loot and now determined to make the best of their good fortune; army contractors grown weary of expeditions which—thanks to the vigilance of the Emperor himself—were no longer as profitable as they used to be, and the nation bled white by annual conscription, actually 'curse these victories the political import of which escapes them'. That magic phrase, the 'national glory', to be made so much of during the coming Restoration, meant little or nothing in France at that time. During the Prussian campaign, Metternich was able to judge from direct observation the reactions of Parisians and he found them unquestionably defeatist. The reports he sent to his government throughout the years 1806, 1807, are full of interesting anecdotes all confirming the indifference or actual hostility of public opinion. In the theatres, 'bulletins announcing victories are greeted by the applause of two or three policemen', at the Court of the Tuileries, the Emperor's letters dispatched the day after the victory of Eylau provoked consternation. The public illuminations—ordered for all householders—in celebration of victories in Russia, appeared on ministries and diplomatic buildings only. The repeated successes of the French army were greeted as calamities to such a point that Metternich began to wonder whether he was in Napoleon's capital or in that of one of the Emperor's enemies.[1] 'Never was a war less national than this one', he wrote.[2] 'The whole of France has only one opinion, one desire, one prayer, to see the collapse of her master's plans.'

Metternich thought that Napoleon had only one army, the famous *Grande Armée*, then operating in Spain; he thought the new attempts at conscription would raise untold difficulties, he thought in the circumstances that in a war between France and Austria, forces would not be evenly matched—France would be outnumbered. 'Whenever Napoleon decides to attack, we shall find ourselves with a majority.' (July 13th, 1808.)

Austrian historians, even those who were the most friendly to Metternich, such as Srbik, have reproached him with his 'fatal mistakes' during his period at the Paris Embassy, a period which led up to the war of 1809. But is it really fair to say that Metternich had urged war? Didn't he rather consider it as an inevitable scourge, outcome of a situation which appeared to defy all notions 'of civilisation and humanity'? He made a mistake in his estimate of the results: and yet it was not so much his responsibility as that of the Vienna government—unmistakably bellicose—to estimate correctly the rival armed forces. In one way or another, the young

1. Vienna, Secret Archives.
2. September 24th, 1806. (Vienna, Secret Archives.)

41

D

ambassador had made every effort to postpone the flare-up. 'It would be sheer madness', he wrote on August 2nd, 1808, 'to do anything to provoke war. Napoleon will continue to threaten us but we must hold back the explosion as long as we can. . . . To put off the war as long as possible is an objective of the highest importance.'

One question only obsessed him, in 1807, 1808 and 1809. 'Does Napoleon want an immediate war, or not?' Conscientiously he noted every symptom of a pacific nature. He even interpreted in an optimistic sense that famous scene when, on August 15th, 1808, Caesar harangued him in front of the whole diplomatic corps, reproaching him with Austria's precipitate rearmament. ('Well, Monsieur l'Ambassadeur, what is your master, the Emperor, up to now? Does he by any chance wish to see me back in Vienna?')

Metternich wrote to his government—in contradiction to the attitude he was to adopt later—that the whole of this conversation (which must have lasted more than an hour) took place in an atmosphere of 'great frankness and absolute calm', that the Emperor never once raised his voice and never departed from 'a quite astonishing reasonableness', even, it seems, when the presumptuous diplomat remarked: 'Rest assured, Sire, if you have counted our soldiers, we also have counted yours.'

But each day, each week, brought new causes of alarm. That French society which Metternich had believed so little disposed to uphold the Napoleonic ambition, was becoming warlike again. Field-Marshals promoted to the rank of Duke were now wishing, said Fouché, to become Archdukes. A whole horde of climbers and agitators began to get busy. Small German principalities were stirring up anti-Austrian propaganda hoping to pocket some of the spoils of the fray. And all these influences acted on the Emperor as the proverbial drop of water wearing away the stone. He was in any event never reluctant to pursue some new hope of conquest.

Such information as Metternich was able to collect in the course of a short visit to Vienna was no more reassuring: the population there was in a state of fever, of exaltation. In the spring of 1809, the Austrian army prepared for war: 300,000 men (regulars, reservists and men of the *landwehr*) were moving towards the frontier. Regiments marched through the capital to the sound of pipes and singing. The Empress Maria-Ludovica, in the Cathedral of Saint Stephen, solemnly distributed the regimental *colours*, partly embroidered by her own hand. And the Emperor Francis, in his study, working absent-mindedly with his thoughts fixed on Napoleon, repeated: 'that man is a terrible anxiety to me; he will never be satisfied until he has destroyed my Empire'.[1] Was he so wrong? Didn't Napoleon write to Jerome: 'The Emperor of Austria will have ceased to reign, two months from now. . . .'?

Metternich found himself reduced to the role of an impotent onlooker: the Viennese government was treated more and more as an entity not worth consideration.

In the course of long conversations with Talleyrand, Metternich had harboured a design for the Emperor Francis' participation in the conference of Erfurt. It was suggested that Francis should take a journey into Bohemia: the sovereign would be so near the meeting-place that he might appear there as if by chance. But the authorities at Vienna would not allow their Emperor to be put in so humiliating a position, and the suggestion that some Archduke be dispatched in a similar manner met with no better reception. Thereupon, Metternich requested permission to go himself: the French government categorically refused even to consider the proposal. In these circumstances the Ambassador was obliged to admit that 'there was little chance that the conference at Erfurt would prove conducive to a general pacification'. 'Napoleon has no such intention', he wrote, and could never be induced to consider peace otherwise than by stress of circumstance, for reasons of *force majeure*.

On his return, Napoleon treated Metternich with a marked coolness. He pretended not to see him during receptions of the diplomatic corps. Whenever he did address a remark to him it was always to ask the same question. 'How is Madame de Metter-

1. Telegrams from Andreossy, French ambassador, February 18th, 1809, and from Dodun, French chargé d'affaires, April 4th, 1809.

nich?' to which the Ambassador replied with his usual unruffled calm that 'her health was much the same as usual'. Metternich asked Talleyrand: 'Do you think Napoleon is grateful to us for not creating embarrassing situations at the present juncture?' He got this categorical reply: 'Not at all, he hates you with a deadly hatred.'

The representatives of other countries, about this time, heard some ill-disguised threats against Austria from the mouth of the Emperor of the French. Metternich was aware that a formal declaration of war would not be long now. 'Napoleon seems only to be moved by the spirit of destruction and universal domination', he wrote to his government. 'Napoleon's genius seems to impel him to make laws for the whole world.'

But Metternich was by no means pessimistic about the final issue. He visualised Austria 're-established in the European scene, stronger, more powerful than ever'. And reiterating his favourite theme: it is now no longer the French nation that will be fighting us, this is purely Napoleon's war—not even that of his army. 'If there is little enthusiasm for war in Austria, they have a horror of it here. Foreigners cannot imagine the extent to which France is weary.'[1]

And Talleyrand piled it on: 'all Germany will be on your side and you will have a number of partisans—but less—in Italy. Napoleon is well aware of that, but the force of circumstances has dragged him beyond his original calculations.' The treacherous French statesman even went so far as to advise Austria to wait four or five months and then declare war: 'Napoleon will inevitably be much weaker by next May.'[2]

The Russian Cabinet made a last-minute effort to preserve peace. Austrian independence would be guaranteed by Russia and France in return for which the Emperor Francis should agree to reduce his armed forces. Negotiations began between Metternich, Champagny and Count Roumianzoff, Russia's Foreign Minister

1. Metternich to Stadion, January 25th, 1809. (Vienna, Secret Archives).
2. Metternich to Stadion, January 11th, 1809. (Vienna, Secret Archives.) In another telegram, dated January 17th, Metternich suggested a possible *coup d'état*. 'I am watching Talleyrand and his friend Fouché. . . quite determined to seize any opportunity that occurs but not sufficiently courageous to make one.'

who had for some time been resident at Paris. But such last-minute negotiations were not to alter the course of events.

Metternich's own position was becoming more difficult every day; he would soon no longer be in a position to get his diplomatic mail through safely. He wrote: 'an Ambassador no longer able to correspond with his headquarters, banished from the presence of the sovereign to whom he is accredited, is unquestionably justified in asking for his papers.... Personally I should not be surprised by any violation of elementary rights or freedom, here, now; so much the better, I shall know how to live up to the character with which His Majesty has been pleased to credit me. Let the enemy do what they will ... if it's my official documents they're after, they won't find a single sheet. At the first shot fired, I shall ask for my passport.'[1] 'Nothing would surprise me now', declared Metternich in a letter addressed to Schwarzenberg, Ambassador at Saint Petersburg. 'But even more peremptory methods with my person, or a few weeks at Vincennes would be well worth it from the standpoint of our common cause. Rest assured, I shall make it plain on every occasion who and what I am. Goodbye, dear Prince, you may shortly learn that I have been *put inside.*[2] In that case, rejoice with me; if you hear that I have been shot, rest assured that I shall first have accounted for quite a number of those sent to arrest me and remember an old friend who is sincerely attached to you.'[3] Was he play-acting? Did he want to impress the Cabinet at Saint Petersburg? Or had he really lost his head?

Metternich was to escape the fate of the Duc d'Enghien, he was neither imprisoned nor shot; Napoleon had never intended that he should play the role of martyr. Before parting, the two adversaries faced each other preserving all the amenities.

The fateful day arrived. The Court, ministers, ambassadors were all assembled in the *grande salle des Tuileries* to hear the master's verdict. All eyes were fixed on Metternich as the Emperor

1. Metternich to Stadion, April 9th, 1809 (Secret Archives of Vienna.)
2. Imprisoned.
3. Metternich to Schwarzenberg, manuscript letter of April 10th, 1809. (Vienna Secret Archives.) See also: C. de Grünwald: 'La Fin d'une ambassade' (*Revue de Paris*, October 1st and 15th, 1937).

approached him to announce that he would march on Vienna via Ratisbonne and Munich. Humboldt was to remind us some ten years later of 'the nobility, dignity and really admirable sangfroid', displayed at that historic moment by his Austrian colleague. [1] A few minutes later, the Emperor went down into the Palace courtyard and there, mounted on a white horse, harangued the troops. He instructed Champagny to inform Metternich that he bore him no ill-will whatever, that the scene which had just transpired was only designed for the gallery. 'Monsieur,' replied the Ambassador, 'tell the Emperor, your master, that I never took him seriously. . . .' [2] That was the last word.

On the fields of Eckmuhl and Wagram, however, Napoleon was shortly to prove how ill-founded was this pert reply. For in spite of all her preparations, of popular enthusiasm, in spite of her unquestionably heroic army, in spite even of occasional victories, Austria in the long run was again to prove her inability to stand up to the *Grande Armée*.

'Use the enemy's own tactics', Metternich finally advised. 'Turn his own methods back upon him. . . . Expect hard knocks and above all be prepared for the unexpected. Oppose him with an adaptability equal to his own, use the same procedure. Never regard any battle as a victory until the following day, never admit ourselves vanquished until four days later. Let us always keep the sword in one hand and an olive branch in the other.'

But the Austrian generals, with the Archduke Charles as their leader, had not made good use of these wise precepts. The sword indeed was to fall from their hands but—prudence or calculation —it was Metternich who was always there at the right moment to tender the olive branch. His departure from Paris was delayed: the Austrian authorities having arrested the French chargé d'affaires, Metternich was held as hostage.

It was only during the first days of July—after an exchange with the French diplomats—that he was able to reach the Emperor of Austria's headquarters. He arrived there just in time to

1. Previously unpublished letter, quoted by Srbik, Metternich. Vol. I, page 118.
2. Memoirs of Graf Fitzthum-Eckstaedt (a conversation with Metternich at Dresden, October 1828).

be present at the battle of Wagram, and to witness the resignation of the Foreign Secretary, Stadion, appalled by this tangible evidence of the failure of his bellicose methods. In this moment of general chaos, the eyes of the Emperor turned towards his young Ambassador 'fresh from the lion's den' and who had turned up full of confidence and optimism, well groomed, fresh as a daisy, just as if nothing had happened. Francis could hardly wait to put into power the only man of all his suite who hadn't lost his head. Once more, fate had played a trump card for Metternich.

# IV

# HAPPY AUSTRIA

### A.E.I.O.U.

*Austria erit in orbe ultima*[1]

'THE WORD AUSTRIA', wrote Baron Andrian, in 1840, 'is an illusory term; it stands neither for a country nor a people nor a nation. A mere convention, it is used to describe a complex of nationalities bearing no relation to each other. Italians, Germans, Slavs, Hungarians, combine to constitute the Austrian Empire, but there is no such thing as an Austrian nation.'

Like many another paradox, this much-quoted remark by a typically Austrian commentator contains a grain of truth. It might be countered by the equally effective retort of the famous Slav patriot, Palácky, instigator of the Czech nationalist movement: 'If the Austrian Empire did not exist, in the interest of Europe and the whole human race, we should have to invent it.'

It is evident that no Austrian nation ever existed in the sense that we apply that term to France, to England or to Germany—and this is not surprising, since the nature of the conglomeration was itself the very essence of the Empire. But an Austrian national type of thought has, in fact, persisted through the centuries. The Empire of the Habsburgs was not merely an historical fact: it was the tangible expression of certain geographical, political, cultural and economic necessities. That became strikingly evident when after the horrors of the Great War, the Empire disappeared from the map of Europe.

---

1. 'Austria's dominion will stretch to the ends of the earth.' It was also said, *'Austriae est imperare orbi universo'*.

Since the dawn of history, since the earliest days of the great migrations, and almost up till our own time, the Continent has been continually over-run by nomadic peoples from the steppes of Asia. The Grand Duchy of Russia was the first line of defence against these incursions; it was easily overcome. The Habsburg Empire was then called in to organise a second line.

The most diverse races, Celts, Cambrians, Marcomans, Visigoths, Huns, Ostrogoths, Lombards, Avars, Hungarians, Turks, not to mention Slavs and Roumanians, spread in the course of centuries over the fertile Danubian plains, moving back and forth, coming to grips with each other, settling down. On the borders of the river up-stream from Vienna, we find a picturesque district—hills and valleys—which for a thousand years has been known by the name of Niebelungengau: and it was there that that half-legendary German people—made famous by the Wagnerian Trilogy—came face to face with Attila and his Huns.

This ethnological instability persists throughout the Middle Ages up to the beginning of the eighteenth century. Now and again it is the germanic peoples who advance victoriously: Charlemagne destroyed the Empire of the Avars and created the Eastern frontier provinces (that Ostmark which was to give the name of Oesterreich to the future Austria). Then again, the Hungarians advanced towards the West, or the Slav Kings of the new Bohemia extended their dominion over a considerable part of the Danube basin. Later, in the sixteenth century, the Turks were to seize the whole of Central Hungary, were to dig themselves in at Buda for two hundred years and besiege Vienna in 1529 and 1683.

And yet, from the very beginning a kernel was forming and it was racially German. It was grouped round Vienna, geographical and thus natural centre of the whole Danubian basin. The native dynasty of the Babenbergs, on whom had been conferred the marquisate of Austria in 976 (subsequently raised to a Duchy) died out at the end of the thirteenth century. Rudolph I, of Habsburg, elected Emperor of Germany in 1273, bestowed these lands upon his sons thus creating an unbreakable link between the countries of the Danube and the arrogant sons of Habichtsburg. [1]

The Habsburgs were a strange race, essentially a race of masters; they had kept their individuality and even their physical traits intact for hundreds of years. The type has become classic: long narrow head, wide-open nostrils, small eyes with thick lids, wearing a perpetual air of surprise and reserve, thick lips and protruding chin. As for their character, their temperament, that was an eccentric mixture of humility and pride, of rapacity and prudence, wild flights of fancy combined with all the limitations of obstinacy. From time to time the line threw up men of genius who in the span of a very short life, a few years' reign, marked out a course for their successors. But these were exceptions; most of the dynasty were pretty mediocre, narrow-minded, prone to quite exceptional longevity: the latter reigned for many decades and slowly and patiently put into effect the plans of their more gifted ancestors. And all had the same object: to build up *Domus Austriae*, the House of Austria. It was always the same system, the same methods: to harness the resources of the whole German Empire, to achieve by peaceful means what could not be won in battle, to maintain in a state of equilibrium all those discordant elements which formed their Kingdom; to conceal their own arid natures under a cover of *bonhomie* and spurious good-will.

For eighteen generations, without a break, the Imperial Crown of Germany was in their hands. The successors of Rudolph I ceded it to the dynasty of Luxembourg, but at the end of the fifteenth century, under Frederick III, the Habsburgs got it back and held it until the dissolution of the Holy-Empire (with the sole exception of the short reign of Charles VII of Bavaria). And still today, the crown once worn by Charlemagne is given pride of place at Vienna among all the treasures of the Habsburgs.

German and Catholic, the Habsburg Princes made the best use of the material and spiritual forces of the German race to acquire immense new territories and impose a 'Christian order' within their borders, 'Christian' as they themselves conceived the term.

1. Habsburg is short for Habichtsburg—Hawk's castle—home of the Arch-family. This castle was in Swabia, not far from the Swiss frontier.

The central agglomeration, with Vienna as its capital, grew through the years. It quickly absorbed all the middle course of the Danube; gradually an immense natural fortress came into being. An Alpine chain, the forests of Bohemia and Carpathia, was to form nature's protection for these fertile plains, combining with the Tyrol, Bohemia and Transylvania as bastions, with the Swabian, Silesian, Galician, Serbian and Lombard lands as glacis. Then more distant possessions were added: Flanders, Burgundy, Spain, the Americas, until the day when Charles V reigned gloriously over an Empire on which the sun never set. Thus the power of Austria fulfilled prophecy and 'stretched to the ends of the earth'.

Strangely enough, this impressive edifice owed its existence less to the force of arms than to clever diplomacy. The matrimonial alliances of the House of Habsburg were mainly responsible for its growth and power: *Bella gerant alii, tu felix Austria nube*. And while others had waged wars, happy Austria indeed had married to good effect.

Rudolph von Habsburg was descended from an unpretentious and rather poor line of knights but his father had made a brilliant marriage. Thus Rudolph inherited rich feudal lands in Swabia which in turn smoothed the way for his election to the imperial throne and assisted his victory over Bohemia and his subsequent acquisition of Austria. His successors, by means of direct purchase, by marriage and inheritance, further acquired the Tyrol, Corinthia, the *Krain*, and added a section of ancient Frioul to Styria. Then weakened for a while by re-partitions, temporarily deprived of the Imperial crown, the House of Habsburg nevertheless came into the limelight again with Prince Albert who married the daughter of Siegmund of Luxemburg, Emperor of Germany, thus becoming his heir. Prince Albert's son, Frederick III, in turn managed to gather together all the family possessions, then in the hands of lateral branches: *Time is a great avenger* was his favourite motto. Rudolph IV, the Magnificent (1358-1365) raised the status of the House by means of a doubtful document, known as *privilegium majus*. From then on, followed a plethora of marriages: Maximilian, by his union with Princess Marie, heiress of *Charles*

51

*le Téméraire* and *Phillipe le Hardi*, secured Burgundy and Flanders together with certain rights in Savoy; his son became King of Spain. Under his grandson, Charles Quint, Hungary and Poland returned to the Habsburgs: for when the young King Louis, last scion of the Jagellons, fell on the field of Mohacs mortally wounded by the Turks, it was his brother-in-law, Ferdinand of Austria (brother of Charles Quint), who inherited the crowns of Saint Wenceslaus and Saint Stephen (1526).

But the seventeenth century perhaps marked the culmination of the power of the Habsburgs. It was then that the Cardinal de Retz compared the courage of Richelieu with that of Caesar or Alexander because he had dared to 'attack the formidable House of Austria'. After that, the Spanish branch of the dynasty died out. The Bourbons moved into Madrid, Naples and Parma (treaty of Utrecht, 1713); they were united by a 'family pact' with the Bourbons of France. But the politico-matrimonial policies of the Habsburgs were still operative. Maria-Theresa, last direct descendant of the Austrian branch, married François de Lorraine who brought to the ancient House the Duchy of Lorraine itself and considerable new blood and vigour. The couple had sixteen children; their second son, Leopold, also had sixteen and their grandson, Francis II, not less than ten—a fine crop of new marriages in perspective.

'Without the expenditure of so much as one soldier or a shilling piece, the House of Austria, far from squandering the Bourbon alliance, actually turns it to profit; enough that it can instal its daughters at Naples, Parma and even at Versailles' (Masson). The union of Louis XVI and Marie-Antoinette, supreme achievement of the great chancellor Kaunitz, thus appears as a logical link in a vast and secular design. For the instinct of the Parisian populace was not unsound when as a final injury they launched at Marie-Antoinette the hated name of 'Austrian'.

But this extension of their influence through matrimony which had strengthened the Habsburgs had its counter disadvantage. The House had managed to create a state outside its own borders, supra-national, but it lacked cohesion. The task of the Sovereign at Vienna had indeed been simplified since another branch of the family had been installed at Madrid. But they still had the German Empire on their hands, a Germany torn by religious strife and weakened by the individual ambitions of her princes, especially those of the House of Prussia. As Germany disintegrated, the Habsburgs turned their attention more and more to those lands which were in fact their family possession. And while the Empire became more and more a kind of German League of Nations, the *domus Austriae* grew increasingly conscious of her individual ends. A Chancellery of the Austrian Court, distinct from the Imperial Chancellery, was created in 1620; a permanent Austrian army in 1650. In the year 1669, a 'secret conference' was inaugurated; this was designed to forward specifically Austrian ends, known only to a few initiates. Pragmatic Sanctions in 1713 put the final stamp on the work of many generations by declaring 'an inseparable and indissoluble union' between all the hereditary possessions of the House of Habsburg. At least, that from now on would be the fictitious legal aspect. But what was the actual situation? How could one find any link binding, in fact, the Tyrol and Transylvania, Bohemia with Illyria, to say nothing of Flanders, Mantua or the land of the Milanese? Where indeed? For apart from the 'sacred person' of the Monarch himself, no organic link existed. Each country had its Diet, its laws, its own Minister resident at Vienna, political centre of the 'Imperial and Royal States'. Thus, there was a secret Chancellery for Bohemia, another for High and Low Austria, there was a supreme Commission concerned with the affairs of Hungary, and even a 'supreme Court' for Spain. Up to the time of Maria-Theresa, Vienna boasted two aulic Chancelleries: one Bohemian, the other Austrian; a Hungarian aulic council; three Departments (Transylvanian, Dutch, Italian); an Illyrian 'Deputation', to which must be added a Gallician aulic Chancellery; one got lost in the maze.

The language used between all these diverse local and central institutions was Latin, universal medium—up to the eighteenth century—for diplomats, the Church and Science. The Emperor Maxmilian I, last of mediaeval knights who was fond of saying 'My pride is German, and German is my pride', had, in fact tried to stress the German element, to make the German way of life predominate. He wished to found a central administration to control foreign affairs, the army and finance. He had even called together the elected representatives of each country in order to unite in 'fraternal' discussion of their common problems. But his effort was vain. The German element had indeed been sufficiently powerful to subdue vast territories under the domination of a national dynasty. It had succeeded in crushing Czech aspirations to political and religious independence at the battle of the White Mountain. But complete assimilation of millions of Slavs, Hungarians, Italians (all living in compact agglomerations) was not to be contemplated. The German racial avalanche, spreading Eastward along the Danube, had stopped short at the time of Charlemagne on the Leitha, not far from Vienna: it was never to go farther except in occasional sporadic movements by small groups.

And yet if the Habsburgs did manage to create something in the nature of an Austrian attitude of mind, it was precisely by utilising such diverse racial elements. Austrian civilisation was a peculiar mixture which one might compare with Viennese cooking, composed of Italian *pasta*, Slavonic sweetmeats, and highly spiced Hungarian national dishes, all mixed up with the heavy, indigestible products of the German *delicatessen* stores.

Already, at the beginning of the sixteenth century, after the death of Maximilian, the 'Countries' had snorted their independence and refused to obey the lieutenants of the Crown: Low Austria was already coining her own currency. Hurrying from the depths of Spain, the Emperor Ferdinand restored order in the various Austrian Duchies after a savage tussle resulting in the appalling massacre of Wiener-Neustadt. This was followed by a rising of Bohemian nobles, defeated—after a few transitory successes—at the famous White Mountain. The Bohemian nobles were dispossessed of their lands and replaced by a 'Court nobility' of German origin. From then on, an absolute *régime* was in operation for two centuries over all the 'hereditary' countries, including Hungary: an autocracy in the Spanish manner. 'To a pompous ceremonial, strict and closely observed rules of social hierarchy, was added the severest rules of discipline combined

with certain traditions then current in Madrid.' The Jesuits made
their appearance and acquired considerable influence. In the early
days of the Reformation, about one-twentieth of the Austrian
nobility and bourgeoisie had remained Catholic; but the arrival
of the Jesuits reversed the situation: heresy was sternly put down,
there was soon not a single Protestant in the King's Councils, or
other public offices: no more Protestant Church, or schools—no
more Bible. The Jesuits even filtered into the administration,
controlled police and censorship, monopolised the education of
the ruling classes and inculcated that traditionalism and taste for
splitting hairs which were to become the leading characteristics
of the Austrian mind.

If they mercilessly destroyed the last vestige of Czech culture,
at least they contributed in a remarkable manner to a flowering
of the arts and science, notably of the theatre and Viennese
music. The *baroque* style came into fashion: transplanted in the
first place from Italy, it soon became indigenous. This style,
theatrical, decorative, sumptuous, essentially allegorical, combining painting and sculpture, high colours and much gold, with
its over-decorated façades and extensive use of marble in poly-
chrome, became all the rage.[1] After architecture and sculpture,
music in turn began to show Italian influence. The Archbishops
of Salzburg initiated the first German Opera House; their example was soon followed at Vienna, and the capital of the Habsburgs became what it has remained to our day, the greatest musical centre in Europe.

In Maria-Theresa, the Austrian point of view found its most
perfect incarnation. 'She combines all the qualities of a Catholic
and an Austrian: piety, veneration for the natural order which
she esteems Divine, a cult of tradition, respect for authority, a
horror of rationalism.' She was one of those historic figures which
leave a trace not easily wiped out in the public memory. The
ghost of a great Queen still lingers today in the Austrian capital,
just as the spirit of Louis XIV hovers over the gardens of Versailles. At Vienna, the influence of her taste was everywhere

1. For greater detail we refer the reader to André Tibal's well-documented
book: *L'Autrichien. Essai sur la formation d'une individualité nationale*, 1936.

apparent: in the pompous decoration of the Hofburg; of Schoenbrunn and the Belvedere, in the style of the churches and their many altars erected by her, in the choice of pictures and statues in her collections. Her tomb is the focal point of that dark crypt of the Capuchin Chapel where the heavy metal coffins of other Habsburgs are all huddled together in nondescript array, and the caretaker-guide never fails to point out to visitors that such and such a prince was 'the grand-father of Maria-Theresa', that another was 'her great grandson'. The struggle then waging against Frederick II had made her fully conscious of an 'Austrian point of view', an outlook steeped in that essentially southern amenity which she felt was the complete antithesis of the rigid and implacable ideology of Prussia, based only on a principle of blind obedience.

Her son and successor, Joseph II, fervent disciple of the Enlightenment, felt it incumbent upon him to break with the old traditions. He tried to build a state in the abstract: he wanted centralisation, unity, without taking long-established provincial privileges or local ways and customs into account. There were to be no more Tyrolians or Hungarians—all his subjects would be Austrian—'the various provinces of the monarchy will be combined in a single unit'. He was filled with reforming zeal, but unfortunately ignorant of the realities of human life, and so he abolished with a stroke of the pen all Provincial Diets and moved the jewels from the crown of St. Wenceslaus and St. Stephen to the Hofburg. 'Great things must be done with decision', he said. But he found himself in opposition to the nobility and the clergy, up against the passive resistance and lack of comprehension of the peasants, faced with the complicated mechanism of a state which had never been national but *supra*-national. He was soon obliged to retrace his steps. Reforms were held up, the crown of St. Stephen returned to Buda. 'All my cherished schemes have come to nought!' cried Joseph on his death-bed. Leopold II, who succeeded him, immediately revived the right of the 'Countries'. And Austria remained what she had always been: an Empire without rigid national frontiers, with no stereotyped institutions, no common language; a polychromatic empire, composed of bits

56

and pieces, and yet itself called upon to maintain the cohesion, equilibrium, stability of Europe.

Happy Austria! land of many races, subject to diverse and contradictory influences, Europe in miniature, microcosmic portrait of a continent. Was she really happy? Although happiness, of course, is not easy to define, one can safely risk the statement that she was, at least as much as other countries, perhaps a little more. Up till the end of the eighteenth century, until the moment when Joseph II, by his attempt at centralisation, roused the opposition of the different races that formed his monarchy, the problem of nationalities had never arisen. Deprived of their nobility and other cultured classes, the Czechs had temporarily lost all race consciousness: even their language was in danger of becoming a local idiom, used only by serfs and people of no standing. Among other Slav peoples, race consciousness was almost non-existent. The troubles that arose in Hungary between the master race and the Slav minority did not involve any question of language since Latin only was spoken in courts of justice, by all administrative bodies, and by educated people in general.

Thus at this period the Empire of the Habsburgs was still unaware of the terrible conflicts which in time were to tear her to shreds and bring about her final collapse. As long as a certain equilibrium was maintained within the bosom of the great family itself, all went smoothly. Neither did *the countries*, calm and docile, experience any particular heart-searchings as to their lack of political freedom. An enlightened autocracy maintained order, with the help of a loyal clergy, rigorous censorship and a zealous police force. But their rule was infused with a patriarchal spirit: the sovereign genuinely looked upon the various peoples as his children, and since no political opposition existed, the government's procedure shocked no one. 'I have always thought,' wrote Leibnitz, about 1683, 'and I am still entirely convinced, that all is well within the Empire, and that whether we are happy depends upon ourselves alone. . . . For our government is as mild and merciful as His Majesty himself is great. Such leniency is a hereditary virtue of the House of Austria.'

These were not merely servile phrases: Austria, the world of the

E

Habsburgs, was no more perfect than any other human insti-
tution; but one breathed a certain atmosphere of humanity and
goodwill which reconciled the most subversive spirits with
authority.

The Emperor appeared, according to Leibnitz, as something
like a 'lay chief of Christianity'. Economically and culturally, the
territories concerned: arid alpine slopes, rich river valleys of the
Danube, the Carpathians and mountains of Bohemia with their
inexhaustible mineral resources, were mutually complementary
and gave promise of great future prosperity. The nobility were
powerful. They were still largely feudal in character: their
domains were as extensive as their privileges. Freer, nearer to the
soil than any courtier of Versailles, less addicted to notions of independence, less prone to individual arrogance than the German
nobles, less conscious of 'rights' than the English lords, Austrian
aristocracy—Jesuit trained—constituted an ever loyal and solid
support for the throne of the Habsburgs. In comparison with the
nobility, the bourgeoisie just emerging played an inconspicuous
part. As for the peasant, he certainly was poor, down-trodden,
exploited, he was crushed by taxation and ruined by conscription.
When he was not lucky enough to belong to the master race—
Hungarian or German—his situation was even more unfortunate.
But he was not conscious of his misfortunes. The government
under which he lived seemed to him established for eternity; he
never questioned his submission. He lived in the lap of a smiling
and generous nature: he owned the sun, the green hills, corn and
vines.... that was enough for him.

In short, Austria rather resembled some comfortable old house
where there was room for everybody. But dry rot had set in.
One had to be careful what one touched; the old place might
hold together for many a long year; yet on the other hand, the
slightest shaking might bring it crashing down.

And the shaking came . . . when Francis II, Metternich's
'august master', succeeded to the throne in 1792. We already
know something of the very special atmosphere in which the
pomps and ceremonies of his coronation took place. The great

Revolution was knocking at the door of ancient Europe: the voices of pioneers reverberated like a tocsin among the world's enslaved masses; they called to a new life.

Francis II was born in 1768; he was thus exactly the same age as Napoleon Bonaparte, his future enemy; he was four years older than Metternich.

Tall and thin, long angular face, dull, expressionless eyes; his sharp features, white tunic and high boots have come down to us in innumerable pictures of the Napoleonic era. His character was entirely compatible with the role he was to play in history. For if Maria-Theresa had personified Austria in the days of her glory, Francis personified little but the hereditary principle; he was 'heir' to the dynasty, little more. Metternich said of him that never had monarch to such an extent possessed 'official' entrails! For half a century he fought the Revolution without ever understanding it. But this lack of comprehension, this closed mind was his strength. He was in danger of no mental contagion. He certainly had none of the genius of Napoleon, nor was he capable of occasional soaring in the manner of Alexander I. But he was never craven like Frederick-William III and so many other German princes. This mediocre man did not entirely lack greatness, and to that he owed the devotion of his suite and of his people.

Francis had an uncanny natural instinct when it came to courting popularity with the masses. He was a strange mixture of simplicity and despotism, Jesuitical ruse and debonair frankness, gross selfishness and sentimental good nature. 'To see him driving in the streets of Vienna', writes a contemporary, 'in his old green barouche, with two horses, dressed in a shabby brown cape, with hat to match, to watch him as he smiled amiably to right and left, or chatted familiarly with his Grand Chamberlain, one would never have suspected him of an ounce of pride.' The Emperor was also an adept in the use of the current witty Viennese slang; he often amazed his hearers.

Fundamentally, Francis was lazy and his natural tastes inclined him to fiddling tasks. 'He spent much time stamping seals onto sealing wax, carefully spreading it out to insure handsome effects; in adding impressive signatures to innumerable unimportant

59

documents. He loved to pore over the details of a hundred and one minor matters, which he liked to consider his special prerogative, such as: ranks, titles, privileges, pardons and benefactions; to say nothing of holding an incredible number of military reviews.'

Such a sovereign obviously needed counsellors to guide him, to enlarge his horizon beyond the limits of his apartments in the Hofburg where Joseph II had installed him and where he was to live without moving for half a century. He had a clear plan from the beginning as far as home affairs were concerned: he would establish order over his whole Empire—order as he conceived it. But he was a novice in the field of diplomacy and in coping with the wider European issues; he fell under the influence of a few men around him and allowed himself—contrary to all Habsburg tradition—to be drawn into a policy of war.

Three men, three different characters. Thugut, the war baron, 'of modest origin, narrow and reactionary, opponent of every freedom, of all superior knowledge, hating the French as bitterly as that "infernal race", the Prussians'; Cobenzl, lazy, unprincipled aristocrat, 'without opinions, without character, incapable of grasping any great idea, adept above all in the art of temporising or of sliding out by means of trickery'; finally, Stadion, old-fashioned politician of the romantic type, 'Knight of the Empire', idealist and patriot, anxious to follow the example of Prussia and to inculcate an acute national consciousness in the Austrian people. And all three ministers, so different in temperament and in every way, concurred as to this one impossible objective: to crush revolutionary France and Bonaparte, heir of the Jacobins.

Their influence prevailed with Francis. One must, of course, admit that his counsellors' views were in keeping with his own inclinations. He had family ties with all the deposed crowned heads. He was the son of an Infanta of Spain, nephew of Marie-Antoinette, son-in-law of Marie-Caroline of Naples; in the circumstances he could only feel a kind of religious horror of those who were proclaimed 'enemies of the human race'. He visited his army in the field and was present at the battle of Turcoing where his troops were beaten, as usual. Later, we see him at

Austerlitz and Wagram but he took no part in the direction of operations. But neither under canvas nor in the committee rooms of the Hofburg did he show any particular enthusiasm for this struggle which he himself had sponsored and the whole of his suite had urged upon him. It seemed as if some hereditary caution was stirring in the deep recesses of his unconscious mind. Had he really chosen the right path? Is it really the function of Austria to make war? Doesn't she lose, each time, in war, a part of that glorious heritage which his ancestors had handed down? [1]

Already in 1801, Francis was writing: 'I have so exhausted my monarchy, so drained it of men and money that it is no longer in a position to play its natural part in maintaining the balance of power in Europe. I have lost all my erstwhile diplomatic relations and cannot—in the present exhausted condition of Austria—count on the sincerity of a single ally.' [2] He was, up to a point, a fatalist. 'The French will soon attack us again—and then again; they will rout us and we shall have to start negotiating once more.' These words, spoken during the French campaign, must often have come back to mind. After the appalling result of Wagram, his mind was made up. 'I will try once more', he said to the Burgomaster of Vienna; 'if that is not successful, I shall pack up and go.' [3] The House of Austria was in grave need of returning to a political procedure more in keeping with its traditions, more supple, more conciliatory, more realistic. It was Metternich who would be called upon to put this into effect.

'The relationship between the Habsburgs and their advisers', said the historian Tschuppik, 'has always been rather unusual. The members of that egocentric dynasty were convinced that the universe, the whole human race, had no other function than to cater to their glory. Proceeding from such a basis, their choice of counsellors was not easy. That is why they have always shown a marked preference for the refugee, the man-without-a-country,

1. At Campo Formio, Bonaparte seized the Low Countries, Lombardy, Brisgau and the left bank of the Rhine. At Luneville, he took Tuscany, Presburg, the Venetian States, the Tyrol and forced Francis to surrender the Imperial crown of Germany. The treaty of Vienna was further to deprive Austria of Salzburg, a portion of Galicia, Trieste, Fiume, Carniola and a portion of Carinthia.
2. V. Bibl: *François II, le beau-père de Napoléon*, 1936.
3. Otto to Champagny, October 20th, 1811. (Arch. aff. etr.)

the man who might be disposed to limit his horizon to that of the Habsburgs themselves—to merge his own fate in that of the dynasty.' Prince Eugène of Savoy had been their prime discovery in the eighteenth, Metternich was to be their dynastic phoenix in the nineteenth century.

He was not Austrian, he was a Count of the Rhenish country; the predatory expeditions of the post-Revolution period had destroyed his German patrimony. Up to the time of his marriage with Eléonore von Kaunitz, he had no link whatever with feudal Austria. Since then, he had lived abroad and had remained aloof from intrigues periodically stirred up by the bureaucrats and aristocrats of Vienna. He was thus in a position to devote himself exclusively to the great House.[1] He was to bring to it his worldly wisdom, his experience of German and Eastern Courts, his elegant and subtle mind, persuasive eloquence, a distinguished pen, all the arts of the charmer. But his working programme, its framework, were predetermined, marked out for centuries by all those others who had created and built up 'happy Austria'.

1. 'My fate will always depend upon the Austrian monarchy; I shall stand or fall by that.' Metternich to Stadion, March 17th, 1809. (Vienna, Secret Archives.)

# V

# THE MARRIAGE OF
# MARIE-LOUISE

*A virgin of the house of Austria had to be sacrificed to appease the Monster...* — LADY CASTLEREAGH

'WE have a great deal to restore', said the Emperor Francis to Count Metternich when, on July 1st, 1809, he appointed the latter to be interim Secretary of State for Foreign Affairs (it was the evening of the bloody rout of Wagram).

And the young statesman, who finally assumed permanent ministerial functions the day after the disastrous treaty of Vienna, had indeed taken on a legacy sadly impaired. 'It is no small matter to be Foreign Secretary in Austria today', Metternich wrote to his wife on November 28th, 1809. 'What happenings all around me! In the midst of what incredible predicaments have I been called upon to play the leading part: I am caught in a maelstrom.' But he was by no means cast down. Gentz indeed was surprised at 'the confidence, really quite shocking, with which he is preparing to tackle so terrible a task. I shall never forgive him the frivolous indifference with which he let his predecessor Stadion go.' Gentz was far from realising what fiery zeal impelled the young Minister. 'I shall do three times as much work, and in much less time than it has taken others—including my predecessors—to do it', he declared in a letter to a friend. He also had realised that any further struggle against the apparently invincible Napoleon would be futile, and already by August 10th, 1809, he was addressing to his Emperor a report (later to become famous)

63

in which he exposed the principles of his new political technique. 'We can only consolidate our own position', he wrote, 'by coming to terms with victorious France. . . . Our principles remain unaltered but one cannot battle with the irrevocable. We must reserve our strength for better days and seek our immediate salvation by gentler means. . . . As from the signing of the peace, our policy will consist exclusively of tacking, avoiding commitments, and of flattery. Only so can we hope to carry on until the day of general liberation.'

At the end of November, Metternich took the first step towards some kind of practical accommodation with France. A certain M. de Laborde, ex-emigré, then living in Vienna, had at one time been in the service of Austria but had since rallied to the Emperor of the French. During the campaign of 1809, Napoleon had given Laborde a kind of liaison job with the French army, counting probably on the usefulness of the emigre's social connections in influential Viennese circles.

After the departure of the troops, Laborde had stayed on in the Austrian capital to clear up certain matters of administration. He was about to leave when, on November 29th, Metternich summoned him in order to outline his point of view as to what the future relations of Austria and France ought to be.

'The Emperor Francis', said the Minister, 'has for a long time been distressed by his people's misfortunes. He knows my own desire for peace—a desire from which I have never wavered except when circumstances forcibly dragged me in the opposite direction. I have every reason to hope that a policy of peace will keep me at the Ministry and that my presence at the Ministry will maintain a policy of peace. It is, however, essential that no insuperable obstacles should arise as from the French side, particularly such minor irritations as tend to wound national susceptibilities without any tangible advantage. We, on our side, shall be particularly careful to avoid similar discourtesies, and France, I am convinced, will have no cause for complaint in this respect. It is essential, however, to distinguish between the official attitude and irresponsible chatter in Viennese drawing-rooms. The latter for the most part arises from purely internal party considerations and cliques: opposition, for instance, to individual members of the government, to some Archduke or General. The Minister cannot know everything or exercise a comprehensive censorship, but the really essential factor is that his own conduct should be loyal, sensitive and frank. You know how we discharged our war indemnities: other secret agreements will take care of themselves. All the generals who were *non grata* to the French Government have been retired; the soldiers of the *landwehr* have gone home, the one battalion that came to Vienna was immediately disbanded. Finally, let me assure you that we shall even refrain from jealousy! I mean from any displeasure at the marked preference which the Emperor Napoleon seems to feel called upon to extend to Russia, recurrent proofs of which might tend to wound us.'[1]

Metternich well knew that statements of such importance would immediately be reported to the Emperor of the French. In themselves, they constituted a complete reversal of the Austrian state of mind.

Now securely installed at the desk of his great predecessor Kaunitz, he wished to revive the old politico-matrimonial policies of the House of Habsburg.

Can the circumstances surrounding Napoleon's second marriage even now be completely understood? The motives which induced him to separate from Josephine and marry a foreign princess are generally known. The reasons which precluded his marriage with a sister of the Tsar are clear and universally accepted. There remains, however, one point which has never been satisfactorily explained: the origin of the Austrian project and the manner in which the final realisation of that marriage came about. Who was the prime mover in this scheme? What part was played by the Viennese Cabinet and what by Napoleon himself?

German distortions, catering to popular taste, have found an elementary answer. Drunk with his victories, convinced of his omnipotence, the all-conquering Corsican is supposed to have

1. Archives du Quai d'Orsay, Vienna, 1809. No. 343. Unsigned copy. This part of the Laborde report has not previously been published.

inflicted on the proudest of European dynasties this unparalleled humiliation: a sudden and brutal demand for the hand of the heiress of the Habsburgs.

Powerless, the Austrian Emperor is said to have offered a supreme sacrifice on the altar of his country, to have delivered the new Iphigenia bound hand and foot to the embraces of an adventurer; immolated the nineteen-year-old Archduchess, Marie-Louise who had grown up in fear and hatred of the tyrant. Metternich's own *Mémoires* indeed have contributed, not only in Germany but up to a point in France, to confirm that legend.

In contradistinction to this theory, discredited by all contemporary evidence, we find another—rather more subtle—beyond the Rhine, which suggests that Napoleon was the victim of Machiavellian machinations, that Metternich, in short, made a fool of him.

The young Austrian minister was pursuing an inspired plan. 'Nobody suspected the truth,' wrote Countess Lulu Thurheim in her *Mémoires*, 'nobody had considered how this new daughter of Aeneas might avenge her people—except, perhaps, one man. That man was Metternich. And Marie-Louise was in fact predestined to avenge Austria.'

It is important, once for all, to scotch all fantasies by means of authentic contemporary documents. And these give ample proof that Metternich himself was the original instigator, and most zealous worker in behalf of the marriage of Napoleon to the Archduchess Marie-Louise.

What could have been his motives in urging this marriage with a man from whom, in his own words, he wished to 'deliver the civilised world'?

First, there was the memory of that glorious period (the Austrian matrimonial system in reverse) when Kaunitz, with the help of Mercy d'Argenteau, had guided the political policies of the royal couple in France. Metternich sincerely believed that the influence of an Austrian Empress in France might mollify the tyrannical demands of the conqueror, that she might succeed in lulling his suspicions, perhaps even accomplish something behind his back.

Furthermore, he proposed to treat his sovereign's daughter as a means of barter. The marriage would offer an excuse to retrieve at least some of the lost provinces, thus rehabilitating the tottering prestige of Austria. But there was still a third consideration which carried more weight than all the others. By a strange aberration, Metternich had concluded that to offer the hand of the Archduchess Marie-Louise was the only way of averting a matrimonial alliance between France and Russia, and that appeared to him an irrevocable disaster both for Austria and the whole of Europe.

For, long before Bismark, Metternich had been obsessed with a nightmare of 'coalitions'. He feared Russia at least as much as he feared France. Political thought in Austria and Germany has always fluctuated between the two tendencies: to turn towards Russia or the West. Metternich had categorically chosen the latter. He knew London, he had lived a long time in Paris. In spite of his grudge against Napoleon, he was filled with admiration. On the other hand, he saw in darkest Russia, the Kingdom of the Tsars, a murky influence, little less than barbaric. If such an influence were to become actively attached to France, subjected to the impetuous genius of Napoleon, he felt it would be all up with Europe.

Later, Metternich frankly admitted that this fear of Russia had governed his attitude to the marriage. His admission is not to be found in the *Mémoires*, which were 'cooked', but occurred during a conversation with Finkenstein, the Prussian diplomat, in March, 1810. That conversation took place in an atmosphere of 'detachment and great frankness'. 'Our interests are absolutely identical with those of Prussia, hingeing essentially on her conservation and general well-being', Metternich declared. 'This cannot be altered in any way by the family ties which we have just contracted with France.' Whereupon, Metternich let the cat out of the bag: 'The imminent danger of a family union between France and Russia ... threatened Austria with destruction and the whole of Europe with being shared out between those two powers.'[1]

1. Telegram from Finkenstein, March 14th, 1810. (Berlin-Dahlem Secret Archives.)

The same point of view appears in a memorandum addressed to the Viennese Chancellery designed for its own use and a few days after Napoleon's divorce. This document affirmed that a marriage with the Archduchess would be Austria's only hope of salvation since the alternative Russian marriage would lead to 'anarchy, the destruction of all intervening states, the triumph of despotism, in short to an age of barbarism'.[1]

Metternich thus decided to play his trump card. In November 1809, as the last shots of the campaign died away, the Austrian General Bubna, acting on instructions from the young Minister, declared to Guilleminot (Eugène de Beauharnais' chief of staff) that in the case of a divorce, Marie-Louise would be the only Princess in Europe worthy of the Emperor. A few days later, on November 29th, Metternich himself showed his hand at the end of a memorable conversation with Alexandre de Laborde. 'As a means of greater harmony, a means of uniting two peoples', wrote Laborde, M. de Metternich slid into the conversation the words 'a family alliance'. After some circumlocution and diplomatic niceties, he spoke straight out: 'Do you think the Emperor has ever really considered a divorce?' he said. I was not expecting such a question and thinking that he only had in mind its relation to some princess of the French Imperial family, I answered vaguely and waited for him to become more precise. He returned to the question and spoke of the possibility of a marriage between Napoleon and a Princess of the House of Austria. '*This idea*', he said, '*is my own*. I have not yet had occasion to test the Emperor's opinions. But apart from being reasonably assured that they would be favourable, such an event would have the universal approval here among all those whose names and position carry weight, in fact with the whole population. Of this I have no doubt and I should regard it as a great good fortune for us and a proud achievement of my own ministry.'

During the last days of November, diplomatic relations be-

In a previous telegram, dated February 29th, Finkenstein already suggested that Metternich had done everything possible to induce Francis to give his daughter because he feared the 'abnormal influence that Russia would have acquired by the marriage of a Grand Duchess'.
1. Quoted by E. Wertheimer in *Der Herzog von Reichstadt*, 1902.

tween France and Austria were resumed. Prince Schwarzenberg arrived at Paris accompanied by the Counsellor Floret, a young diplomat who enjoyed Metternich's full confidence and who wrote to him in private.[1]

Without more ado, Floret assured the Senator Semonville, whom he met in the *salon* of the Empress Josephine, 'that Vienna would consider giving an Archduchess: And your Ambassador? replied Semonville. I will guarantee his approval. And Metternich?—No trouble there. And the Emperor?—Even more certain.'[2]

Napoleon, informed of all this, now knew exactly where he stood. He would lose little, should Alexander refuse. He made up his mind. On November 22nd, 1809, the Comte de Champagny, French Foreign Minister, instructed Caulaincourt, Ambassador at Saint Petersburg, to open formal negotiations with the Tsar concerning marriage between Napoleon and the Grand Duchess Anne. This telegram was to reach Saint Petersburg on December 14th. Absent from his capital, Alexander only gave audience to the French Ambassador on December 28th, and the telegram recording the Ambassador's first impressions did not reach Paris before January 26th, 1810. It was during these weeks of delay that Metternich's state of mind reached fever pitch. If one wishes to understand his tactics during this period, one must see him convinced that Napoleon's request would be accepted by the Russian Court. He based his opinions on reports received from the banks of the Neva. These were sent by the Comte de Saint-Julien, recently arrived at Saint Petersburg to re-establish long interrupted diplomatic relations between Vienna and the capital of the Tsars. But the young man had gained a completely wrong impression of the state of mind prevailing at Alexander's Court.[3]

1. Floret seems to have been one of the first partisans of a marriage with an Archduchess. He had already mentioned it at the French headquarters during the Peace negotiations. (*Floret's Journal*, Vienna, Secret Archives.)

2. Ernouf: Maret, *Duc de Bassano*.

3. 'Always actuated by the distressing sentiment of fear', wrote Saint-Julien, 'they pile one craven act upon another; they seem ready to make any concession if only it will stave off war with France. Fear dominates the Tsar in... all humility, he acknowledges the superiority of his ally... one condescension entails another, and the indignation of the public has no effect.' (Vienna, Secret Archives.)

Certainly, they feared Napoleon at Saint Petersburg; they were unquestionably nervous about war. And again, Napoleon could always count on the good offices of a Roumianzoff, now completely sold to the French state. But to conclude the possibility of a marriage with a Russian princess, with one who had scarcely reached the age of puberty into the bargain, was to take too much for granted. Metternich was ready to play ducks and drakes with the pride of the Habsburgs and thought to do as much with the haughty Romanoffs.... He had not taken into account the almost mystical reverence felt for the Tsar and all his family throughout Russia. He knew the weaknesses of Alexander as they appeared from day to day, but he discounted the long-term influence of the Empress-mother, her hatred of Napoleon, her watchful eye when it came to the fate of her daughters. Letters exchanged, during this period, between the Austrian Ambassador to Paris and Count Metternich convey a curious light on the situation. Napoleon's divorce and the respective chances of the Russian or Austrian marriage appear to have been their sole concern.

Prince von Schwarzenberg had arrived at Paris toward the end of November. The future commander-in-chief of Leipzig was a slow-thinking fellow, heavy and pompous. He did not fit easily into the Parisian scene; everything upset him, the favours showered by Napoleon upon his Russian colleague reduced him to the last pitch of exasperation. His second report, under date of December 21st, was a long list of grievances. At the end of it, Schwarzenberg announced that Napoleon's divorce was now a *fait accompli*. 'Napoleon', he said, 'has designs on Madame, the Grand Duchess Anne, of that there is little doubt. Prince Kouakine denies all knowledge of any such intentions with regard to any Russian princess, but we all know that for a long time the two sovereigns have been in private correspondence, that a considerable number of letters have been exchanged, and it is commonly rumoured that General Savary might leave for Russia at any moment on a special mission. One can only conclude that Napoleon would never go so far in that direction were he not reasonably assured of ultimate success.'

70

But sponsors of the Austrian cause by no means laid down their arms. On the same day, Schwarzenberg sent a long postscript to his report in which he gave a detailed account of his extremely curious negotiations with the zealous Laborde: 'M. le Comte de Laborde came to see me yesterday morning', he wrote. 'He began by inquiring in a discreet manner what the reactions in Vienna would be in the case of a proposal of marriage for the Arch Duchess Marie-Louise by Napoleon. I told him in confidence that *such an event seemed to me by no means impossible, since I knew that our Emperor's dearest wish was to establish some more intimate relation with France....* He begged me to ask for categorical instructions in this matter so that he would be in a position to reply without ambiguity, with absolute precision, to such proposals as might at any moment arise. I replied that I myself was convinced that Russia *would accept or even had already accepted*; but he insisted that the matter was by no means yet decided.'

But the most glaring evidence of the state of mind which prevailed at the Austrian Embassy, Paris, at the end of 1809, is a private letter which Floret appended to the official mail-bag on December 21st. It supplies conclusive evidence; it leaves no shred of excuse for that legend which has since grown up, for any claim that Napoleon himself forced the marriage upon Austria. 'Most of the ministers seem to accept the new ties which are about to be formed, but were their choice entirely free, it is by no means certain that they would prefer a Russian princess still too much of a child to play any appreciable part in state affairs; there is also a feeling that the slightest delay in the negotiations would make Napoleon withdraw, and it is not yet considered impossible that he might change his mind in a direction which many influential persons desire. You must, then, *keep this eventuality in mind and be well prepared in order to be able to give an immediate answer to any overture or proposition that might be made*; the Prince should be informed that anything is possible.' [1]

Metternich replied without delay; on December 25th he officially instructed Schwarzenberg not to hold back in any way should overtures be made to him in the matter of a French alliance with the House of Austria. 'The Emperor, our august master, has always shown that the good of the state was his first consideration. What sovereign has ever given evidence of a greater devotion, a greater willingness to sacrifice his personal happiness?' [1]

It was then that Countess Metternich came into the picture. Not having been able to leave Paris at the beginning, she had remained there with her children throughout the war. But since the arrival of Schwarzenberg and the renewal of normal diplomatic relations, there was nothing to keep her in France, and yet we see her preparing for an indefinite stay. What had happened? We find an explanation in a report which M. Piquot, Prussian *chargé d'affaires* at Vienna, sent to his government after the marriage had taken place.

'Napoleon back in Paris, the question of the marriage was revived, and Countess Metternich, wife of the Minister, assumed the role of confidante. She therefore made a point of saying good-bye to all her friends but still continued to go to Court where the Emperor said to her, quite straightforwardly and in such a manner as to be heard by all present, that it was impossible for her to leave at such a season, on account of the December cold. At which the Countess—having already been primed—appeared to give way to the monarch's wishes, assuring him in turn in such a way as to be heard by the gallery—that she was much touched by his kindness and that she would postpone her journey until the following spring if her husband agreed. That same evening, the Emperor arranged with Countess Metternich a time and place where they could meet to discuss the marriage project. Shortly after this, the monarch, in order to throw dust in our eyes, again said openly: 'I like Madame de Metternich, she is a really charming woman because she never meddles with politics'. [2]

By the end of December, the Austrian Minister's wife had seen Napoleon and at *la Malmaison* had actually received certain confidences from Josephine herself: 'I have a plan with which I am seriously preoccupied,' said the ex-Empress, 'the success of which

1. Metternich: *Mémoires.*
2. Report of February 21st, 1810. (Berlin, Secret Archives.)

alone would make the sacrifice I have just made appear to me worth while; I mean that the Emperor should marry your Archduchess; I spoke to him about it yesterday and he told me that his choice was not yet fixed—she added: I think that it could be, were he sure to be accepted *chez vous*.'[1] Madame de Metternich replied that 'she would regard such a marriage as a great honour'.

A letter dated January 13th, one that Metternich's son has not seen fit to include in his collection, is even more explicit and brings out in no uncertain manner the official nature of the part played by the Foreign Minister's wife at that period: 'I can tell you nothing more about the all-important matter. I have seen neither the Queen of Holland nor the Empress, since. Only La Borde, the tame domestic spy, came to see me and repeated what he had already said to Schwarzenberg. . . . He is very much afraid that the Prince might act too slowly in the case of an official proposal. He ought to be in a position to reply immediately, without hesitation.'[2]

We find an echo of these conversations with Laborde in official diplomatic documents and particularly in Schwarzenberg's long report, dated January 13th. 'Monsieur de La Borde', wrote the Ambassador, 'still visits me with every show of assiduity. The subject of his conversation is invariably the marriage between Napoleon and Madame the Archduchess Marie-Louise, he considers it the only means of establishing a solid alliance between our two nations and thus securing peace for the whole continent . . . La Borde insists that Napoleon has decided to ask for the Archduchess immediately should the Russian mail—expected from day to day—not only fail to bring a categorically affirmative answer but furthermore announce the imminent arrival of the Grand Duchess Anne herself. . . . he added that I ought to be in a position to reply immediately to any official feelers such as might shortly be put out. . . . La Borde's frequent conversations about this question of the marriage appear to have a rather more

1. Metternich: *Mémoires*.
2. This letter was published by Fournier in his study 'Zur Heirat Napoleons and Marie-Louisens' (*Historische Skizzen und Studien*, 1912) but was never known in France. See also A. Becker: *Der Plan der zweiten. Heirat Napoleons.*(Mitteilung des Instituts für oesterreichische Geschichte Bd. 19.)

than semi-official character. I beg you to believe that should this very interesting matter reach a point of serious negotiation, I shall make every effort to carry out the orders of my August Sovereign.'

The die was cast. The Austrians were prepared to suffer—by no means reluctantly—this 'outrage'.... Metternich himself wrote to his wife on January 27th. 'At the moment I consider this matter of first importance for the whole of Europe.... From the moment when I first heard of the dissolution of his marriage with a wife who will not easily be replaced, I began to turn over in my mind a possible successor. It was natural that first among all available princess, Madame the Archduchess should spring to my mind.... I found the Emperor in this instance, as in all others, without prejudice, honourable, trustworthy, resolute, a man of principle.... From then on, I felt that I could safely pursue my plan.'[1]

But what would Napoleon himself decide? The Austrians had put their cards on the table, but the Emperor of the French was still holding his hand. Schwarzenberg, also, was torn between hope and fear as we see by the three reports which he sent to Vienna at the end of January.[2] Every step taken by the French Government was watched: dates on which the mail arrived were known, as also the hours at which documents were opened. Thanks to the deliberate indiscretions of Laborde the Austrian Embassy was also kept in touch with the trend of discussions in the *Grand Conseil*, presided over by Napoleon himself.

Schwarzenberg thought he knew everything, but in fact he ignored the only really important factor, that evasive, virtually negative, reply from Coulaincourt which had reached Paris on January 26th. He was also completely to ignore the frankly unfavourable nature (for Napoleon) of two telegrams sent by Coulaincourt on January 15th and 21st respectively.

It was when he had received these telegrams that Napoleon reached his final conclusion and sent Eugène de Beauharnais to Schwarzenberg to demand an immediate contract of marriage with Marie-Louise, stipulating that it was to be signed within the

1. Published in *Mémoires*.
2. See C. de Grunwald: *Le mariage de Napoléon et de Marie-Louise*.

next few hours. In turn, Napoleon played his trumps, turning failure into victory. He ran no risks, he was well aware that Austria would refuse him nothing.[1]

The Viennese archives are singularly reticent when it comes to the events of these decisive days. The dossier 'Reports-France' contains very few documents concerning the marriage as between the dates of February 1st and 17th, 1810. It is inadmissible to conclude that Schwarzenberg did not send a whole series of reports on the very day when the great event occurred. We can only find one in which Schwarzenberg justifying himself with the authorities at home, wrote: 'If I had hesitated one moment to sign, he [Napoleon] would have thrown over the whole thing, and said good-bye to both the Russian and the Saxon. . . .'[2] What happened to the other reports? To whose interest was it to remove them? We do not and we shall never know.

E. Wertheimer, the eminent Austrian historian has, however, unearthed a document by Metternich's own hand, related to these two weeks. It is a report from the Minister to his Emperor, under date of February 7th, 1810. Consent to the marriage had been signed by Schwarzenberg the day before, thus Metternich still knew nothing about it. What was he then thinking? He drew his sovereign's attention to the nomination of Narbonne as French ambassador to Munich. 'This appointment is very important', he wrote, 'since it may be considered as an effect of the letter to Fouché, already known to Your Majesty and which was concerned with the chances of the marriage.' Metternich subsequently affirmed that his instructions to Schwarzenberg had been strikingly successful: 'The marriage issue, I feel, will certainly be decided in our favour.'[3]

Here, then, is proof. The marriage project which was almost

1. He actually said to Prince Eugène that 'Vienna was already quite prepared'. (*Mémoires de la Princesse Edling*, page 132.) While he was in the Isle of Elba, he was even more explicit: 'The Austrian Court! The marriage negotiations were not generally known. I have often wished to write my memoirs, now I shall not do so. . . But what treacherous tricks in connection with that Marriage! Vienna, it struck me, was behaving like some middle-class mother, trying to marry her daughter to a Grand Duke.' (Boutiagine to Nesselrode, February 9th, 1815. Quoted by Commander Weil: *Les Dessous du Congrès de Vienne*.)
2. Quoted by Masson in *L'Impératrice Marie Louise*.
3. E. Wertheimer: *Der Herzog von Reichstadt*, 1902.

universally judged as a brutal gesture by the Corsican despot had in fact been anxiously, feverishly, awaited and desired by the other side: everything possible (and almost impossible) had been done in order to achieve it. And if the shadow of a doubt remained, it would be dissipated by a private letter from Countess Metternich to her husband the day following the signing of the contract. 'At last, the all-important matter is accomplished; may God be thanked and afford it His blessing! I do not want to boast but I was able to help not a little. . . . Your letter made an excellent impression on the great man who actually saw it . . . but for Heaven's sake, don't mention this. Prince Schwarzenberg knows nothing about it, and was opposed to my using it. I acted entirely out of my own little head; it was successful and that is all we need to know. But how many sleepless nights I have had! How anxious and worried I have been!' [1]

It is interesting to compare authentic documentation which has now come to hand about 'the all-important matter' with the official version given by the Austrian Cabinet to diplomats accredited to the Court of Vienna.

Count Finkenstein wrote in a letter to the King of Prussia (dated March 11th, 1810): 'As proof to Your Majesty that the principal motive actuating the Viennese Court in concluding this marriage of the Archduchess Marie-Louise with the Emperor Napoleon was the fear of an alternative marriage with a Russian Archduchess [*sic*], I will give Your Majesty an account in a few words of Count Metternich's behaviour in the matter. The first tentative enquiries from the Emperor Napoleon designed to discover what his chances were in asking for the hand of the Princess Marie-Louise were made through the intermediary of the Countess Metternich; the Count only took a hand when he saw the imminent probability of a marriage with the Grand-Duchess Anne. Then, however, he began to make overtures which increased in frequency in proportion to the likelihood of the other marriage. The Minister only finally gave way to the Emperor Napoleon when he became certain that the Russian marriage

1. Vienna; Secret Archives.

would otherwise certainly take place and that there was no other way to prevent it.'[1]

Did Metternich himself believe this erroneous version? That would not be impossible. Napoleon knew how to keep a secret.

It seems, then, quite evident that Metternich made a poor bargain. What would have happened if he had not so unduly hurried the march of events . . .? Had he waited for the Russian reply with all that patience and sang-froid which are indispensable qualities in a great diplomat, had he been able to foresee that any reply from the arrogant Muscovites must inevitably be negative, the history of Europe might have taken a very different turn.

There are certain political formulae which tend to become an obsession with statesmen, often unknown to themselves; *Tu felix Austria nube* was of the number. Metternich, inheriting a tradition of centuries, had become its prisoner. The prospect of 'turning a military defeat into a political victory' was too tempting. Metternich had been caught by the *mirage*—he had hoped to make tangible profit out of a marriage between the Emperor of the French and Marie-Louise; but in rushing Schwarzenberg, in demanding a signature on the spot, Napoleon had effectively checkmated the Austrians, deprived them of all bargaining capacity. Instructions given to Schwarzenberg on February 17th, 1810, show us the extent to which Napoleon's manœuvre had upset the Viennese Cabinet and set all their plans awry.[2]

But whereas members of the Viennese Cabinet were indulging such bitter-sweet observations, news of the marriage was received

1. Berlin, Secret Archives.
2. 'M. de Floret', Metternich wrote, 'has forwarded Your Excellency's telegrams of approximately the 14th or 15th of this month. The French mail, which left Paris a few hours before the departure of M. de Floret, reached here two hours after his arrival. I showed the Emperor your report, M. l'Ambassadeur. His Majesty, our master, could only see in the extreme haste shown by the officials of the French Court in this matter, a new proof of the normally exaggerated tempo of their sovereign. But if, as Your Excellency will unquestionably have understood from previous communication, His Imperial Majesty has done me the honour to consult me in a matter vitally affecting the well-being of his people, it is no less true that he had every reason to be surprised that the signature to a contract of marriage was required, before any formal demand had been made for the hand of the Archduchess, his daughter. He has nevertheless not seen fit to take offence at this informality. We feel that it can to some extent be modified by considering the document of February 7th as merely the preamble to the real marriage contract, to be signed later, at the house of the august *fiancée*.' (Vienna, Secret Archives.)

with joy by the Austrian nation. Indeed, certain socially exalted persons had been 'dumbfounded' to learn that the great-grand-daughter of Maria-Theresa was to occupy, in the bed of a *soldier of fortune*, the place recently vacated by that little creole, Josephine, ex-mistress of Barras. But the masses were unaware of such 'cries of dismay, the curses and smothered sobbing' of distinguished protesters. The crowd now acclaimed the marriage with exactly the same enthusiasm that had appeared in its anti-French manifestations the week before.[1]

But stranger still were the reactions of the so-called victim of the 'tyrant' (or at least so considered through the years), of Marie-Louise, herself. On February 15th, Metternich hastened to reassure Count Otto de Mosloy, the French Ambassador: 'we inquired as to the feelings of Madame the Archduchess in this matter some three days ago, since naturally the Emperor would never have consented to impose a distasteful union upon her, and we found our Princess *exceedingly well disposed*'.

Admittedly, we also are acquainted with a series of letters from the Archduchess herself (written prior to the demand in marriage) in which she discusses Napoleon with little indulgence. The conqueror alarmed her, but we are perhaps permitted to wonder whether she was not a little interested by the man. In any event, she accepted without noticeable protest the great destiny imposed upon her. Furthermore, before leaving Vienna she seemed to be intrigued, enchanted by the prospect of Paris.[2]

1. Such an explosion of popular approval is in fact not difficult to understand. 'Everybody thinks that this alliance will afford a long term guarantee for the peace of Europe, that it will force England to make peace, that it will give their own Monarch all necessary leisure to organize—according to his own inimitable plans—that vast empire which he has created. Finally, that it would have a beneficial influence on the destinies of Turkey, Poland and Sweden.' (Archives of Foreign Affairs.)

2. What could be more significant than her very lively conversation with Count Otto, in the course of a gala dinner given at the Palace: 'Madame the Archduchess', he wrote, 'has asked me a number of questions which suggest the serious nature of her preoccupations. Here are the most striking: "Is the Musée Napoléon near enough to the Tuileries to allow me to go there often and study the antiques and other beautiful objects to be seen there? Does the Emperor like music? Would it be possible for me to learn the harp? It is an instrument of which I am very fond. The Emperor is so good to me, do you think he would allow me to have a botanical garden? Nothing would please me more. I am told that there are some very wild and picturesque spots at Fontainebleau, I know nothing more enthralling

On February 22nd, Napoleon had obtained the Austrian Government's agreement to the marriage contract, signed by Prince Schwarzenberg. From then on, the affair was to go post haste in the same tempo as it had started. February 27th, a message from the Emperor to the Senate; March 4th, arrival of the Duc de Neufchâtel at Vienna; March 13th, departure of Marie-Louise; March 27th, the royal couple meet at Compiègne; April 2nd, the religious marriage to the pealing of the bells of Notre Dame; April 3rd, impressive reception for fifteen hundred guests.

On the following day, the fourth of April, a guest of no small importance arrived at the Tuileries: Metternich, himself. The Emperor's marriage with an Archduchess of the House of Austria which he had so much desired and which was largely of his doing, was now a *fait accompli*. But had it in fact been a triumph for his political strategy? Metternich did all he could to convince those around him to that effect, and wished to believe it himself. But he knew enough about diplomacy to realise that he had been checkmated in his plans by the Emperor's brusque decision. The life of the Austrian Empire was now saved—but had it, in fact, ever been in danger? The nightmare of a Russian marriage was no more, but would that marriage, in fact, ever have taken place?[1]

The fact remained that Austria's consent to the marriage had been given without conditions. There still was hope, of course, of getting compensations *post factum*, but such an aim could only be pursued in a friendly atmosphere. Above all, however, than lovely country. . . . I hope the Emperor will be patient with me: I do not know how to dance quadrilles, but if he wishes, I will take a dancing master." I told Her Imperial Majesty that the Emperor was very anxious to know something of her tastes, and the way in which it pleased her to conduct her normal life. She replied that she was pleased with anything, that her tastes were very simple, that she could adjust herself to any type of living, that she would conform hers entirely to those of His Majesty, since her chief wish was to please him.'

See also Helfert: *Marie-Louise*, Ertz-Herzogin von Oesterreich, Kaiserin der Französen, Baron de Bourgoing: *Le Cœur de Marie-Louise*. (Calmann-Lévy, 1938.)

1. On March 14th, Count Finkenstein wrote from Vienna: 'The Austrian Government claims to know that Count Czerniczeff, who came for a moment to Berlin, during my stay in the capital, arrived three days after the signing of the contract of marriage with the Archduchess Marie-Louise, bearing a formal and complete assent from Tsar Alexander.' (Berlin, Secret Archives.) This was pure fabrication. Why did Metternich feel he had to lie? Perhaps in order to disguise his own bloomer.

Metternich hoped that Napoleon's schemes might to some extent be influenced by the new Empress of the French. Both objects would require his presence at Paris. He suddenly decided to go and informed Schwarzenberg on the very day that a telegram from the Ambassador, announcing the signing of the marriage contract, reached Vienna.

The day before he left, on March 14th, he presented to the Emperor Francis a report which outlined an extensive programme. The Foreign Minister stated that the object of his journey was to procure for Austria the means to resist future attack by any possible enemy power. That is why he wished Napoleon's consent to annul those secret clauses of the peace treaty which prevented any increase in the Austrian armed forces. He was aiming to obtain a port on the Adriatic sea and permission to establish a commercial highway along the Littoral, or in any event, power to control commercial movements in transit. Francis appended the following resolution to his Minister's report: 'Having complete confidence in you, I have commanded you to go to Paris and there, to the best of your ability, to safeguard the interests of my monarchy and to secure all possible advantages for our dominions.'[1]

And it is here that we begin to chronicle that extraordinary adventure which constitutes the real epilogue to the diplomatic story of Napoleon's marriage. For ten months the Austrian Foreign Secretary was to be absent from his post. For ten months he was to try to circumvent Napoleon's plans and attempt to realise his own ambitious schemes. For ten months he was destined to go from one disillusion to another. For Napoleon's plans were cut and dried: Metternich was to be overwhelmed with attentions and courtesy, the Emperor was willing to conduct interminable conversations on almost any subject, without of course committing himself to any basic idea, but when it came to concessions, he would get exactly nothing—or near enough.

Had Metternich only come to Paris for private amusement, he would have had little cause for complaint. As representative of the Emperor Francis whose daughter Napoleon had just married,

1. Vienna, Secret Archives.

he was now more than ever entertained and made much of by Parisian society. He had renewed a number of old ties, he wore on one arm, it is said, a bracelet plaited with the hair of Caroline Murat. This anecdote, at least, is reported by Stendhal: one is permitted, however, to doubt its accuracy since Metternich, in fact, had little reason to publicise his by-gone intimate association with the Emperor's sister. Madame de Metternich, of course, had no illusions as to the infidelities of her flighty husband: it was in fact thanks to her that the threat of a considerable scandal, provoked by Junot (who happened to be a jealous husband), had been averted.

This incident had occurred before the renewal of diplomatic relations, while Metternich was living in Austria. In the course of a fancy-dress ball given by Caroline, some figure in a mask, (conceivably the hostess herself, inspired by jealousy) had gone up to Junot and talked to him of his conjugal misfortunes: 'go home, open your wife's desk and you will find a packet of letters tied up with pink ribbon—then you'll understand'.[1]

Junot had followed the advice of his perfidious informant and an appalling scene with his wife followed; of this she has given us a melodramatic account in her diary: 'I know all', said he, grinding his teeth. 'M. de Metternich has been your lover: since he left here, you have kept up an active correspondence.... You can commit your soul to God, you are going to die.' Having changed his mind about his original intention, Junot considered challenging Metternich to a duel: 'Prince, you have brought despair to a man who had done you no wrong, you have fouled his honour; he demands satisfaction. On February 15th, I shall go to Mayence.... any weapon will suit me, if only it bring death to one of us.' But changing his mind once more, he administered a thrashing to his wife and rushed to the house of ... Countess Metternich! The latter had taken the whole situation in the grand manner, with considerable calm and dignity. 'The role of Othello really doesn't suit you', she said. 'It is scarcely becoming for a man whose behaviour has scandalised the whole of France

---

1. *Mémoires de Mademoiselle Avrillon* (p. 339). See also Capefigue's article (signed M.P.), 'Diplomates Européens', in the *Revue des Deux Mondes*, October, 1835.

to adopt such an attitude.' And she went immediately to Junot's home and, exercising all her powers of pursuasion, put an end to the quarrel. The couple's reconciliation, however, was scarcely less violent than their falling out. ('Beside himself,' writes Laure Junot, 'he seemed to wish to hold in his arms a blood-stained wife, half-dead and torn to pieces by his own hand. . . . Great heaven, what terrible embraces!') And Napoleon, who had heard the story, said to Countess Metternich: 'You are a good little woman and have saved me from a very difficult situation with that noisy lout, Junot.' As the hero of this much publicised adventure, Metternich came more than ever into the limelight in Parisian circles.[1]

But was it for mere trifling, such triumphs as these, that he had come to Paris? Hadn't he the interests of Austria, indeed of all Europe to defend? Alas, too many favours turned his head. 'Received with the cream of hospitality, the very perfection of good manners, such as no foreigner had ever encountered before',[2] Metternich sent enthusiastic reports to Vienna and failed to see through the game of the French government. 'The position of Your Majesty's Ambassador, at Paris, today', he wrote to the

1. The Viennese secret archives revealed a letter, hitherto unpublished, sent by Madame Metternich to her husband and dated February 7th, 1810. 'I do not', wrote the indulgent wife, 'think that your affair with Madame Junot—which unfortunately has occasioned a good deal of comment—need prevent your return; I actually know that no harm has been done, as regards the Emperor, himself. He said, "this only goes to prove the inaccuracy of rumours which have been current about my sister". There are a variety of versions, as to how Junot discovered the letters: some say that at Marescalchi's fancy dress ball, a certain masked person gave him an anonymous letter, telling the whole story, and that—being fully informed—he forced his wife to give them up, promising not to use them. Another version has it, that having followed her at the same party, he heard her give a rendezvous to M. de L.; that he tried as a result to provoke that gallant to a duel and, since the individual in question has a host of friends, they immediately thought of turning his rage onto you. They knew you were away, and in no position to tackle this blue-beard, who has now gone off with his amazon (never, we are told, to return). It is said that Savaz will replace him here and that he will stay in Spain.' And Madame Metternich again takes up the incident in her letter of February 14th. 'I have just returned from a visit to Princess Pauline who sent for me. She would like you to accompany the Archduchess. The Princess also talked to me about the fantastic Junot incident, and asked me if it was really true that he had tried to make that row with me. She—like everybody else—was scandalised. Good-bye, dear friend, come back to us soon. . . I embrace you. . .'

2. Count Nesselrode to his father, Paris, December 8th, 1810. (*Archives de Comte Nesselrode*. Vol. III, page 279.)

Emperor Francis, on April 4th, 'is now that which the Russian Ambassador enjoyed before the last war. No favour is too great. . . . There seems to exist a general enthusiasm, and which grows daily, among all classes of the people. I am forced to acknowledge that the French Court could scarcely show us a more delicate consideration.'

Napoleon suggested that the past was now wiped out, spoke of the dawn of a new era, happy and calm, and Metternich immediately had visions of concluding a loan, signing a commercial treaty, using the good offices of Austria between France and the Vatican, even indeed between France and England.[1]

He was then convinced that Napoleon would allow himself to be guided by Marie-Louise: 'The Emperor is very much in love with her and everything suggests to me that she is beginning to understand him perfectly. He has, perhaps, more susceptibilities than most of us, and if the Empress continues to make the best of them. . . . *She might be able to achieve much, both for herself and for the whole of Europe.* He is so much in love with her. . . . She has very frank eyes—and seems devoid of bias.'[2]

But weeks and months were to go by and nothing was to change either Napoleon's political intentions or in the immediate relationship of France and Austria. Metternich, who thought he knew the Emperor so well, should have known that he would never allow himself to be influenced by any woman. There was a wall between the Empress and her country, and it was not ripe for scaling.

In October 1810, Metternich went home to Vienna with empty hands. His hope to influence, as intermediary, the destinies of Europe had floated away into thin air. He had not even succeeded in establishing relations with the English Cabinet, and as far as Austrian intervention between Napoleon and the Pope, that, too, had come to nothing. Napoleon had forced him to

1. A. Baer: *Zür Sendung Metternichs nach Paris* (mitteilungen des Instituts für oesterreichische Geschichte, Bd. 16).

2. Metternich to Francis I, April 16th, 1810. Quoted by E. Wertheimer in *Der Herzog von Reichstadt*, 1912. This author mentions another letter from Metternich, under date of July 20th: 'The Empress', he said, 'is beginning to exert a by no means negligible influence on her husband.'

write as follows: 'The Emperor does not require our intervention as regards the Pope—since he does not need him. The Emperor is now in so unassailable a position that in a few years' time the Pope will end by doing everything that he wishes.[1] The diplomatic mission of Lebzeltern, Austrian delegate to the Vatican sent by Metternich to Savone, had indeed lost all *raison d'être*.

Negotiations for a loan had been equally sterile. The Emperor's permission was not enough: French and Dutch bankers would have had to underwrite it and these remained coy. Even in so small a matter as that of the bad paper money once issued by France, Napoleon tricked him again: instead of returning the offending notes, he had the Minister informed that 'the currency required no longer existed and that he personally had ordered its immediate destruction'.

Negotiations for a commercial treaty brought him an even crueller blow. This time, it was the Viennese government itself which, advised by Count Wallis, Minister of Finance, refused to ratify the convention already signed by Metternich and the qualified representatives of France. Wallis had declared that the treaty would destroy all Austria's commerce and place her completely under the heel of France.

Metternich obtained satisfaction on two points only. Napoleon conceded a delay for payment of war indemnities incurred under the treaty of Vienna and consented to annul a secret clause of the same treaty which limited the Austrian army to a strength of 150,000 men.[2]

The Metternich and Schwarzenberg families also obtained personal favours in the shape of restitution of certain properties of which they had been despoiled by the King of Württemberg. Count Metternich himself, on leaving, received an official present:

1. Metternich: *Mémoires*, Vol. II.
2. This was in fact little more than a platonic concession. 'The obligation imposed on Austria to limit her army to 150,000 men', wrote Bignon, 'was one of those measures easier to enjoin than to have carried out. The cancellation of this clause was little more than a gesture, but precious nevertheless as an act of recognition of the independence of a great Empire. As a matter of fact, had the Austrian Court not been completely bankrupt, it could easily have eluded even Napoleon's sharp eye and considerably increased the country's military strength. But given its financial straits, it had not been possible to maintain an army, even up to the limits imposed by the treaty.' (Bignon: *Histoire de France*, Vol. IX, page 161.)

a bust of His Majesty, some Gobelin tapestries valued at 2,400 francs and certain Sèvres vases and other china, valued at 8,600 francs.[1]

For the hand of an Archduchess, the price was certainly not too high....

Metternich's open attachment to the French cause at the beginning of his ministry, and above all at the time of the marriage of Marie-Louise, had made him many enemies. His long absence surprised Viennese society and turned many against him. 'Count Metternich would be well advised not to put off his return much longer', wrote the Prussian Ambassador on August 29th, 1810, 'that is if he wishes to keep his present job without being forced to depend on Napoleon's direct support—and such dependence, as I know him, would be little to his liking. The number of his enemies, here, grows daily, and all the most important people are among them [*sic*]. Everybody remotely connected with the Schwarzenberg family are, of course, furious at the way in which he has forced the ambassador to play second fiddle at Paris. The Liechtensteins, above all Count Jean, against whom Metternich took a very firm stand at the signing of the Peace of Vienna, are now taking their revenge. Others, who have an eye on his job, are trying to undermine him with the Emperor, by calling him the *foreigner*.[2]

It was true that a savage opposition to Metternich had grown up among those who were closest to the throne. His predecessor, Stadion, summarily dismissed, had now joined forces with Baldacci and Count Zichy (ex-courtiers, also in disgrace), and with Count Wallis, Minister of Finance, with a view to concocting intrigues against this brilliant advocate of a political outlook which seemed to them incomprehensible.

The Archduke Charles, his brother Joseph, Palatin of Hungary, and the Empress Maria-Ludovica, herself, took sides with the malcontents. The Empress, something of a stormy petrel, frankly declared that she 'would never be able to view with calm the

---

1. The Duc de Frioul to M. de Champagny, October 18th, 1810. (Archives of Foreign Affairs.)
2. Berlin-Dahlem, Secret Archives.

man mainly responsible for her step-daughter's marriage'. Metternich seemed to her to be 'too frivolous, too much of a gambler' to be worthy to perform the highly important task entrusted to him.

Strong in the unwavering support of his master, Metternich might well, on his return, have disposed of his enemies, might well have taken reprisals. He did no such thing: he was to disarm them by an appearance of friendliness. He became a frequent guest at the palace of Count Razoumowski, then the centre of all the *cabala* directed against Napoleon. He spent his evenings in the salon of Madame de Bagration, one of his ex-mistresses who was generally considered to be spying for the Tsar; he pacified with vague promises the English, Prussian and Russian representatives.[1] And nothing better reveals Metternich's innate talent for diplomacy than his masterly tactics—different in each case—towards these different powers. The nickname of 'comte de la Balance', which was given him in diplomatic circles at that time, was indeed well earned!

'To put the policy of the Cabinet of Vienna in a nutshell', wrote the Hanoverian, Hardenberg (Münster, March 15th, 1811) 'one must realise that nothing would please the Minister better than to see the power of France decreased, brought within its proper bounds. But he believes it would be difficult to achieve this result during the life-time of Napoleon, and does not wish to endanger the realm by taking a false step.' Poorly expressed, the idea was nevertheless quite clear. Metternich was looking forward to the days when France, finally divorced from all Jacobin influence, governed by a new and legitimate dynasty in whose veins would run the blood of the Habsburgs and that of the great Corsican combined. He saw a France once more the symbol of stability and balance for the whole of Europe, finally, a France with whom Austria might be on terms of absolute equality, as in the great days of Kaunitz and Choiseul.

But, of course, the finely balanced movement of the scales—Metternich's chief preoccupation—could only continue for as

---

1. W. Oncken: *Oesterreich und Preussen in Befreiungskriege*, 1879. C. S. B. Buckland: *Metternich and the British Government, 1809-1810*.

long as Napoleon refrained from any attempt to drag Austria into war with all its attendant complications.

When, on January 17th, 1811, he had handed to the Emperor Francis an official report on the results of his stay at Paris, the Minister wrote: 'At the moment we can do little more than hope to ward off catastrophe (and any new war would mean exactly that). . . . Recently, Austria has been entirely free in relation to France; that is the situation which we must try at all cost to prolong.'

But already by the end of 1811, Napoleon had asked his father-in-law for material assistance in the war he was then preparing against Russia. Forced by circumstance against his private convictions, Metternich with 'deep regret' consented to an alliance, dated March 14th, 1812, which called upon Austria to supply the Emperor of the French with 30,000 men.

The interview between Napoleon and Francis I at Dresden, at the beginning of June 1812, might be called the high-water mark of Metternich's Francophile policy. He seemed completely overwhelmed by the greatness of Napoleon and the latter—if we are to believe Caulaincourt—'for the first time, and perhaps the last time, made it known that he thought highly of M. de Metternich'.

He was then convinced, as indeed was the whole of Europe, that the first Russian engagement would be a walk-over for Napoleon.[1] By the end of March, he had written to M. de Saint-Julien, his representative at Saint Petersburg: 'Russia is done for; her army could never stand up to such a task; her finances are inadequate. . . . Alexander is counting on his Polish partisans; he will be gravely disillusioned, the whole nation will turn against him. . . . A crushing defeat would put him out altogether whereas a decisive victory would take his army no farther than the Vistula.'

Early successes of the French troops confirmed the optimism of the Austrian Chancellery. A series of letters, about this date, written by hand to Otto and Bassano, display a really surprising

---

1. See Demelitsch: *Metternich und seine auswartige Politik.*

solicitude on Metternich's part for the French cause.[1] At one moment, he was sending the Ambassador news which he himself received via the Balkans. Then he would inform him about the state of mind in Russia, propose an effective propaganda among the populations of Illyria or suggest some common policy in Turkey. He tried to smooth out the difficulties which arose between the French high command and the Austrian authorities; he tried, but was completely unsuccessful, to increase the Austrian contingent; he went so far as himself to write bulletins of the first victories. He refused to believe Boutiagine, a young Russian diplomat who had been sent on a secret mission to convey to Vienna the story of the first reverses of *la Grande Armée*.

It was only at the beginning of December, when Napoleon abandoned his army in rout, that the full horror of the situation dawned upon the Foreign Minister.

And yet even then, when all passions were let loose, when Alexander in his mystic dreams saw himself as the liberator of Europe, when a Stein was feverishly planning to revive the old Germany, when Napoleon himself (only just back in France) was planning new and impracticable campaigns against Saint Petersburg and Kiev, Metternich, perhaps alone among European statesmen, managed to keep his head. For him, there was no urge to destroy 'the beast of the Apocalypse' but merely to re-establish the European balance of power.

As soon as Metternich learnt by telegram from Bassano that Lauriston had set out for the Russian H.Q. in order to propose cessation of hostilities, he raised the question of a 'general pacification', easier to achieve than a separate peace with Russia, and, on November the fourth, sent definite instructions to Floret to that effect. He cautiously laid his plans before Count Otto, stressing the important role that Austria might play in the circumstances, connected as she was with France by dynastic ties.

As gradually the full significance of the catastrophe dawned upon the whole of Europe, Metternich grew more urgent. On

1. See C. de Grünwald: *Metternich et Alexandre* dans *Le Monde Slave*, January, 1938.

December 9th, 1812, he sent a telegram of unusual eloquence: 'Unquestionably', he cried, 'the resources of genius are prodigious.' Could the Emperor of the French, however, contemplate a second campaign on the same ground which has just witnessed the rout of combined forces?.... There would seem nothing to induce the Tsar Alexander to effect a separate peace.... 'The Emperor of the French appears to have foreseen what is now happening when he said to me that his marriage had changed the face of Europe. The moment is approaching, is perhaps already here, when Napoleon might reap the real benefit of that alliance.... Austria must speak to the great powers of Europe, Austria holding out an olive-branch to all and sundry, speaking to France as an ally, offering the other powers their complete independence.... On account of her unwavering firmness and her calm, Austria alone among the great powers, today, is in a position to raise fifty million men for a cause which at one word from our monarch would be regarded as a general obligation.'

The year drew to an end, at Vienna, as everywhere else,[1] in an atmosphere of feverish anxiety. 'Scarcely a day goes by', wrote Otto to Bassano, 'but that M. de Metternich talks to me of the urgent need for a general peace.... The most heartfelt wish of the Austrian Emperor, he tells me, is to preserve the present French Government and the new dynasty.... He is alarmed for the dynasty and for his grandson towards whom he feels a deep affection.'[2]

On December 31st, Metternich addressed to Otto a letter by hand. 'It would be superfluous for me to talk to Your Excellency of the interest which His Majesty of Austria feels about anything that might tend to safeguard the throne of France (from even remote dangers). Your Excellency knows our Emperor's thoughts in this matter as well as I do.... I hope that the Emperor Napoleon will find our most recent communications and proposals at least *as French* in feeling as they are Austrian.'

1. Otto to Bassano, November 10th, 1812. (Archives of Foreign Affairs.)
2. December 28th and 30th, 1812. (Archives of Foreign Affairs.)

G

And so we see Metternich attempting not by any means a treachery but a formidable attempt to rescue the husband of Marie-Louise. His hopes, we know, were not to be realised. Was that his fault alone? Only an impartial posterity will be able to judge.

# VI

# AT THE MARCOLINI PALACE

T HAT impressive structure, the Marcolini Palace, near Dresden, has now been converted into a civilian hospital. But visitors are still shown two rooms on the ground floor (leading straight out into the garden) where the famous interview between Napoleon and Metternich took place, on June 26th, 1813. The door used by Metternich on that occasion is now walled up; the palatial ante-rooms, then lined with rows of anxious courtiers through which he passed to the audience chamber, have been turned into wards, but memories of a great historic past still linger in the air.

Both men—the conqueror and the diplomat—had come a long way since their last encounter, since they met in this same city of Dresden at a time when Napoleon had appeared as a second Alexander setting out for the conquest of new worlds. Metternich had then been obsequiously modest—lost among the crowd of fascinated courtiers; but today, he came almost as an equal to meet the fallen idol after the retreat from Moscow.

Human life—as both poet and wise men agree—is often little more than a tissue of dreams. For we tend to retire into a dream world as soon as reality becomes intolerable. The greatest genius, like the rest of us, will succumb to this psychological urge. How could one otherwise explain those incredible blunders committed by Napoleon in the course of the year of 1813?

For Bonaparte, as we all know and as Metternich himself has so frequently told us, was positive by nature. He had little use for vagaries, in practice as in theory he went straight to the point—

91

and the same applied to all his conversations. He was only interested in the core of the matter, disdaining non-essentials, and was furthermore convinced that no man—whether called upon to play a part in public or merely engaged in the pursuits of a private life—could ever be actuated by anything other than self-interest. How then could a man with such views bring himself to believe that the Emperor Francis would stay loyal to him merely on account of family ties? After the defeats of Borodino and the Beresina pass, how could he still count on the terror of his name, on the reputation of his erstwhile invincible army? Did he fail to realise—when the docile Prussian population itself rose in revolt —that these no longer conveyed the same salutary fear? We can only assume Napoleon was also seeking compensation in a dream.

Historians have made heavy weather, alleging cunning and duplicity by Metternich before the final line-up of Austria with the anti-Napoleonic coalition. He certainly manœuvred during those decisive months of his career with supreme ability: he veered and changed his course and changed his mind, trying to gain time, trying to get all the trump cards into his own hand. Certainly, he lied and finessed and coated the pill of menace with soft words. But in fact his tactics were clear from the start. We need not be surprised that those hysterical patriots, the Germanophiles, mistook his intentions and subsequently heaped opprobrium upon him accusing him of craven cowardice or of treachery to the national cause. But that Napoleon himself did not see through the ambitious diplomat's game can only be explained by his reluctance to see things at all in their true light.

For Metternich had made his intentions as clear as could be, even as far back as December, 1812. Could anything have been more explicit than his instructions then to Floret and Bubna, or— above all—than his conversations with Otto, the French ambassador.

It has been suggested that Napoleon was badly served by his immediate advisers; that Count Otto was not competent and that it was only after he had been replaced by Narbonne that the Emperor was able to get a proper picture of the situation. But contemporary correspondence belies that theory. Otto was indeed no brilliant ambassador, but he was conscientious and wary, he was thoroughly at home on the Danube and had watched the opposition grow to a point at which the French cause had only two remaining sponsors, Francis I and Metternich himself. This he did not hide in his despatches. If he also punctiliously recorded Count Metternich's honeyed and often ambiguous words, that was little more than his duty. The Austrian Minister, on his side, was pursuing his own: for is it not in the tradition of the best diplomacy to continue those polite and hollow exchanges right up to the eve of war, as was also apparent in 1914?

'Austria is in no position to play a belligerent role' (by the side of France), Otto was already writing on January 3rd, 1813; 'but if it came to mediation, we could count on an important contribution from that quarter. Indeed only her exercise of such a function could calm public opinion here and make the people accept sacrifices to which they are now little inclined.'[1]

On the same day, Metternich outlined his own views in an extremely friendly letter, written by hand and which Otto forwarded to Paris: 'The Emperor's victories [*sic*] are as little open to discussion as the total incapacity and lack of organisation of the Russian generals. . . . What you have been told about the Emperor's war-potential, is undoubtedly true. . . . But a second campaign would necessarily involve appalling losses for France, to say nothing of the complete exhaustion of her allies, after which a third campaign would inevitably be required. Why not use all this energy in a direction more compatible with the hopes and general interest of Europe? Why not make the present situation a basis for negotiating a general continental peace. . . . ? When it comes to anything which touches the soil of France, Napoleon and the Empress' father—grandfather of the successor to the throne—must inevitably think alike. It is there, at the very centre of all he has created, that the head of a new dynasty should feel most secure. It is also there that he will best realise how important his own life is to the future monarch and the general good of the state. Let the Emperor once for all renounce any step which might involve in his person a major catastrophe for France,

1. Archives of Foreign Affairs.

93

a tragedy which no man who had the real interests of Europe at heart could contemplate without alarm.'[1]

On January 21st, Otto analysed the situation in a way which showed that he was by no means taken in by specious gabblers. 'The Cabinet', he said, 'having often deceived us in the past, it would be unwise to pay too much attention to their assurances today. In judging their intentions, one must take into account their basic interests, the means immediately at their disposal and the general orientation of their policy. Their interests obviously lie on the side of peace and the full capacity of their resources would only be available in that contingency.'

At the beginning of February, Otto noted that Metternich would—in certain circumstances—be prepared to put a considerable military force at the disposal of France. He even seemed willing once more to subordinate Austria's own freedom (that freedom which was so near his heart) if only the Emperor of the French would show a more generally pacific purpose. 'Until now', he said to Otto, 'this has never really been an Austrian war; if it were at any time to become so, it is not with a force of 30,000 men but with every ounce of the monarchy's strength that we should fight Russia!'

A little later, on February 18th, Metternich sent the following instructions to Floret, still accredited to the court of France: 'The whole situation is becoming daily more urgent and we fear that our ally is not looking at it in the only way which might preclude catastrophe.... The French themselves admit that they cannot conquer Russia, that their renewed efforts allow no hope of making a breach in the Russian provinces. A first, second or third campaign, then, has little to offer beyond the destruction of the forces concerned. If the governments refuse to take account of this, the peoples will pretty quickly do so, and such a realisation cannot fail to entail prodigious upheavals in those countries which lie between the Vistula and the Rhine. One must have been at Vienna, at Berlin, or anywhere in Germany lately, to realise the universal state of tension, and it is growing day by day.'

1. This hitherto unpublished document and those which follow, have been taken from the Archives of the Quai d'Orsay.

Otto, on his side, saw that Metternich's own position was getting worse: 'every day we run the risk of the Emperor being publicly insulted or I myself, assassinated', Metternich told Otto during the first half of February. Shortly after, his fears were justified. 'The Foreign Minister has shown me evidence of a plot to assassinate him. Two officers were involved; they were to surprise him at night, on his way back from a house to which he goes frequently. The officers have been arrested, as also other members of the committee to which they belonged.'[1]

One week later, a new incident, even more alarming: the project for a rising in the Tyrol was discovered; 'I have learnt', wrote Otto, on March 8th, 'that M. de Metternich was working all day yesterday with the chief of police, and that a large number of persons—some of them of considerable importance—were arrested last night, among them the Baron de Hormayr, Councillor of the State Department, well known for his past associations with the Tyrol. The Minister was very much disturbed; he told me that the Emperor now stood between a powerful faction of men in his own country who are violently opposed to his policies and an ally who gives us no indication of his plans and intentions. M. von Bubna sends us no mail, probably because he himself fails to get news from the French Cabinet.'[2]

In March, Otto was superseded by Count Narbonne. From his first interview with the new ambassador, Metternich again urged with some insistence that France should take the path of peace. 'If only the Emperor of the French would be satisfied to be a monarch three times more powerful than Louis XIV, to be the master of Europe by virtue of his present position, his strength and his genius, all our difficulties might easily be smoothed out.'[3] 'What is essential', he said on another occasion (despatch of April 10th), is that the Confederation of the Rhine should not be allowed to extend to the Niemen. . . . Austria really cannot fight in order to help France to keep her present hold on the Con-

1. Archives of Foreign Affairs.
2. Otto, did not know that the Archduke John, brother of the Emperor, was also connected with the plot. See A. Robert: *L'idée nationale autrichienne et les guerres de Napoléon. L'apostolat du Baron Hormayr et le salon de C. Pichler*, 1933.
3. Archives of Foreign Affairs. Telegram of March 24th, 1818.

federation of the Rhine. . . . we in Austria only want peace. . . .
Do you know what France wants? The Emperor will make
absolutely no concessions.'

And Narbonne himself was obliged to admit (in his despatches
of March 24th and April 1st) that 'the Austrian Minister displays
a maximum of goodwill in his relationship with us . . . as long
as the general objective remains pacific'.

On May 1st, Narbonne received from Metternich and forwarded to Paris this solemn appeal: 'One is permitted to hope
that the Emperor Napoleon feels some confidence in the man
who is mainly responsible for the present close relationship of
Austria and France. . . . I am forced to reiterate what I have now
said some twenty times to your master, the Emperor, that it is his
task to consolidate the governments of Europe. . . . For if His
Majesty has now little chance of success in a foreign war, he
could do much in the direction of a general pacification.'

Was it possible to be more frank, more insistent than Metternich during the first five months of 1813? He no longer wished
to fight by the side of France but alternatively had no desire to
place Austria on the side of France's enemies. He wished to leave
open, as Narbonne said, a decision which 'he himself had not yet
made'.[1] It was indeed this capacity for taking the middle way
that was Metternich's outstanding contribution.

At the beginning of the 1812 campaign, Tsar Alexander is
reported to have said, 'Napoleon or I! One of us will have to
surrender', and this conviction was shared not only by the
Prussian trio, Scharnhorst, Gneisenau, Stein, but also by Napoleon
himself. All these men saw themselves as engaged in a life-or-
death struggle. But Metternich, for his part, wished neither party
ill. For him, one thing only mattered: he wanted peace, the
general stabilisation of Europe. If France would only consent
to remain within her borders (her proper geographical limits),
if Napoleon would forgo his dream of world domination,
Metternich would have been well satisfied to keep the Emperor
on his throne and to maintain friendly relations with him. Mixed
motives lay behind his point of view. The Kaunitz tradition, the

1. May 5th, 1813. Archives of Foreign Affairs.

personal ascendancy of Napoleon whom he could not help admiring, an inveterate fear of Russia,[1] fear of nationalist insurrections within the Empire, lack of confidence in Austria's war potential, the easy-going cynicism of a typical aristocrat, of a man little disposed to lose his head over 'noble causes'.

Napoleon, on his side, misunderstood the reasons for the Austrian compromise, refused to admit any eventual collusion between Austria and the coalition as possible, and replied to all Metternich's advances in a manner rather more than casual.

Admitted, the Emperor had not entirely rejected proposals made by Bubna at an audience given on December 31st, 1812. 'Well, if that's how things stand,' Napoleon had said, 'let's make peace. I have no objection: let your Emperor approach the Russians.' But Bonaparte had hastened to add that he did not believe in any possible *entente* between Russia and England. He rejected the programme devised by Metternich, and yet this was modest in comparison with Alexander's claims, or that of the Prussians or the English. He had made no comment about the adjustment of German boundaries. He remained mum as to any question of compensation for his allies: a vague promise to relinquish the Illyrian provinces (nothing more than before the war with Russia) was all Austria got. Napoleon's consent, then, meant little more than his own immediate way out.

The letter from Napoleon to the Emperor of Austria on January 7th, as well as one sent the following day from Bassano to Metternich, could only be interpreted in that way: 'I am not prepared to take any steps for peace. . . . I shall not surrender a single village of the Duchy of Warsaw', said Napoleon. 'There is one point on which France will never give way, that must be considered incontrovertible: no single one of the territories now united by senatorial decree must ever be separated from the Empire. Any such separation could only be interpreted as a dissolution of the Empire as a whole; to achieve it would require a force of no less than 500,000 men surrounding the capital and bivouacked upon the heights of Montmartre.'[2]

1. 'Russia is a natural enemy of Austria', he said to Otto. Otto to Bossano, February 17th, 1813. (Archives of Foreign Affairs.)
2. Bassano to Otto, January 8th, 1813. Only the first sentence has previously been published.

It is only fair to say that it was scarcely possible for Napoleon to act otherwise than he did. 'To have agreed to peace in these circumstances would have put an end to his career and to his dynasty, would have entailed the break-up of his Empire. His reign would not outlast any sign of weakness, strength was his *raison d'être;* he governed from a background of *Te Deum* sung and re-sung at Notre Dame; his power was rooted in those shouts of *Vive l'Empereur* when on the evenings of his victories he passed down the lines of his assembled troops. But at the moment, he had nothing of all this to offer to his peoples.... He could not lay down his arms; had he done so, he would not have been himself, would not have been *the Emperor.*' (d'Ussel.)

And so, he would continue the fight. He would raise a new army, inflict new defeats on Russians and Prussians alike. But having admitted the principle of mediation—although against the grain—he had already weakened his position, already prepared the way for Austria's revival which would in turn allow her, when the moment came, to align herself as she chose with him or his enemies.

For the interview with Bubna freed Metternich's hands. Napoleon himself had now consented and Austria was free openly to negotiate with the enemies of France, was absolved from obligations hitherto inherent in the Austro-French alliance.

Metternich was to take full advantage of his new freedom for the whole of the first six months of 1813. Frigid, calm and imperturbable, a schemer *par excellence*, he conducted in a masterly manner negotiations which began with Lebzeltern's mission to the court of the Tsar and that of Wessenberg to England, and which ended the day after his meeting at the Marcolini Palace. It was then that he achieved his reputation as the century's greatest diplomat, but it went hard with his popularity. From that moment, he was censured by both French and Russians for his 'duplicity', by the Austrians for 'weakness'. And the implacable hatred with which the German patriots always regarded him may also be said to date from the events of this period. They wished the Minister to throw himself unequivocally into the country's fight for freedom. But which was his country? Stein was then declaring that he himself knew but one, and that one Germany. But Stein was a visionary, a 'prophet', the quasi-occult adviser of a foreign king. Metternich was a minister on his home territory, overwhelmed with great responsibilities. With as good a claim to probity as Stein himself, he could afford to ignore Germany as 'a mere geographical concept', non-existent on the chessboard of diplomacy. Strange destiny, that of a man reproached at the height of his career with having failed the French or having failed the Prussians, whereas in fact he was pursuing the only political line incumbent upon him: safeguarding the interests of Austria and all Europe.

It was not in Metternich's character to come to a rapid decision even after the defection of General Yorck, the uprising in Eastern Prussia and the conclusion of an alliance between Frederick William III and Alexander I. The door was still open to peace, furthermore, Austria was by no means prepared. Already on February 27th, Otto had informed his Government 'the country is actively pursuing preparation for war. Regiments designed to reinforce Bohemia and Galicia are on the move; requisitions of a stringent nature are being enforced, even in Hungary; the munitions factories are working full pitch and certain fiscal projects designed to revive the treasury, are afoot.'[1]

These were only the first preparations for war; in the opinion of General Radetzky, it would take another three months to complete them. Metternich was convinced that 'a single initial defeat would compromise the whole campaign, before we hurry into war we ought to be sufficiently strong to conduct it, if necessary, on our own account'. For he was not counting on the Russian army 'badly organised and with a low morale', nor on the Prussian, 'an army in name only'. He was depending entirely on Austria. And in spite of innumerable obstacles arising within her borders (the fact that Francis I was temperamentally opposed to war, the bad state of the country's finances, the intrigues of his personal enemies) he raised an army of 120,000 men. He was playing for time, and he allowed the flower of German manhood to perish at Möckern, Lutzen and Bautzen without raising a

1. Otto to Bassano. February 27th. (Archives of Foreign Affairs.)

finger in the common cause. And while Napoleon and his enemies mutually wore each other out on Silesian battle-fields, he, Metternich, was negotiating. He negotiated with England, Russia, Prussia, Bavaria, Württemberg, Sweden, Denmark—and above all, with France.[1] For the conditional permission originally given by Napoleon had now, thanks to Metternich's ability, become complete. Schwarzenberg indeed arrived at the French headquarters, sent by Metternich, to negotiate 'on the basis of a proper balance of power in Europe'.

And what exactly was this 'proper balance'? During the month of May, Austria's conditions became more explicit: the Duchy of Warsaw was to be relinquished and all conquered territories on the right bank of the Rhine and in Italy restored; Illyria and perhaps the Tyrol were to be evacuated. Was Austria still allied with France, or was she not?—nobody seemed to know.

'If Napoleon accepts these terms Austria is prepared to defend her platform by force of arms' (despatch from Narbonne on May 11th). 'But if—as all would lead us to suppose—he rejects them, then Austria will pursue a new path (already arranged with the coalition) and will declare war on France.' (Conversation between Metternich and Hardenberg, May 9th; conference between Stadion and the Tsar, on May 16th.)

Events took on a new impetus just after the battle of Bautzen. Beaten once more, the armies of the coalition retreated towards Silesia. Metternich felt that the time for a decision was at hand. On his advice, the Emperor Francis hurriedly left the capital, accompanied by his minister. They were to stay at Gitschin (a château belonging to the Prince von Trautmansdorf), which lay half-way between Dresden where Napoleon then was in residence, and the headquarters of the Russian and Prussian armies. Before leaving he gave Narbonne his 'word of honour that the Emperor Francis would not visit any of the allied sovereigns', a purely gratuitous assurance since Metternich himself could well replace him.

1. See Klinckowstroem: *Oesterreichs Teilnahme an den Befreiungskriegen nach Aufzeichnungen von Gentz*. Vienna, 1887. A. Veltze: *Die Politik Metternichs*, 1813-1815. *Vienna-Leipzig*, 1911. O'Lanna: *Metternichs Politik bis zum Sturze Napoleons*, 1897. D'Ussel, J: *L'intervention de l'Autriche* (December 1812-May 1813.)

In the meanwhile, an armistice of six weeks was arranged on June 4th, at Peuschwitz; an unexpected respite during which Metternich could continue his negotiations. But the atmosphere was growing worse: the hopelessness of any attempt to come to terms with France increasingly apparent. 'One gets nothing from the French by threats', Napoleon declared to Bubna; 'I shall relinquish nothing, not a single village.'

'Being called upon at this juncture to save Europe, we shall do so', was a conviction now taking definite shape in Metternich's mind.[1] He informed the Tsar that he would visit him. 'Sire,' he wrote immediately on his arrival at Gitschin, 'we are now here. Be patient and have confidence. I shall visit you in three days' time, and six weeks from now we shall be allies.' He kept his promise and went to Alexander's headquarters at Opotchno. When the Tsar asked him: 'What tactics shall we adopt should Napoleon accept the offer of mediation?' Metternich replied with complete sang-froid: 'If he refuses, the armistice will automatically come to an end and you will find us among your allies; if he accepts, we are sure to discover in the course of negotiation that Napoleon has no intention of being either reasonable or just, and so the result will be exactly the same.' 'I am not unduly suspicious,' remarked the Russian monarch, 'but what guarantee have I of your Emperor's good faith?' 'A knowledge of his character and of mine,' replied Metternich; 'I am no Haugwitz.'

In the second half of June, Russian and Prussian delegates met those of Austria at Reichenbach and jointly drew up a treaty whereby Austria undertook to declare war on France should Napoleon not have accepted their terms by July 20th. The conditions were decided on the 24th June.[2]

It was then that Napoleon, becoming anxious about the coming and going of the Austrians, invited Metternich to visit him at Dresden, at the Marcolini Palace. Metternich accepted with alacrity; before putting his sovereign's signature to the treaty of Reichenbach he would make one last effort to convert the

---

1. *Mémoires*, Vol. I, page 160.
2. This treaty was only signed after an interview with Napoleon on the 27th of June.

Emperor of the French. For didn't Napoleon control the issues of peace or war? A word from him would put an end to hostilities, at least on the continent of Europe. But were words of wisdom and prudence likely from such a source? How changed, if at all, was Bonaparte since his defeat in Russia?

As soon as the Emperor spoke, his visitor realised that he had 'neither learnt nor forgotten anything', 'So, there you are, Metternich', he cried, just as if they had parted yesterday. 'You're rather late. If you didn't want to continue our alliance, if it was hanging heavily upon you, why didn't you say so? I should not have tried to force you. I might even have modified my plans. You come to us and talk "arbitration" .... You go to my enemies and talk "alliance", it's a muddle all round.... !'

Napoleon could not have chosen a worse preamble. He was no longer in a position to talk in such terms to the man who then saw himself as 'the representative of all Europe'. Flattery rather than bluntness was called for; sobriety and reason combined with gravity and calm. Instead of this, for eight hours on end, going from one paroxysm of rage to the next—Napoleon raved and menaced and reproached. He waved innumerable French victories in Metternich's face, vaunted his own destiny without a qualm, showed his usual complete disregard for the value or dignity of human life. He accused Austria of treachery, or merely wishing to take advantage of a temporarily embarrassed France.

He 'accepted the challenge', he said: 'They would meet at Vienna, next October.' He expressed regret at having married an Austrian Archduchess. 'I had hoped to combine the present with the past. . . . I was wrong and today I realise the full extent of my mistake. It may cost me my throne, but I shall drag the whole world down with me in my fall.'

He refused to consider any reasonable terms of peace. 'Do you wish to strip me to the bone? Perhaps you would like Italy, Brabant, Lorraine? I refuse to cede a single inch of territory. . . . I shall give you nothing, because you have not yet beaten me; I shall give nothing to Prussia because she has betrayed me. You are no soldier', he went on, roughly, 'and don't know what goes on in a soldier's mind. I grew up on the battle-field and a man of my mettle attaches little importance to the lives of a million men.'

Once, such language might have impressed Metternich, now it merely left him cold. At that moment, Napoleon seemed to me a very 'small' man, he said later—to the extreme indignation of a number of historians. 'The man who wrote this', declared Albert Sorel, 'wouldn't have understood Shakespeare. The puppy here is showing off and has completely lost his head.... Metternich had all the stamp of a cad.'

Such a judgment is profoundly unjust. Metternich had something to defend: the hope of peace, of European order, the concept of a social structure shaken by the Jacobin onslaught, but by no means yet destroyed. With what, on the other hand, was Napoleon concerned? His own reputation, his own glory, at a pinch, perhaps, the interests of the dynasty he had so recently founded—but nothing more. How far he was from those real Jacobins of the early days, from Roberjot, from Treilhard, Debry, who confronted Metternich at Rastadt, builders of a new world! They might have lacked distinction and good manners, those men of the revolution, but at least they were sincere and thought they were working for the good of mankind. But for whom was Napoleon working—for what cause was he preparing to sacrifice a million lives?

Memories of another conversation came back to Metternich: one night at Compiègne, when Napoleon had boasted the superiority of the Bonaparte family over the Pozzo di Borgo. But the Emperor then, as he talked, had struck the Habsburg's ambassador (Count of the Empire, Rosenkavalier, the husband of a Kaunitz), as little more than a vulgar upstart. The tragic isolation of the great Corsican defying fate might have moved Shakespeare as it still moves today all those who try to fathom the depths of the human spirit, but Metternich had not come to Dresden in poetic mood. For eight hours they walked up and down through the great reception chamber and in and out of the library: the man in a grey frock-coat, short and stocky, lock of black hair falling over his forehead, and the super-elegant diplomat, slender, distinguished as always, impeccably dressed, large white linen jabot and blonde curls, eyes smiling, but always with the slightly disdainful pout of the aristocrat and courtier. 'The issues of war or peace lie in Your Majesty's hands,' he told Napoleon, 'the fate of Europe, Europe's future and your own, you alone can decide. Between the aspirations of all Europe and those of Your Majesty there is a vast hiatus ... today, you can still make peace; tomorrow may be too late.... Your peace treaties have never meant much more than an armistice. Defeat as well as victory seems to drive you into war. The moment is upon us when you and Europe will mutually throw down the gauntlet; you will both pick it up, but it will not be Europe that goes down in the struggle ... the stars might well be against you as they were in 1812 ... and when that army of raw youths which you have now assembled has disappeared, what will you do ...? You say you are prepared to sacrifice a million men; open the doors and windows and let all Europe hear those words!'[1]

To such intelligent and prudent counsel, Napoleon had no answer. It merely inflamed his anger, incited him to fresh violence, to more threats. Lacking all self-control he flung the hat which he had been holding in his hand into the corner of the room.

But Metternich (Sorel's cad!) stayed imperturbable and calm throughout; leaning nonchalantly against a console set between two windows, he left the hat on the floor and waited for Napoleon

1. Metternich: *Mémoires*, Vol. I, pages 164–170. Since nobody but the main protagonists was present at this historic interview, we are necessarily confined to their own accounts. That of Metternich is to be found in his autobiography and also in a 'short compendium', addressed to the Emperor Francis, on the day of the encounter. Napoleon gave his account to Maret: it was reproduced by Baron Fain in his *Manuscript* of 1813. The two versions complete, rather than contradict each other, each of the interested parties reporting mainly his own words. Both accounts, in fact, contain passages which strike us as highly improbable. It seems unlikely, for instance, that Napoleon should have greeted the Austrian Minister with: 'Ah, Metternich, and how much has England paid you to turn against me?' An insult the more gratuitous in that Metternich was still on very distant terms with England, a fact which Napoleon could scarcely ignore. On the other side, we might well question the reply that Metternich claims to have made to Napoleon, when the latter boasted of having sacrificed, in the Russian campaign, 'ten times more German lives than French'. 'You seem to forget, Sire, that you are speaking to a German.' That does not ring true to the Metternich tradition. He probably added it to please his old enemies, the German patriots. But otherwise it is easy to fill in any gaps in the conversation.

himself to pick it up. 'Your Majesty is lost', he said, before taking his leave. 'I thought so when I came, but now as I go, I know it . . . !'

It had been dark already for some hours. Outside in the dim-lit ante-chambers, French generals were anxiously awaiting the illustrious visitor. Metternich passed through their ranks in silence—not a word: Berthier alone went with him as far as his carriage. At the moment of parting, when nobody could hear them, Metternich whispered into the Maréchal's ear: 'The Emperor has given me all the information that I require; he is a lost man.'

The die was cast. Napoleon might still deceive himself: 'I have had a long interview with M. de Metternich', he told his suite, on regaining his own apartments, 'he made a good fight. Thirteen times I threw down the gauntlet, and thirteen times he picked it up again . . . the last time, it stayed in my hands.'

But after living through these unforgettable hours, Metternich now knew exactly where he stood. Armed neutrality was un-questionably doomed to failure. The only hope of re-establishing the balance of power in Europe was for Austria to join the coalition when the time came. When would that be? Was Austria ready? Didn't she need a few more weeks to bring her forces up to full strength? To satisfy himself, he sent a courier to Prince Schwarzenberg asking whether a prolongation of the armistice might be opportune from the military point of view. He demanded a reply within thirty-six hours. But before this time limit had expired, Schwarzenberg sent his answer: 'In twenty days from now, my army will have been reinforced by 75,000 men. I should be happy to be able to count on the delay you mentioned, but one day longer would embarrass me.' And when the Emperor Napoleon summoned Metternich for the second time and stated that he was willing to meet the pleni-potentiaries of the armed coalition, at Prague, and willing to extend the armistice until 10th August, the Austrian Minister accepted without hesitation what in fact coincided with his own desires—although he had no authority to do so.

H

One hour later, he left Dresden.

The agreement which Metternich brought back in his pocket was in direct contradiction to the terms of the treaty of Reichenbach. An immediate declaration of war was expected from Austria, and instead of that, the Minister came home bearing a prolongation of the armistice which neither Prussia nor Russia had authorised him to conclude. There was consternation in the camps of the allies. Furious invective was hurled at 'the traitor', the indignation of Baron von Stein knew no bounds. The contrast between these two men and their political tactics never stood out more clearly: on one side, the advocate of violence, obsessed by a notion of his patriotic mission, wishing to forge ahead in a hectic dream of annihilating Napoleon and re-establishing the German Empire,[1] on the other, a protagonist of peaceful means, cold and calculating, determined not to come to grips before holding all the trumps in his own hand. Yet both men wanted to destroy the Bonapartist sway in Europe and to weaken France. From our own more favourable perspective, as we look back, we may well ask ourselves which was in fact the more dangerous policy.

Today in very different circumstances, political men who are called upon to negotiate Franco-German relations, must often ask themselves the same question.

Had the over-impatient elements of the coalition been slightly more perspicacious, they would have found no difficulty in interpreting the Austrian Minister's intentions which were now quite clear.

The interview at Marcolini Palace had convinced Metternich that it was impossible to destroy Napoleonic illusions otherwise than by force of arms. The course of the Prague negotiations only confirmed this theory. In despite of common sense, the Emperor of the French and his advisers had not yet abandoned hope of intimidating Austria and forcing her to maintain a position of neutrality by prolonging the negotiations.[2] The French Pleni-

1. C. de Grünwald: *Stein, l'ennemi de Napoléon*. (Grassett.)
2. Maret to Narbonne, July 28th, 1813. Napoleon, himself, had written a month earlier, on June 30th, to his father-in-law: 'I hope that Your Majesty will not allow yourself to be dragged into a war which would be a calamity for your country.'

potentiaries came to Prague without credentials: 'they were marking time: formalities, manœuvring, stage entrances and exits—all this is a spectacular attempt to throw dust in the eyes of their opponents'. (Sorel.) The fateful date of August 10th was drawing near. Three days before the end of the agreed delay, Metternich handed an ultimatum to Caulaincourt, stipulating as part of his peace objective: the dissolution of the Duchy of Warsaw, a demand that Napoleon should relinquish his protectorate of the Confederation of the Rhine, a complete rehabilitation of Russia and the cession of Illyria to Austria. Caulaincourt was convinced that an affirmative answer from Napoleon would insure peace, and he urged his sovereign in that direction. 'It is now a matter of hours.' The tenth of August passed without any sign of a message from France. The Russian and Prussian delegates—Anstett and Humboldt—were waiting watch in hand. At midnight to the minute, they notified Metternich that the period of their mandate had now expired. Metternich declared the congress closed and immediately returned his passports to the Comte de Narbonne. He then had the beacon flares lighted from Prague to the Silesian frontier, announcing that negotiations had broken down and that the allied armies were now free to cross the passes into Bohemia. Caulaincourt arriving the following day with counter-proposals and full power of implementation, found himself too late and was politely bowed out. The die was cast. . . .

Napoleon's reaction was curious. We can see in the dossiers of the period remarks which he dictated during the reading of that document which bore Metternich's own signature and which concluded with a declaration of war. Rage and possibly fear of what the future might bring had clouded his mind. Like Lear, he was sublime but blind. The Emperor seemed unable to grasp that his day of domination was over, that the peoples of Europe would no longer tolerate his yoke. Neither would he realise that in the camp of his adversaries there was one man—and one man only—who did not desire his fall, who would never have refused him a helping hand. That man was Metternich.

And Metternich informed Stadion, on July 25th: 'Napoleon is struggling against negotiation, like the devil in a stoup of holy water.'

107

As soon as Austria declared war, Humboldt, the Prussian delegate, wrote to Hardenberg: 'We have achieved our aim, dear Baron, all that we have been negotiating since January 4th, is now a *fait accompli*.' But the representative of Frederick William III was also wrong about the situation. The desires of Russia and Prussia were far from being realised. Metternich had no notion of making himself the instrument of liberationist theories for which he had a profound distaste. He had no sympathy whatever with the great national movement (to some extent revolutionary) which then fired the hearts of the German patriots. He considered all such enthusiasms as part of a false political concept, and saw it above all as dangerous to the social order of Europe. He was also fundamentally opposed to any increase of Muscovite power, to anything that might resemble a Russian hegemony in Central Europe.

Whilst the others clamoured for action, Metternich merely tried to put on the brakes. The Germans have never forgiven and always held it as a grudge against him. But what else could he do and remain true to himself? His future 'system' was not yet fully evolved but it was developing during the storms of this climax in European affairs: Metternich's war was to be conducted by Çabinet ministers and their monarchs; decisions—all decisions —would be taken by them and not by the masses. But as far as Russia was concerned he—as an Austrian diplomat—could not envisage a type of relationship which came naturally to Prussian statesmen. Hohenzollerns and Romanoffs had sealed a dynastic *entente* with the blood of their soldiers on the battle-fields of 1813 and 1814, which was to survive throughout the nineteenth century and up to the accession of William II: and in this alliance they found every mutual advantage. But that a similar tie could ever exist between the houses of Romanoff and Habsburg was out of the question. Everything ran counter, not only the temperamental peculiarities of the two most arrogant families in Europe, but also considerations of political realism. The Austrian Emperor reigned over millions of Slavs in a state of serfdom, to whom the *orthodox* Tsar might well some day appear in the light of a liberator and natural protector. The Emperor of Austria, on the other hand, could not remain indifferent to the lot of the Danubian principalities and that of the Balkan peninsula; in these regions there existed a special antagonism between the interests of Vienna and Saint Petersburg.

And so, no sooner was the duel between Metternich and Napoleon over, than one between the minister and the Tsar began. From the start, Metternich had tried to make Austrian influence paramount among the allies. He appointed the Austrian Prince Schwarzenberg commander-in-chief. Alexander's candidate was Moreau. But Metternich unequivocally opposed that nomination, even threatening to withdraw from the coalition. 'Two days later', said Metternich, 'the general was mortally wounded as he stood by Alexander's side. When the Tsar met me, the following day, he remarked: "God, Himself, has given the answer; He seems to have agreed with you"!'

Metternich then decreed that the allied monarchs and their ministers should follow in the wake of the armies. Not that he was over-fond of the sights of war, but: 'One must keep an eye on one's allies', he said, 'no less than on the enemy.' He felt that he had to curb Alexander, that man 'whose ideas and plans were alike unstable', 'surrounded by revolutionaries' [*sic*] who exercised, it seems, a fatal and decisive influence on a mind 'entertaining projects which might well bring the world to perdition'. Yes, put the brake on . . . hold back, more and more. . . .

Undoubtedly Metternich contributed as much as the other Chiefs of the Fourth Coalition to their military success. It was thanks to his moderation that Bavaria joined up with them, bringing in her train the other countries of Southern Germany. Agreeing to bury the hatchet which for a century had kept Bavaria and Austria apart, Metternich even decided to grant that country 'an appreciable service' by recognising her independent and sovereign rights and justifying her claim to substantial compensation. It was also thanks to Metternich's ability (and, it must be admitted to his lack of scruple!) that the Tsar was prevailed upon to violate Swiss neutrality. Swiss historians have made much of this and are still reproaching him today with what was at that time an act of the highest strategic and political importance. It allowed the allies to harry Napoleon's flank and to make Switzerland—hitherto a buyer on French markets—into an economic barrier against France. It was above all, thanks to his incomparable sagacity, that Metternich succeeded in creating trouble in Paris itself. He achieved this by certain bogus 'overtures', reported from Frankfort by M. de Saint-Aignan and by the distribution of a manifesto which promised France her 'natural frontiers'. 'Only Metternich could have written that. To speak of the Rhine, the Alps and the Pyrenees, needed a past-master in the art of guile. Such an idea could only have originated in the mind of a man who knows France as well as he does.' That, according to Metternich, was Napoleon's own complimentary opinion of an act by no means devoid of treachery.

But after that—incredible as this may seem  it was in defence of the Napoleonic cause that Metternich was to devote most of his time and energies.

The great historian, Albert Sorel, who in general has been a harsh critic of the Chancellor, was yet obliged to admit that after the battle of Leipzig neither Metternich nor his master wished to dethrone Napoleon. 'A beaten Napoleon, humiliated, thrown back within his former boundaries, reduced to impotence, brought to bay (presumably by some kind of constitution which would clip his wings), a Napoleon just "husband and father" and so, at last, a true successor and nephew of Louis XVI . . . that kind of Napoleon would have suited Austria down to the ground.'

And, 'humiliation' and 'impotence' apart, wasn't this also what the majority of Frenchmen wanted? What more could one ask of the Coalition's Minister!

Be that as it may, it is a fact that Metternich, throughout these hectic and agonising months—tragic high-water mark of his career—did all in his power to save the husband of Marie-Louise before it was too late. When he parted with Caulaincourt, he had said: 'although formal negotiations are now at an end, the Emperor Francis would nevertheless always be prepared to use his influence with his new allies in the cause of peace. . . . but it must be a real peace.' At the same time he wrote to Bubna who was

then at French headquarters: 'If Bassano should object to you
that our new alliance is an obstacle to peace, tell him flatly that the
way is still open, that it would not take longer than sixty hours
to arrange it. He has only to make proposals to the three Courts
concerned and we would throw in all our weight on his side.'

Through all the vicissitudes of the campaigns of 1813 and 1814,
in victory or defeat, throughout the interminable conferences at
Langres, Troyes, Chatillon, Metternich stayed true to his original
idea: to make peace as soon as possible, to save Napoleon and his
dynasty before the irreparable happened. He energetically opposed the Crown Prince of Sweden, candidate favoured by the
Tsar: 'we have no intention of sacrificing a single life in order to
put Bernadotte upon the throne of France', he wrote to Schwarzenberg, on January 16th, 1814. At first he stood firmly against
any invasion of France. 'Metternich has done all in his power,
since we were at Fribourg, to halt the army's progress. But the
Tsar Alexander has always managed to slip through his fingers
and advance', Münster reported on January 30th, 1814. Whatever
he might have said later, he also opposed the plan to dethrone
Napoleon, to reinstate the legitimist dynasty—and particularly
objected to a suggested popular referendum in this respect. He
wished to extract every possible advantage from the mere 'existence of Napoleon still tolerated by the French nation'. He foresaw that 'it would be easier to destroy Napoleon than to come
to any general agreement when sharing out the spoils'. He wanted
to 'reduce Napoleon but to keep him where he was'. That was
the very key-stone of his policy.[1] 'Bonaparte', he remarked to
the Tsar, 'mastered the Revolution . . . this proposal to consult
the nation, thereby reviving something in the nature of another
Convention, would only unleash a second revolution; and that
must neither be the object, nor does it enter into the general
intention of our Alliance. . . .'

He even again threatened to withdraw from the coalition
should the allies persist in their plan to consult the French people.

On February 12th he handed to the Allies a memorandum

---

1. See Metternich's conversation with Princess Bagration, on February 2nd,
1815. (Weil: *Les dessous du Congrès de Vienne*.)

declaring: the Emperor of Austria is of the opinion that the purpose of the war has now been achieved. 'The Powers are agreed [*sic*] that a change of dynasty in France is by no means their final objective. H.M. the Austrian Emperor would never permit himself to deviate from a principle which he considers the cornerstone of the social structure. He would not consider himself justified in interfering in the internal affairs—as to its form of government—of an independent sovereign state. . . . His Majesty does not agree that Parisian opinion can be read as an expression of the national will. . . . He furthermore refuses to admit that an enemy invasion, the presence of foreign troops surrounding or inside the capital, would be conducive to free expression by the people. A general appeal to the nation would seem to him to invite incalculable dangers. The Emperor (of Austria) feels that any foreign intervention in this matter of a choice of dynasty would be to create a dangerous precedent equally applicable to other countries.'[1]

And even in March, when Vitrolles came to Chatillon as delegate of the French royalists and declared that there could be no peace with Bonaparte and that there could be no France without the Bourbons, Metternich snapped back at him: 'But we have gone through your France, we have lived there for over two months and we have seen no indication of what you suggest.'

Metternich was well aware that if he hoped to save the dynasty, peace must be declared quickly. But what kind of a peace? The demands of the different members of the coalition were becoming more exaggerated. When Metternich, in a memorandum dated January 26th, put this straightforward question to Alexander: 'Do you consider that the Alliance of last August has now achieved what it set out to do?' the Tsar replied: 'The terms of the treaty do not necessarily compel us to relinquish all the other advantages which Providence and our own immense sacrifices might lead us to expect. . . . The unofficial discussions at Frankfort were based on conditions very different from those of today; opinions expressed at Fribourg were not those of Bâle, and the latter might well be found to differ substantially from anything

1. Berlin-Dahlem, Secret archives.

we heard at Langres.[1] 'Surely there would be no end to their demands when once they were encamped outside the walls of Paris.'

And Napoleon, on his side, was equally unreasonable. But at least, in his case, there was more excuse: 'Leave France smaller than I found her? Never.... Reply what you will, I shall not sign', he cried, during that dramatic vigil at Nogent-sur-Seine. And always the same recriminations against Metternich: 'Has he forgotten that my marriage with an Austrian princess was his doing?' he asked, before releasing Wessenberg, brought to him as a prisoner on March 28th. 'Your Emperor does not seem to care much for his daughter; if he did, he could not fail to feel for her anguish now. I committed a grave mistake when I married her.... I never imagined that the Empress could become estranged from her father.' And the same hope in the ultimate intervention of 'Papa François' can be read between the lines of letters, recently published, from Napoleon to Marie-Louise. For the Emperor cherished till the last that Corsican notion of family ties which must have made the Habsburgs and their ministers smile.

Metternich's own position became invidious. His attitude alarmed the Allies. The Russians and the English suspected him of treating with the French behind their backs. On February 11th Münster could already write: 'The French want to bring the negotiations to an end with peace at any price. It is more than possible that Metternich would not be averse to that, either.' Every day brought an increase of tension in the Foreign Minister's relations with the allied generals. 'You cannot imagine', he wrote to Stadion, 'what we have to put up with from our military headquarters. They are all mad. I am at the end of my tether and it has made the Emperor quite ill.' Between the two camps, Austria stood in danger of complete isolation.

On March 8th, Metternich addressed a final appeal to Caulaincourt: 'If peace is not made quickly, no further opportunity will arise . . . those who desire to annihilate the Emperor of the French will have their way . . . the world will be turned upside down and France will be at the mercy of every wind that blows. . . .'

1. Berlin-Dahlem, Secret archives.

Caulaincourt transmitted this message to Napoleon, pointing out that it was a last desperate feeler put out by his Austrian relations. 'Austria, Your Majesty, is on the point of repudiating you.' And, in fact, on March 20th, 1814, the day after the Congress of Chatillon (that final effort at conciliation) had been dissolved, Metternich openly espoused the cause of the legitimist Comte de Provence. 'When one cannot stem the tide of events, one must direct their course', he said. 'We no longer have a free hand; a majority in France has declared against Napoleon. These people now consider him an obstacle to peace, and are convinced that quiet and security are incompatible with such a temperament.' Napoleon's doom foretold by Metternich at the Marcolini Palace was imminent. Several hundred thousand men were about to camp upon the heights of Montmartre, to impose their will, as he had once suggested, on a defeated Emperor. . . .[1]

1. Memories of Napoleon haunted Metternich throughout his life. If we judge from his own notes and letters, the Chancellor's feelings towards his illustrious adversary were a mixture of disappointment, repressed anger and affectionate admiration. He claims that 'Napoleon was as ignorant as the average non-commissioned officer'. He evokes 'that squat, square face, his untidy appearance, combined with an obvious desire to look impressive'. He deplores the Emperor's lack of *savoir vivre*. 'It would be hard to imagine a more awkward man.' But he could not help admiring a certain greatness, 'cold and calculating, marvellously precise', this Caesar who felt nothing but contempt for the sovereign masses, for parliamentary discourse, the liberty of the Press, 'who disliked the dreams of visionaries and all ideological abstractions. . . . who had vowed undying hatred to the false philosophy and even more false philanthropy of the eighteenth century'. (*Mémoires*, Vol. VIII, page 307.)

Capefigue has pointed out that 'Metternich always speaks of Napoleon with considerable respect, and the prestige attached to that great figure appears to have made a lasting impression'. 'How many times', said Pauline Metternich, 'has grandfather repeated that he never knew anyone whose conversation was more entertaining, more seductive. He could only deplore that a man of genius should have had so little self-control, and that after getting the better of the French Revolution, he did not confine himself to maintaining order in his own country.' ('I spent with Napoleon, or near him,' Metternich wrote on October 18th, 1809, 'the best years of my life.') And how many times he referred to the Emperor, when the date of August 15th—Napoleon's birthday—came round. 'For many years,' he wrote in 1823, 'that day of the year was for me, the occasion of some Napoleonic outburst: either the ill-humour of the prisoner at Saint-Helena was directed against my person, or somebody else was the victim before my eyes. Years have gone by since those fateful days; but that date of August 15th so stands out in my memory that each year, as the day comes round, the past revives with clarity and vigour.' And a year before that, he had written: 'I am convinced that Napoleon never understood me. And the reason for this is obvious, he had a complete contempt for the human race, a remarkable faculty for seeing through men's weakness. . . . Being accustomed to speculate on the result of human passions, my

Austria alone was to profit by the treaty of Paris (May 30th, 1814) which ended that tussle of Titans. France came out of it sorely bruised, Russia gained nothing, the future of Prussia remained problematic. Austria did in fact recover her lost provinces: Illyria, Dalmatia, the Tyrol; better still, the Habsburg Empire had acquired Lombardy and the Venetian territories.

Metternich, mainly responsible for these extraordinary results, gained immensely in personal prestige, and not by reputation only. For during all those months of agony and labour, of hectic days and sleepless nights the man had grown in stature, mellowed and opened out. Never in his life before had he been so single-minded, so conscientious. Women—his major weakness—were completely relegated to the background: no reference even to the treacherous Duchesse de Sagan who nevertheless persistently followed in the wake of the high command. He lived as a man among men, among soldiers, among crowned heads—and was treated as an equal by the most eminent among them. He made a deep impression on so profound and noble a thinker as Goethe. On October 26th, 1813, after a long interview with the Austrian minister, the poet wrote: 'What an inspiration for heart and mind, to hear the opinions of such a man, of one who deals with situations of such magnitude while we ourselves are daunted by an infinitesimal part. For Metternich belongs to the favoured few who achieve both the highest peaks of human destiny and of culture. . . . From such a type we may well derive comfort, and assurance that reason and humanity will at last prevail, that a clear intelligence will some day arise to order and correct the chaos amidst which we live.'

The signs of appreciation now showered upon him made him conscious of his own achievement. 'Europe will be saved,' he wrote to his father on October 1st, 1813, 'and I flatter myself that in time no small part of the credit will come to me. For years

particular brand of phlegm, put all his calculations out.' And on August 15th: 'Today is the birthday of the illustrious exile: were he still on his throne, and were he the only other inhabitant of this planet, what a happy man I should be!' Napoleon's supreme achievement, according to Metternich, lay in having defeated the Jacobins; his greatest failure, to have let them loose again, through the circumstances of his own downfall. (A. Hudelist, July 20th, 1850.)

now my policies have never been altered, and a great power like Austria must eventually triumph over all obstacles if properly directed.' 'Heaven entrusted me with the mission to put an end to so much misery', he declared on the same day in a letter to his daughter. . . . 'Napoleon must be continually thinking of me; I must appear to him as conscience personified; I said all I could and forecast his future accurately at Dresden; he would not believe it. . . . *Quos Deus vult perdere dementat.*' And six weeks later: 'We can all be wise after the event. . . . I can at least feel that my policies were justified—and that was much, in 1813. . . . I have now the satisfaction of knowing that the Emperor Francis is aware that my zeal in his service has not been unsuccessful. He feels that he owes to me no small part of the happiness he now enjoys after twenty years of misery.' The sovereign's gratitude, in fact, took tangible form: the day after Leipzig, the title of 'Prince' was conferred upon Metternich and his descendants.

Metternich's return to Vienna assumed the nature of a triumphal entry. On the open square in front of the Palace of the Chancellery, Prince Palffy organised a serenade in his honour. The combined forces of performers from the Court theatre and the *Wiener Theater* executed Beethoven's *Prometheus* overture. And to crown the festal proceedings, a cantata specially composed for the occasion was sung: 'homage to the illustrious statesman whose perspicacity and untiring patience, whose caution and moderation have produced results of which no man would have dared to dream one year ago'.

'Hail to thee, great Prince,' cried the singers, 'to thee whose prudent wisdom guided the royal course, leading us and all our brothers to freedom. . . .

'Hail to thee who reinforced the sword and brought us to great triumph. . . . !

'The whole world now extols thy name and blesses such mature and vigorous counsel.

'When all wounds have been healed, when towns and villages arise once more from their ruins, we shall see the golden sheaves and fertile gardens where once lay only the corpses of our soldiers. . . .

'Then proudly turn thine eyes upon us, and in the far future of thy declining years, consider the immortal splendour of thy work, and smile.'

Thirty-three years later, on an icy winter's night, Prince Metternich, pursued by the cries of a maddened populace, was to flee that same city of Vienna which today acclaimed him as 'outstanding victor of the age and a model among great men'.

# VII

# THE

# CONGRESS DANCES

*Après une longue guerre*
*L'enfant ailé de Cythère*
*Voulut, en donnant la paix,*
*Tenir a Vienne un congrès.*
*Il convoque en diligence*
*Les Dieux qu'on put réunir,*
*Et par une contredanse*
*On vit le Congrès s'ouvrir.*

THAT immense and dingy edifice, the Hofburg of Vienna, is made up of a heterogeneous collection of minor buildings and courtyards. The official residence of Austrian Emperors is now deserted, but visitors are allowed to wander through the state apartments (prune-coloured damask on walls and chairs) in which the monarchs lived. They can also visit the *treasure* of the House of Habsburg and the stables with their famous strain of white Arab horses which were the special pride of the old Austrian Court.

At the time of the Congress of Vienna, two Emperors with their consorts, four Kings, one Queen, a round half-dozen Archdukes, Archduchesses and Princelings slept beneath its roof. And all day long the curious crowds besieged the castle gates, hungry for a sight of the many august mortals lodged within. Three hundred two or four-horse barouches, all exactly alike, waited day and night at the disposal of their Highnesses and circulated in one continuous stream to and from the palace. As soon as the first snows appeared, these gala equipages were replaced by sleighs, ornately carved in gold with armorial bearings. Swift thoroughbreds, caparisonned in tiger-skins with ribbons in their manes, drew all these illustrious visitors through the streets of Vienna. On special occasions the sledge convoys were preceded by a band and escorted by a detachment of the Emperor's body-guard, in full dress. The outing would terminate with a march-past of the troops: assembled sovereigns reviewing some twenty thousand picked grenadiers resplendent in new uniforms, massed for the occasion in the capital.

But the real centre of the Congress was not in that sombre imperial palace on which the eyes of the curious were focused. For just opposite the wing in which the Tsar had his quarters, stood a great house of distinguished proportions, built by the late Prince Kaunitz and since inhabited by Prince Metternich. The building is unimpaired to this day; it has a notably pleasing façade of white stone with rococo ornamentation. And it was there, in that famous mansion of the Ballhausplatz, that the major activities of the Congress of Vienna in fact took place. In a spac-ious audience chamber, white and gold (five doors allowed the five Monarchs a simultaneous entrance should they so desire!), Metternich received all Europe. Here, he was at home, on his own ground: his study and private apartments (since then the home of the Austrian Chancellery) were close at hand, under the same roof. The Congress was his own particular achievement, he was its actual president, master of ceremonies and chief planner. Posterity is still agog at the preposterous extravagance of that vast programme of social festivities. Most European countries had just come through an appalling test of endurance. After twenty years of war, of revolution and invasion, now at last there was peace. The several monarchs were taking a 'holiday' and their subjects rejoiced with them in celebration of a new era of calm and prosperity. We, in our time, have also known them —those happy periods which followed sanguinary war-years in which men who had come too near to death were hysterically determined to secure their full meed of life and pleasure. But the joys of our aftermath of war were less spirited: too much had been sacrificed, too many ruins remained in permanent protest, political and social world order had been shaken to its foundations. In 1815 the situation was somewhat different. For if the number of victims (although a bagatelle compared with the casualty lists of the Great War) was nevertheless appreciable, the foundations of society, at least, had scarcely moved.

It was due to this comparatively fortunate background that the Congress of Vienna was able to operate in a spirit of careless gaiety which is unique in history. 'Strange to say, and as far as I know the first experience of its kind', said the elderly Prince de Ligne, 'the pursuit of pleasure is here achieving peace.' In the wake of a brilliant constellation of monarchs and diplomats, all the great nobility of Germany, Bohemia, Hungary and Russia had come post-haste to Vienna. And women were there: the most famous beauties of Europe suddenly appeared in the Austrian capital. A galaxy of female charm and capacity surrounded the crowned-heads, ready to play their part, if need be, in deciding the fate of nations. There was coquetry in the person of Caroline Szecheny, frivolity in Sophie Zichy, endless surprise in Rosine Esterhazy, the sublime in Julie Zichie, the springtime in Countess Saurma, and finally there was the 'only one for whom a man might seriously care', Gabrielle d'Auersperg. In the drawing-rooms of the Princesses Esterhazy, Colloredo and Liechtenstein, one found good breeding, a gracious smile, a thousand and one details that mark the perfect hostess; in that of Princess Fürstenberg, a wide culture combined with the extremes of old-world etiquette. The elderly Princess Lubomirska, cousin of King Stanislas, true to the traditions of the *grand siècle*, surrounded her guests with an opulent if somewhat oppressive luxury, half European, half Asiatic. The Princess of Hesse-Philippstal combined beauty with great dignity, Countess Theresa Apponyi was chiefly remarkable for her slimness and expressive eyes, and finally Lady Castlereagh for the extreme eccentricity of her garments. But among all these women, 'these matadors of hospitality', none created such a stir in diplomatic circles as Metternich's two particular friends who had rushed to be present at the Congress: the ultra-thin and highly incandescent Duchesse de Sagan, his more or less official mistress, and Catherine Bagration, more radiant than ever, enchanting in her native costumes and much admired in the Russian national dances. She was surrounded by a permanent court of young gallants (the Counts Schönfeld and Schulenberg, Prince Charles of Bavaria) for whom she intermittently 'fell'—such attractions were of short duration. The Tsar, in person, undertook to console his beautiful subject for Metternich's defection: he went to see her often, and stayed on late into the night. By a strange coincidence, the two Egerias, Madame de Sagan and Madame de Bagration, lived in opposite wings of the same house: Palm Palace, in the Schenkengasse. But in fact this was by no means the only place where political intrigue and affairs of the heart seemed often to coincide. In the *salons* of the Comtesse Edmond de Périgord, sister of the Duchesse de Sagan, the second of the Courlande 'Three Graces' and Talleyrand's *confidante*, one could always find a group of the friends of France. Princess Thurn-und-Taxis, sister of the late Queen Louise, made her house a centre of activities on behalf of Prussia whilst King Frederick William III preferred to languish at the feet of Countess Julie Zichy. Lady Castlereagh pleaded the English cause with her accustomed eloquence and Countess Bernstorff that of Denmark. The dowager Countess of Pergen-Grosschlag gathered around her those who wished to intrigue for intrigue's sake; and a whole gang of elderly ladies, the Countesses Schoenburg, Chotek, Hoyos, Cobenzl, and others, met every evening with all the latest news of the *goings-on* of crowned heads and their suites, to say nothing of envenomed comment on the Prince von Metternich.[1]

This drawing-room diplomacy, however, has been somewhat exaggerated—the ladies had enough to do apart from politics, overwhelmed as they were with a never-ending sequence of receptions, balls, masquerades and entertainments of all kinds.

Contemporary records (particularly those of Count de la Garde-Chabonas) help us to reconstruct the social programme of the Congress from day to day. Theatricals, followed by a ball at the Hofburg, come to life for us in these delightful sketches. We

1. Report by the Secret Police of Vienna, November 9th, 1814.

121

J

see Tsar Alexander, deaf in his right ear sitting next to the Austrian Empress, deaf in her left, making desperate but futile efforts at communication. We see groups of young aristocrats, with their lovely partners, in a *tableau vivant:* a banquet of gods and goddesses. This is followed by a reproduction of Teniers' scene in the life of the Troubadours showing a meeting between Maximilian I and Marie de Bourgogue. The orchestra played symphonies by Haydn and Mozart and many a famous *diva* was applauded in sentimental ditties (*Partant pour la Syrie, Fais ce que dois, advienne que pourra*).[1]

One colossal entertainment took place in the castle's riding-school, the capacious state apartments being no longer large enough to hold the crowds: the assembled sovereigns in full uniforms were seated on a dais surrounded by a decoration of regimental standards and other war trophies; the most beautiful women of the Congress were grouped together on benches; in the centre of the ring, a group of masked children played a Venetian pantomime lighted by 8,000 candles.

On another occasion, we see a mammoth tournament: in the galleries of the riding school sat ambassadors, ministers of state, generals and the bearers of some of the most famous names in Europe. Royal personages were enthroned on a large tribune, and on another smaller and lower stage sat the wives of the twenty-four 'paladins' of the tournament dressed in Renaissance costumes of unparalleled splendour (in the colours of France, Hungary, Poland and Austria), the sum-total of these ladies' jewels amounting to no less than thirty million *livres* (of which six million belonged to Princess Esterhazy, *née* Thurn-und-Taxis, alone). And the whole of this distinguished gathering was there to acclaim the convolutions of the twenty-four paladins, dressed as Knights of the Court of Francis I and mounted on the pick of Hungarian horses.

Then again, one notes a simple family reunion bringing together innumerable monarchs and attendant highnesses to celebrate some birthday: that of the Emperor of Austria or the King of Denmark. Tokay wine (a hundred years old and costing 150

1. 'When duty calls. . . whate'er the cost. . . .' TRANS.

gulden a bottle) is served, and all the guests describe themselves as brothers and cousins.

After those of the Emperor, receptions were given in turn by lesser men: foreign diplomats and lords of high finance competing with the local aristocracy. Popular rejoicing alternated with all this formal ceremonial.

Caught up with the others in a whirlpool of festivity (of which he was mostly the instigator) Metternich was in his element. He could always combine 'well-chosen luxury with an infinite care for detail'; such qualities confirmed his position as a leader and gave his entertaining 'a unique character quite in keeping with his person'.

Countess Metternich's invitations (she seconded her husband to good effect) were eagerly sought: all Vienna was to be found in her *salons*, every Monday. For larger gatherings, Metternich used a villa which he owned on the Rennweg, then a suburb of the capital. And there he gave two gala entertainments which stand out with an almost historic significance.

The first of these took place on October 18th, anniversary of the battle of Leipzig, in the presence of a crowd of sovereigns and other notabilities: it had as its central theme 'to celebrate Peace'. The programme was arranged by an *inspecteur général de l'Académie royale de musique de Paris*. Among other attractions, a balloon was let loose to the sound of drums and trumpets; a visit of the gardens was accompanied by both vocal and instrumental music; a pantomime on the spacious lawns showed the triumph of Peace over Discord, and was lit by a magnificent display of fireworks. All the ladies, including the Empress, were dressed in blue relieved only by crowns of olive or oak leaves. A magnificent combined theatre-and-dance-floor had been built for the occasion in the gardens: 'the steps of this building were covered', writes La Garde, 'with lovely women superbly dressed. The eye could with difficulty be lured from that enchanting sight and then only to rest on one even more brilliant: that rich variety of uniforms, gold braid and decorations, displayed by the privileged circle at the centre of the hall.'

The second entertainment was in the nature of a fancy-dress

ball. 'The guests had decided, in honour of their illustrious host and his sovereign, to wear the national costumes of all those countries and provinces which were united in the Austrian Empire.' Once more the occasion was a complete success: the traffic congestion was such that Countess Bernstorff, who had left home at nine o'clock, only arrived at the gates of the villa by eleven—happy, even then, to have escaped safe and sound from the crush. Normally, it would have taken a quarter of an hour to accomplish the journey. (Gräfin Bernstorff: *Erinnerunger*.)

'Dressed in the national costumes of Austria, with heavy bodices and bright-coloured scarves, our cheerful and fresh young faces made a charming contrast with their rustic headgear', notes Countess Thurheim in her Memoirs. Twenty years later, that sprightly Viennese lady still remembered the fantastic apparition of the scraggy Lady Castlereagh, who had concocted for the occasion a 'national' costume of her own vintage. To the amazed eyes of the Congress, she appeared swathed from head to foot in a garment of *hobble* proportions (revealing all such contours as she possessed) and wearing round her head her husband's Order of the Garter with *Honi soit qui mal y pense* inscribed in diamonds on her forehead.

We all know how Metternich has been despised and blamed for turning the European Congress into a smart jamboree; for having—five memorable months on end, from October 1814 to March, 1815—frittered away his time and energy in pleasures as frivolous as they were futile. The lode-star for all eyes, central figure of the Congress, he roused hostility on all sides: to cope adequately with his detractors, he would have had to belong to every camp in turn. There were the Russians: 'Metternich', said the Tsar, 'is the best master-of-ceremonies in the world, but it would be hard to find a worse Minister.' 'What on earth is Metternich doing?' echoed Capo d'Istria. 'Why, he is doing nothing: he just drags on from week to week. In the meanwhile he intrigues, whispering first into one ear and then another. Where is he heading? He confuses everyone—including himself.'

On another occasion, Capo d'Istria speaks of Metternich's

'bad faith, poor judgment, frivolity, lack of principle'. 'One cannot negotiate, he is too unstable. He distorts everything, and denies today something he said yesterday. He has forced us all to make suspicion a *sine qua non* of our procedure.'

And La Harpe, the Tsar's old tutor, exclaims: 'How dangerous for Austria to have a Minister despised by his own countrymen and hated by foreigners!' He recognised in Metternich 'with his elegant bearing and sparkling wit' the qualities of a successful Ambassador—but nothing more. Anstett, back-bencher of the Russian clique, was furious not to have been honoured by some Austrian decoration. [1] Others went so far as to accuse Metternich of having received a bribe of 500,000 *thalers* from the King of Prussia. But this did not mean that the Prussians, themselves, were any better disposed towards him. The King of Prussia, indeed, in the presence of General von Knesebeck, let out a furious sally against the Minister. ('He described him as a scoundrel; he accused Metternich of ruining his pet schemes, and of having sown dissension between Prussia and Austria.') [2] And Humboldt contributed to the chorus: 'All that interests Metternich is to arrange entertainments and *tableaux vivants* for the Court. He is capable of keeping two Ambassadors waiting, while he watches his daughter dance and chats affably with the ladies. For him, only trifles are serious, and he treats serious matters as trifles.'

Each delegation had its grievance. M. de la Tour du Pin claimed that 'Metternich was only enterprising when it came to the ladies'. Count Solms, envoy from Württemberg, sneered at the carelessness and lack of method with which Metternich conducted official business. 'Metternich never goes into anything whole-heartedly. He is incapable of concentration and seems to think it unnecessary to give any matter his serious attention.' [3] Hacke, Minister of the Grand Duchy of Baden, went so far as to hold Metternich responsible for deterioration in rates of

1. Police reports of October 13th, November 10th and December 28th, 1814, and of January 24th, of February 5th and 12th, 1815. (Weill: *Lesdessous du Congrès de Vienne.*)
2. Police reports of December 19th, 1814, and February 9th, 1815.
3. Reports of November 20th and 30th, 1814.

exchange.[1] The King of Denmark was offended: Metternich was really too casual in his manner with crowned heads, 'speaks to us sitting down and is offensive in his whole bearing'. The mediatised Princes were furious because they did not get their compensation as quickly as they hoped: 'They all appear to think that the fate of the House of Austria hangs on their own upkeep and insist that it is Metternich who has dragged his Emperor into this hornet's nest.' The Abbé Evangelisti, secretary to Cardinal Consalvi, who had insisted in vain on the return to the Vatican of all lost territories, described Metternich as a dangerous Proteus, a worse monster than Bonaparte, a pitiless enemy of the Holy See, and finally as an initiate of the mysteries of Isis and Ceres and of freemasonry to boot!

And the Chancellor fared no better with his own countrymen. Stadion, the Foreign Minister, under whom he once served, Wallis, who had been his colleague when at the Exchequer, Count Wrbna, Lord High Chamberlain to the Emperor, now revived their former intrigues. . . . Even the Counsellors of the Austrian Chancellery: Hudelist, Baron Kruft and Baron Hope, three men on whom Metternich had showered favours, 'were at no pains to avoid criticising the Minister's policy'. Gentz, himself, that most devoted of secretaries, was outraged by the time that Metternich wasted in amorous brawls with Madame de Sagan, 'that damnable woman', who was playing fast and loose, first calling him to her side, then making a fool of him with young Windischgraetz, and dragging him from scene to scene until their final distressing rupture.[2]

1. Report of November 1814. See also N. von Humboldt: *Gesammelte Schriften.* (Herausgeg, Von W. Richter, Berlin.) Freiherr von Stein: *Tagebuch waehrend des Wiener Congresses* (Historische Zeitschrift, 1888). H. C. E. Freiherr von Gagern: *Mein Anteil an der Politik.*

2. A whole legend has been built up around the fact that Austria lost Bavaria because on the decisive day Metternich, who had passed the night with Madame de Sagan, did not turn up at his office. During the morning, the King of Bavaria—who was to have received certain Italian territories in compensation—is said to have changed his mind. The date has even been given: November 11th, 1814. One can well imagine the scene: the harassed diplomats met together at the Kaunitz Palace, feverishly await their president throwing anxious side-long glances at the clock while Metternich disports himself in a dressing-gown, taking breakfast at the feet of the beautiful Duchess. But we seem here to be leaving the field of history for that of cinema—it is surprising that no scenario writer has yet laid hands on this gem.

Finally, the campaign of vilification spread to the masses. As from November, the Viennese public, 'who had always been enthusiasts for everything in the way of pageant and entertainment, began to tire of this ceaseless stream of social dissipation'. They blamed the presence of so many foreign sovereigns in the capital for their rising cost of living.[1] All these royalties lodging at the Hofburg might well be made a pretext for fresh taxation.

By this avalanche of passion, Metternich remained unmoved. Once only he is said to have departed from his usual calm, when he heard that the treacherous Duchesse de Sagan had joined the chorus of his enemies and was saying to all and sundry that 'a Foreign Minister who has lost the confidence of other European powers is no longer fit for his post'.[1] But apart from this his general bearing never changed: phlegmatic, haughty, disdainful; the attitude of a great nobleman and a great statesman. For the Minister was well aware that were he disposed to say 'amen' to all the demands and proposals of the assembled parties, the work of the Congress might indeed be rushed through in twenty-four hours.[2]

Better than anyone else concerned, however, he also knew the potentiality (properly directed) of such a gathering of plenipotentiaries as he was then presiding.

Today, when we speak of a political congress, we imagine an enormous hall with some hundred diplomats and ministers sitting round a table covered with green baize; and these surrounded in turn by a whole army of secretaries and journalists. But no such congress as this—and one cannot too much insist upon that fact—ever sat in Vienna in 1814-1815. The men of that period could never have conceived such a type of procedure. Many years later, indeed, Metternich was still asking himself whether it would not be ridiculous to enforce upon European diplomacy anything of a 'representational' character. In 1822, he wrote: 'Would such complicated and delicate matters really gain by being submitted to forty or fifty ministers and members of parliament, all bearing no relation to each other? Are such men

1. Police report of November 4th, 1814.
2. Police report of November 15th, 1814.

127

really qualified, voting by a show of hands, [1] passing by majorities
—sometimes problematic, often ill-advised—motions which the
combined experience and wisdom of three or four Cabinets
(accustomed to work together) find it hard to bring to any
reasonable conclusion?' And in this, everyone then agreed. The
notion of a congress had been rather lightly undertaken by members of the Coalition during the negotiations at Paris and London
following the defeat of Napoleon. Nobody had stopped to consider exactly what this term 'congress' would entail, but invitations had been sent to all the European powers without exception.
An incredible number of plenipotentiaries had thus set out for
Vienna with vague aspirations and ill-defined projects in their
bags. In the meanwhile on the banks of the Danube, no steps
had been taken to weld them into a coherent whole. They, in
fact, had only been called so that they might ratify the decisions
of a limited number of the greater powers; they were called upon
to supply a background—picturesque if somewhat expensive—to
that so-called 'panorama of Europe'. 'If the majority of these
envoys had never come to Vienna, it would not have altered one
jot of the decisions finally reached there.' [2]

'The Congress—or what it had been agreed to call by that
name—had opened with a conference between the representatives of the four powers who signed the treaty of Chaumont.
France was debarred from the conference: it had been arranged
to admit her later together with Spain, thus creating the big *Six*.
Talleyrand's undying claim to distinction in the eyes of Frenchmen—an achievement which won his pardon for many a fatal
error, for much disgraceful treachery—is to have succeeded, as
soon as he arrived at Vienna, in securing full recognition for his
country and in getting the committee of *Four* transformed into
one of *Five*. From the moment Talleyrand was admitted to the
executive committee, he abandoned all pretence of a general
Congress. No more was heard of the rights of small powers. . . .
The Committee of Five became the *de facto* Congress of Vienna.'
(Webster.)

1. They really stood up or remained seated.
2. C. K. Webster: *The Congress of Vienna*, London, 1934.

Sure enough, a working and workable machinery had been found with which to operate; for didn't the Committee of Five represent all the forces which had then any practical say in the government of Europe? Metternich himself was obliged to admit —as Talleyrand ironically noted in his Memoirs—that 'the Congress was not a congress; that its opening had opened nothing; that the committees were not committees; that in bringing the powers to Vienna, the only advantage gained was the suppression of distance'.

Talleyrand had nevertheless insisted that a second committee be formed, consisting this time of the eight signatories to the treaty of Paris. But all that the *Eight* were ever asked to do was to confirm by their own signatures decisions already reached by the more restricted committee of the five great powers. Metternich presided at the committee of Eight and thereby became known as President of the Congress, although he laid no official claim to that title.

The nature of the Congress absolved Metternich from any need to pay attention to the clamour of delegates from second- and third-rate zones. He could afford to snap his fingers when the Kings of Bavaria or Denmark were not pleased: offended not to have been consulted when Napoleon was declared 'ostracised by all Europe'. He was totally indifferent as to the impatience of this or that princeling; didn't give a fig for such nonentities as Count Nostitz, the Saxon delegate, who questioned the Austrian Chancellor's diplomatic capacities and called him 'the butterfly-minister, incapable of any point of view, devoid of objective or of character'. The only men who finally concerned him, whom he had to conciliate, to treat with tact, convince and hold together, were the few really great figures then speaking in the name of England, France, Russia and Prussia. To achieve this was his real function.

In Castlereagh, representing England at the Congress, Metternich had re-discovered an old and tried friend. That bony Anglo-Saxon, whose thin legs had a natural predilection for dancing Scottish jigs, was one of the most remarkable figures ever known to English diplomacy. Savage enemy of the Revolution, he was much disliked by the English Liberals; he could count on no support from his colleagues of the Liverpool Cabinet, men who knew nothing whatever of the affairs of Europe and had no inclination to know more. But among Continental statesmen, by his courage, intelligence and ability as a negotiator, Castlereagh had already made his mark; he was perhaps 'the least insular of all the ministers who had ever directed English foreign policy'. (Webster.) His lack of geography (it seems that on arriving at Vienna, he was not aware that Dresden was the capital of Saxony!) did not in any way hamper clear and precise convictions. His programme for Europe coincided exactly with that of Metternich: he wished to insure against any further imperialist encroachments on the part of France and to establish a stable balance of power on the continent of Europe. In opposing the designs of the Tsar and the immoderate appetite of Prussia, Metternich was always able to count on the support of the English statesman who had inherited from Pitt a deep suspicion of Russia and who had only one desire—to see peace and order revived.

The relationship between Metternich and Talleyrand was delicate and complex. But in spite of a general conviction to that effect, accepted even by certain historians, the Congress of Vienna was no cock-pit in which the two greatest diplomats of the century tried out their strength. A certain rivalry did, of course, exist, but it was one of personal prestige. When it came to politics, Talleyrand was to be found more often than not on Metternich's side. But Talleyrand this time had the better part as Metternich after Wagram: he represented a defeated country, always an occasion for the display of diplomatic ability. The frontiers of France had been fixed by the Treaty of Paris; thus there only remained for the French Minister to insure his country's general prestige and to make her voice felt in the council of nations in a manner befitting her high estate. But a congress which stood unanimously for legitimist theories could scarcely have treated a country now governed by the Bourbons as an enemy—nor excluded France, in the circumstances, from its deliberations designed to establish a new order in Europe. Furthermore, France was unquestionably a nation with a glorious past and actually one of the richest and most powerful in the world. The fact that Talleyrand was able to make his point in a few days (from September 23rd to October 3rd, 1814) proves not only his ability but also the lack of any appreciable resistance; any opposition there was came from Alexander I and very little from Metternich.

Talleyrand's second intervention in the affairs of the Congress —and it came with a bang—was when he insisted that France should have a say in the affairs of Saxony. As a result, he became the instigator of the triple alliance—France, England and Austria —directed against Russia and Prussia. A great victory for French diplomacy but by no means scored at the expense of Metternich. On the contrary, it supplied the Austrian Chancellor with a formidable weapon against the northern powers. For Metternich welcomed the Triple Alliance as soon as Talleyrand suggested it. The whole affair was despatched in twenty-four hours. The importance of that treaty of January 3rd, 1815, has however been much exaggerated (first by Talleyrand himself and then by later historians). It remained a secret and had no influence on later events, concessions which Russia and Prussia subsequently offered having made it unnecessary.

Talleyrand's third achievement at the Congress, on the other hand—the enforcing of his point of view with regard to the Kingdom of Naples—might be considered a victory over the policies of Metternich. The Frenchman was here concerned—as were the other delegates—to bring back in the south of the peninsula (as indeed everywhere else) the legitimate dynasty, in this instance, of course, the Bourbons. 'I have no knowledge of such a person', Talleyrand snapped out when reminded that the throne of Naples was now occupied by Joachim Murat. But for a variety of political and—one must admit—of sentimental reasons, Metternich supported a different point of view. He did not wish to see the Bourbons strengthened to the detriment of Austrian influence in Italy. Also, he had never forgotten Napoleon's sister. These discussions revived the past: a beautiful head, brown locks thrown back in languor among the cushions—his former mistress was now the Queen of Naples. During the Wars of the

Coalition, Metternich had kept up a correspondence with Caroline Murat; she was largely responsible for her husband's defection after the battle of Leipzig. In this she was more than a mere accomplice, she was, in fact, the prime mover: a letter from Metternich had actually persuaded her to join the Coalition. [1] The Treaty of Naples (January 11th, 1814) had guaranteed to Murat his rights over the Kingdom of Naples, over Sicily and territories seized from the State of Rome. A clause added to the treaty of Chaumont had granted him further benefits. [2] It was not easy for Metternich to forswear his own signature and betray the confidence of a woman he had once loved. And yet, from the political angle alone, his position was illogical: what reason could there be for refusing to the Bourbons in Sicily what they were unanimously conceded elsewhere? Metternich's endeavour on behalf of his protégés had no success; he was obliged to give way to Talleyrand in the course of a stormy session: Caroline and Murat were to be dispossessed.

But this one passage of arms apart, Talleyrand was to remain what he had always been, no adversary of Metternich but a most helpful partner. [3] Their past association drew them together as much as their activities of the moment: they now lived under the same roof (Talleyrand was staying at the Kaunitz Palace); they were collaborators in the Congress; both aristocrats, by birth and upbringing, they had the same tastes and prejudices and were even mutually complementary in their temperamental contrasts. [4]

Talleyrand had the finer wit ('Europe is always on the *qui vive* for fear of his latest *bon mot*', wrote the Baronne de Montet), Metternich had more charm, was more gracious, more attractive. Talleyrand could sit back, with his customary sardonic smile,

---

1. This is confirmed by a letter from the Duke d'Otrante to Prince Eugène. See Arthur Lévy: *Les dissentiments de la famille impériale*.
2. According to Pasquier (*Mémoires*, Vol. III) the clause in question had all the appearance of 'a lover's homage'.
3. See Duff Cooper: *Talleyrand*; Sainte-Aulaire: *Talleyrand*; also Talleyrand: *Correspondance diplomatique*.
4. Talleyrand was well aware of Metternich's weaknesses. ('He spends three-quarters of his time dancing and at other social festivities.' 'He takes his phlegm for a sign of genius.' 'When it comes to intrigue which he thinks to direct, he is often duped like any child'.) These were Metternich's failings—but Talleyrand was wise enough to be conscious of his own. . . .

watching the great human comedy unfold before his eyes, and he could remain comfortably ensconced in his armchair, a privileged guest, chief delegate of the King of France. But not so Metternich, his host, never for a moment free of his obligations, forced to rush hither and thither dispensing minor favours, performing a plethora of small tasks. They both had an eye for women (at one time, pursuing two sisters), but Talleyrand, on the verge of old age, was well satisfied with mere friendly attentions from Madame Edmond de Périgord, whilst Metternich, some eighteen years his junior, was still in the throes of amorous upheavals with Madame de Sagan. Neither was indifferent to money, but Talleyrand would sell himself to the first bidder whereas Metternich only accepted 'presents' from friends![1] They were both entirely devoid of scruple, had intrigue in their blood and lied as they breathed, but Talleyrand was an out-and-out opportunist whereas Metternich had certain fixed political principles from which he never departed. The nobleman from Périgord, who was 'organically' a Frenchman (according to Baronne de Montet), 'the *Frenchiest* Frenchman of them all', (according to the Prince de Ligne), fought for his own country and for that alone, whereas the Rhenish Count was impelled by a concept which far transcended the frontiers of Austria, his adopted country. Against the considerable background of the Congress of Vienna, one was pursuing mere tactics, the other a major strategy; one was behaving like a good Frenchman, the other like a good European—and therein, perhaps, lay Metternich's superiority.

But in any event, the two *compères* of the show hit it off to perfection. With the emaciated Castlereagh beside them, they proceeded hand-in-hand, symbolising in their persons the union and solid qualities of the three great powers of Christendom, standing like a rock against the dynamic pressure of young Prussia and young Muscovy.

It was with the Tsar that Metternich had his most formidable tussle, in the winter of 1814-1815; the issues which arose between

1. For instance, a gift of ten thousand ducats from the city of Frankfurt.

them, supply—according to Gentz—'a key to most of the pre-occupations of the Congress'.

As soon as the Tsar arrived at Vienna, their relationship had begun to be strained. 'Alexander liked to cut a figure, that was his chief ambition.' (Gentz.) He wanted pride of place in the drawing-room no less than at the conference-table, he wished to make an impression (at least platonic) on all women [1] and become a kind of umpire among the diplomats. But wherever he turned, he came up against Metternich, who had no intention of conceding the leading role to anyone. Jealousy and irritation combined: the gossip of Countess Bagration—not a little pleased to score off a faithless lover in what she confided to her new protector—did much to fan the flame of disagreements which had started as political. [2]

Alexander was fully determined to enlarge the Duchy of Warsaw and make it into an independent Kingdom. This had been a project of his youth; he wished to wipe out an historical injustice, to implement a solemn promise made as an adolescent to his friend Czartoryski and recently renewed to the whole Polish nation. But in the eyes of Metternich any reconstruction of Poland under the aegis of the Tsar meant something quite different: a threat to Austrian Galicia, a formidable increase of Russian prestige and, unquestionably, a further disruption of that balance of power in Europe so dearly bought by twenty years of war with France.

These diametrically opposite points of view were irreconcilable and could not fail quickly to bring about a sharp conflict. Alexander lost his temper and Metternich refused to budge. 'You are the only man in Austria who would dare to oppose me', shouted the Russian autocrat on one occasion. Another day, beside himself with rage, the Tsar threw his sword on the table, called Metternich a 'rebel' and challenged him to a duel. According to

1. 'Viennese morality will suffer nothing from the Russians', wrote Count Alexander Nostitz. 'The Tsar is not very exacting; words and looks apparently are all he requires. His advances, in fact, are often addressed to as many as six beautiful ladies at the same time.'

2. 'Alexander loves to converse about military matters and can be heard to remark on all occasions: "We soldiers. . ." especially when he wishes to annoy Metternich who is anything but military.' (Countess Thurheim: *Mémoires*.)

Talleyrand, the Chancellor came out of that interview 'in a state in which his most intimate friends had never seen him'. But he soon pulled himself together and, calm restored, offered explanations which might well have passed for apology. Instead of seeking the Chancellor's blood, Alexander merely refused to attend his ball and cut him consistently when they met, which was almost daily, at other people's houses.

This was the climax in a state of affairs watched 'with curiosity and amusement' by frivolous elements but with a certain anxiety by the more responsible.

Feeling now secure in his knowledge of the support of England, France, and Francis I in person, Metternich was able to force the Tsar to yield ground: Poland was sacrificed to the cause of peace; a compromise arrived at as to frontiers. Tarnopol, acquired by Russia in 1809, was given back to Austria. Matters had reached this stage when Napoleon, escaped from Elba, and back at the Tuileries, lost no time in communicating to the Tsar the text of an alliance concluded on January 3rd, 1815, between Austria, France and England, a flagrant proof of treachery by the old Coalition of Chaumont. One scarcely knows which to admire most in relation to this dramatic episode: the Tsar's magnanimity or Metternich's sang-froid. The unpleasantly revealing document was placed before the Minister, in his Emperor's study, in the presence of Baron Stein who, as an eye-witness, has furnished us with this account. Metternich examined the document in absolute silence; not a flicker passed over his face. Just as he was about to speak, the Tsar interposed: 'Metternich, this incident must never, in our life-time, be mentioned again. We have more serious matters to attend to. Napoleon is back and our alliance should be firmer than ever.' Having said this, he threw the incriminating document into the fire. [1]

With no more loss than a slight wound to his vanity, Metternich's policy in fact had triumphed. From that day, he was on

1. Metternich gives a slightly different report and does not admit that he was faced with the treaty. 'There is still a personal quarrel outstanding between us. We are both Christians; as you know our holy religion insists that we forgive those that trespass against us. Let us kiss and let all be forgotten', Alexander is supposed to have said according to Metternich's *Mémoires*.

the best of terms again with the Tsar. They were to part as friends from the Congress and their relations would grow closer and more cordial as the years went by.

But no such tidy conclusion was available with regard to the issues raised by Prussia. In that instance, the settlement was unsatisfactory. For there, too, Metternich found himself faced with something in the nature of a *mystique*, but accompanied by unmistakable and quite tangible greed. The obstacle was what Metternich liked to call *Teutomania*, the German cult of nationalism which had evolved during the wars of liberation. As for Prussia's greed, she coveted Saxony first and foremost but *faute de mieux* was prepared to accept a slice of Poland or even Rhenish territory. Metternich tried to compromise: he offered a part of Saxony including 430,000 inhabitants (described as 430,000 'souls' of the population). This was rejected as 'insulting'. 'The storm was such', wrote Friedrich von Gentz, 'that for a fortnight—and even till the end of 1814—those who had inside information regarded war as inevitable.' But Metternich would have regarded such a war as an unthinkable catastrophe. 'Austria is not in any way jealous of Prussia', he wrote to Hardenberg on September 10th, 1814; 'indeed, we consider that power as one of the most valuable assets of a well-balanced Europe.... Prussia and Austria are both building up their defences; united they constitute an impregnable barrier against any over-ambitious Prince who might some day come out of France, again, or Russia.'

Once more, Metternich's presence of mind and the magnanimous intervention of Alexander saved the situation. Prussia would be allowed half Saxony with 800,000 subjects and, in addition, 1,400,000 'souls' in the Renish country. Her population would thus consist of over ten million inhabitants, nearly all of German origin. The old quarrel which had destroyed the Holy Empire had cropped up again. It is not surprising that the Emperor of Austria, guided by the prudent Metternich, should have refused the Imperial crown of Germany, offered by Pan-German parties at the beginning of 1815. With Prussia's new gargantuan proportions, he would have had less chance than ever of exercising effective control: as things stood, the two monarchies—

Austria and Prussia—exactly balanced each other. Vienna, never-theless, could claim a certain moral prestige, which was hers alone, and a tradition of authority which Metternich used to the fullest advantage when the statutes of the new German Confederation were being drawn up at the Congress.

But the German patriots felt badly let down—all those fanatic supporters of the new Imperial concept. Stein left Vienna dis-appointed and embittered before the end of the proceedings—it was a heartbreak for many others who shared his convictions. Already, in 1812-13, such circles were in the habit of vaguely considering Metternich a traitor to the German cause. For the future that reputation was definitely to be pinned upon him; for the moment, he was quite indifferent to the accusation. For if, in his tussle with Prussia, he had not exactly had his own way, he could scarcely be said to have been beaten. The Kingdom of Saxony—although diminished—would continue to act as a buffer state between Prussia and Austria. King Frederick-William left Vienna on good terms with Metternich and was to be in-fluenced by him in the future as much as the Tsar.

In the course of the first few months of 1815, most of the difficulties arising between the great powers had been smoothed out: the special problems of Saxony and Poland were settled; the negotiations were coming to an end. A final solution came with a crash: *Deus ex machina*, Napoleon reappeared on the European scene. 'We were all at a ball given by M. de Metternich', reports La Garde, 'when we learnt of the landing at Cannes and the Emperor's first military successes. The news had the effect of the proverbial fairy's wand (or the scene-shifter's whistle), changing Armide's Eden into a desert in the twinkling of an eye. It seemed as if thousands of candles immediately went out. The news spread like wild-fire. Waltzing stopped short, in vain the orchestra tried to go on with the tune. . . . The King of Prussia made a sign to the Duke of Wellington, and both went out of the ball-room. They were immediately followed by Alexander, the Emperor Francis and M. de Metternich. . . . Most of the guests faded away. Only a few scared chatterers remained. . . .' The story is un-doubtedly picturesque but not entirely accurate. It is quite

K

possible that an important message did, in fact, disturb the Metternichs' reception. It is also possible that the sudden departure of all the crowned heads revealed Napoleon's escape to the public. But the general situation had been known for several days and the public were prepared for all eventualities. The only point which was not yet generally known, and which might well have transpired on that memorable evening, was the exact spot where Napoleon had landed.

Metternich, himself, has told us in his *Mémoires* exactly how the news reached him: by an urgent message from an Austrian consular agent, late at night. One can still see the original missive in the Viennese archives, sent from Leghorn, under date of March 3rd, 1815, and signed by Julio Grifi, Austrian consul at Portoferraio. Napoleon Bonaparte, it seemed, had set sail with a small flotilla for some 'destination unknown'. Misled, no doubt, by the insignificant aspect of this communication from a subordinate official written on square-ruled paper of the cheapest commercial format, Metternich had left it lying on the table until morning: he only read it on waking.[1] 'I dressed in the twinkling of an eye and before eight o'clock was with the Emperor Francis.... By nine o'clock, following brief interviews with Alexander, Frederick-William and Schwarzenberg, it was decided to resume military operations against France....' Maybe, things did not go quite so quickly; if we are to believe certain other reliable witnesses, it took two or three days to get a unanimous decision. But in any event the old coalition was soon presenting a united front again.

The celebrations came to an end, the various sovereigns went off in haste with their armies, but the work of statesmen carried on. 'The Congress is dismissed', Napoleon had cried when he set foot upon the soil of France. But the saying—which has come down to history—proved to be little more than a *bon mot*. The allies foresaw the Corsican's defeat and this was soon to be confirmed. Even before the final blow was struck at Waterloo,

1. An almost identical message was sent to Metternich on March 3rd by the Comte de Bellegarde, in command of Austrian troops at Milan, who in turn had received the information by express messenger from Leghorn: it seems, the general added, that Napoleon 'was headed towards the coast of France'.

representatives of the eight great European powers signed, on June 8th, 1815, a final decree put out by the Congress of Vienna: it was to form the basis of the international *entente* in Europe for half a century. Simultaneously, the *Four* signed separate treaties relating to Poland and Saxony. And in the course of the following weeks all the other European powers joined in—not always without protest.

In the last phases of the negotiations, Metternich, now free of meddling monarchs, had categorically assumed the reins. Sometimes he continued to pursue his old policy of marking time, watching for eventualities which might arise according to the fortune of the armies. But none of the old criticisms were revived. 'Ministers and representatives of the German Princes are praising his circumspection', said a police report of June 6th. 'It seems that the Prince von Mecklenburg, in the house of Count Zichy, delivered a terrific oration in praise of Metternich. He admired the manner in which the Chancellor had handled German affairs, his impartiality, his integrity, the more praiseworthy in that he himself had been *mediatised*.' At last all had come to recognise the soundness of his procedure, the necessity for delaying tactics, for patience and caution in getting things done. The signing of the final decree marked also the climax of a personal triumph.

'What is a peace treaty?' Talleyrand had once asked, in a curious memorandum inscribed under date of *le* 3 *Nivose*, of the Year IV, and addressed to the Directorate. 'It is something which while achieving a settlement of the specific objects concerned also succeeds in replacing hate by friendship.' Did the closing gesture of the Congress of Vienna live up to this *desideratum*? Gentz, secretary to the Congress, judged it with some severity. 'The real object of the Congress', he wrote, 'was to divide the spoils of victory among the victors. Such impressive phrases as reconstruction of the social order, revival of the political traditions of Europe, lasting peace established on an equitable balance of forces, were just so much bluff designed to impress the masses and to give dignity and a high moral tone to the proceedings.'

But whatever Gentz might think, it was by no means mere

cupidity that inspired the negotiations at Vienna, nor even mere traditional legitimist theories (these, in fact, were more than once disregarded). It was something infinitely more important: Metternich's guiding principle, a European equilibrium. And he enjoyed this fortuitous advantage: that while putting the general notion into effect, he was able simultaneously to advance the particular interests of Austria, his special responsibility. After the destruction of the Napoleonic Empire, Europe needed a strong and powerful Austria. Thus Metternich was in the happy position of being able to pose as the benefactor of Europe while often advancing the merely selfish interests of the House of Habsburg— 'to talk like Plato and to act like Philip of Macedonia' (K. Th. von Heigel). With such a programme his success was a foregone conclusion.

Having, by the first treaty of Paris, retrieved most of her lost provinces from France, Austria induced the Congress to order Bavaria to return the Tyrol and Salzburg as well. She then established her right to preside over the Pan-German Confederation: in fact the Austrian Emperor resumed his historic role as the first German sovereign of Europe, a supremacy which he had traditionally enjoyed until the dissolution of the Holy Empire. Added to this, Austria was extending her dominion over the whole of Italy. The Duchy of Parma having been given to Marie-Louise, Tuscany and Modena to Austrian Archdukes, Austrian garrisons established in the towns of Ravenna, Bologna and Ferrare (now returned to the Pope), the House of Habsburg became all-powerful at the centre of the peninsula. Farther north, the provinces of Lombardy and Venetia were already directly under her sway. There only remained for her to ally herself with the Bourbons of Naples and so establish a complete 'Italian League' under her effective domination.[1]

This arrangement, of course, was not perfect, even considered from the purely selfish interest of Austria. It was comparatively easy for the Habsburgs to console themselves for the decisive loss of Flanders, territory which had always been topographically

1. See Karl Grossmann: *Metternichs Plan eines italien. Bundes* (Histor. Blätter, 1931).

detached, too far away. But, when it came to Alsace, retained, according to this arrangement, by France, and to the Rhenish territories sacrificed to Prussia and Bavaria—! For, in giving up her hereditary interests in these places, the House of Austria was also relinquishing her right to defend the German eastern frontiers. Stadion went so far as to say that Austria was 'now no longer a German power', and Stein ventured the prophecy that 'she would become progressively Italianate'. Metternich, subsequently, felt called upon to justify this supreme concession by a varied list of excuses: He had not been entirely free: the German high command had insisted that he get from Bavaria the chain of mountains north of Salzburg, and he claimed that to obtain this glacis (which they considered indispensable for the national defence) he had been obliged to cede the Palatinate to Bavaria. He had also wished to land Prussia into an awkward position by putting her directly up against France.

All the Chancellor's excuses strike us now as superfluous, for unless one were taking the strictly narrow view of the German nationalists, one must admit that his arrangements were ingenious. No human intelligence was then in a position to foresee the incalculable consequences of installing Prussia on the banks of the Rhine. But by these means, Metternich had obviated—for Austria—any danger of war with France for several generations. He was even taking a supplementary precaution (on behalf of the whole of Germany) in giving back Alsace and thus warding off any immediate desire for reprisals by the French.

In 1853, just before his death, Metternich, looking back to that Congress which is now inseparable from his name, attempted to assess its achievement with all the impartiality that a long-range perspective allows. 'It is perhaps enough to say', wrote the elderly statesman, 'it set the foundations of a peace that has lasted now for thirty-eight years and that its main decrees have not only withstood all intervening storms but were able even to survive the upheavals of 1848.'

For the Congress which 'danced but never took a step forward' had finally achieved, perhaps quite unintentionally, a work of such solidity that many an international gathering since might envy.

# VIII

# PORTRAIT BY LAWRENCE

*At seventeen—a little experience more or less—I was
what I am today, exactly as I am now: same qualities,
same faults, but my heart has come down to earth again.*
METTERNICH to Madame de Lieven, 1819

IN Lawrence's famous portrait of Metternich we see the Chancellor, chest rather prominent, shoulders slight, oblong head receding towards what is commonly known as a noble brow. He is wearing a skin-fitting uniform, tight-waisted, heavily embroidered. The Order of the Golden Fleece is round his neck, a broader ribbon in red and black worn in the manner of our own Order of the Garter, across his chest. Sitting comfortably in a large armchair, the whiteness of his tight Court-breeches and silk stockings show up in striking contrast to the red velvet. One aristocratic hand with its long, slender fingers lies nonchalantly on the arm of the chair. Blue eyes, blond curls, the nose suggestive of an eagle's beak. But most startling is the enigmatic expression: a piercing look, satanic smile, disdainful upper lip. Typical portrait of an aristocrat of the early nineteenth century, of a man accustomed to soar continuously above the swarming crowds whose destiny lay in his hands, typical portrait of a statesman of that time, a period now gone for ever, brilliant, frivolous—one which our contemporaries can hardly understand.[1]

1. This portrait, which until recently hung in Metternich's old study at the Ballhausplatz in Vienna, was painted by Lawrence at the beginning of 1819.

We find evidence scattered in a variety of places—in memoirs, diplomatic memoralia, in private correspondence—to confirm that 'speaking likeness' left by the masterly brush of a great English painter. And the stories all come from people who knew the great statesman well, who, themselves, spent long hours with him in discussion of complex political issues, problems of art or love.

Opinions all coincide. They show us a man of impressive appearance, outstandingly intelligent, a well-ordered mind, unsurpassable charm of manner. 'He had finely chiselled features', says La Garde, 'handsome, with a delightful smile, his face was distinguished and good-humoured . . . he moved with elegance, had great nobility of bearing . . . one saw at a glance that here was a man supremely.gifted, by nature, with remarkable capacities of attraction.' 'I was struck by the Prince's distinguished appearance', notes another sound observer, Baron Peter von Meyendorff (Russian diplomat) in his diary. 'I found fine feeling underneath the stiffness, it came through all merely superficial politeness and countered the somewhat ironic expression of a face which never departs from dignity and calm.'[1] And he continues: 'Metternich's curly blond hair, aquiline nose, well-drawn mouth, high forehead and unusually high eyebrows, combine in an agreeable ensemble although its harmony is perhaps a little strained by the fact that one pale blue eye is immobile. But when he laughs, this normally calm and inscrutable face becomes rather too animated, almost as it were, goes to pieces. An enormous mouth then opens in a circle, the eyebrows rise unevenly towards the forehead and seem to come apart—there is something satanic in this grimace—and as soon as he begins to joke, the

---

Lawrence had begun by 'taking up three hours of my morning', the Chancellor wrote, on January 12th. And then again on January 17th, 'The mouth has been changed; its sardonic expression has now disappeared: it seems to me to be a perfect portrait'. On February 13th: 'a two hours' sitting with Lawrence sketching in my right hand. As I make no claim whatever to having beautiful hands, I find it insufferable to waste so much time in getting them painted. . . .The portrait, however, is excellent in every way.'—Correspondence with Princess Lieven.

1. Peter von Meyendorff: *Politischer und privater Briefwechsel* (1923). (Notes from the diary, July 15th-17th, 1827.)

Prince's voice, normally rather a drawl, immediately loses its character, becoming harsh and squeaky.'[1]

'The Prince is of medium height and slim', says an English-woman who met him in 1836, 'refined and regular features . . . he normally has a gentle and kindly expression, but his pale blue eyes convey the impression of a profoundly thoughtful man. He is gracious and dignified, both innately and in manner; he imparts by his whole bearing an air of tranquillity, of philosophic calm.'[2]

And finally, the remarks of the inimical Sealsfeld, Austro-American publicist who went by that name and who for years devoted a savage energy to fighting the policies of the Austrian Cabinet. Even he was obliged to note that 'Metternich, although slightly effeminate, has great charm'. He specially points to 'beautiful blue eyes, an agreeable mouth with always a ready smile'.[3] 'Nobody knows how to make better use of natural gifts. He can entertain fifty people at once with ease and amiability without ever lapsing into the obvious . . . a skilful courtier to his finger-tips; however critical or thorny a situation, he never loses mastery and poise. He has a unique flair for situations and temperaments.'

And what was behind all this, behind that impressive deportment and studied gesture, behind those formal manners (affable yet haughty), the supercilious yet good-natured smile? Appearances are rarely wholly deceptive, one doesn't make a silk purse of a sow's ear. In this instance, too, the exterior did not belie the content: Metternich's character was essentially equable, healthy and balanced. 'His characteristics', said Countess Lulu Thurheim, 'have been well mixed—it would be hard to dissociate them. One would have to be a very knowing analyst to be able to dissect them.' 'Metternich needs "space", he "cannot bear to be cramped" ' (letter of November 20th, 1820). 'I am rather like the orange-flower,' he said, 'always in bloom.' 'I am a child of the light.'

---

1. Varnhagen von Ense also talks of 'Metternich's nasal and drawling voice'.
2. Mrs. Trollope: *Vienna and the Viennese.*
3. 'He seems always to be smiling', wrote the Englishman, J. Russel.

In 1817 he wrote to Prince Hardenberg: 'The last few years have nearly killed me. I really need, now, to think a little of myself. I must take some steps to insure my future. I have now arrived at one of those peaks where the future may easily be deduced from the present. . . . when nature warns and man is given his lead.'[1] And yet he was rarely ill; he only suffered 'slight indispositions, catarrh, perhaps, or rheumatism which would lay him low for some nine to thirteen days'. (Letters of October 2nd and 17th, 1823.)

For many years he suffered severely from his eyes, but managed to get cured.[2] Marshal Marmont, who observed him closely in 1835, noted 'a terrific appetite'; he saw Metternich devouring 'enormous slices of rye-bread'. In fact, the great statesman was to last till a ripe old age, with full use of his faculties, retaining his dignified bearing until the end. Only a slight deafness bore witness to declining physical powers in his last years. Young or old, exuberant gaiety was always a leading characteristic. During his first audience with the Pope, 'he made His Holiness laugh for at least a quarter of an hour'. (Letter of April 2nd, 1819.) He was fond of joking. He liked to mix the serious and burlesque and often played harmless practical jokes on his suite. If we are to believe Marmont, he 'derived considerable relaxation from mere nonsense'. 'He likes to create an air of mystery,' said Countess Thurheim, 'he is then in his element—but of course it is also one of his failings.' Prince Puckler-Muskau called him 'an amiable Mephisto'.

1. From Metternich's own letter under date of September 7th, 1817. (Berlin, Secret Archives.)

2. In Metternich's personal dossiers, among the secret archives of Vienna, we found an amusing correspondence between the Chancellor and a certain M. Julian, junior, a merchant of Bordeaux: 'I write as the proprietor of a pomade for the eyes (invented by my father, M. Julian, the elder, merchant of Bayonne and at one time *commissionnaire* at the Court of H.M. Charles IV of Spain). Concocted from a secret family recipe, now fifty years old, I hasten to send Your Highness four pots, the certain efficacy of which I can guarantee after at least thirty years of experience in treating more than three thousand persons—all treated freely, with the sole object of doing good.' Metternich replied that, being now cured of his indisposition, he would keep the pots for others similarly afflicted, 'and shall not forget to let them know that it is to your generosity they owe these benefits'. Then he concluded a little maliciously: 'I feel that I ought to add for your satisfaction [*sic*] that the formula I am actually using seems (after analysis) to be identical with yours. . .'

To understand Metternich properly, one must never forget that this cosmopolitan *grand seigneur*, this 'Frenchman' by education, was by race a German—although certainly of the best type. And it is to his German blood that we must ascribe most of his good qualities and not a few of his faults.

And one who is so often presented as just a man-about-town, *bon viveur*, a drawing-room darling, became as he grew older the most hard-working of Ministers, absorbed in his work, living for little else. It almost seems as if during the brilliant period of the Congress of Vienna, he had supped his fill of social gaiety.[1] 'I never seem to have a minute to myself', he wrote on March 23rd, 1819. After sitting for Lawrence, for instance, he spent the next three hours in the following manner: considering what proposals to make to the German Diet; running through the news from Paris; taking stock of impertinences by Weimar pamphleteers; making decisions about the Bavarian Concordat, or the flight of the Hospodar of Walachia. And no sooner did he begin to look into some tender letter from a woman friend than he found himself obliged to receive: 'the Papal Nuncio, Golovkine, de Caraman, seven or eight "political athletes".' 'The rascals kept me for three hours', he complained. 'If I had been their mother I should have spanked them!'

Then, suddenly, his daughter was at the point of death. During a Conference the news was brought that the doctors were all gathered at her bedside: 'When I tried to get up, the man who was then speaking insisted: "Allow me to say a few more words in relation to the toll-houses of the Rhine country".' 'I am obliged to leave you, Sir,' replied Metternich, 'should the Rhine itself return to its source', and he left his disconcerted questioner flabbergasted by such methods of conducting affairs of state. (Letter of May 2nd, 1820.) 'He labours without stopping', wrote Lord Stewart, the English Ambassador; 'his whole mind and all his time are given to his work—he scarcely ever leaves his office.'

We are far removed from the days when a Stackelberg could

1. 'Metternich is a completely changed man', wrote Lord Stewart to Castlereagh, in January 1820, 'he is no longer what he was during the Congress of Vienna; he seems to have given up all trivial occupations; neither gambling, nor women, nor entertaining seem to interest him any more.'

write: 'What can one think of a minister who is scarcely ever at his job?'[1] But was he really lazy, as often stated during those years of his youth? Wasn't he even then one of those men who find time for everything, for work and for pleasure, too?

In a conversation with Varnhagen bon Ense, Metternich described at some length his method of working: 'I find that I cannot concentrate on one single subject for two or three days on end, as some of my colleagues seem to do. A hundred and one matters rush into my mind and I forget the main points. If I am really preoccupied with any subject, it goes on stewing inside me. I work it out while I am ostensibly attending to other matters; results come to fruition in the midst of seeming distractions; my best ideas, my most witty retorts have come to me while eating, or perhaps, while chatting with a visitor or travelling. But when by this method the subject has fully matured in my own mind, I begin to write and I find that a logical development automatically ensues. Also when I have reached that point, no interruption can break the chain of my thought: I am able to pick up my work again, at any moment, exactly where I left it.' A method cut out to be *non grata* to surly bureaucrats, but that of a genuine intellectual![2]

'I do nothing that others could do equally well.' That was his consistent principle.... His subordinates often complained that it was difficult to get a quick decision from their chief in secondary matters: either questions of administration or finance. But for anything really important, he spared neither time nor energy; to the despair of officials of the Chancellery, he worked far into the night. A formidable number of urgent messages, memoralia, instructions or whatever bear his signature. And all documents of any importance were literally studded with marginal notes which grew noticeably longer as the years went by. Often, he himself translated messages sent in a foreign language, for instance, those

1. Stackelberg to Roumianzoff, November 15th, 1810.
2. 'I can never delegate my work because it is essentially a matter of the mind—of my own mind and nobody else could do it for me. How could I ask another to think for me, to write for me, to follow my particular train of thought, to pronounce tomorrow, the word I thought of today?' (Metternich to Madame de Lieven, March 3rd, 1819.)

from Lord Castlereagh. He was an incredibly quick worker: he wrote in two hours what it took his secretaries six hours to copy. He, himself, said (March 23rd, 1822): 'If I had to re-read all that I have written during the last ten years, it would certainly take me more than four years to do so!' 'And yet', says J. K. Mayr, Keeper of the Archives, 'the letters Metternich wrote with his own hand represent only an infinitesimal fraction of the work turned out by the Chancellery under his direction.' To conduct the affairs of a great Empire is certainly no sinecure!

But that was not all. He had an insatiable curiosity; all kinds of interests. Up till an advanced age, he continued those scientific studies which had been among the chief pleasures of his youth, and kept up with all the latest discoveries and inventions. During the war of 1813, he found time for interminable philosophic discussions with Gentz and Humboldt. In 1832, he actually took part in the debates of a scientific Congress, in the departments of botany, mineralogy and anatomy. He kept up a lively correspondence with Liebig, the famous chemist. He was able to repeat almost word for word, for the benefit of Marshal Marmont, a long conference given by the physicist Baumgartner concerning some new theory of acoustics. 'One might almost have thought him a professional.' (Memoirs by Dr Jäger.)

He had actually a scientific cast of mind, somewhat pedantic, typically German. Many of his love-letters read like philosophic theses; he shows a marked interest in processes of analysis, in differentiation or generalisation. 'Prince Metternich', said G. von Usedom, 'had a more scholarly cast of mind than any other statesman of his time.'[1]

His reading, also, was wide; he assiduously followed the world's Press and that of his own country—not disdaining the fiction. And in his own home, we find the same preoccupation

1. See also appreciation by Marshal Marmont: 'M. de Metternich is a man of learning and wide culture. . . without claiming to be exactly a scholar, there is probably no other nobleman of our time—occupied as he is both with state and social duties—who has studied so widely and is as conversant with recent discoveries and the general march of science and the arts—at least as to results and application.' (Duke of Ragusa, *Mémoires*. Vol. VI.)

with literature, 'substantial daily bread' (Srbik). 'The Chancellor reads Voltaire aloud to his wife; Montaigne, Pascal, Goethe, Jean-Paul, are all familar authors.' Those who met him in 1825, wrote Capefigue, were surprised to discover considerable literary ability. 'M. de Metternich knew all our good authors and displayed remarkable critical acumen when it came to contemporaries. One found it hard to believe that a man who had spent his life dealing with international issues of such magnitude could still be interested in the comparative futilities of literature.' [*sic*!]

Ten years later, for the benefit of an English visitor, Mrs Trollope, he embarked on a long dissertation about poetry and methods of composition in general, showing unusual perception and sensibility. 'He recited by heart, for Grillparzer, with all the right nuances, the *Ode to the Sea*, from the *Epilogue* of *Childe Harold*, some hundred verses, or more, and declared Lord Byron to be "the brightest star in all the firmament of poetry in our time".' He wept, as any good German should, on reading Heine's lyrics.[1] He even took an interest in certain political verse: 'It is lucky', he once said laughingly, 'that the police are not aware of the *liberal* nature of some of my reading, or they would certainly have denounced me to the Emperor!'[2]

Another essentially German trait—Metternich was extremely musical. 'Nothing moves me like music', he wrote.[3] 'After love, or, more exactly, combined with love, it is probably the best of all possible influences. Music both stirs and calms me; it revives the memory; it lifts me out of the narrow circle of daily experience; the heart expands, its urges become timeless; all comes

1. Always perspicacious, the great German Jew returned the compliment: 'I feel a certain affection for Metternich,' he wrote in *Reisebilder*; 'I don't take his political theories too seriously and I am certain that a man who knows the heady wines of Johannisberg, a man who can be so liberal, cannot at the bottom of his heart approve all this slavery and obscurantism.'

2. But there was one literary style he had always disliked: the novel. Historical fiction exasperated him by its inaccuracy and romantic fiction bored him. 'When the heroes of fiction are good lovers, they are no better than I am; when they are bad, they are merely my inferiors—no more, no less!' In this, he shared the taste of his master, the Emperor Francis, who, on his side, had never read a single novel, having given up his sole attempt by the end of the eighth page. Metternich went as far as page 12! (Reminiscences of Princess Pauline von Metternich.)

3. To Princess Lieven, December 18th, 1818.

to life: the joys and sorrows of the past—those which I desire and those for which I wait.' A reasonably good performer, he was mad about playing the violin. As a young delegate to the Congress he took part in a concert in an unexpected capacity: 'I conducted the orchestra, symphonies and concerti, and played in a *quatuor* so successfully that people still remember the occasion today . . . the public paid a small fee to come in.'

(Who would have thought to see a Metternich performing for money! History treats us to many such surprises.) In later years, he was satisfied to play at the Emperor Francis' musical receptions, frequently to attend the opera, and to listen to the great virtuosi of the age, to Paganini, Thalberg and Liszt, in his own house. The tragic genius of a Beethoven was not to his liking: he was infatuated with the Italians, with *bel canto*, with la Catalani.[1] At the age of eighty-six, he wrote to Rossini: 'Dear *Maestro*—I must call you that because the title fits you to such a point that no human agency—not even you yourself—could ever deprive you of it. The world needs music.' His interest in architecture was no less acute, and in painting and all the plastic and graphic arts.

When a young ambassador at Berlin, he learnt to engrave on brass. At Vienna, he would have liked to become a great patron of the arts, had his means permitted. 'Our people must know how to get the best from our own artists', he declared, in 1812; 'we must not be inferior, in any field, to other countries.' He was outraged by the lack of talent of the Viennese architects and of the aesthetic indifference of the aristocracy whose feeling for significant form was confined to '*ballerinas* and race-horses'.[2] His study was full of *objets d'art*, of pictures, busts in marble, bronzes (among others, the works of Thorwaldsen and Canova[3]). Even

1. 'What a happy experience Italian opera has been for me, and how glad I am to have got it established here! You can well understand, for a music-lover like myself, what a triumph that has been. Such moments are the rays of sunshine coming through my prison wall; that exactly describes my feelings.' (Letter, April 8th, 1822.)
2. Reminiscences of Dr. Jäger.
3. 'I have just received a group in marble by Canova, and have installed it in the pavilion. . . . The marble, under his hand, has become Love and Beauty personified. The group represents Cupid kissing Psyche for the first time. And the two

in his bedroom, one saw a large table on which lay a carton 'full of drawings and etchings', all pell-mell, mixed in with a lot of maps. [1] It was rather like being in Goethe's home, for Metternich had this in common with that great man, a taste for collecting *per se:* astrolabes, all kinds of instruments, manuscripts, 'any old rubbish', as he himself admitted, and this was confirmed by Marshal Marmont. [2]

But we mustn't exaggerate: Metternich, who liked to dip into every pie, was a mere dilettante. In spite of his literary and artistic preoccupations, he remained the aristocratic amateur with wide interests. 'His knowledge, in general, is superficial', said his enemy, Sealsfield, for once not without reason. 'He is an indifferent jurisconsult; a dunce in economics.' And in fact he managed his own fortune in a desultory and absent-minded manner. 'I'm all over the place and I'm nowhere', he wrote on April 18th, 1820. 'I own a lot of property that I have never visited: travellers often describe some estate of mine that I have never seen as "a little paradise".'

In these circumstances one can scarcely be surprised that a man with naturally extravagant tastes, incapable of meanness, should suffer from the traditional aristocratic malady of being short of cash. His position obliged him to keep open house, to cut a figure in society, to receive some dozens of people every day and, on occasion, to offer lavish entertainments for which he engaged not only well-known actors but hundreds of 'supers'.

We have come a long way since the days when this young scion of a ruined noble family first came to Vienna to revive his fortunes. The Metternichs' properties on the left bank of the Rhine were never given back. But after a brilliant career, having climbed to the top of the tree, the Chancellor—in the Empire's service—obtained rich compensation. He enjoyed a regular salary of 98,000 florins a year—to which was added a supple-

children are managing very creditably: they might have had a long life experience. . .! If these charming creatures weighed a little less, I should have had them mounted on wheels. But anyhow, I am pleased to know that—in spite of his wings —Cupid will now be obliged to stay with me.' (Letter, February 10, 1822.)

1. Letter, February 7th, 1820.
2. One can still see at the Schloss Koenigswart Museum some of the collections which are, indeed, totally devoid of interest.

mentary allowance for expenses in the case of a Congress or travel amounting often to as much as 4,000 florins a month. [1] He received rich gifts of lands: not only the family seat, Koenigswart Castle, in Bohemia, but later also the celebrated Abbey of Johannisberg with its famous Rhenish wines which Baron Stein had coveted before him. [2]

Like Goethe, he had a passion for building and generally improving his properties. At Koenigswart, he laid out a superb park with costly roads designed to link the estate with Marienbad. He added a variety of farm buildings, coach-houses and stables, he had a pond dried out and converted into a meadow, he built public baths to exploit the local mineral and curative waters. [3]

The Johannisberg estate was in a miserable condition when he took it over. He rebuilt the famous wine-cellars, redecorated an enormous hall and installed ventilation ('a new invention, and I flatter myself quite original'). In 1819 he bought a country house at Baden, near Vienna. In 1826 he acquired another great monastic domain, Plass (also in Bohemia), where important iron foundries had been installed. This last was 'a big speculation'. 'I am mad', he wrote, 'mad to have spent nearly four million francs for something I have never seen. It's like marrying by proxy. They say my wife is beautiful, but one feels one ought at least to know her.' All that acquisition and reconstruction required money—a great deal of money—and Metternich did not always know where to turn to get it. At first, the Emperor Francis granted him mortgages or even at times allowed him to dip into the treasury against his simple note of hand. Later, presents from the Tsar and the King of Naples saved the situation. The latter endowed him with the Duchy of Portella, carrying an

1. J. K. Mayr: *Geschichte der Oster.     Staatskanzlei im Zeitalter des Fürsten Metternich.* (Vienna, 1935.)

2. It seems that the Emperor Francis, exasperated by innumerable demands from high functionaries all of whom aspired to the lands of the dispossessed abbey, one day shouted: 'I'll give it to the first comer.' At that moment, Prince Metternich was announced—and without hesitation the monarch handed him that princely gift at the same time explaining what he had just said. This story, accepted by the family, has been handed down to us by Princess Sophie Oettingen, the Chancellor's grand-daughter.

3. The Koenigswart waters still attract a number of visitors to the *cure*, today.

annual income of 60,000 florins. [1] Presents from the two Tsars, Alexander and Nicholas, are harder to estimate. Some people put them at an annual figure of 50,000 or even 75,000 ducats. [2] As a last resource, he was helped by certain great bankers (such as Eskeles) and principally by the house of Rothschild whose Viennese branch by no means restricted their benefactions to mere 'Christmas presents' to the Metternich children and grand-children, but for years established a much more solid claim to the Prince's gratitude. [3] All rather a muddle, but it has scarcely im-proved the Chancellor's reputation: his enemies were to remem-ber this when the time for a settlement came, and accused him—without ever producing absolute proof—of venality and mal-versation. [4]

But so much negligence, excessive disregard of normal caution, or lack of any proper concentration, must be admitted as weak-ness. Always the 'china doll', Metternich lacked moral stamina, energy to make decisions, the dynamic courage required to get things started, in short, lacked enterprise. The pallid aristocrat (that 'pasty-face', said Talleyrand) was fundamentally—in spite of his robust appetites—a lymphatic. He seemed devoid of emotion, was always calm; he neither loved nor hated. He couldn't stand up to obstacles, always tried to go round them. He could never reply frankly to an indiscreet question. The slightest thing seemed to hold him up; 'he was often alarmed by the merest futilities', says Marmont. Flattery and 'tricks' were the foundation of his arsenal. Admitted, he was past-master in the

1. The Viennese enjoyed a good laugh; 'Duc de *Bordella*', they called him, and said he was well named.

2. It seems that this sum had been paid directly by the Russian Cabinet in recog-nition of certain confidential reports that Metternich sent them (with the permis-sion of his sovereign). Note also, a letter sent by the Tsar to his sister Catherine who was then at Karlsbad and who, as he put it, was also 'working for the common cause'. 'I am sorry that you have not yet told me anything about Metternich or how much it would cost to ensure his services absolutely. I have all the money we need, so don't try to economise. I return the 1,700 ducas and authorise you to proceed along these lines (always the most reliable) whenever it might be necessary.' (N. A. Elisseeff: *La Grande Duchesse Catherina Pavlovna en Bohême*, in 1813, Prague 1937.)

3. 'He owes half a million to Rothschild', says Baron Meyendorff. See also Corti: *The House of Rothschild*.

4. His accusers specially insisted that he had shared with Nesselrode a sum of two million francs paid by Louis XVIII in recognition of their services at the moment of the restoration of the Bourbons.

former, his flattery was exquisitely subtle, witty, full of charm, discreet and delicate. 'He is one of those men who know how to stroke the lion's mane' (Talleyrand: *Memoires*). And if in spite of all this, the adversary still held out, Metternich could always resort to cunning, another weak man's weapon. Trickiness, duplicity, a taste for splitting hairs were certainly among the least ingratiating of his characteristics. 'Lying with him has become second nature', said Meyendorff; 'it helps him to cover up his indiscretions, to mitigate the worst errors of his tortuous political system.' Baron Stein's conclusions were much the same: 'Metternich likes complications; they keep him busy, also he lacks the strength of character, is too petty, to work things out in the simple straightforward manner of the truly great. He really creates all these complications by his laziness and lies.'

A questionable method which by no means always achieved its end. There were times, of course, when he was quite unable to evade a direct question, was obliged to give a categorical reply. 'With a modicum of judgment and considerable patience', said M. de Sainte-Aulaire, 'one can dig out the truth from all this enigmatic verbiage.' 'Nobody can trust him', writes Lord Liverpool, 'he thinks politics in terms of *finesse* and tricks, and so doing has created more trouble for himself and his government than more straightforward methods could ever have produced.' 'Richelieu often misled other men', said Talleyrand, 'but he never lied. Metternich never stops lying and misleads no one.' And that was also Napoleon's opinion about him: 'Metternich thinks he's a diplomat; he's nothing but a big liar.' Stendhal, alone, depicting him in the person of Count Mosca, paid tribute to 'those blue eyes, that urbanity with which M. de Metternich would inveigle God Himself'.[1]

But if he lacked some of that volcanic drive which seems to

1. An interesting point for those concerned with the comparative psychology of nations: In France, men consider lying and a general absence of sincerity as essentially a German characteristic. But that, of course, is not the opinion of the Germans. One is told by them that men of the Teutonic race take pride in being brutally straightforward: such frankness, they add, tending not infrequently to rudeness. 'The German language', says Herder, 'is only suitable for expressing the truth.' Metternich, who always preferred a tacking course, who like Talleyrand 'used language chiefly to disguise his thought', was in this not consistent with his national traditions.

distinguish genuinely creative minds, the real leaders of men, at least he was also exempt from their pride and brutal arrogance: at the opposite pole from a Napoleon's abrupt and peremptory ways. All who ever met him agree in recognising 'his affability; that he made no distinction in his courtesy between the great and humbler men; his amazing good temper, to which must be added the complete absence of any spirit of revenge'.[1] (Marmont.) 'He is gentle and easy to get on with in daily social intercourse.' (Meyendorff.) 'His manner with his collaborators was always charming.' (Prokesch.) 'He shows everybody, without distinction of person, the same benevolence and affability.' (Baron Andlau.) 'He is completely free from aristocratic insolence.' (Dr Jäger.) 'He knows how to talk to children, to the young and to simple folk.' (Princess Pauline von Metternich.)

These ingratiating traits, however, were somewhat offset by one unpleasant and irritating failing. A German writer devoted a whole book to the vanity of Prince Metternich.[2] The word is not exactly well-chosen. Vanity is a characteristic of the parvenu, of the man who throws his weight about and makes a vulgar display of his fortune. But Metternich was always a *grand seigneur* even when slightly ridiculous. 'He is fatuous under a mask of pedantry, that is what shocks one most in him.' (Chateaubriand.) He displays a self-sufficiency (sometimes quite naïve) on all occasions. This agreeable egoist, 'the most logically egotistical man one could ever hope to meet' (Jäger), suffers from 'an inflated ego, considers himself unique.' Well-balanced but cold and unemotional, Metternich was certainly well pleased with himself. 'He believes that he is lucky; has faith in his stars.' (Gentz.) All that concerns him seems to him of capital importance —he considers himself infallible, that he is and always has been right. And one gets a notion of such pretensions when reading extracts from his own letters: 'I came to Frankfurt as a kind of Messiah to save sinners; I became something in the nature of a moral influence in Germany, perhaps in all Europe; my absence

1. Note also these words of Francis I reported by Countess Metternich to Mrs. Trollope: 'Metternich is a better man than I am, he forgives at once, without any effort. . . I, too, forgive in the long run, but it's not always easy.'
2. Karl Groos: *Fürst Metternich. Eine Studie zur Psychologie der Eitelkeit*, 1922.

will be felt when I go.' 'My presence in Italy has had an incalculable effect on political developments.' (June 10th, 1817-June 4th and September 11th, 1818.) He saw his own destiny as unique in world history. 'It is my special privilege that every eye is focused on my person, wherever I might happen to be at the moment.' 'There is nothing petty about me, I am always above and beyond the preoccupations of other politicians; my scope is infinitely wider than anything they can—or even wish to—see.' 'Why must I, among so many millions, always be obliged to think and act and write for others who seem incapable?' (July 27th and October 23rd, 1819.) 'For ten years I have never ceased to ask myself why it was my lot—among so many millions— always to be obliged to face Napoleon?' (To Countess Lieven, January 13th, 1819.) According to Marmont, he also entertained 'the fantastic notion that he was born possessed of military genius'. When trials and awkward situation closed in upon him, and drove sleep away, he always finally heard 'an inner voice. . . . I seem to become greater . . . and end by believing myself to be immense'. (August 20th, 1820.)

He is convinced that his associates share his admiration of his person: 'Floret would never get over it if I let him go out of my life.' 'My death would kill my daughter.' 'Nesselrode is very fond of me, and it dates a long way back.' 'The Emperor Francis regards me as his staunchest friend.' 'The Tsar Alexander often says to me: "Great Heavens, why are you not my Chancellor? Together we should conquer the world".' 'The King of Prussia really likes me very much.' And Kaunitz, his cousin by marriage 'adores me'. The painter Lawrence, 'cries like a child when he leaves me'.

In success or failure, in triumph or defeat, Metternich never changed. 'I know the whole world and the whole world knows me; every single word I ever said or wrote has been justified.' And Guizot reports that in 1848, while they were in exile together in London, 'he used to say to me with a half-smile—as if to excuse that egregious statement: "Error never had access to my mind".' In those words Metternich's fatuous self-satisfaction attains the sublime: the vainest of Frenchmen would have boggled at their enormity. Germans, it is generally admitted, have no such terror of the shafts of ridicule.

'The style's the man', and Metternich's style may be said to reflect pretty accurately that peculiar blend of intellectual acumen and moral weakness which distinguished the Chancellor. The subject almost calls for a special study: 'god of boundaries for the Cabinets of Europe'. (Sorel.) Hadn't Metternich indeed served as a model for generations of diplomatists? Isn't there still a trace of his 'style' among political leader-writers today? And whereas he disclaimed 'any talent as a writer', Metternich himself attached a certain importance to the manner in which he expressed his thoughts. He was indeed well pleased with it, as with all his other activities. 'As I see it, anything of real value must be expressed clearly. Intelligence should give light without smoke.' (October 29th, 1820.) 'Above all I seek clarity, the exact and the true expressed with objectivity and calm. Exaggeration is always disastrous: that's why I hate and refrain from superlatives—every superlative is an untruth, it distorts the sentence. I avoid also anything in the nature of a flowery style: intelligibility is the only kind of eloquence one can admit in politics. Obviously, in certain cases, precision itself is best served by some figure of speech; that is why I frequently resort to metaphor. And when, on re-reading, I find some passage obscure, I follow the expert advice of Baron Thugut: I do not attempt to replace what I have written with something better, I merely delete any word which is not indispensable to the sentence and I find that what remains expresses my thought exactly.'[1]

A good critic, however, would be able to pick quite a number of quarrels with Metternich's style. His use of German in memoralia addressed to the Emperor Francis is heavy and completely without charm. One senses a language to which he is unaccustomed. His French is certainly much better, more considered, more distinguished, more precise.[2] In his early messages, those

1. Varnhagen von Ense: *Denkwurdigkeiten*. Vol. VIII, pages 111-112.
2. As to his pronunciation of French, there are contradictory reports. 'His accent, essentially that of the Empire, had a special charm for French ears', remarks the

associated with his *débuts* in diplomacy, we find a lot of awkward phrasing, but once steeped in a Parisian atmosphere, his style improved, grew more subtle and more sure: Talleyrand's influence is felt, and that perhaps of Napoleon still more. And in later life, one might claim for Metternich as a writer rather more than amateur status. He knew how to dramatise, how to be both lively and impressive in his opening words. He was peculiarly happy in the use of antithesis. Nobody, of course, writes like that today: accustomed as we are to something more straightforward and more simple, we find Metternich's style too artificial, too pompous, often obscure. It strikes us as a thoroughly outmoded method of showing off; as an artist he lacked imagination. Even his contemporaries objected to such abuse of emphasis and metaphor. Treitschke, who disliked him at best, made a list: 'the volcano, the plague, cancer, the deluge, conflagration and the powder-magazine'. Others noted 'his involved phraseology' (Meyendorff), the platitudinous nature of his 'long ambiguous messages' (Nesselrode) with their too-frequent repetitions. 'The die is cast', 'the destiny of Europe is at stake', 'the tricky dealings of the English Cabinet', and a host of other clichés are to be found on every page of his correspondence.

As he grew older, this tendency to a flatulent, pompous and exasperating style became more marked: he seemed more pleased with himself, more egotistical, more fatuous than ever.

And yet what Metternich wrote was always interesting. He had a natural facility, a certain force of persuasion. He was always inclined to 'bring the light of analysis to bear on whatever he tackled; he had a very happy knack of getting to the core of any subject, a felicitous choice of words and a clarity which stamped all his thought with a remarkable precision'.[1] Capefigue: 'he has good and simple taste and displays nobility of style even in those diplomatic exchanges whose sense is so often concealed by professional jargon. Into that somewhat earth-bound medium indeed he manages to infuse a literary flavour which distinguishes every

Baroness du Montet. Was it by chance that *creole* intonation peculiar to Josephine? Meyendorff, on the other hand, claims that his pronunciation was bad. 'He always puts his accents in the wrong places.'

1. Mrs. Trollope: *Vienna and the Viennese*.

document from his Cabinet.' La Garde calls him 'one of the most delightful story-tellers of our time', and Meyendorff sums up the whole question when he says: 'few people know better how to develop a line of thought and present it in such a way as to carry conviction'. The Portugese succession, tussles with Bavaria, troubles in Syria, revolution in France, a new Cabinet in London or the death of a Tsar, Metternich always rose above the petty details of the occasion: each administrative detail became linked in his mind with the evolution of Europe, indeed with that of the whole human race. But he writes best in his more intimate letters to members of the family, to friends or mistresses. One really cannot agree with Treitschke according to whom the great statesman's description of a journey through Italy was 'worthy of any commercial traveller'. Metternich was certainly in ecstasy before the beauty of the South, as many a middle-class German before him. But as soon as he begins to speak of the people he met, of the monarchs who gave him audience, when he laughs good-naturedly at elderly Englishwomen or Italian cooking, he is amusing, witty and very human. One can read these original, caustic and subtle remarks without the slightest boredom.

Passion, as we have seen, never ceased to play a considerable part in the life of Metternich. For this self-satisfied, superegotistical man was by no means incapable of losing his head about a woman.[1] Sometimes he seems rather scornful of the fair sex: listening to him one might imagine no greater disaster existed than to be born a female. But if that indeed were so, a witty commentator pointed out, he at least devoted a considerable portion of his own life to consoling the sex for their original misfortune.

Metternich came out of his liaison with Madame de Sagan broken-hearted. He assured the world that his treacherous mistress had tried to kill herself the day after their final break. But since she had refused to accept his surely very moderate conditions:

1. The Tsar, Alexander, denied this. He said to Princess Bagration: 'Metternich never loved you, neither you nor the Sagan. . . . He is a cold-blooded creature. With that face of a priest, can't you see he never really loved anyone?' (Police report of October 3rd, 1814.) But these were the words of a jealous man.

'six months of fidelity'—that seems highly improbable. She had, in fact, quite a number of 'consolers' to hand. Metternich, on the other hand, was left high and dry. His sentimental life, as he himself said, continued on the pattern of his first liaison: he only looked for amorous adventure in the highest social circles. To disperse his energies in a multiplicity of affairs was not to his taste. 'I have never been unfaithful(!) . . . the woman I love is the only woman in the world for me.'[1]

As a distraction, Metternich began to pay court to Countess Juliette Zichy, that 'celestial beauty' of the Congress of Vienna who had so infatuated Frederick-William III, King of Prussia. But here he came up against one of those 'great souls' who are not open to seduction. With a subtle observation that did honour to his amateur talents, a secret informer of the Viennese Prefect of Police wrote, on October 14th, 1813: 'Juliette Zichy is too pious, too sincerely virtuous; Prince Metternich will have no success in this direction.' The man was right. However much Metternich might write: 'She loved me as only so ethereal a being can love: the world scarcely knew . . . we alone were in the secret . . .'[2] there was in fact little to conceal. 'She had come down to earth only for the spring-time . . . her later years were passed in a kind of religious ecstasy'. She died shortly after, in the prime of life, leaving to her executor a small sealed box. When he opened it, Metternich found the ashes of his letters burnt by her and a ring that she had broken. A touching and tearfully sentimental idyll in the manner of the period!

It was not until 1818 that Metternich found solid consolation in the person of Dorothea Lieven. Their romance became history. A preposterous legend has tried to present this couple in the guise of such immortal lovers as Anthony and Cleopatra, of a Romeo

1. 'My name has been associated with many women to whom I never gave a thought', he wrote. A certain number of illegitimate children have also been ascribed to him, among others, M. von Neumann, a Counsellor of the Chancellery. It has been said that he had two children by Madame de Sagan: a boy, subsequently ambassador at Hamburg, a girl who was married to a Polish nobleman. But all this gossip has no proof to show. On the other hand, Metternich never hesitated to recognise Clementine Bagration (mentioned in a former chapter) as his daughter. She was brought up at Vienna under his personal supervision, married General Count Blome, and died on May 29th, 1829.

2. Metternich to Princess Lieven, December 1st, 1818.

and Juliet. Nothing could be farther from the truth. Great passion cannot be divorced from those extremes of joy and suffering which it invariably entails. But the liaison between Metternich and the famous Russian Ambassadress to London showed neither the heights nor depths of a true and all-absorbing love. It was short and essentially worldly. The easy, flowery path: two people of equal rank and similar upbringing met, were attracted to each other, enjoyed their strictly evanescent transports: senses no less than pride, to say nothing of their several interests, were satisfied.

And yet, we repeat, their romance came down to history. Luck, and not improbably her own well-developed sense of publicity, favoured Princess Lieven. Of all the women loved by Metternich, she alone had posterity in mind: for her, this liaison with the famous statesman assumed the importance of an historic event. Thus, whereas we know nothing of what Metternich wrote to his other mistresses: to Caroline Murat, to the Duchesse d'Abrantes, to Madame de Bagration and Madame de Sagan, Princess Lieven preserved—to good effect—every letter addressed to her from the Ballhaussplatz of Vienna: these, that distinguished scholar M. J. Hanotaux published, with valuable notes, in 1896.[1]

The lady also re-copied in her characteristically energetic and decided handwriting a large number of letters which she had written to her lover and which were returned to her through the good offices of the Duke of Wellington after the break. 'To whom shall we leave our correspondence? Some worthy man we shall never know will stumble on this fortune', she wrote to Metternich on March 1st, 1822. And again: 'It seems to me that our correspondence ought to be of the greatest value to an historian of our times.' For a whole century, the last part of the Metternich-Lieven correspondence was not available: It has only recently been published in an English translation.[2] So all the details of a famous liaison which intrigued the diplomatic world of the nineteenth century are now for us an open book.

In 1818, when Metternich first met Dorothea Lieven, he was

1. J. Hanotaux: *Lettres du prince de Metternich à la princesse de Lieven.*
2. *The Private Letters of Princess Lieven to Prince Metternich,* 1820-1826, edited with a biographical foreword by Peter Quennell, assisted in translation by Dilys Powell (John Murray, London, 1938).

looking for a woman who could both love and understand him. The Sagan, and the Bagration, although socially impeccable and received in Court circles, were both somewhat light ladies; Laure Junot and Caroline Murat were nobodies who had been hoisted by fortune to vertiginous heights. He needed a woman of his own rank, of his own world, and one with whom he could converse on equal terms, a woman not likely to prefer some handsome nincompoop of an attaché.

Madame de Lieven exactly answered all these requirements. The haughty ambassadress, *née* Benckendorff—a family intimately associated with the Romanoffs since the end of the eighteenth century—had been married for many years to Count Lieven (later created Prince and even Serene Highness). He was the son of a lady who had been governess to the two Tsars Alexander and Nicholas. And the Countess, having spent her childhood at the foot of the throne, was received as by right into the highest international circles.

She was not exactly beautiful: an abundance of soft, silky hair and vivacious black eyes did not entirely make up for a sharply pointed nose, a neck too long and a chin cut off too abruptly, a frankly unpleasant mouth and 'that disastrously bony silhouette'. But 'she impressed one by her dignity' (it is Talleyrand speaking), 'by a rather haughty graciousness, by supreme good breeding'. A peculiar mixture of qualities, as she herself admitted, she was alternately 'energetic and lazy, gay and melancholy, courageous or a mere poltroon'. She was remarkably intelligent, a good linguist, excellent pianist, tactful, flexible, witty and perspicacious. She talked in a clear, incisive manner, had a happy knack of *repartie:* she knew how to draw others into conversation and never allowed their interest to flag; she seemed to deal with men as they might turn the pages of a book. [1] Another of her qualities, invaluable in the case of so verbose, so long-winded a chatterer as Metternich, she was a good listener.

She was caustic and could be malicious, but, like Metternich himself, was generous and indulgent toward human weakness.

1. A. Chuquet: *Episodes et Portraits;* see also the portrait by Lytton Strachey in *Miniatures.*

She adored the game of politics, not for the sake of any special principle; she had few convictions: what intrigued her essentially restless and warped nature was the game itself, the technique of diplomacy, the complex struggle of Cabinets; for her, all this was something in the nature of 'art for art's sake'. [1]

From a certain standpoint, she must have been insufferable: ambitious, arrogant, determined to cut a figure, domineering. She was a shameless snob: 'I enjoy the society of kings', she stated categorically. In one of her letters (December 9th, 1824) she condemns the eccentricity of Canning, who, at a reception at the Russian Embassy, buttonholed and remained for a whole hour with M. Labenski, a mere 'fourth' secretary, 'a little man to whom I have never addressed a word except to say good-morning'. [2] In short, taking into account both her virtues and her vices, she seems to have been exactly the woman that Metternich required.

The affair with Madame de Lieven started during a Congress at Aix-la-Chapelle. The great statesman himself, in a letter addressed to her under the date of November 28th, 1818, gives us a detailed account of all that led up to the explosion of their passion. True, it might well have been the preliminaries to a treaty between the powers; nothing was left out: no encounter was too brief, no conversation too trite. 'On October 29th', he concludes, 'I didn't see you. On the 30th, I discovered that the day before had been both cold and empty. I forget which day it was that you came to my house. [3] You also caught the fever, my dear, and at last were mine. Don't ask me all that I have felt since then....'

1. On October 20th, 1823, she wrote, 'I think that one wishes to live mainly out of curiosity, from a desire to know what is going to happen. I should not like to die, for instance, without knowing the results of the Congress of Vienna.'

2. The following story, told by an old Russian Chamberlain, shows something of the mentality of circles who managed—up to the end of the XIXth century—to preserve a type of snobbery that Princess Lieven considered smart. As a young diplomat, he got lost in the corridors, during a ball at the Court of Berlin. He landed up in the boudoir of the Empress Augusta (to whom the great French poet, Jules Laforgue, was reader). The sovereign looked him up and down in a menacing manner as, abashed, he announced his name and diplomatic standing. 'Sir', said the wife of William I, 'I often speak to ambassadors, *occasionally* to *chargés d'affaires*, but *never* to secretaries or attachés.' This was worthy of Madame de Lieven herself.

3. Metternich lived in a house belonging to a certain Demoiselle Brammertz; he paid a sum of 20,000 francs for the duration of his stay at Aix.

The lovers' dream was short: the Congress was coming to an end. Already, on November 18th, the Countess left Aix-la-Chapelle with her husband. At Brussels and Paris they again had brief encounters, after which they separated for three years. In 1821, the visit of George IV of England to Hanover supplied another occasion for their meeting—but for a week only.

The following year another Congress, this time at Verona, afforded a pretext: they met again, but from then on their ways were forced apart. To sum up, it was little more than a passing fancy: all the evidence goes to support that version. After that, any personal association was replaced by an animated correspondence. Into this they both put of their best, revealing their most intimate thoughts and feelings, exchanging endless opinions in relation to a subject which interested them at least as much as, if not more than, love—the political destinies of Europe.

Metternich's early letters overflowed with feeling. ('Such an association as ours only comes once in a lifetime.... At eighteen years of age, my heart was seeking what it found at forty.... How the man of ice melted in contact with you.... Am I still that cold and unapproachable fellow who so alarmed you?') But his letters soon grew cooler. Soon he was talking of 'a sacred love, the only one worth while', he recommended a union of souls, a communion of the spirit. ('What binds me more than anything to you is a kind of quiet confidence. I never question our complete understanding.') He never ceases to be surprised that men should think so much of 'women' but so little of any one woman. 'If you were a man', he wrote, 'you would have reached great heights. With such a head and heart as yours, nothing could have stopped you.'

As time went on, the correspondence became increasingly intellectual and literary; the love affair turned into a diplomatic alliance: statesmen were severely criticized, others approved; gossip current in the houses of the great was passed to and fro. Metternich tells the story of his life, pours out his woes, describes his travels or launches into dissertations on such subjects as presentiment or 'the dual principle in human nature'. Surprisingly enough, he also offered much good advice as to the lady's conjugal relations. In this respect, the lover wrote: 'I want you to be kind, gentle, a good wife in every way to your husband.... I never caused any couple to fall out. I, myself, am law-abiding and I like others to be the same.' And when Madame de Lieven, who appears to have put his counsel to good effect with some promptitude, announced the imminent birth of a child, he congratulated her warmly: 'You think I ought to be displeased to learn of your condition, or rather the cause of it', he wrote. 'My dear, what can I say? Didn't I myself urge you to be a good wife? I have no right even to wish that your husband should refrain from his normal conjugal rights.... You will have, I am sure, a beautiful child.... you will love your child, and I also shall love it because it is yours.'

Madame de Lieven's letters, on the other hand, kept their passionate note throughout the correspondence.

For however much she might talk about politics, in spite of an extreme reserve, of the severest editing (by her) as she copied her letters, what remains reveals sincere feeling, sometimes a genuine hurt. We note many terms of affection, some compliment inspired by obvious admiration, a point of *coquetterie*, perhaps, then a cry of impatience of even simple jealousy. 'Why are you not in England?' she wrote once when at the seaside there.... 'Why are you not here, at Brighton, staying at the same inn, or perhaps next door? Yes, why are you not my neighbour? Everything would then be so simple! But now I am getting foolish.' And one day, walking in the English countryside, at Woburn, she exclaims: 'I have never seen two trees growing together without regretting that I was not one of them; wouldn't you have liked to be the other?' But she added quickly, as if to offset the ironical reply she knew she would get from him: 'Can you imagine us two static, two pieces of wood?' Sometimes she even tried to rouse his jealousy: 'If you hear anything about my supposed intimacy with Castlereagh, do not conclude the worst.' Again, with real emotion she recalls some happy memory: a drive, for instance, 'when I made room for Nesselrode between us'; sometimes she seems lost in admiration of the Chancellor's letters which strike us today as not a little pompous and pedantic. 'Your letters are delightful', she declares. 'You seem to have an inexhaustible fund of gaiety. You are the most good-humoured man I ever met—and I love to laugh.'

One night, she saw Metternich in a dream: he had taken her on his knee to whisper into her ear and she felt the beating of his heart; it was so loud it woke her. 'My heart was responding to yours.' She sent him a gold ring which was to be the 'seal of their union'. She asked him about the shape of his ears, at the end of one of her letters. She begged him to be tender, very tender. She wrote: 'My dear, how sweet it is to love you! It is a wonderful experience!' 'Love me, my sweet Clement, love me with all your heart; day and night—and always.' And when she was told to expect him in person soon: 'I began to tremble all over. All the happiness, all the pain that your visit here will cause me, burst upon me at one blast.... My dear, to see you for so short a time, to see and lose you again, to revel but to tremble every instant of every day!'

But their meetings grew more rare; Metternich was drawing back; his replies were long delayed, he allowed occasions for a meeting to slip by. Was absence in itself the reason, or was it the state of Europe? 'As long as Austria and Saint Petersburg pursued the same policy', wrote J. Hanotaux, 'no cloud came between the Ambassadress and the Chancellor. But would their love survive the shock of the Eastern question?' In 1823 Madame de Lieven set out for Italy firmly determined to meet her beloved there. But although she spent months at Milan, at Florence and at Rome, Metternich never turned up and often left her for a long time without any news. Her disillusion was complete. 'And so you are not coming to Italy. Then why did you ask me to come here? There was no mistaking what you said in your letter. I left all my comforts behind, my agreeable daily round, all my interests, to live in a foreign climate which assuredly warms the body but leaves the mind quite blank.' (October 20th, 1823.) But she will not confess herself beaten: she wheedles, becomes more tender: 'We could both be so happy in Rome. You are already mad about it; I am quite ready to go mad; together we should certainly make a happy and harmonious couple.' But the post from Vienna arrived without any word from the lover. Madame de Lieven went completely to pieces. 'Oh, how unkind you are, how hateful! I am really furious. I shall be hostile in my dealings with Austria, today . . . it is very bad policy not to write to me.'

Even after her return from London, to take up again, as she herself described it, her 'official duties', Madame de Lieven refused to give up hope and was on the watch for any opportunity of meeting (in May 1821, in March and June, 1825). 'The months go by', she wrote, 'and many more will go the same way before we find a chance of meeting. It is a sad thought, but there is some consolation in being faced with the inevitable. On the whole, it seems to me that hope more often kills than consoles us. . . .'

On November 22nd, 1826, Princess Lieven sent out her final SOS . . . 'you ought to write to me more often. Let's start again from the beginning. We should be hard put to it to find in the whole world anyone of our particular mettle; our hearts are well-matched, our minds also; and our letters are delightful. . . . I repeat: you will find no one better than me. If you ever meet your like, don't fail to let me know. Good-bye.' It was all in vain: their liaison had reached its natural end.

In their manner, the amours of the Chancellor pursued an even course. Taking stock, we find that he had affairs with three Frenchwomen (Madame de Caumont, Caroline Murat, Laure Junot) and three Russians (the Princesses Bagration, de Sagan, and Lieven). He also contracted three legal marriages, all three with women of the Austrian aristocracy. He was dazzled by the charms and finesse of the French, by the languor and fantasy of the Russians—but when it came to conjugal virtues, he sought them in his own country: it was there he found that gentle peace and devotion which were to adorn his hearth.

During the first part of his life, he had in Eléonore von Kaunitz a devoted wife and loyal friend. Nesselrode found her 'insipid'. Metternich himself could see 'no charm' in her. But he appreciated her 'admirable intelligence' and did not disdain to consult her in political matters. Husband and wife had long gone their separate ways. 'When I was appointed to Dresden', he wrote, 'we decided that we would never part but agreed in certain matters to leave each other absolutely free.'[1] A supremely well-bred woman, Eléonore seems to have accepted her husband's infidelities with amused resignation. She went so far as to say she 'could not imagine any woman remaining impervious to her Clement's charms'. Did she return him as good as he gave, which Count Nesselrode rather crudely asserted . . .?[2] Did she, for instance, when at Berlin in 1802, carry on an affair with the handsome Marquis de Moustiers, Secretary at the French Embassy, as Strobl von Ravensberg reports?[3]

We are faced with a number of suppositions which seem to argue in favour of the Princess. Eléonore always behaved as a great lady: Napoleon, who was no novice in such matters, had a very high opinion of her;[4] during the Congress of Vienna, we have seen her acting hostess in the grand manner. Besides, she was an excellent mother and the upbringing of seven children required her constant care and attention. She enjoyed very poor health: she suffered from lung trouble for which there was no cure and the disease, alas, was hereditary. Her children died off one after the other in the prime of life, causing their father infinite distress. For this busy man, whose interests were so wide, and often frivolous, was also a model father. The world might think he had no heart under that official frock-coat, but in fact he has described the joys and sorrows of paternity in a deeply moving manner. 'My real vocation lies in the nursery', he once said. When grown up, his sons and daughters became his friends and *confidantes*. And no words can express his despair as the inexorable consumption carried them off one by one, those beloved children, their father's dearest earthly tie.

1. Quoted by Strobl von Ravensberg with no indication as to date.
2. Count Nesselrode to his father April 25th, 1806. (*Archives de Comte Nesselrode*. Vol. III, page 131.)
3. This historian-biographer refers his readers to page 180 of the Baroness de Montet's *Souvenirs*. We have tried to confirm this, but the name of Madame de Metternich does not appear there at all.
4. 'The woman about whom there is no gossip must be a model of her sex. Napoleon often praised your mother in some such terms as these, and he was right.' (Metternich to his son, Victor, February 13th, 1829).

On May 6th, 1820, he lost his daughter Clementine who has also been immortalised by Lawrence. And a few months later her elder sister, Marie Esterhazy died: she had been described as 'one of the queens of love and beauty at the Congress of Vienna', a woman as warm-hearted as she was chaste. 'My loss is beyond measure', Metternich wrote: 'how I loved that child! For many years she has been my closest friend, there was no need for me to tell her what I was thinking, she always guessed it. She knew better than I know myself, she never uttered a word which might not have been spoken by me.... I never ceased to bless and thank her for being mine.' (July 25th, 1820.)

After each successive catastrophe Metternich seemed to plunge more deeply into his work. Following the death of Clementine he wrote: 'The thirty delegates who gathered daily round the green baize of the conference table had little notion of what was going on inside me as I spoke (sometimes for three or four hours) or dictated some hundreds of pages.' And the day after the death of Marie: 'In the throes of my great sorrow all the troubles of the world seem to be weighing me down. On the very day my daughter died, I was obliged to attend six hours at the council chamber and eight at my own department. But I shall continue to do my duty; from now on, indeed, duty will supersede the joy of living for me.'

As time went on, bereavements seemed to affect him less. In 1819, speaking of his son Victor, a young man of great promise, about to enter the diplomatic service, he wrote to Madame de Lieven: 'I have only one son, but had I sixty-five—like the Shah of Persia—I should not love him less. The idea of losing him, or of seeing him become a permanent invalid, would kill me.' But the merciless disease pursued its course and Metternich became resigned. In 1829, poor Victor's flame flickered out and we find Metternich noting quite calmly: 'The moment of death was for him, as for us all, a release.... His protracted suffering and his death surely entitle him to a martyr's crown.'

The death of his wife, Princess Eléonore, in 1825, does not seem to have disturbed the Chancellor unduly. After losing two daughters, Princess Metternich had made her home in Paris with

M

her three remaining children. 'I shall be all alone', Metternich then remarked, 'but in my solitude I shall console myself with the thought that my family will be together and will not be subject to this baneful Viennese climate.... We are making still one more sacrifice in the interest of duty and common sense.' From that moment, Metternich no longer had a home—a relation, Countess von Wrbna-Kagenegg, came to keep house for him as best she could. When serious misgivings began to be felt about the Princess' health, Metternich showed no particular eagerness to join his wife. He never stirred from Vienna in spite of repeated assertions that her condition 'grieved him more than anything else on earth'. 'I shall only move', he said, 'when I begin to see more clearly....' Political considerations were in fact over-weighing those of affection. 'Were I obliged to go to Paris, it might produce a bad effect on Canning: he would certainly find some pretext for my journey apart from its real and sad—and only—motive. But what he thinks is really a matter of indifference to me, and of course it might not even have any repercussions.'

But the journey became inevitable. Metternich went to Paris and wrote from his wife's bed-side: 'In the meanwhile the French Press is busy with my arrival; here, they are making their own comments. At London, even more importance is attached to my sudden appearance in the rival capital.' And when at last 'the best of mothers had left her children', and 'never a complaint throughout her illness', Metternich, still doing lip-service to 'that beautiful soul who has gone to Heaven, returning to the bosom of her God with a gentle and quiet confidence in His fatherly goodness', nevertheless concludes a letter of so touching and intimate a nature as follows: 'My presence here cannot fail to have good results....' Sad epilogue to a union which had lasted thirty years and 'never for one instant been clouded'.[1]

Two years later, Metternich remarried, and—surprising as it was unexpected—he made a love-match. 'I am not blind', he wrote during the period of his *fiancailles*, 'I am no longer actuated

1. Eléonore died on March 19th, 1825. 'Her heart and conscience were as pure at the moment when she breathed her last as they had been for every hour of a life-time devoted to duty.'

170

by the fatal ascendency of passion—my heart is warm and calm, serene and austere. . . . I have a terrible hunger for repose—that is my heart's real secret.' And yet it was in a very storm of love that he sought that 'repose'. A St Martin's summer for this elderly statesman: he had fallen desperately in love with a girl some thirty years his junior.

It would be hard to imagine a creature more charming than that young Viennese with a touch of Italian blood, 'lovely as an angel, and angelic in every way': a delightful silhouette, pure oval face, a tiny mouth, blonde curls, the soft look of a melancholy doe, an active mind, artistic tastes, in fact a figure that might have been drawn by Lamartine.

To any unprejudiced observer, Marie-Antoinette von Leykam might well seem to have had quite an honourable background: grandfather an official of the Foreign Office, her father in charge of some diplomatic mission, a mother with artistic tastes, of Italian origin. But that was not the opinion of the leaders of Viennese society. Marie-Antoinette was not the *crème de la crème;* she was neither a princess nor a countess, but a mere baroness, and that of very recent creation. What a windfall for the gossips! Hadn't some Leykam ancestors once worked for Prince Thurn-and-Taxis' Imperial Posts? From that to turning them into coachmen was but a step. And then the mother, *née* Pedrella, who was so fond of music and only seemed to entertain the male sex, hadn't she been a *prima donna* at the Naples Opera—or perhaps even worse? How could the highest Minister of State, the President of the Congress of Vienna, marry into such a family?

Metternich snapped his fingers at all this. 'When it comes to important decisions, I consult no one; I put myself right with my conscience and that's enough.' Wasn't he also, perhaps, listening to the voice of passion?

He arranged for the Emperor to confer on his lovely fiancée the title of Countess Beilstein, the name being taken from one of his hereditary estates. He married on November 5th, 1827, almost secretly; on that same day the news of the battle of Navarin reached Vienna. The marriage was celebrated at Hetzendorff, a small village on the outskirts, in the presence of a few persons only: Metternich's mother, his sister (now married to a Duke of Württemberg), his brother Joseph and his brother-in-law Kaunitz—the last two signed the register. The church doors were kept closed, the curious remained outside.

With Marie-Antoinette, sunshine and youthful gaiety came to the Chancellor's Palace. The young Princess won all hearts; she entertained artists and scholars, and even diplomatists. There was conversation and music. Metternich at last had found what he had always looked for: 'a human being who would belong to him entirely and in connection with whom he need suffer no pangs of jealousy'.[1]

But his happiness was short-lived. Fourteen months later Marie-Antoinette died in child-birth, after being delivered of a boy, 'fat and very ugly, healthy and well set-up'. He was called Richard and was later to shine as Austria's Ambassador at the Court of Napoleon III by the side of his world-famous wife, Princess Pauline. 'The most horrible calamity has fallen upon me', notes the appalled husband. 'What God gave, He has the right to take away—man can only bow his head and not question. I believe . . . and I worship His immutable decrees.'

'Yes, my friend,' he wrote to Princess Lieven, 'I have suffered the most terrible blow that fate could possibly deal me. I have lost more than half my life. I have lost my home, my domestic happiness, all that part of my life which really belonged to me, the part that helped me to bear the rest—which is not mine; everything for me has crumbled. . . .' 'My life is finished', he wrote elsewhere, 'and if I am not yet physically reckoned among the dead, in the spirit I am now enrolled in that great army.' But the Prince's amazing vitality rose once more triumphant over fate.

His hair was growing white and his sight beginning to decline —but he still had the same proud bearing, his slim figure and sardonic smile were exactly as they had been handed down to posterity by Lawrence. Some years later the Comte de Falloux, who had expected to find Metternich looking like the great Frederick, 'with his powdered wig, pretty-pretty and over-

1. Letter of February 25th, 1829, published by M. Jean Hanotaux.

dressed', was surprised to find one of the most handsome and distinguished men of his time, 'who has a regard for fashion only in so far as it is compatible with dignity', and who talks in a manner 'both impressive and up to date'.[1]

Although approaching the sixties, with his attractive personality and important position he was still a matrimonial prize, and his friends were determined to get him married for the third time. But now it was to be a super-social alliance, a marriage which would put the final stamp on Metternich's already exalted position in Viennese society. And so it was in the arms of the daughter of a Hungarian magnate, of that spirited brunette, the haughty and passionate Mélanie von Zichy-Ferraris (third Princess Metternich), that the great statesman pursued his quiet journey to the tomb.

1. Falloux: *Mémoires d'un Royaliste.*

# IX

# THE SYSTEM

*One must have known life's cruelties to see that, in a*
*world continually shaken by the forces of destruction,*
*to preserve is to create.*

GEORGES DUHAMEL

IVORCED from biased interpretations (spiteful or more often ignorant), Metternich's 'system' strikes this biographer as an essentially rational political concept, and one which finds its roots in eighteenth-century philosophies.

It is usual to identify the system with the Holy Alliance. In 1827, Princess Lieven, in a jealous rage at the marriage of her former lover with the young Baroness von Leykam, launched the following *bon mot* on the salons of Paris and London: 'The Knight of the *Sainte-Alliance* is ending his days with a *mésalliance.*'

Nothing, however, could be more erroneous than to associate Metternich, as instigator, implementer, 'knight' or 'provost marshal' of that semi-mystical association for which he never felt the slightest sympathy. And if any doubt as to this remained, it is easily disposed of in the light of extensive documentation published during the last few years.

The theory of a Holy Alliance, designed to safeguard the liberty of the peoples of Europe on a basis of Christian charity (the chief protagonist of which had been the Abbé Saint-Pierre), owes its emergence into practical politics solely to the generous initiative of Tsar Alexander.[1] He presented the idea, during his visit to Paris in the autumn of 1815, to Frederick-William and to

1. See W. Schwartz: *Die Heilige-Allianz*; E. Muehlenbeck: *Etudes sur les origines de la Sainte-Alliance,* 1887; W. P. Cresson: *The Holy Alliance,* New York, 1922; Näff: *Zur Geschichte der Heiligen Allianz*; Bueckler: *Die geistigen Wurzeln der Heiligen Allianz.*

174

Francis II. According to the Tsar, this was a problem for sovereigns only. 'What I have in mind', he told Metternich, 'is of such a nature that Cabinet ministers could be of no assistance.' And if Francis I had agreed with this opinion, the treaty might well have been signed and sealed by the three monarchs without Metternich knowing anything about it. But the Emperor of Austria took no decision without consulting his Chancellor, and the latter immediately set about an editorial intervention, made certain vigorous amendments to the original text, bringing down to earth the transcendental aspirations of the Russian autocrat.

Thus Metternich astutely managed to transform a fraternity-of-peoples into a pact of their respective sovereigns: the supreme competence of the monarchy in every eventuality, all the old patriarchal notions, were re-affirmed, Alexander's theocratic aspirations, his repudiation of discredited outworn methods were eliminated. Thus a programme originally designed as a forerunner of better things to come had been turned into a political manifesto which merely confirmed long-established methods of government.

But, even then, Metternich always considered the document as 'something abstract', 'an example of sublime nonsense', 'a loud-sounding nothing', 'a philanthropic[1] aspiration masquerading under the cloak of religion'. 'The Holy Alliance', said Metternich's collaborator and stool-pigeon, Gentz, in 1818, 'is only an inadequate and inaccurate symbol of a union—later described as a "trades union"—of Princes'. In his old age, recapitulating the events of 1815, Metternich wrote: 'There was never any question of its being seriously entertained by the various Cabinets concerned, nor would any such consideration have been possible.' This is a categorical statement and there is no known docu-

---

1. It is perhaps advisable to remind English readers (lest the translator be blamed for writing nonsense) that for Continental conservatives the term 'philanthropy' had an invidious meaning. Pope Leo XIII only published his startling Encyclical, *De Rerum Novarum*, in 1891; Mastaï-Ferreti, Pope Pius IX, with his abortive liberalism, had not yet appeared upon the scene. In 1815, it was normal for a Continental Roman Catholic to consider 'philanthropy' as inevitably connected with the 'dangerous' opinions of the Encyclopaedists, with the savage anti-clericalism of the new Enlightenment—and therefore incompatible with religion.—TRANS.

mentation to refute it. Furthermore, there is no single evidence, in all Metternich's subsequent performance, of any intervention of the Christian ethic in the domain of international politics. But Metternich's actual procedure and his repeated insistence upon the principle of fraternal union between the three sovereigns (which was also one of the tenets of the Holy Alliance) tended to make people forget the fundamental incompatibility between his personal ideology and that mystic pietism which had originally inspired the famous treaty of September 1815.

Son of a freemason, pupil of a future Jacobin, Metternich himself remained always and in every way an aristocrat of the old school. His religious convictions were exactly those which we should expect, *a priori*, in a man of his period and rank. A faithful son of the Church, he nevertheless maintained towards the Vatican 'an attitude that was correct and active', but nothing more. 'No other Catholic power is as independent as we are of submission (in any narrow sense) to the opinions of the Holy See. . . .' And when he admitted the Jesuits (who had been driven out of Russia) into Galicia, he put severe restrictions on their activities and refused them residence in any other province of the Austrian Empire. 'I admire the Jesuits, as even many protestants do', he said to Varnhagen von Ense, in 1834, 'but that does not prevent my hating Jesuitry like the plague.' 'I am suspicious of the light that shines in vestries', is another statement attributed to him by Dr Jäger. Later, after his third marriage, as old age was creeping on, such anti-clerical tendencies seem to disappear. He began to go regularly to Mass and wished 'to put an end to that clandestine war with the Church and its official headquarters' which the Austrian Empire had been waging since the reign of Joseph II (noted on April 6th, 1844). He was later to favour a renewal of the concordat and a revision of the laws relating to mixed marriages. All such measures, in fact insignificant, needless to say provoked the fury of the liberals[1] and free thinkers. But

---

1. Refer also to relevant Translator's note on page 252. English readers should also note the special and invidious meaning given to the term 'liberal' by certain thinkers on the continent since it bears little relation to our own traditional usage. The distinction is perhaps best illustrated by a study of the Vatican's historic attitude towards 'voting liberal'. The works of Don Luigi Sturzo are helpful.—TRANS.

basically he remained the same: a man for whom the Church was a means to individual morality, a consolation of pious souls, but never an influence applicable to political action.

For in the realm of politics, the only one that ever really counted for Metternich, it was reason which reigned supreme. 'We can trace the origins of his political theory', says Srbik, 'to the writings of the XVIIIth century, to that age of rationalism, of an abstract *ideal*, of reason transcendent. That century proclaimed its faith in certain immutable principles, based upon reason, applicable to every age and every nation.' And the Chancellor's methods proceed from a similar concept. 'What is generally called the Metternich system', he declares, 'is not so much a system as the simple application of laws which govern the universe.' 'Political science', he says again, 'can be reduced to terms as exact as those of chemistry: if only men would refrain from theorising and take the trouble to note the similar nature of results traceable to identical causes.' (Mrs. Trollope.)

He was not the only man of his time to hold this conviction. It had been accepted by such different personalities as Kant and Frederick of Prussia, by Robespierre and Napoleon.

Two main currents of thought were concerned. First, the ideology of the French Revolution: the Jacobins had made reason their divinity. They had installed the goddess of Reason on the altar of Notre Dame, they wished to apply rationalist principles to every detail of their work of reformation. For them, the triumph of reason entailed the triumph of the individual, freed from fetters imposed by centuries of superstition and barbarism. The individual, of his own free will, was to enter into a new 'social contract' and was thus to establish the corner-stone of a new social order.

A second current was the line then adopted by conservatives in Central and Northern Europe. Hierarchy, for them, was a fundamental law, the state was the basis of society; the state with its restrictive authority, its 'divine right', which is nothing more nor less than a law of nature. Such doctrine, although in a sense rationalist, could nevertheless conveniently be grounded on the doctrines of the Fathers and other great religious teachers: 'All law is founded on the first of all laws, on natural law, that is to say on right reason and natural equity.' (Bossuet.)

For Metternich, the choice was easy; his whole experience of life imposed it. In his eyes the revolutionary spirit had been once for all identified with evil; it was destructive, incompatible with peace, with order, with prosperity, with life itself. And this for him had assumed the importance of dogma, but dogma based on very different premises from those of Alexander's mystico-evangelical concepts.

Metternich indeed postulated for his assumptions the same scientific exactitude claimed by his adversaries, the Jacobins, for theirs. The Chancellor was always willing to compromise when it came to action, but never with regard to principle.[1]

Starting from the premise of an eternal struggle between two opposites, the forces of destruction and those of conservation, Metternich built up a system of *defence*: defence of the old and natural human rights against new and arbitrary rights; defence of the old against the new and revolutionary human order.

Contrary to accepted opinion, the Chancellor never wished to be thought reactionary; he claimed to be constructive by nature and tradition. He knew full well that 'one cannot resist currents of thought'. (Dr Jäger.) Growing-pains are inevitable; they are the sickness proper to any social body. But to prevent such convulsions becoming fatal we need defenders of the old order to hold the fort against those others—always more numerous—who are working for the new. Society must evolve in an atmosphere of calm, in a well-ordered equilibrium.

Domestic combined with international stability summed up the Prince's *credo*. After the fall of Napoleon, it was important to insure a proper balance of power and maintain a kind of spiritual league of nations. For 'political units can no more be independent of each other than individuals living in the same society'. 'There is no such thing as an isolated state. One must never lose sight of a community of nations, the one essential condition of the modern world. Each state, apart from its domestic concerns, has common interests either with the whole federation or with some

---

1. Guizot: *Mémoires*, Vol. VIII, page 120.

more limited group. Axioms of political science are derived from
a knowledge of the real political requirements *of all states*. It is
only on the basis of mutual interests that survival can be guaranteed. . . . This tendency to co-operation between states is characteristic of the modern world and what most distinguishes it from
the social concepts of antiquity. It is a kind of family of states such
as once existed for individuals in the bosom of Christendom. To
re-establish good international relations on a basis of reciprocity,
with a guarantee to respect existing rights, is the essence of a wise
political system.' Fine principles, and which make Metternich a
worthy precursor of the founders of the League of Nations.[1]

But the Habsburgs' Chancellor did not stop there. He believed
that international and domestic order must go hand in hand, each
nation contributing to the life blood of the whole. 'We wish to
maintain a general peace, not that we have become addicted to
the utopian theories of the Abbé de Saint-Pierre, but because we
know that as soon as that peace is broken, the dogs of liberalism
will be unleashed, they will take the power in their teeth and tear
it to bits as is their wont.' And again: 'The first principle of a
concert of great powers is to maintain intact all legally established
institutions; it is only on that condition that a general peace can
be maintained.' (To Francis I, October 9th, 1829.) 'The populations of the world', he said, 'wish to live at peace not only
today but tomorrow also; security is the most important boon
humanity could wish for.' (To Apponyi, May 7th, 1835.) The
chief object of political action in Europe must be to suppress any
effervescence which might endanger tranquillity and order.

Sovereign intervention in the domestic affairs of any individual
state must be considered as a sacred duty, a natural right: it is the
inevitable concomitant of membership in this society of nations;
it entails both the rehabilitation and preservation of good social
order. 'Liberty, divorced from order, would inevitably develop
into tyranny, and tyranny, for me, has always been synonymous
with madness. The undisturbed functioning of law and order

1. See the illuminating treatise by Robert de Traz in his excellent book *De la
ligue des rois à l'alliance des peuples* (Ed. Grasset, 1936). The author has certainly
understood Metternich better than any other historian writing in French.

179

can alone insure national stability.' As to the nature of institutions best qualified to safeguard stability Metternich has no doubt: he is categorically committed to the principle of a social hierarchy with one man at the top. But the Chancellor's monarchist opinions were by no means dictated by sentimental loyalty toward some particular dynasty. In this, he differs radically, for instance, from the French legitimists—at whom he never ceases to poke fun. By origin a Rhenish Count, he was in fact serving a foreign dynasty. And if he felt genuinely attached to Francis I. he had a poor opinion of crowned heads in general. On January 6th, 1821, during the Congress of Laibach, we find this entry in his notebook: 'A number of kings seem to imagine their throne is an armchair into which they can sink comfortably and doze.' And on December 19th, 1820, in an emphatic missive addressed to the Tsar Alexander, that 'revolutionary with a crown on his head', Metternich proclaimed: 'The revolution was already well hatched in the palaces of kings when it was still in its infancy among the common people.' Legitimacy was certainly the best basis for a monarchy, but it was not the only one: hadn't Napoleon shown the world that an unorthodox sovereign could also restore and maintain order? One cannot, with impunity, live continuously in the wake of a very great man, and Metternich had been much more influenced than he himself supposed by the theories of Bonaparte.... The iron hand, a centralised government legislating by means of a strong police, a submissive clergy, an efficient bureaucracy, subordinating everything to the good of the state—wasn't this exactly the model favoured by the Austrian Chancellor?

He was anyhow convinced that a monarchy (acting with moderation) was an essential symbol of the eternal moral order. This rationalist politician accepted without reservation the traditional theses of an Aquinas or a Bossuet.[1] The masses need 'authority', not 'majorities'. The presence of heterogeneous elements in the legislature merely entails a permanent struggle which destroys the body politic. 'I am accused of not caring for Con-

---

1. Saint Thomas Aquinas: *De Regimine Principum*, Chapter XV. Bossuet: *Of Hereditary Monarchy*.

stitutions', he once said to a French diplomat, 'but there is a distinction to be made there. I do not, in fact, care for Constitutions which grew up over night and have to be imposed by violence on populations to whom they are pre-eminently unsuited. But I do favour those which have had a natural organic growth, a legitimate origin, and I should, if occasion arose, be prepared to safeguard them, as indeed I am prepared to protect everything which has been legally and properly established.' 'England, alone, possesses a Constitution', he said, 'of which *Magna Carta* is only a secondary element; the English Constitution grew.... What passes today for a Constitution is little more than the principle of: "Get out, and let me take your place".'

Thus it is for the sovereign and his ministers gathered in council, responsible only to their own conscience, to impose a unified procedure upon the whole machinery of government,[1] to direct the destinies of peoples 'in a manner more enlightened than anything of which the peoples themselves are capable'. 'Expedient changes in legislation and in the general administration of the state ought only to proceed from the free will, the considered and declared intention of those responsible under God for government. Any departure from this line of conduct brings inevitable disaster, general upheaval and ills far worse than those which it claims to cure.'[2]

Our leaders are in a better position than the man-in-the-street to acquire the necessary information on which to act. That is why the activity of the Press, however useful, must often be stemmed, and in general controlled. If every man be free to think what he pleases, that does not involve the right to 'an indefinite multiplication of conclusions'. Repressive measures against the Press do not, however, achieve the desired end; they only exasperate the public. (August 7th, 1835.) Metternich much preferred a 'preventive censorship'. In this he was again guided by the example of Napoleon, who used to say: 'I am now master of France, as you can see, but I would not undertake to govern

1. The lack of anything in the nature of centralised government, at that time in Europe, was patent.—TRANS.
2. Circular letter addressed to Austrian Legations accredited to foreign Courts. (Laibach, May 12th, 1821.)

her for three months if we had absolute freedom of the Press.'[1]

Under the supreme power, Metternich presupposes an aristocracy participating in the legislation and administration of local affairs. His was an aristocratic world. Throughout his life, Metternich moved only in aristocratic circles: apart from a few doctors and university professors he knew no other stratum of society. He wrote automatically 'M. *de* Fouché'.[2] With Metternich, as in the *Bibliothèque rose*,[3] 'all the good men have a particle and the bad have not; like that it is easy to distinguish'. (Montherlant.) According to Metternich, it had been one of the most fatal errors of the *ancien régime*, in France, to have 'undermined the aristocracy' and disposed of that intermediary body which originally stood between the King and the lower orders, leaving the King isolated and 'face to face with his people'—an error which Napoleon tried to remedy by creating a new nobility.

Like all rigid aristocrats, Metternich had a horror of the middle classes. Below the nobility, he could see only the people, 'those good creatures who only ask to be allowed to live and to work, who never wish to change as long as their material conditions are reasonably assured'. Unfortunately, 'the advance in industry and commerce has developed that middle class whose members have adopted dangerous views and sown discontent among the masses to their own eventual undoing'. Much sooner than other statesmen among his contemporaries, Metternich realised the significance of the socialism then emerging. He claimed to be a 'socialist' himself, and contested the right of Proudhon, of Louis Blanc or Robert Owen to annex the term; but he called himself a 'conservative socialist', one committed to preserving the social order and thus an enemy of revolutionary socialism.

'It is a long time now since the doctrines of Saint-Simon attracted our attention', he wrote on December 27th, 1831. 'The

1. See also, Metternich's letter to M. de Kaunitz, (April 16th, 1846): 'I know no statesman in England or in France who does not consider the liberty of the Press (a liberty which by its very nature can never be anything but licence) an evil, the scope and consequences of which are beyond calculation.'

2. The author once knew an old Russian general who always conferred the particle on heads of state under the third Republic, saying 'M. *de* Poincaré', 'M. *de* Clemenceau.'

3. Books for children.—TRANS.

opinions of Saint-Simon's followers are subversive. They attack
the social order at its roots; in attacking the family and property
they try to rouse the proletariat and set them at the throats of
the landlords. Followers of all these sects anathematise both the
principles of religion and those which lie at the root of all social
order. They incite and open up facilities for sensualism un-
restrained, and easily corrupt weak minds. A class which has
nothing to lose is always prepared to try any foolhardy scheme
in the hope of getting rich. And that class already numerous is
growing and present an ever-increasing danger in proportion
to the growth of civilisation.'[1]

The Chancellor was well aware that for the moment the
revolutionary proletariat was an infinitesimal minority; the masses
were not yet on the march. The movement was then restricted
mainly to the middle layer of society whose members seemed
unaware that political must always be followed by social upheaval. 'The gangrene has so far mainly contaminated the middle
classes; it is there one finds the star protagonists of the new party.
Intellectuals, professors full of their ideologies, barristers without
a brief, radicals who wish to throw dust in our eyes, sentimental
drawing-room philanthropists, drawing-room politicians— that's
where to look for the enemy. It is these who will open the breach
and let the radicals inside.' The danger lies in the *presumption*
of certain individuals; for the people as a whole it lies in
'those vagaries of thought which lead constantly to over
generalisation'.

'Facts and justice must lie at the base of world government',
said Metternich, 'not fine phrases and theories.'[2] It is against the
preachers of such nefarious doctrines that one must take a stand
for the 'eternal right'. Let the various governments silence these
miscreant doctrinaires inside their own dominions and show
their contempt for those of foreign culture. 'All such presumptuous weaklings will be ground to powder if stronger men than
they arise, make common cause and push on to victory.' 'Let
Europe place at her four corners, four energetic men who know

1. Metternich to Count Apponyi (Vienna, Secret Archives).
2. To the Tsar Alexander (Troppeau, December 15th, 1820).

exactly what they want and how to get it; let them know both how to lift their voices and, if needs be, a strong right arm, and I guarantee that the whole pack of ideologists will melt away into thin air.' (Vienna, January 6th, 1823.)

One of these men was already to hand, Metternich in person. 'I have only one passion in life', he said: 'to maintain justice and equity.' (October 1st, 1820.) 'I have arrived half-way along the course pursued by one generation, and fate has designed me to prevent (in the measure of my ability) the next generation from taking a wrong turning.' (Koenigswart, September 3rd, 1819.) The three or four strong men required must be furnished by the Coalition.

'A pact between monarchs is the only possible means, today, of saving society from total disintegration.' 'The masses are like children or like nervous females. Their leaders must agree in order to insure the peoples' happiness.' (March 20th, 1820.) 'What is Europe?' the Tsar had once asked a French ambassador. 'Europe consists of you and me.' And Metternich was coming to agree; it was only a matter of increasing the number of those who would have a right to speak for their fellows. At his instigation, the Treaty of Paris, signed on November 20th, 1815, was reinforced by a clause revising the Chaumont alliance and it became the practical means of implementing a pact of sovereigns. The monarchs of Austria, Prussia, Russia and England undertook, 'in order to consolidate their mutual relations', to hold at certain fixed periods conferences designed with a view to federal interests. They undertook 'to examine such measures as, in each relevant period, might be deemed expedient for the tranquillity and prosperity of the peoples as also for the maintenance of peace in Europe'. In fact, a European *Directoire* had been constituted. Four years later, at Aix-la-Chapelle, France was to be admitted, but this did not in any way modify the original alliance of the Four. The same old formula as that of the Committee of Five which had operated during the Congress of Vienna, was now revived. And this is what at a pinch one might call Metternich's Holy Alliance, one which had nothing in common with the original other-worldly document of that name. This was an alliance which envisaged no odour of sanctity but a purely practical federation, and had in mind not the brotherhood of man but the preservation of things as they were.

All philosophies, said Leibnitz, are true in what they affirm and false in what they deny. And one might make the same claim in relation to Metternich if one approaches the problem with an open mind. To our Western contemporaries, inoculated since childhood with what Metternich terms 'the illusion of democracy', his ideology might well seem monstrously out of date. But any proper understanding of the Austrian statesman requires us to remember what he himself said of Napoleon: 'One can only properly judge any man by setting him in the framework within which he moved and considering all the circumstances which played upon him.'[1] The political evolution of the populations beyond the Rhine cannot profitably be compared with those of England or France. In our time, the principle of the sovereign rights of the people (which Metternich so strenuously opposed) is universally accepted. And what has it led to in Central and Eastern Europe? To the installation of totalitarian governments, with whom the good of the state is the supreme and only law. We see a familiar pattern very similar to Metternich's own system. Today a new kind of master replaces the former 'monarch by the grace of God', directs the people 'for their good', leaning for that purpose upon a new 'aristocracy'— that of the party in power. Metternich's name is not very popular in Germany, in Italy or in many of the Danubian countries, but his ideas have been justified there to a truly amazing extent. Indeed, our present anti-communist campaign might be considered an up-to-date replica of his crusade, of the steps advised by the Chancellor Prince when he invited his league of sovereigns to fight all subversive elements, those mortal enemies not only of civilisation but of humanity itself.[2]

At the opening of the XIXth century, after the unsettled period of the great Revolution and the Napoleonic wars, Metternich

1. *Mémoires.*
2. It is impractical to speak of the pre-war situation in countries under an autocratic *régime*, for instance in Russia. The ideology of a Pobiedonostzef, adviser of Alexander III and preceptor of Nicholas II, is exactly similar to that of Metternich.

185

could justifiably claim that his system met the requirements of the moment, of the state which he was called upon to govern, and that it was pre-eminently in keeping with his own temperament.

Europe was sick to death of constant social upheaval, of wars, of ruined cities and the spilling of blood. Men had urgent need of tranquillity and rest. In our time, speaking on the occasion of his induction at the Académie, M. Duhamel said: 'It is conceivable that at certain periods a complete transformation, spiritual or material, might appear desirable even to the most balanced minds. But when, in the throes of frenzy, society loses sight of any tradition other than disorder, it is time for all sane men to seek salvation in stability.' Metternich himself might be speaking.

And of all the states of Europe, Austria had certainly most need of that stability which the 'system' held out. There are countries so composed that they must inevitably live in a permanent state of evolution. The British *Commonwealth* of nations is a case in point: however much administrative ties between England and her overseas possessions relax, or even dissolve altogether—the ties of blood and of a common civilisation will always remain. But where centrifugal forces are powerful, such evolution would endanger the very life of the state. Thus the Empire of the Habsburgs, composed of heterogeneous elements, of a variety of different races—Germans, Slavs, Italians, Hungarians—might have been unsettled by the slightest shock. In our time, certain nationalist writers have insisted that the Empire could have been saved from disintegration had its leaders, beginning with Metternich, energetically pursued federation. We are permitted to doubt this: having achieved a relative liberty, peoples who had lived in a state of serfdom for centuries would not have been satisfied by any such arrangement in the long run. Their attachment to the dynasty would not have prevented them sooner or later demanding their complete independence, thus breaking up an edifice already crumbling with decay.

For a man who essentially wished to preserve the edifice in question, there could be no worse heresy than the claim to self-determination by national units. And if stability were needed in

Austria, it would have to be maintained in the whole of Europe: revolutionary ideas soon cross frontiers.

With a complacency easy to understand, Metternich in a letter dated November 25th, 1819, quotes one of Talleyrand's innumerable *bons mots:* 'Austria is the House of Lords of Europe; as long as she remains intact, she can absorb the Commons.'

Nothing could have pleased him better than to apply the brakes, calm the hot-heads, put a stop to agitation. 'Leader of a Cabinet whose political philosophy and procedure (pre-eminently suitable to the geographical position of the power they represented) was inclined to moderation, to conservatism, he followed the more readily this line in that it coincided with his natural bent.' (Marmont.)

What Metternich could never understand was that neither the schemes of some outstanding personality nor the intervention of a group of determined men, nor the requirements of a single state nor even the fatigue of a whole continent, could indefinitely hold up the process of evolution. He was little justified in claiming that he had been 'dyed in a sense of history'. (February 7th, 1820.) Historical sense is probably what he most conspicuously lacked.

His conception of statecraft was purely formal; all irrational, subconscious, emotional elements were excluded. His was an abstract state, utilitarian and mechanistic. It was no living organism, animated by a mystical union with the *Divine essence*, as were those of the theologians and legitimists. Nor was it infused by the rich blood of the people, as held by the historical school, by those who realise that every nation pursues its own destiny and creates its own social pattern.

The inevitability of lasting social changes was ignored by Metternich. 'The eternal pursuit of progress in human societies' struck him as 'sheer nonsense'; just as the dynamism inherent in the idea of nationality was equally beyond his comprehension. 'There is nothing to prove', he wrote to Prokesch, 'that the national state is essentially superior to one founded on tradition and legality.'

'Italy is a mere geographical notion!' This statement more than

187

any other written or spoken by Metternich throughout his long life achieved a disastrous celebrity. It established in perpetuity his reputation as an oppressor of the Italian people. But Metternich certainly never saw himself in that light: 'Our Viennese wise-acres', he wrote to his wife, 'wish to treat Italians as if they were Germans. Personally, I cannot help feeling that Germans and Italians are as different as chalk from cheese.' (June 16th, 1819.) Immediately after the Congress of Vienna, he had sent a long report to the Emperor Francis I setting forth his notion of how the Lombardo-Venetian state ought to be governed. 'It is important', he wrote, 'to dispose, as soon as possible, of the deficiencies and actual vices of administration in this most interesting section of the monarchy. We ought to develop business activity, to make concessions to public opinion and to national sentiment, we ought to give these provinces a new kind of administration. This will prove to the Italians that we intend to differentiate them from the German provinces, that we are not seeking to absorb them.' (November 3rd, 1817.) How many times during the thirteen years following did he not deplore the actions of over-zealous Austrian prefects and generals, or alternatively, the narrow-minded and tactless behaviour of some Italian princeling? But he never understood the high moral and intellectual qualities of the Italian people.

In spite of those delightful people living in a landscape of unparalleled beauty, surrounded by the grandiose heirlooms of antiquity, Metternich considered Italy absolutely incapable of becoming a united nation. This prejudice he shared with a majority of his contemporaries, including Napoleon himself. 'The old Romans no longer exist', he wrote to his son Victor, 'the inhabitants of the Eternal City today are no longer Romans, and never again will be. Let all the visionaries in the world have a go; they will only fail.' (January 1st, 1819.) He was convinced that local and municipal traditions would always dominate in Italy. 'A Milanese', he said to Cobden, in 1847, 'will not place a mortgage in Padua or Cremona; he cannot see their steeples.'

And he remained convinced to the end, in spite of his denials before certain foreign diplomats[1] that a federation of Italian Princes, under the aegis of the Austrian Emperor, was the only way to govern the country and dispose of recurrent anarchy.

And when it came to German nationalism, his sentiments were just as hostile, although in that case he was dealing with people of his own blood. 'Certainly', says Srbik, 'the German nation was the nearest to his heart, he felt German but in the rather *universalist* manner of the eighteenth century: his point of view was roughly that of Goethe.' 'My remark which so exasperated Palmerston, "Italy is no more than a geographical term", has now become a household word, but one might say the same of Germany', he wrote to his friend Prokesch on November 19th, 1849.

The history of the Holy Roman Empire confirmed his opinion. The wars of liberation, although he had been an eye-witness, had left him cold; he had never wholeheartedly supported any liberationist movement.

'I alone', he wrote in old age, 'envisaged the German problem clearly during the transitional period of 1812 and 1813. I realised what would be possible in the event of Napoleon's downfall. My long experience allows me to say that the German problem has no solution other than the one I postulated in 1813 in the following formula: not a Reich (an Empire) but a federation of states.' 'There can be no Germany without Austria and Prussia.' (To Prokesch, January 2nd, 1850.)

'I am convinced', he also said, 'that Austria alone serves the true interests of Germany and would be able to maintain her domestic peace—and that without any ulterior motives. This can best be understood by reference to the facts: The size of our Empire, as a political unit, has reached saturation point; we have nothing to demand of Germany except her own tranquillity. Prussia, on the other hand, has an urge to expansion which could only be satisfied to the detriment of other German states.' (To Prokesch, November 15th, 1849.) 'When Prussia professes her devotion to the German idea, to *Deutschtum*, she advances as her final end what is in fact merely a means.' Mortal enemy of a subtle and

---

1. Gordon to Castlereagh, July 12th, 1819.

aggressive Prussianism, ruthless opponent of *Teutomania* in any form, Metternich nevertheless continued to regard himself as 'the best of all Germans'.

He underestimated, in this as always, the vital forces of racial feeling, ideological movements, enthusiasms which no official decree—be it ever so intelligent—could hope to hinder or snuff out.

At the very moment when Metternich thought he had the destiny of Europe in his hands, the *romantic* movement sprang into significance, giving birth to a flood of new ideas, to a fresh crop of 'universals'. The romantic philosophy being diametrically opposed to the classic, its followers denied that any one system could be imposed with success in every circumstance; it roused that passion of national feeling which was to become the real revolutionary force of the century, and it was finally to overthrow the Metternich system.

The Chancellor's great mistake probably lay in seeking to create an absolute of theories which were essentially relative. He who had always accused the revolutionaries of being doctrinaire, who always offset their ideologies with 'principles', does not appear to have realised the full subtlety of this distinction. His own principles became as dogmatic as those of his adversaries. 'The political system of H.I.M. has all the character of a religion', he once wrote to Prince Esterhazy, Austrian ambassador to London, thereby making exactly the same mistake as his enemies on the Left, of those 'who think they have embalmed truth in their theory of *progress*'.

The ten years that followed the Congress of Vienna saw the most complete (and the most efficacious) application of the Metternich system. This period is generally known as the 'Congressional era'; innumerable historians have presented it in detail. The initial suggestion of a periodic meeting of sovereigns and ministers of the greater powers seems to have come from Castlereagh, who had always believed that 'it would be useful occasionally to bring the principal Cabinets into touch with each other'. But it was Metternich who put the notion into practice, who formed what he called 'a real moral *fasces*' of this small group of men who held a monopoly of power in Europe.

Five great Congresses, in all, assembled between 1818 and 1822. It was to Aix-la-Chapelle that Francis I and Metternich first took their way, passing through the Rhenish country, greeted as if the Holy Empire had never been dissolved, with a loyalty and enthusiasm reminiscent of 1792 (year of the coronation), greeted in short as if the banks of the frontier river had never become Prussian.[1] It was actually only a 'little Congress', a miniature replica of Vienna. It assembled the Austrian, Prussian and Russian monarchs and some dozen diplomats: the Duc de Richelieu represented France. There were no great social festivities. Walks in the town and its surroundings were taken during the day, and in the evening the notabilities met at the houses of a privileged few who happened to dispose of large reception rooms. All were bored, in turn, *chez* Castlereagh, or played whist *chez* Metternich. Small *thés-dansants* were organised by Princess Thurn-und-Taxis. Nesselrode's house was the only one conducted in the grand manner: it was a meeting-ground for the French and Austrian delegates. 'Greater and lesser affairs of Europe and America were there discussed over a fragrant cup of tea.' (Gentz.) Metternich had occasion to hear and applaud the *diva*, Catalani, also to meet Madame Récamier, whom he found 'beautiful but dull'. Actually, it was under Nesselrode's hospitable roof that his liaison with Princess Lieven started. The results of the Congress of Aix-la-Chapelle were important: it was decided to evacuate coalition troops from French territory and France was admitted to the quadruple alliance.[2]

After Aix-la-Chapelle came Troppau, a simple burgh-hamlet in Silesia, and there the same group gathered in 1820. The background was even more modest, more intimate; both sovereigns and ministers were housed in small villas and their deliberations took place in the shady avenues of the picturesque old market-town. The question of the Kingdom of Naples was discussed;

1. Metternich wrote to Gentz from Mainz, on July 7th, 1825: 'As all preparations had been made for a gala reception to the Emperor and he did not turn up, the inhabitants made do with a demonstration in favour of my humble person. Illuminations, fire-works, operas, deputations, I had to swallow the lot.'
2. Ernst Molden: *Zur Geschichte des osterreichisch-russischen Gegensatzes: die Politik der europaischen Grossmachte und die Aachener Konferenz, Wien*, 1916.

whether or not a military intervention was called for against the revolutionaries who had seized power and were forcing the hand of the old King Ferdinand. [1]

Intervention was decided a few months later, at the Congress of Laibach (in Carniola), the King of the Two Sicilies being present. Under a European mandate, the Austrian armies, in March 1821, were to restore an absolutist regime throughout the whole of Italy. [2] Then, in autumn 1822, came the Congress of Verona consisting not only of Alexander, Francis I and Frederick-William III but of all the Italian princelings, and also Chateaubriand who was manœuvring (not unsuccessfully) a French armed intervention in Spain. [3]

This brief picture of the four congresses, of those who took part and their decisions, is designed to show the extent to which Metternich had succeeded in imposing his system on the political leaders of Europe. The Habsburg's Chancellor was becoming increasingly 'the mentor of the Continent'.

His position in Austria itself was also noticeably more secure. Since the Congress of Vienna, the Emperor Francis had shown him unbounded confidence. In 1821 he gave a startling demonstration of this by raising his minister to the supreme dignity of Chancellor of Court and State, a title which had lapsed with the death of Kaunitz. The monarch and his adviser met daily and worked for hours together. 'Metternich had realised', said Meyendorff, 'that both the Emperor's personal predilections and his dynastic interests were against the Revolution.... To keep himself in good odour, he found it advisable to give way to the Emperor about points on which the latter was adamant.... But by remaining within the limits prescribed by his master's principles, he was able to develop all the projects he thought necessary: his sovereign was indifferent to the means he employed to carry them out, and he himself by no means scrupulous.' And so

1. Bignon: *Du Congrès de Troppau.*
2. 'Our army', Metternich wrote, 'has not lost a drop of blood but has covered itself with glory, for no excesses of any kind have been committed, not the slightest sign of disorder.'
3. Chateaubriand: *Le Congrès de Vérone*; Bignon: *Les Cabinets européens*: 1815-1822.

one might say that Austrian policy was based on the Emperor's character and intelligently directed by Prince Metternich. And the fire-eater, Sealsfeld, did not differ. 'There exists a remarkable similarity of views and temperament between Francis and Metternich: *Francis has found his man*, and that is why he follows his advice and clings to him in all eventualities.' Metternich, himself, described the situation as follows: 'Heaven placed me beside a monarch who seems, so to speak, to have been especially created for me. The Emperor Francis never utters a superfluous word; he knows what he wants and imposes upon me only what duty compels me myself to desire.' (July 26th, 1820.) 'The Emperor always does what I wish, but I never wish anything except what he ought to do.' 'If he overwhelms me with favours, if he has confidence in me, it is because I follow the path that he mapped out. Were I so unlucky as to deviate from that path, Prince Metternich would not remain Austrian foreign minister for twenty-four hours.'

But the general situation at that moment was such that Austria could have no strictly individual preoccupations: 'Our country, or rather I should say our countries', Metternich wrote, 'are conspicuously peaceful because, without revolutions, they are now enjoying some of the perquisites which (and they unquestionably do) rise from the ashes of Empires thus overthrown. Our peoples see no need for agitation when they can enjoy in peace and tranquillity all that such agitation has secured for others.' (To Madame de Lieven, February 4th, 1819.)

The effective influence of the house of Habsburg stretched far beyond the limits of its hereditary possessions. Since the Congress of Vienna, Austria had dominated both Italy and Germany. Order was maintained in Lombardy and Venetia by force of arms; and in the independent states of the peninsula, Metternich could count on the unconditional support of their rulers. The King of Naples, as we have seen, appeared humbly before the tribunal of the great powers and immediately annulled, at their bidding, the constitution which he had granted to his subjects. At a meeting, in 1825, the King of Sardinia asked Metternich: 'Well, are you pleased with me, and do you consider that I have

fulfilled my undertaking towards the Emperor and his minister?'
Cardinal Consalvi, secretary of State to the Holy See, signed
himself 'the most devoted and zealous of your faithful servants'
and assured Metternich of his boundless devotion.[1] And the
Pope, having heard from Cardinal Albani that Metternich had
a predilection for the colour red, interpreted this innocent remark
in his own way and invited the Chancellor to become a member
of the Sacred College,[2] in other words, to wear a Cardinal's hat!

In Germany, the Chancellor could count on the unconditional
support of Frederick-William III and on the long-tried friendship
of King Maximilian of Bavaria who, long ago, when a young
colonel, had housed the youth Metternich at Strasbourg and kept
a paternal eye on his education. He could also count on the weakness of the other princes and princelings, since with them 'the
question of self-preservation would always supersede any matters
of secondary importance or any vague disposition to liberalism'.

The Tsar Alexander, himself, had gradually adhered to his
rival's 'system'. Not that he had entirely abandoned the humani-
tarian notions of his youth: he felt some sympathy with the
aspirations of young Italy; he proclaimed before the Polish Diet
'his devotion to liberal institutions' and did not rebel as often as
Metternich could have wished against the influence of Capo
d'Istria, his adviser on Eastern questions and a firm believer in
the emancipation of the masses (a man described by the Chancellor as an 'arrant fool'). 'Alexander is the most childish of all
the world's children', Metternich also wrote.

But the child was growing old: a slow change was taking place
in his heart and in his disillusioned mind. About 1820 the Tsar
declared to Lebzeltern: 'Since 1814, I have been much mistaken;
what I once thought true seems to me wrong today. I have been
responsible for much evil; I must try to make amends for it now.'
The Congress of Troppau sealed his conversion. Alexander
greeted Metternich as 'an old companion-at-arms' and said: 'it is
not you who have changed me; I changed myself. . . . You have

1. Charles van Duerm: *Correspondance du Cardinal Hercule Consalvi avec le Prince
de Metternich*, 1815-1825 (Louvain, 1899). Letter of January 1st, 1819.
2. Metternich to Gentz, July 3rd, 1825. (The Pope concerned was Leo XII;
Metternich at the time, of course, was a widower.—TRANS.)

no cause to reproach yourself; I cannot say as much for me'. And during the Congress of Laibach, Metternich was able to note with considerable satisfaction: 'Russia is not leading us, we are leading the Tsar.' And a year later, when Alexander refused to intervene on behalf of the Greek insurgents, Metternich felt justified in writing to Esterhazy: 'The work of Peter the Great has been shaken to its foundations.' 'Tsar Alexander both thinks and acts as we do', wrote Lebzeltern, Austrian Ambassador to Saint Petersburg. 'You alone, Prince, were capable of bringing about this amazing change of mind.'

English reactions, as regards George IV and Castlereagh, were equally favourable to Metternich and Austria. The head of the Hanoverian dynasty even went so far as to call Francis I 'our Emperor' (Metternich to Francis I, October 24th, 1821). Indeed, he was counting on the Chancellor's visit to London to achieve in a few days 'the moral re-education of his own ministers'. (Metternich to his Emperor, March 17th, 1825.) Didn't His Majesty consider the Austrian Chancellor as 'the leading statesman of Europe'?[1] As for Castlereagh, Metternich felt in him a faithful ally in a good cause, a firm friend, 'devoted heart and soul to me not only for personal reasons but even more by conviction'. Those convictions were at any rate shared at that moment by the whole of British public opinion. According to C. K. Webster, one could have found few members of the Commons or of the House of Lords who would not wholeheartedly have endorsed Castlereagh's opinions.[2] There was Wellington, for instance, 'ultra to his finger-tips', who had always advised Metternich to launch a punitive expedition against the rebels of Naples and congratulated him in advance on the brilliant part he was called upon to play in this connection.

There was nothing, however, more curious than the relationship which developed at that period between the Austrian statesman and France under the Restoration.

The restored monarchy was obliged to be true to its origin; it could not betray the cause of law and order inherent in the legi-

---

1. Esterhazy to Metternich, January 3rd, 1822.
2. C. K. Webster: *The Foreign Policy of Castlereagh*, 1934.

timist principle. Neither Louis XVIII nor Charles X, without destroying themselves, could forswear the Metternich system. The Chancellor, on his side, considered the rehabilitation of France, the strengthening of ties between throne and people, as a *sine qua non* of the balance of power in Europe.

In his *Mémoires d'Outre-Tombe* Chateaubriand stated: 'The men of the Restoration laughed when they heard talk of the balance of power—*balance* in which the dice had been so unfairly weighted against themselves.' And yet, France did all she could to insure its survival. Prince Polignac, for instance, was quite justified, in 1830, in thinking: 'In spite of all the ministerial changes that have taken place since the Restoration, our foreign policy has been able to maintain a uniform direction, always towards the general objective of conservation and peace.' Anxious to wipe out much old ill-feeling, His Majesty's government, since that time, had confined itself to watching over the general interests of the great European federation.[1]

We should thus not be surprised by the friendly atmosphere which then existed between Vienna and the Tuileries. France swallowed her resentment and received with apparent eagerness all those counsels of political wisdom with which Metternich condescendingly favoured her. One can picture the situation as one reads the despatch sent by Count Caraman, Ambassador at Vienna, to the Duc de Richelieu after his first interview with the Chancellor on July 12th, 1816. 'In the course of that long discussion which lasted from nine o'clock till past midnight', wrote the French diplomat, 'Prince Metternich reviewed the whole of our present administration and very justly analysed both its weakness and its strength. He would like us to be able to wipe out all evil memories of the past. He even pointed out certain advantages which the King might now reap from the old upheavals of the Revolution. . . . And in general, I cannot sufficiently insist, Monsieur le Duc, on how satisfied I was with the results of our long conference and the principles expressed by the Prince with such firmness and clarity.'[2]

1. Circular letter to diplomatic agents, April 7th, 1830. See also G. Grosjean: *La politique extérieure de la Restauration et l'Allemagne.*
2. *Archives des Affaires étrangères*, Paris.

Was it surprising that Paris gave Metternich a warm welcome when he went there in 1825, at the time of his wife's death? Louis XVIII decorated him with the Order of the Holy Ghost; he entertained the visitor to dinner, *en famille*, the party including the Dauphin, the Dauphine and the Duchesse de Berry; and His Majesty 'completely relaxed all formality on this occasion'. 'The King, his ministers and all the right people have received me in a manner which shows how high the prestige of Austria stands today', he wrote home on April 17th, 1825. 'The present ministry is full of good-will; what they lack is the tangible means of achievement; they are trying to create them.' (To the Emperor Francis, March 28th, 1825.) 'My relations with the King are certainly unique', he told Gentz. 'People seem to look upon me as a kind of lantern to which they come to be guided in a rather dark night . . . the leaders of the *pure* party gather round me with the fullest confidence.' (April 11th, 1825.) 'Recently, the Archbishop of Paris; the Bonapartist, Martholon; the legitimist, Bonald, and a *Septembrist*, were to be seen together in my drawing-room—one could scarcely push catholicity further . . . a perfect "valley of Jehosaphat".' 'If a number of circumstances', he wrote fatuously to Lebzeltern, 'had not already convinced me that I hold a special and indeed unique position in society, my present visit would have done so. . . . My stay in this capital has been an outstanding event in my life as a public man.' (June 18th, 1825.) 'At Paris', he said again, 'the behaviour of people towards me is rather that of sponges, anxious to absorb ideas. . . .'[1]

---

1. Of all the Restoration ministers, the *romantic* diplomat Chateaubriand was the only one who did not find favour in Metternich's eyes. The Chancellor had always reproached him for his muddled mind and petty pretensions. He considered the Frenchman 'a complete nonentity' and he did not disguise his satisfaction when the Viscount resigned. 'I judged him a long time ago; I recognised a "bonnet" man, and I care little whether the bonnet be red or white. Of the two, indeed, I prefer the demagogue to the royalist variety of Jacobinism. The first makes a frontal attack on the monarchy but the second will strangle it.' (To Lebzeltern, July 15th, 1824). And when he heard that Chateaubriand had begun 'to write some disturbing pamphlets', he said: 'An able poet and pamphleteer, M. de Chateaubriand, has none of the qualities that go to make a statesman. . . . Obsessed with an immoderate vanity and ambition, he worked with M. de Villèle only as long as he thought he could control the Prime Minister. Today, as the enemy of an administration to which he once belonged, he disgraces, daily, the pages of the *Journal des Débats* with diatribes that can only turn to the advantage of the socialists.' (To Lebzeltern,

But could this somewhat grandiose scheme for the 'preservation' of Europe persist indefinitely?

In July 1820, from the other side of the Atlantic, the great American statesman, John Quincey Adams, opined: 'the European alliance will last as long as the states that compose it',[1] thereby singularly misjudging the fluctuations inevitable on our continent.

In December 1825, Alexander I made his exit from the world scene. 'Fiction is no more', cried Metternich. 'We now turn to the pages of history.' The new Tsar was deeply suspicious of Metternich, and his advisers did all in their power to fan the flame. Nicholas I had no experience, but he had a strong will and considerable ambition: he was not prepared to tolerate exterior pressure from any direction. The uprising in Greece was to furnish him with a pretext for interference in the East and Metternich saw once more the phantom of his old terror rising before his eyes: 'a bellicose despotism prepared to tear the world to pieces'. In the circumstances, the attitude of the Cabinet of Saint James would become a decisive factor. 'Russia will never dare to do what England does not want.'

But England, too, had changed. Castlereagh's days had ended in a tragic suicide. 'This is one of the worst calamities that could have struck me', Metternich wrote. 'It will take years before any other English statesman will feel the same confidence in me.' (August 22nd, 1822.)

That desideratum was never to be satisfied. Castlereagh's death coincided with the beginning of a new era in the history of England. Rid now of the spectre of revolution as of the fear of Napoleon, England reverted to her normal self; new social classes emerged; the power of the aristocracy diminished. Canning, succeeding Castlereagh at the Foreign Office, personified a point of view diametrically opposed to that of Metternich. Over-night, the direction of British foreign policy was reversed. Not that Canning had any sympathy for 'subversive elements' or with

July 24th, 1824.) But after Chateaubriand's tragic downfall 'an ever-growing understanding was definitely established between Vienna and Paris', and it was to survive in spite of a few passing clouds up to the eve of the revolution of 1830.

1. W. C. Ford: *Writings of J. Q. Adams*, Vol. VII, p. 477.

democratic principles of freedom. Essentially insular in outlook, the Tory minister was merely reverting to an old English tradition and was opposed to any meddling in the domestic affairs of foreign countries. No more devastating blow could have been dealt the Metternich 'system'. That system could only work as a totality; it was not enough to profess or uphold conservative ideas in one's own country. 'The evil' must be fought wherever it appeared without regard to frontiers, otherwise it would spread all over the world. Sovereign intervention wherever the revolutionary danger might arise was axiomatic, an absolute necessity.[1] But Castlereagh himself had already shown signs of rebelling against such a wholesale principle of intervention.

Intervention, in his view, ought to be considered as an exceptional method, applicable only in special cases, where the safety, for instance, of a neighbour state might be involved. He considered it 'supremely dangerous to incorporate the principle into ordinary diplomatic procedure or to admit it within the concept of normal human rights'. (Circular letter of January 19th, 1821.) Canning, for his part, rejected the theory categorically. 'Prince Metternich's claims', he said, 'are absolutely unreasonable; they are based on a strange misunderstanding of our obligations, of our interests, and of our sentiments. England is in no wise called upon to intervene in the domestic affairs of other nations or to lend her aid to any such intervention.'[2]

A clash between two completely different concepts was inevitable.

Metternich had been able to adjust himself to England's recognition of Mexican independence and that of other South American states. These were all very far away; no direct repercussion was to be feared in Europe. The Greek rebellion, on the other hand, seriously challenged his system. He did not set out to be an enemy of the Greeks but for him the rising had 'a revolutionary character inadmissible however grave its causes'.[3] He feared

1. In our time those who preach the crusade against communism do not differ from those opinions.
2. Canning to Sir H. Wellesley, English Ambassador at Vienna, September 16th, 1823.
3. Metternich to Vincent, January 5th, 1826.

'a further crop of annoyances and dangers in the already critical condition of Europe'. He was apprehensive of any extension of Russian influence in the Near East, a revival of rivalries between the powers, the final destruction of that European equilibrium, so dearly bought. [1] With an amazing tenacity, with consummate ability, he sought concessions from the Sublime Porte and endeavoured to avert an armed conflict. He refused to be discouraged, and pursued an enormous correspondence with all the European Cabinets: he tirelessly spun his diplomatic web 'like my friend the spider', he said.

But the true significance of events began to escape him. For the first time in his life, he realised that an important political issue might transcend the sphere of diplomacy. 'We cannot understand what the three courts (England, Russia, France) intended, or what they now want. We are faced today with the imminent danger of a general collapse.' (To Apponyi, November 13th, 1827.)

In April 1826, Wellington at Saint Petersburg signed a protocol which unmistakably allied England and Russia: establishing Greece on a basis of tributary vassal state under Turkey. A further disagreeable surprise came in July, 1827: representatives of France, at London, solemnly endorsed the Saint Petersburg arrangement. The disappearance of Canning, in August 1827, changed nothing as to policy. Without any general European mandate the three countries lined up with the rebels; in October, their navies—in Navarin Bay—destroyed the Egyptian and Ottoman fleets. ('An appalling catastrophe', wailed Metternich.) The following year, the Russian army beat the Turks. In March 1829, Greek independence was declared at London.

Was this an irreparable defeat, a final collapse of the 'system'? In spite of considerable disillusion, Metternich did not think so. He pursued his propagandist mission with all the faith, determination, the energy (and let us admit, the fanaticism) that the word implies. And the apostle of social order found it quite natural that the miscreants should seek to crucify him. 'One arm nailed to

1. Mendelssohn-Bartholdy: *Metternich's Orient politik. Historische Zeitschrift.* (Bd. 18). Beer: *Die Orient politik Oesterreichs seit 1774* (1889).

Constantinople and the other to Lisbon; while domestic policies occupy the centre. Mr Canning has been my executioner and the Hungarian Diet, the sponge soaked in vinegar.' (December 11th, 1826.) But he never for a moment questioned his own infallibility: 'I know what ought to be done today, and I shall know what ought to be done tomorrow. My policies are those of eternal reason. Happy the man who can claim never to have deviated from that path!' He cared little for attacks by his enemies. 'The world needs me, if only because I perform a unique function; to be what I am requires a long term of preparation.' (May 15th, 1828, to his son Victor.) From contemporary judgments, blinded by party passion, he appealed to the tribunal of history. 'Few men have understood me, and few understand me now. I assure you that writers a hundred years hence will judge me very differently from those of today.'[1]

'What can easily become very dangerous', he said to M. de Rayneval, French ambassador to Vienna, 'are such bilateral alliances as that which the Greek affair engendered.... The salvation of Europe depends on general not partial federation.... We are not thinking here in terms of the Holy Alliance (which in any event was never anything but a pious fiction) nor in terms of "Chaumont", drawn up for one special occasion, nor even in terms of the congress of Aix-la-Chapelle. All I ask is a moral understanding between the five great powers whose strength and great prestige make them the natural arbiters of European destiny. I ask that they take no important step, do nothing which might endanger the general peace, without a previous joint understanding. I should like them above all to be guided by the thought that purely ideological considerations are not always the most important today, that each country must take into account what its actual domestic situation requires. A spirit of innovation, we might better call it disorder, threatens the tranquillity of every state. We must oppose it with the spirit of preservation, we must seek to strengthen and stabilise existing institutions, whether old or new does not matter; if such

1. March 21st, 1819, to Madame de Lieven.

O

institutions have a proper legal standing, they deserve our support.'[1]

In short, Metternich was convinced that he was right and Europe was wrong. Events were to confirm that opinion.

1. Rayneval to Polignac, May 12th, 1830. (*Archives des Affaires étrangères*, Paris.)

# X

# THE CARBONARI

D URING the evening of February 2nd, 1824, an unusual liveli-
ness could be noted in the dreary old building of Police
Headquarters at Vienna. At five o'clock the authorities had
been notified that the all-powerful Chancellor, Prince Metternich,
was coming before nightfall to visit a political prisoner, Count
Confalonieri, arrived from Italy the day before (the Count had
been condemned to death but his sentence had been commuted
to life imprisonment).

Weakened by previous long detention, in a bad state of general
health and subject to epileptic fits, the aristocratic Italian patriot
had promised certain revelations. Metternich was coming in person to receive them.

At precisely seven o'clock the Chancellor entered the condemned man's cell. 'You wish, it seems, to explain your conduct.
The Emperor might have sent an official of the secret police or an
examining magistrate; he preferred to entrust the task to me, to
enable you to talk more freely. Your affair has two aspects: the
judicial, you have broken the law; the Court has given its
verdict but there are also political—or if you prefer the term,
European implications. I have read your evidence: you mentioned
foreign influence to the judges in connection with revolutionary
movements in Italy. *That concerns me.* If you were disposed to
reveal the ramifications of your organisation on home territory,
to reveal the names or activities of subjects of the Empire, I should
refuse to listen. But you have confessed to inside knowledge of an
organisation which you yourself described as a *European conspiracy*.

203

I frankly admit that I should like to hear what you have to say about that.'[1]

An excellent opening, astute to a degree. For two hours, the representatives of rival ideologies: the 'provost marshal of the Holy Alliance', the fettered revolutionary, faced each other in heated argument. Two different concepts of life were clashing in this symbolic encounter. We are reminded of two recent bouts of a similar nature: the Grand Duchess Serge of Russia confronting her husband's assassin; the meeting of the Viceroy of India with Mahatma Gandhi.

But Confalonieri was not going to 'talk'; he confined himself to declaring the integrity of his patriotism, he promised replies to questions in writing—the promise was never kept. He made no complaint, asked no favours: 'One could get nothing from him unless we were to promise a general amnesty', was the Chancellor's final conclusion.

But Metternich had revealed himself completely during this talk. It was he, not the prisoner, who was stating his *credo*. 'There is much talk in liberal circles of patriotism and the brotherhood of man', he said to Confalonieri. 'Such patriotism distinguishes between the country and its monarch and if that is your own contention you must naturally consider yourself innocent. But we who are convinced monarchists, cannot separate the terms God, King, and Country. These three constitute for us an inseparable unity.' It was he again, and not his opponent, who was revealing his most secret preoccupations: that spectre which never ceased to haunt him, the terror of some dark and vast conspiracy directed against sound government and the existing social order which he had sworn to defend. Gentz, his perspicacious collaborator, always considered this tendency to see the hand of secret societies behind all revolutions and social upheavals as his master's greatest weakness, *sein Urlüge*. It was certainly an over-simplification, but understandable if one considers the nature of the times in which he lived.

1. Report of the Chancellor Metternich to the Emperor Francis I, February 3rd, 1824 (Vienna, Secret Archives Reports, number 348). This document was reproduced in Alessandro Luzio's book: *Antonio Salvotti e i processi del Ventuno.*

Always and everywhere, secret societies have made their influence felt, for good or evil. Sometimes men have tended to exaggerate their importance, but more often to underestimate them. Ideas, as well as action, sprout in the shade. Secret groups of initiates (intellectuals or conspirators), in certain periods and given the required conditions, have unquestionably played an important, even a decisive, part. The most striking example of this was the outbreak of *carbonarisme*, of which Confalonieri was a leader. This society overshadowed the whole of European history from 1815 to 1835.

It was just when Napoleon's star began to wane that the 'union of coal-heavers' (*Carboneria*) first became known. This was a secret society formed in the southern States of Italy. Its founders were probably merely dreamers, or even freemasons dissatisfied with the purely speculative activities of the quasi-mystical associations to which they belonged: imbued with the ideas of the French Revolution they sought an effective medium for their political creed. 'Get the wolves out of the forest', was their chief slogan. 'Wolves stood for despots: Austria and her vassals, all those princelings who lorded it over the length and breadth of crucified Italy.' The *Carbonari* Lodges were known as *vendite*, or sales-centres (sale of coal), members referred to each other as 'Good Cousins'. Delegates from twenty cells formed a central cell; representatives of this central cell constituted first the High and then the supreme *Vendite*. Admission to the *Carbonari* and to its higher branches was accompanied by a solemn and complicated ritual, partly inspired by that of the freemasons.

Initiation ceremonies were performed in a sanctuary known as the *baracca*, or coal-heavers' hut, which had been arranged with ostentatious austerity. High officials sat round on square logs. A hatchet in the hands of the president replaced the better-known masonic mallet; over his head, as in the lodges, hung an iridescent triangle. A crucifix on a log covered with a white linen cloth, symbolised the purity of their cause evoking 'Jesus Christ, our Saviour, first of the Good Cousins, Grand Master of the Universe'. A ball of thread recalled 'the linen woven by the Mother of God and the mysterious link which bound the *Carbonari*'. The neophite was called upon to drink 'the cup of forgetfulness' and pursued a series of symbolic journeys through 'the forest rustling with leaves' and the purifying fire. When admitted later to the second degree, to the status of master, he put on a crown of white thorns and took his oath. 'If my sufferings can be useful to mankind, may I never be delivered from them.' Condemned symbolically to crucifixion, he was pardoned after a solemn dedication to the cause and returned to his new life bedecked with black, blue and red ribbons symbolising mourning, hope and faith. The rites of initiation to the higher grades combined an even stranger mixture of the *mystique* of Golgotha and the ideology of revolution. The political objectives of the society came gradually to light: the crucifix came to signify the crucifixion of tyrants; the ball of cotton, a hangman's rope for the enemy; the hatchet was to be seen as a typical weapon of revolution; the 'wolves of the forest', as all foreign oppressors. At the initiation to the highest grades, the 'two thieves' were crucified symbolically as traitors to the order; men dressed in German uniforms burst in to the proceedings and prepared to give the *coup de grâce* to the victim. But the Good Cousins chased the intruders away to cries of 'Victory! Death to Tyrants! Long live Liberty!' [1]

These peculiar rites will make our supercilious contemporaries smile. But they were unquestionably well adapted to the fevered exaltation of their time.

When we begin to examine in detail the history of the movement as presented to us by impartial critics today, one is truly amazed by the scope of its activities, by the number of its ramifications and the quality of its adherents. With lightning rapidity, *Carbonarism* spread its octopus growth over the whole of Italy and was noticeably powerful in the south. Masonic lodges fed it daily with new recruits; the youth of the nation tumbled over each other to gain admission. A few years after its foundation, there were at Naples alone some twenty-eight *Vendite*, some of

1. Eugène Lennhoff: *Histoire des Sociétés politiques secrètes au XIXe. et au XXe. siècle*, 1934; Albert Falcionelli: *Les Sociétés secrètes italiennes (les Carbonari, les Camorra, la Maffia)*, 1936.

which had thousands of members belonging in the main to the upper classes of society. The army of the Kingdom of the Two Sicilies was peppered with neophites. In Piedmont, the chief *Vendita*, between 1815-1821, had succeeded in enlisting a considerable number of men of the aristocracy, of the middle classes, University students and officers of the army. The movement spread through Romagna, through Venetia and Lombardy. Already in 1819, the Emperor Francis I instituted a special commission to inquire into the activities of the 'Good Cousins': Judge Antonio Salvotti, appointed examining magistrate, immediately discovered the existence of a vast network extending over the whole peninsula. The big uprising against Ferdinand, King of the Two Sicilies, had been entirely organised by the underground activities of the *Carbonari*. The revolt of Piedmont, in which Charles-Albert de Carignan, a nephew of the King, had been involved was also their work, and the same applied to a variety of uprisings in Romagna and the Marches. The *Carbonari* did not work alone. They were in constant contact with a whole web of other societies, such as the 'Guelphs', 'the Friends of Liberty', 'Italian Federates', 'the Adelphi', all united by the one slogan: *Italia reggenerata: vincere o morire*.

Offshoots of the *Carbonari* extended far beyond the Italian frontiers. We all know the amazing part played by members of the brotherhood in the French upheavals at the time of the Restoration. Adapted by Flottard, Buchez and Bazard to local political requirements, the French *Carbonari* enlisted old soldiers, men on half-pay, rich bourgeois, doctors, students, an historian of the standing of Augustin Thierry, such artists as the Scheffer brothers, philosophers like Jouffroy and Cousin, in all something like sixty thousand adherents. Certain deputies and even peers of the realm were also members. Plans for an insurrection were elaborated under the trees of the Luxembourg gardens: the wolves were no longer Austrians, as in Italy, but the Bourbons. The plots of Saumur, of Belfort and La Rochelle, can also be traced to the ubiquitous *Carbonari*. Italian Good Cousins and Adelphi, in exile, kept in touch with their French friends prominent among whom were Laffite, Lafayette, Benjamin Constant and General Lamarque.

An essentially Latin organisation, the *Carbonari* had virtually
no following in Germany. Revolutionary aspirations among the
rising generation there were invariably to be found in the gym-
nasia and *Burschenschaften*, those students' associations which
Treitschke so graphically described. We now know, however,
that their effective management was in the hands of clandestine
groups affiliated in a variety of ways to foreign revolutionaries
and chiefly to the Follen group of French *Carbonari*. In its early
days the German youth movement was more or less inoffensive.
In societies devoted to physical training, a hysterical type of
patriotism was preached, there was a cult of the 'tough guy', a
supposedly German (!) attitude to life, and they encouraged a
hatred of France. Jahn, father of the *gymnasts*, proposed that a
'no man's land' be established between France and Germany to
be inhabited exclusively by bears and aurochs. He it was, also,
who with tragic naïveté declared: 'the man who allows his
daughter to learn French might just as well introduce her to
prostitution'. In the bosom of the *Burschenschaften* a kind of
abstract Teutomania was encouraged: patriotism was combined
with a deep religious sentiment and pure idealism with boundless
presumption.[1]

But soon, through the influence of its underground leaders,
the movement assumed a frankly revolutionary character and
came to a head with the murder of Kotzebue. The victim, author
of a number of harmless comedies, had committed the unpardonable crime of disagreeing with the agitator Oken, and had
supplied the Tsar with criticism of contemporary literature for
which the Russian autocrat was prepared to pay. Sand, the
assassin, who considered himself justified in killing because
Kotzebue 'wished to wipe out the divine spark in him', was
venerated as a martyr. Follen advised his friends to 'set fire to

---

1. This is the opinion of Treitschke, historian-patriot and implacable enemy of
Metternich. It coincides exactly with Metternich's own: 'We can define the disease
of our time', said the Chancellor, 'with the one word *presumption*, a natural effect of
the rapid progress of the human spirit in so many fields. . . . Religion, morality,
legislation, economics, politics, administration, are offering rich benefits to all
mankind. But science appears to be intuitive and experience has no value for the
presumptuous man; while faith to him means nothing: he is prepared to substitute
some kind of private conviction, he scorns alike both study and self-examination.'

the four corners of Mannheim', the town where Sand was imprisoned. He was condemned to death. On the scaffold, his executioner kneeling before him implored his pardon. Pieces of the scaffold itself were used to build a pavilion at Heidelberg where students were in future to hold their secret meetings. Shortly after, anti-semitic demonstrations broke out at Frankfort and in other cities of the south.[1]

In the meanwhile, secret societies were springing up all over Europe: the sect known as Mizraim in Switzerland, the society of 'Free brothers' in Poland, the 'Union for the public good' in Russia. The extent of their connection with the main movement is not easy to determine; in Russia, there was probably none. But all these bodies were inspired by the same basic principles. These young men had generally started by becoming freemasons, but were no longer satisfied with that pursuit of purely ethical values which they learnt in the lodges. Militant politics were more to their liking: humble exiles or members of great families, down-at-heel pamphleteers or officers of the Tsar's Imperial Guard, one and all were dedicated to a relentless battle with tyranny wherever it might raise its ugly head. 'In France,' said the caustic Rostopchine, 'shoemakers have always wished to become princes, but with us, in Russia, all the princes now wish to become shoemakers.'

Metternich was quite convinced that all these organisations belonged to one bloc and that they alone were responsible for the troubles in Europe. 'This simultaneous outburst of revolution all over the place, its activities always taking the same forms, its members speaking the same language, the fact that a similar type of pretext is always involved, all these betray but too clearly a common source.' He saw himself faced with 'a vast anti-social conspiracy'. (A. Lebzeltern, December 20th, 1824.) He saw in all this a connection with Weisshaupt's 'illuminist' doctrines (which had never been stamped out) and with freemasonry. 'The objects pursued by the early freemasons were by no means repre-

---

1. *Quellen und Darstellungen zur geschichte der Burschenschaft und der deutschen Einheits bewegung.* Nesta H. Webster: *World Revolution. The Plot Against Civilisation*, London 1922.

hensible', he said—thinking perhaps about the masonic activities of his own father. 'But they are now split up into a variety of sects and these offer ever-ready media for conspiring against religion and the state. Freemasonry today is being used by agitators as a means of increasing their numbers and furthering their intrigues.' (February 4th, 1825.)

The *Carbonari* seemed to him to be the link between all other subversive elements. 'The higher ranks of the association have categorically announced their objective, their procedure is simple and direct, free from all the esoteric mumbo-jumbo of the masons. This disease is eating at the very vitals of society, in the persons of its noblest members; it has been widely spread and the roots go deep.'[1]

From what we know of the *Carbonari*, Metternich to a certain extent was undoubtedly right. Unfortunately he confused the symptoms with the cause of the malady. In confining his attacks to this one society, he was tilting against windmills.[2] 'He interpreted as mere plotting something that was a general *malaise*, a product of the century, the struggle of an old against a new social order, the fight of outworn and decrepit institutions against the energy of a rising generation.'[3]

The assassination of Kotzebue gave the Chancellor an opportunity for intervention in German affairs and he took action against the 'pseudo-patriots'. A convinced 'European', *habitué* of the Court of the Tuileries, indebted to the Rothschilds, a man with essentially aristocratic tastes, Metternich felt nothing but scorn for the fanatics who boasted their barbarous inflexibility, organised pogroms and burnt in the market-place the works of any author who happened to displease them. It shouldn't be difficult to get the better of such as these. An emergency congress of German statesmen called at Carlsbad would decide what measures were necessary.[4]

Events for a time seemed to confirm his opinion. For no sooner

1. To the Tsar Alexander, from Verona (undated).
2. Gordon to Castlereagh, July 12th, 1819 (Archives of the Foreign Office, Austrian dossier).
3. Chateaubriand: *Mémoires d'outre-tombe*.
4. Dufour de Pradt: *Le congrès de Karlsbad*.

was a Press censorship established, a few professors sacked, and the *Burschenschaften* dissolved, than *Carbonarism* as if by magic disappeared from German life: indeed, the court of inquiry set up to look into a plot against the German Confederation found nothing to do.

Two or three generations later, a Treitschke could say that never since the days of Charles-Quint and Wallenstein had the House of Austria laid so heavy a hand on the German nation. But this does not appear to have been the opinion of Metternich's contemporaries by whom he was greeted as the saviour of Germany. 'Since I was lucky enough to get rid of the *Carbonari*,' he wrote, 'people seem to think that it is enough for me to appear for everything they dislike to be disposed of.' 'From all sides people turn to me, some are just good people and want help; some are weak but get stronger before they leave me; some are just bad and are merely trying to find out what's afoot.' 'Wherever I stop for a moment, a crowd gathers round me . . . everywhere I find a flock of the faithful who are waiting for their shepherd, and I cannot leave them—I should regret it later—without the spiritual comfort they crave.'

And two years after, when he was staying on the banks of the Rhine, at Johannisberg: 'All Frankfort and people from the surrounding towns came rushing towards me. One thing is certain: if Austria—and I permit myself to add Austria's Chancellor—are not well thought of and respected in Germany (as we are constantly being assured by the *Débats* and the *Constitutionnel*), then the Germans are past-masters at hiding their game!'

After that came the turn of the Italian *Carbonari*. The revolt at Naples this time was the pretext for a general and systematic repression. Here too, the first steps proved disconcertingly easy. General Frimont's sixty thousand troops seized Naples on the 24th March, 1821, and brought back with them the old autocratic ruler and his old ministers. Over a thousand 'Good Cousins' were tried and condemned to a wide variety of penalties. In Piedmont, the army of the provisional government set up by the *Carbonari* was completely wiped out by General Bubna. The new King, Charles-Felix, made a triumphal entry into Turin and all civil servants and members of the army were forbidden to belong to secret societies. The Pope launched a bull of excommunication against the *Carbonari, Ecclesiam Jesu Christo,* and the prisons of the Papal States began to fill with thousands of prisoners. In the Austrian provinces, disciples of the fellowship were under pain of death. In a ceaseless round-up the Austrian police achieved results surpassing all expectation. At Milan, the Frenchman, Alexandre Andryane, emissary of the *Grand Firmament de l'Adelphie,* was arrested: he confessed that his association, whose chief Synod sat at Geneva, was preparing to wipe out all European monarchies and replace them with governments of a democratic, republican type.

Other conspirators were soon tracked down (still by the Austrian authorities) at Parma, at Modena and elsewhere . . . the writer, Silvio Pellico, was brought to trial at Vienna with a dozen or so of his collaborators. At Milan, the tribunal condemned some twenty-five people to death, including Andryane and Count Confalonieri. The organisation now seemed completely crushed. Metternich was jubilant: 'In the last analysis, the people of the peninsula are no more inclined than anyone else to become the instruments of their own destruction. As I advance along the path that I chose long ago, new factors come to light, and I see as clearly what seemed dark before as if all the sun's rays were beating down. I made a point of bringing Confalonieri to Vienna. . . . I shall make good use of him and you may hear some funny things about what Russia was up to at Turin just before the revolt in Piedmont broke out.'

At this critical moment of his career, the Minister, covered with decorations, facing his handcuffed victim, thought that he held the strings of the conspiracy at last. It never struck him that he was playing the part of a police agent, he did not even see himself as an instrument of reaction. His activities seemed to him to come entirely within the legitimate scope of diplomacy. He believed himself to be acting solely in behalf of international order and peace. If only Confalonieri could be induced to squeal —the whole thing could be cleared up in a jiffy. A few more arrests in other countries and there would be an end of red revolution, of 'Jacobinism', in Europe. The longed-for reign of order, of stability, might at last be re-installed.

But Confalonieri did not talk—and, in fact, what could he have said?

For *Carbonarism*, merely another aspect of the universal spirit of revolution, was a hydra with a thousand heads; as soon as you cut off one, another would pop up. No sooner was calm restored in Germany and Italy than the Greeks began to clamour for independence, or the officers of the Russian Imperial Guard would incite their troops to revolt against the Tsar with cries of: 'Long live the Emperor Constantine and his wife, the Constitution.' In short, an international conspiracy, continuous and all over the place.[1]

But the root of the trouble was not yet destroyed; the elusive 'revolutionary centre' of it was domiciled in Paris....

For in spite of his friendliness with the ministers of the Restoration, in spite of a genuine mutual understanding, Metternich for some years now had watched with growing apprehension the evolution of affairs in France. 'Everything in that country is unexpected', he wrote in 1823; 'even what on the surface appears most reasonable is often the reverse in fact.... One has never since the world began seen business conducted as it is in France. One might almost feel about that country that its inhabitants were seeking some esoteric method of suicide; they invite the chariot to advance, but at the same time direct it towards a precipice.' And in 1828: 'Since the world began, there has been no instance of a country where intelligence was so general being unable to find a quorum of men fit to govern, as in France, today.'

The day after the assassination of the Duc de Berry, he wrote

1. 'This affair of December 26th (called the *Decembrist* uprising) does not appear to us an isolated issue', wrote the Chancellor. 'All Europe is sick of the same disease. ...We shall learn that the secret societies have been mainly responsible and that they have managed to hide under the cloak of freemasonry. ... And if I use here the word *carbonarisme*, I am only utilising for convenience a term generally in use to designate the thing concerned. We are not misled, we who have had to do with so many of these small political sects, we who have forced our way into so many of their lairs, we are not misled, I say, into giving any one of them more importance than another.' (Vienna, Secret Archives.) See also C. de Grünwald: 'L'Autriche et le Décembrisme', in the journal, *Monde Slave*, February, 1938.

to Marshal Marmont: 'France is very sick, that beautiful country which yet seems to possess within herself so many of the means of salvation.... All that has happened in France was due to happen; one cannot indulge in gross errors with impunity. But evils which have reached such a pitch as is now apparent in your country cannot fail to inspire alarm. To what a pass must you have come for a Lafayette to dare to repeat from the Tribune (and still remain a free man), theses which have been discredited by twenty years of ensuing desolation! And how the debates between June 3rd and 10th in the Chamber re-echoed all the chimera we have learnt to associate with the *Constituante*, all the criminal absurdities of the *Convention*! But I still have hope in the immense majority of the nation, in that majority conscious of its interests old or new, but of tangible not abstract interests. France will not again be overthrown because she has already had that experience and knows the results. I must, however, admit that only a strong will (very strong and thus both enlightened and imperturbable) could, in my opinion, save you from a host of minor upheavals.'[1]

But hadn't France already got that 'strong and imperturbable' government in the person of Polignac? Metternich almost thought so. He wrote to his ambassador, Apponyi: 'Since your last interview with Prince Polignac, I hold more than just vague hopes for France. It is certainly on the firm foundation of the Charter that the government must rest; that is the position they must defend and the one which strikes me as impregnable.'

When Polignac announced his famous measures against the liberty of the Press, the Chancellor expressed his best wishes for the complete success of that important enterprise—'the most direct thrust at liberalism since the congress of Carlsbad'. 'The memorandum to the King, signed by all his ministers unanimously, is a document remarkable for its frankness and as such should make a profound impression on all who still cling to reason.'[2] 'The measures decided and made known to the public

1. This letter was published in a German translation by M. Joachim Kuhn in *l'Oesterreichische Rundschau*, February 15th, 1918. The French original is in the Bibliothèque Nationale. (Estate of the late Lefebvre.)

2. Autograph letter to Count Apponyi, August 2nd, 1830. (Vienna, Secret Archives.)

by the *Ordonnances Royales* are now completed . . . and ought, by all normal calculations, to prove very beneficial, unless some storm arise at the moment of putting them into effect. To calculate probabilities in France seems to me very difficult, and although I am not lacking that confidence which every government has a right to demand, yet still I wonder whether the Minister, with the best intentions, has fully examined his capacity for putting all this into effect.' 'The month of August', he wrote in a report to his Emperor dated July 31st, 1830, 'will be a landmark in history. Whatever happens one will be able to apply: *novus ab integro nascitur ordo.*'

While Metternich was writing these words from his holiday resort of Koenigswart, a 'new order' had indeed already been born at Paris: the elder branch of the Bourbons had been overthrown by the revolution.[1]

It was only on the 4th August, late in the evening, that he received the news: the Rothschilds sent *via* Frankfort a detailed description of the revolt of the masses.[2]

The communication fell from the Chancellor's hands. A footman saw his head collapse upon his desk. Had he fainted, or had a fit? They ran for the doctor, who rushed to the Prince's aid, but was surprised to find his pulse completely normal! Metternich looked thoughtfully into his eyes and said: 'My whole life's work has been destroyed.' A sentimental scene, appropriately dramatic,

1. This letter from Paris, not signed, dated July 31st has been preserved in the Secret Archives of Vienna. Here are some extracts: 'As soon as the Cabinet, wishing to control public feeling which had so far only manifested in the form of shouting and small groups of demonstrators, began to charge crowds and to fire upon them, the momentum became general; the whole population rose as one man and Paris suddenly became a vast battlefield. . . . The Cabinet had only counted upon a weak opposition and in the circumstances all their measures for crushing out the rising were completely useless. No armed force was capable of dealing with a whole population enraged at being threatened with massacre by the order of their King. From first to last the inhabitants of Paris, including women and children, all rushed into the fray; in a few hours, pavements were torn up and barricades erected in the streets. . . . After two days, no more troops were left in the capital. There were no attacks on property, no pillage. . . . During those two days, one has seen the common people giving a most striking proof of disinterested exaltation. Their élan was *unanimous*. . . . Any return of the Bourbons would seem difficult, for if we are to judge by public opinion in Paris and the surrounding counties, the nation is ready to be chopped to pieces rather than submit again to their domination.'
2. Dr Jäger's *Mémoires*.

ensued. Princess Mélanie had also arrived in haste and, throwing herself at her husband's feet, began to kiss his hand.[1] An hour later, Metternich was already writing a report to his sovereign: 'A revolution of the worst kind has triumphed. This fact proves two truths: first, that the (French) Cabinet was mistaken in the means they took to achieve their ends; and secondly, that I was right when more than two years ago I warned them of the dangers they ran. Unfortunately I was crying in the desert.'

But Metternich quickly recovered his sang-froid and began to act.

In his opinion, the alliance of 1813 (reinforced by certain later transactions) was still operative.

'The real, and the last, anchor of hope for Europe lies in an understanding between the great powers based on a conservative outlook. And if France fails us, going over to the side of the *Carbonari*, if England can no longer be considered a dependable ally, there only remains one course: to reinforce the ties now existing between Austria, Russia and Prussia, thus forming a new breakwater against the onrush of revolution.' During the recent interview at Teplitz, Metternich had found Frederick-William III in full agreement with himself 'on all counts'. There only remained to secure the adhesion of Russia.

By a curious coincidence, Count Nesselrode, the Russian Foreign Minister, was also drinking the waters at Carlsbad. Metternich had just had a long discussion with him about the attitude of the Russian Cabinet to foreign affairs. 'I shall bring Count Nesselrode round to my point of view', he wrote to Francis II after that interview. 'This, however, is little more than a negative gain; the positive advantage will be furnished by necessity.' And now the July revolution had created that necessity: without a moment's delay, Metternich would seek the basis for an *entente* between Austria and Russia, 'with a view to getting unanimity into both our intentions and our acts'.[2]

Immediately such a basis of *entente* was found; the Carlsbad 'scrap of paper', scribbled by Metternich's own hand, supplied

1. Dr Jäger's *Mémoires*.
2. Metternich to Francis I, August 5th, 1830.

the formula for the new foreign policy. This rough draft of a convention stipulated that there should be no interference in the domestic affairs and upheavals of France, but that the French government would not be allowed to extend its activities beyond its borders, not allowed to menace the material interests of Europe 'as they are now guaranteed by general usage', nor to threaten the domestic peace of any other European state.

With this assurance in hand, Metternich could afford to wait with comparative calm for the repercussion of events in Paris, could afford to offer Austria's hospitality to the exiled King of France and to count upon certain police measures to prevent the spread of disaffection to Austrian territory: travellers would be forbidden passports; foreigners living in Austria, and especially those who came originally from Paris, would be subject to the strictest supervision. Otherwise, he affected a philosophic detachment.

'The eye of an impartial and enlightened observer today looks out on a whole world in ruins.' 'The men responsible for the present state of affairs are very guilty . . . passions are bad guides', he wrote, thinking of his old enemies, the *Carbonari*. 'To get a right perspective on the influences of the last fifteen years, to trace the part of prejudice, of false theory and false practice, of impudence on the one side and craven fear on the other, seems to me impossible today. History alone can tell. . . .' (August 24th, 1830.)[1] 'My innermost conviction, as a matter of fact, is that our old Europe has now reached the beginning of the end. Determined to perish with her, I shall know how to do my duty, and the thought that word conveys is not mine alone, it is also that of our Emperor. The new Europe is not yet under way; before we come to the end, there will be chaos.'

He refused above all to believe that a government like that of Louise-Philippe, supported by Lafayette, the great conspirator, could last for any length of time. 'Nothing of the existing arrangement in France could possibly last; it is all unstable, built upon the sand.' 'All the men in authority belong to the extreme Left: there isn't a single respectable man among them.'

1. Vienna, Secret Archives.

217

P

'King Louis-Philippe, from the moment of his accession, has been placed in an untenable position, for the basis on which his authority rests is nothing but a farrago of erroneous theories.' 'Through weakness, fear and personal inclination, King Louis-Philippe placed himself at the head of the revolution ... it would only require one spark to plunge France into civil war. May God bring it about; it would be a just punishment.'[1]

Behind this 'phantom government', Metternich only saw anarchy rampant. The scene of reconciliation between Louis-Philippe and Lafayette (recognised leader of world revolution) particularly incensed him. 'A kiss is a fragile gesture to snuff out the memory of a republic, but do you think you will be able to infuse your future kisses with a similar potency?'

And when General Béliard, as emissary from the French King, came to Vienna to announce that the country was no longer the ancient France and must now be governed by quite different methods, Metternich answered in his most peremptory tone: 'Austria will never suffer any encroachment on the part of a government which is the outcome of revolution. That government will find us, and all Europe, wherever it tries to spread its propaganda.'

An attitude frankly hostile, but also based on the defensive. To keep peace in Europe—that was the supreme mission of the Viennese Cabinet. Austria was prepared to await events and keep her powder dry. The Emperor Francis would note the accession of Louis-Philippe to the throne: diplomatic relations with France would only have suffered a short interruption and the clamour for war which had arisen in certain ultra-reactionary Austro-German circles was quickly repressed.[2] Furthermore, Austria would remain neutral with regard to revolutionary upheavals then taking place in Belgium and Poland.

Metternich was reserving his strength for a tussle with Italy since it was there that the movements of the *Carbonari* had their

1. Report to the Emperor Francis, 3–4th October. (Vienna, Secret Archives.)
2. 'One could not be more ill-advised than to rush into war against France', Metternich wrote. 'Those German Princes who desire this are wrong and are producing yet one more proof of how unfit they are to guide the world.' (To Schomburg, Austrian ambassador to Stuttgart, October 24th, 1831.)

origin, there that the interests of Austria were directly involved.

The Chancellor had realised the danger that threatened him in the peninsula when he received the news of the July revolution. 'Italy must be carefully watched,' he wrote to Francis I in his first report of August 5th; 'it is there that the revolutionaries will certainly make their supreme effort.' As soon as he got back to Vienna from Koenigswart he turned his attention to this question.[1]

The insurrections that broke out first at Modena and then at Parma, and spread to the Papal states, found Metternich fully prepared. He wrote to the Emperor on the eve of these uprisings: 'a few Austrian battalions will be enough to reduce them to order', and his anticipation was fully justified.

It was enough for General Frimont to put his troops into action and the insurrection immediately collapsed. 'This revolution is more powerful in words than in deeds', the Chancellor declared.

And didn't the poor show of resistance offered furnish new proof of the absence of any real popular movement in Italy? Wasn't it, rather, certain esoteric circles who had engineered the plot? It was foreign intervention that had caused the uprising—that was Metternich's absolute conviction. 'The French are at the bottom of this, it was instigated by France.... There is nothing Italian about all this, the pattern is absolutely French.'

'If King Louis-Philippe feels unable to live by the side of the Duke of Leuchtenberg[2] as King of the Belgians, our august Master, the Emperor, I assure you is no more disposed to reign next door to a revolutionary Italy', wrote Metternich to his representative at Paris.[3]

Was this attitude acceptable to France? Sébastiani, the foreign minister, was categorically hostile to the behaviour of Austria in Italy. He admitted, at a pinch, that Austria might be justified in interfering at Parma, Modena and Ferrare, in defence of their

---

1. Report of the Cabinet deliberations of August 19th and 29th, 1830. (Vienna, Secret Archives.) See also the manuscript reports from Metternich to the Emperor under date of January 24th, 1831. (Vienna, Secret Archives.)

2. Son of Eugène de Beauharnais, who had been suggested for the throne of Belgium.

3. Metternich to Apponyi, January 18th and February 15th, 1831. (Vienna, Secret Archives.)

reigning princes who happened to be of the House of Habsburg, but he made no secret of the fact that any attempt to send Austrian troops into the Papal states might cause serious trouble between Austria and France. 'We cannot accept any such distinction', said Metternich. 'It is certainly not on a basis of family ties between princes, nor on any other such human and plausible consideration that our attitude is based, but solely on the indispensable requirement of keeping revolution down in Italy.'[1]

'Reduced to its own devices the *Carbonari* movement can, if necessary, be treated as negligible. Sustained by France, on the other hand, it becomes a danger for the world. If Louis-Philippe's government cannot be made to listen to reason, we must find some means of forcing them.'[2]

A young prince, twenty years old, recently promoted to the grade of lieutenant-colonel, was then living in Vienna and waiting impatiently to get a battalion under his command. He was intelligent, astute and precocious. He surprised everyone by the sharp decision of his language; graceful but serious, he moved at times almost with solemnity. In spite of a striking resemblance to his ancestor, Maria Theresa, he stood out from other members of the Imperial family as a being of superior essence. He was 'that man's son', child of Napoleon and Marie-Louise, sole scion of a marriage which Metternich had been used to consider the *chef d'œuvre* of his diplomatic achievement.

1. Metternich to Apponyi, March 12th, 1831. (Vienna, Secret Archives.) In this same despatch, in connection with the principle of intervention, the Chancellor advances some curious considerations which have lost none of their actuality today. Sébastiani had suggested repeating energetic protests to the Holy See with a view to forcing the Pope to certain domestic reforms along liberal lines: 'There is a radical difference between French and Austrian anti-interventionist notions. The first rejects all general political or diplomatic intervention but has no qualms about interfering in the purely domestic legislative and administrative concerns of other states. The opposing opinion admits intervention in matters and situations of general political significance (significant to the world outside) but declaims absolutely any right to interfere in the purely domestic affairs of an independent state. Our Court professes the second opinion and that must direct our policy. Our Emperor claims the absolute right to go to the aid of any legally established power which has been threatened either by invasion or by internal upheaval, but he would never admit his right to attempt to impose upon that power any particular method of legislation or administration.'

2. See Vicomte de Guichen, *La révolution de 1830 et l'Europe*; Vidal: *Louis-Philippe, Metternich et la révolution italienne*.

The day after the wedding of the Emperor of the French, on the occasion of the great banquet at the Tuileries, Metternich, just arrived in Paris, raised his glass to drink a toast to the King of Rome.[1] It was he, the Austrian minister, who first recognised the right of this heir of the Bonapartes to a title which for centuries had belonged to the House of Habsburg. But now there was no more King of Rome; the young man was called Duke of Reichstadt. 'The Habsburg Eagle has many eaglets,' he was told, 'and you are one of them, that's all!'

For centuries the addicts of romance have deplored the tragic destiny of the captive eaglet, *l'Aiglon*. A poetic legend has grown up around his life and the circumstances of his death. 'It is not always legend that lies,' wrote Edmond Rostand, 'a dream can often be much less deceptive than a document.' And a conscientious historian might even subscribe to this if only a dream were in fact involved, if that dream did not also imply a calumny.

Metternich—brutal persecutor of the Eaglet! A rich tapestry has been woven around this apparently inexhaustible theme! It was Metternich, we are told, who deprived him of his mother's love by throwing Marie-Louise into the arms of Neipperg; who turned him over to the care of ignorant professors, who persistently dragged him down, humiliated him, and finally was the cause of the young man's death by pushing him into debauchery and exposing him to the rigours of a military service incompatible with his fragile constitution. So many lies—and provably false by all the evidence of history—so many lies that have been docilely accepted by the crowds.[2]

Metternich—whatever might have been said to the contrary—

---

1. Barante: *Souvenirs*, Vol. I, page 318.
2. A whole book might be devoted to proving how little justified these assertions are. But the public would not read it: they prefer melodrama. And in any case, the *dossier* of this business has been fully established: one can find all the information one needs in the well-known works of Wertheimer, Welchinger, Bibl, Bourgoing, Octave Aubry. But strange to say, a majority of these eminent historians have most disconcertingly accepted the popular story. One is amazed to read from the pen of so conscientious a writer, for instance, as Baron de Bourgoing, the following remark: 'The Chancellor never lost an opportunity of visiting upon the son that relentless hatred which he had vowed against the father', whereas all the evidence the author then adduces (and it is very full) appears to us to prove the opposite contention.

had not the slightest reason to hate Napoleon's son, since he never, in point of fact, had hated the father. He had not much reason to love him either. As the instigator of Napoleon's second marriage, he must have seen in the person of that semi-captive son a living reproach. The Duke of Reichstadt was 'the cancer on his political system'. His very presence was an unpleasant reminder for the Chancellor: reminder of irresponsible actions in the past, of imprudence, failure and disillusion. And his presence was also a source of endless worry to the Austrian government, since it perennially revived suspicion among all those statesmen who had formerly fought the Napoleonic dictatorship, and who were by no means sanguine about the heir now fallen from his high estate.

During those fifteen years spent by the young prince at his grandfather's Court, Metternich had actually encountered him five times; no more. He was satisfied to keep an eye on him from a distance and to conduct interminable discussions with all the European Cabinets about him.

And if Marie-Louise had forgotten her maternal duties in the arms of her one-eyed lover, Metternich had nothing whatever to do with it. Neipperg's nomination had been made without his knowledge (in fact during his absence) and had been entirely due to the recommendation of Schwarzenberg.[1] The fact that Napoleon's son had been deprived of the duchies of Parma and Plaisance was solely due to Talleyrand and Louis XVIII, upheld by England and Spain.

But of all the accusations against Metternich, the one relating to the Duke of Reichstadt's education is certainly the most absurd. The Eaglet enjoyed the best professors that Vienna had to offer. His guardian-tutor, Count Dietrichstein, was one of the most cultured men in Austria: 'a highly intellectual aristocrat, agreeable patron of the arts, descerning bibliophile, and finally a musician of renown who acquired a lasting reputation as the benefactor of Beethoven'. Among other tutors, there were: Captain Forest, 'a good fellow, worthy and cultured', and Colin,

---

1. Six months later, Neipperg was asking Metternich to appoint him Austrian ambassador to Stockholm and the Chancellor was promising his support.

'a writer with a high moral purpose'; the young Duke considered him not only as a teacher, but as a very dear friend into the bargain. And finally, there was Obenaus, so much maligned by Rostand, a professional pedagogue who 'exercised his function with integrity and marked ability'. The last-named had already educated the heir to the Austrian throne and other members of the Austrian Imperial family.[1]

So if the young prince, uprooted from his native soil, consumed his soul in idleness, devoured by ambition and foreboding, if the first germs of a relentless malady were beginning to eat into his already seedy frame, what better reason can we give than an inexorable and tragic destiny?[2]

The Gordian knot had already been tied when France and the coalition deposed Napoleon and refused to accept the Empress Marie-Louise as Regent.

'Since Madame the Archduchess is now separated from her husband, she comes exclusively within the jurisdiction of her father', was the Emperor Francis' decision communicated by Stadion to Metternich. And naturally, the grandson also 'belonged' to him!

In these circumstances, what was the unfortunate Minister of Court and State to do?

He stood for the interests of his country, not only towards the young Duke himself, but towards his grandfather and guardian. He was obliged to listen to the complaints of foreign statesmen, the recriminations of Castlereagh, of Richelieu; he was obliged to convey all this to his sovereign and obliged to be continually alert lest the presence of Napoleon's son on Austrian soil should become a cause of international complications. He was responsible for the young Prince's safety. He had to guard against any attempt to kidnap the Eaglet and at the same time to calm the anxieties of all those who believed in a plot by Austria to restore Napoleon II

1. All the information given here about these tutors has been taken from the writings of Bibl himself, Prince Metternich's chief accuser in this connection.

2. It is scarcely necessary to say that women were not the cause of the Duke of Reichstadt's malady, and that he never even spoke to Fanny Elssler. The unimpeachable witness of Prokesch and of Fanny Elssler herself are there to confirm it.

to his father's throne.¹ Thus the minor annoyances to which the Prince was subject (the removal of all those who had connection with France from his surrounding, an increasingly strict supervision, etc.) were the outcome of foreign insistence; Metternich was a mere intermediary. But it was natural that public opinion—in Bonapartist circles in France and elsewhere—should regard Metternich as the Grand Inquisitor. Didn't the young Duke himself believe that it was to Metternich he owed his sorry fate? Wasn't he convinced that the Chancellor's opposition alone stood between him and the throne of France?

Chiefly concerned with preserving peace in Europe, Metternich did, in fact, show hostility to any idea of a Napoleonic restoration. And yet he knew very well—Gentz has stated this repeatedly—that nothing could have been more to the advantage of Austria than the reign of the Duke of Reichstadt.² But he also knew that the mere name of the Eaglet was enough to cause 'alarm and terror to most of the Cabinets of Europe', that it 'distressed and alarmed the most reasonable of statesmen'. He had once, to the extreme limits of his capacity, attempted to save the Napoleonic dynasty, but in 1815 had declared categorically: 'We have finished for ever with Napoleon, and with his whole race.' And in 1829, again, a discussion had taken place in the presence of Countess Molly Zichy and Princess Grassalkowitch about the chances of nominating the Duke of Reichstadt to be King of Poland. Metternich is then reported to have exclaimed: 'The Bonapartes have once for all been excluded from all thrones.'

But now suddenly his attitude changed. To please the Bour-

1. On January 11th, 1829, Apponyi wrote to Metternich: 'Popular interest in the Duke in France is not surprising. But it is difficult to understand how the government itself, and the Court in particular, can be subject to such anxiety not only about the mere existence of Napoleon's son but also about the fact that he lives at the Austrian Court and the possible plans that Austria might nurse in this connection in the event of a break with France.' And simultaneously Savary told Apponyi that there existed in Paris among a certain set of people a categorical project to get rid of the Duke; they used the slogan: 'This branch must be lopped off.'

2. 'When one thinks', wrote Gentz, on July 19th, 1815, 'when one thinks of the heights to which Austria might aspire if she openly espoused the cause of Napoleon's son! We are really dumbfounded, and our descendants will be so even more that that plan was not adopted since the chances of success were not only probable but pretty well certain.'

bons, to preserve peace in Europe, he had been content to place himself in an invidious position, to appear as the 'oppressor of an innocent young man'. But if Louis-Philippe, at the best of times an unorthodox representative of the Bourbon dynasty, were now to become the patron of world revolution and the trouble-maker of Europe, he would have to think again. There would no longer be any reason to persist in his old line of conduct.

On January 18th Metternich wrote to persons in Paris, through the intermediary of his ambassador, a preliminary warning. 'Has nobody in Paris ever thought of being grateful to us for our extreme tact in the matter of Napoleon II? We are really deserving of some praise in this matter. . . . Forgive these whimsies, but they might in fact acquire some practical import were Louis Philippe to attempt to play the role of conquering dictator or that of chief instigator of revolutionary propaganda. For should we find ourselves with our backs to the wall, I assure you we are no angels, and we should certainly not neglect to play all our trump cards.'

A month later, he resorted to more explicit language; he wrote in his most impressive style to Count Apponyi: 'The essential character of our own government makes us the natural *confidante* of the legitimists everywhere; the family relationship existing between our Imperial House and the late Napoleon have brought us the confidences of adherents of the old French Empire. Napoleon's son lives at Vienna; his father's followers, when casting their eyes in his direction, will very naturally look also in the direction of his grandfather! . . . Our enemy is anarchy, our friends are those who oppose it. And should we be reduced to a choice of evils (among those which anarchy entails), we shall be obliged to plump for the one which least threatens our own existence, and the means to that end *we now hold in our hands*.[1] The threat was clear: Louis-Philippe would have to choose

1. And Herr von Maltzahn, Prussian ambassador to Vienna, wrote virtually the same to his own government on February 15th, 1830: 'If the French government were to support the revolutionaries in Italy, the Austrian government would feel justified in using all the resources of a strong position against the obviously weak one of King Louis-Philippe, going even to the extremity of using a means which it has to hand and setting up the Duke in opposition.'

between the *Carbonari* and the claim of an Austrian Archduke to the throne of France; in the words of a French poet 'of an Archduke whose grandfather was the 18 *Brumaire* and whose grandmother was the French Revolution', who could in fact 'go one better' than the *Carbonari*.

Of all the political machinations of Metternich, none can vie with this in audacity and machiavellism. We can hardly believe that he ever considered seriously the chances of Napoleon II as candidate for the throne of France. He had always believed that the Bonapartist party in France was faced with 'resources by which it was certainly outnumbered'. At the end of August 1830, he had even had a long conversation with the Duke of Reichstadt to this effect.[1] He said to Prokesch: 'In six months' time, the Duke would be surrounded and overwhelmed by ambitions, demands, resentments, hatreds, conspiracy: he would find himself on the brink of catastrophe.... Bonapartism without Bonaparte is an absolutely mistaken notion, and a man of his genius is not easily come by.' Wasn't the Chancellor thinking rather of the throne of Italy? The Duke might well be made an instrument of Austrian policy to bring back peace and order to the peninsula: 'The Italian sovereign would thus not have been chosen by any political party or as the outcome of a popular uprising, but in full agreement with the powers, by an existing legitimate monarchy as in the case of the King of the Belgians and King of Greece.' (Bourgoing.)

But such conjectures are beside the point. The Duke was to die two years later, in the flower of youth, tuberculosis supplying a means of exit from the anguish inherent in his position. He attained neither the throne of France nor of Italy. He was even to await the Day of Judgment in a resting-place chosen for him by Metternich: in the Capuchin crypt where Francis I and Marie-Louise would eventually lie beside him. But the trick had worked,

1. This, it seems, was the only occasion when the two men had an opportunity to talk at some length. Metternich met the Duke in the ante-chamber of the Emperor's apartments and invited him to visit him. But the Eaglet had been evasive and suspicious and struck the Chancellor as 'play-acting'. No real contact had been established, no cordiality. Metternich spoke subsequently of the meeting 'as if he had had to swallow a very bitter pill'.

Louis-Philippe had bowed before the Bonapartist menace.[1]

Orders were given to the Prefect of Lyons to disarm two thousand *Carbonari* refugees in France. Lafayette's activities and those of his *Comité directeur* were submitted to strict supervision. In obedience to the royal command, Sébastiani, the foreign minister, developed a new political orientation and gave the cold shoulder to Italian insurgents. 'Shame and ignominy', an Italian poet was to cry to Louis-Philippe. 'You boasted that you would liberate the earth . . . and now you leave us to our tears and our distress.'[2]

On March 17th, 1831, Austrian troops entered Bologna and Ancona. The situation for a moment became tense. On March 20th the French ambassador to Vienna requested a *visa* for his horses and carriages then ready to start for Paris.[3] On April 2nd Metternich learnt by means of a letter from the Rothschilds that there was disagreement among the members of the French Cabinet as to the question of war or peace.[4] He did not move a hair; he knew that the issue was already closed. 'I do not propose to base my arguments on the fortunes of war', he wrote. 'That would be allowing too much to the insurgents; it would seem to anticipate further trouble where a puff of wind has been enough to blow away the miserable mirage of revolution. If France wants war she must make it, but she must also realise that in so doing she will jeopardise her whole political and social structure, including the throne of Louis-Philippe himself. That is where the solution to the problem really lies.'

A few days later, he was able to record that the revolution in Italy was over. 'It disappeared', he wrote to Apponyi, 'like smoke

1. At the same time Metternich was accused of poisoning the Duke of Reichstadt, but it is only fair to say that the same accusation was made against the French Cabinet who were immediately interested in suppressing a pretender to the throne.
2. Pietro Silva: *La monarchia di luglio e l'Italia, studio di storia diplomatica*, Torino, 1917.
3. Report from Metternich to the Emperor, March 20th, 1831. (Vienna, Secret Archives.)
4. 'Sébastiani was furious, like a mad bear; he told Pozzo: "I'm going to declare war on Austria." It was no good trying to make him see reason. I went to see Perrier who said: "I'm in no hurry; in the Cabinet I stand for peace".' Letter from James Rothschild to Solomon Rothschild, March 26th, 1831. (Vienna, Secret Archives.)

before the appropriate antidotes of nature. It was never anything but the work of a few seditious individuals, all previously compromised either as to their private or political records, the dregs of the population ... this revolution had no strength apart from the weakness of the governments against which it was directed.'[1]

Negotiations between France and Austria about the Italian question were to continue for many years: proposals and counter-proposals were rife, and the Austrian troops later evacuated Bologna and Ancona, returning to the latter as soon as the French took it upon themselves to occupy the town. But these were minor skirmishes and of secondary interest. Metternich had won. The *coup de grâce* was given to the *Carbonari* when the Tsar and King of Prussia concluded with Francis I and Metternich at Münchengraetz a solemn treaty, according to which: 'every independent sovereign, either in respect of domestic difficulties or of dangers threatening from outside his borders, has a right to summon to his aid whichever other independent sovereign appears to him most suitable in the circumstances.' Following upon this a memorandum in no uncertain terms was sent to Paris to inform the French Cabinet that 'the three sovereigns are no longer prepared to accept the erroneous doctrine of non-intervention'. The document was also designed as a warning to Louis Philippe to put a stop to all subversive propaganda, thus 'eradicating the evil at its root'. France with her wings clipped, a triple alliance of Nordic powers solidly established: Metternich's dearest wish had been fulfilled.

It was only a generation later that a new initiate of the sect of the *Carbonari*, Napoleon III, Emperor of the French (*Coalheaver* with a crown on his head), was able to bring to fruition all the noble aspirations of the nationalists who had succumbed in 1831. But Metternich was already in his tomb. . . .

1. Vienna, Secret Archives.

# XI

# 'VIENNA, CAPUA[1] OF THE MIND'

'WHEN I think of that period now gone for ever, and of life in old Vienna', wrote an elderly Austrian diplomat long after 1848, 'I can hear the sound of two violins: Strauss and Lanner are playing. . . . I remember him, that Johann Strauss, small, thin, very dark, always hopping about, making innumerable dancing couples revolve to his magic fiddle . . . and Lanner, too, had his following: his music was compared with the wines of Bordeaux but that of Strauss with champagne. Lanner wrote for the delectation of the mind but Strauss to enliven our legs. Today such charming gaieties are no more; but they have made way for others more up-to-date, since whereas we frequently change their means of expression, fundamentally the joys and sorrows of the world remain the same.'[2]

But our memories are still lively: those two violins which sang for thirty-odd years on the banks of the beautiful blue Danube symbolise for us a period both delightful and unique, high peak of the Romantic movement, in that essentially romantic setting

1. Hannibal's army was accused of having become soft amidst the delights of Capua. 'S'endarmir dans les délices de Capoue', as used in French means: to waste precious time in frivolous amusements.—TRANS.
2. F. Johann von Andlau, *Erinnerungsblatter auisden Papieren eines Diplomaten* (Frankfurt, 1857). Johann Strauss, born at Vienna in 1854, at first belonged to the orchestra of the composer Lanner from which he separated in 1825. In 1835, he was made director of music for the balls of the Viennese Court. He died at Vienna in 1849 having published 250 musical compositions. 'The Blue Danube' was composed by his son, Johann Strauss the second, who in 1844, at the age of nineteen, founded his own orchestra.

229

of old Vienna. All the splendour and pageantry which we associate with entertainments during the Congress of 1815 was now a thing of the past. Foreign monarchs had all gone home, the clanking of arms had faded away in the distance. After the troubles of 1830, all danger of revolution had been warded off. Europe seemed to have regained her normal calm. The Viennese were now once more enjoying their own company, in their natural atmosphere, in that 'quiet and measured cheerfulness which is characteristic of the Germans'. (La Garde.)

It was a small place, when you come to think of it, that Vienna of 1830 and 1840, small if one compares it with our immense modern cities. Willebald Alexis, the German author, could walk round it in three-quarters of an hour, keeping close to the fortification walls 'which still looked warlike but had now taken on a peaceful function'. The old line of defence had been transformed into a magnificent terrace—a wall from fifty to seventy feet high—broken by a number of bastions, by clumps of trees and gardens, and it had become the scene of nothing more alarming than agreeable walks. Some of the most impressive houses of the town—of which Prince Metternich's was one—looked out onto this terrace: the famous *Bastey*.

Inside the fortifications (since destroyed and replaced by a kind of triumphal way known as the Ring boulevards) were the Imperial castle, the Cathedral of Saint Stephen, several palaces belonging to the higher nobility (these were all grouped round the Hofburg in half a dozen dark and narrow streets), innumerable other churches and chapels, small markets, courtyards and large spaces open to the public, with fountains in the *baroque* style. Outside the ramparts was a large moat now also turned into a carriage promenade, there was also a glacis planted with trees and intersected by very well-kept roads, and beyond lay the *faubourgs* (almost suburbs) where a new town was gradually growing up outside the walls, to become that great city of Vienna which we know today.

A happy and calm little people, remarkable for their diversity of type and costume, came and went in streets and boulevards and congregated in the afternoon in the famous *Prater*, there to admire the procession of fine horses with their elegant barouches and also to enjoy a dance in the open air. All the time and everywhere one heard strains of music, light and effervescent. Lanner and Strauss were conducting the merry round of the good people of Vienna. . . .

Yes, a small town, in the last analysis, this Viennese capital in which 'Society' consisted of some two to four hundred families. Of these, only about a quarter could claim to be *crême-de-la-crême*, of that inner circle to which belong princes of the blood and their families, a few important dignitaries of Court and State, a few leading figures of the High Command. Some ten or twelve families eclipsed all the rest by their fabulous wealth, their hereditary prestige and immediate fashionable glamour; their names were Liechtenstein, Schwarzenberg, Lobkowitz, Esterhazy, Czartorysky, Schoenburg, Dietrichstein, Clary, Furstenberg, and naturally Metternich. 'A supremely insolent aristocratic clique', said the Baronne du Montet, 'set inside a wider circle of nobility of at least equal—perhaps even higher—rank.'[1]

The men and women of this select little *coterie* imposed a species of petty tyranny on the rest of society which the latter seemed disposed to accept as one of the phenomena of nature. Certain less exalted mortals, young diplomats and civil servants, artists, the stage, and foreigners of distinction who met generally in the *salons* of the great bankers (Eskeles, Sina, Arnstein, Geymuller) seemed well satisfied with their own circles where one often found more wit and even more elegance. These showed little desire to get any nearer to the elect, to that cream which had so marked a tendency to turn sour.

But in their sumptuous palaces (now converted into embassies or office buildings), mansions which still dominate many a dingy, narrow street of Vienna today, these scions of the great nobility conducted their lives with a pomp and ostentation very little inferior to that of the Imperial Court itself.

Their wives, the Queens of Viennese drawing-rooms, were

1. See also Sealsfeld: *L'Autriche telle qu'elle est, on chroniques de certaines cours d'Allemagne par un témoin oculaire*, 1828; Mrs Trollope: *Vienna and the Viennese*; the Comte de Sainte-Aulaire: *Souvenirs*, edited by Marcel Thiébaut, 1927. (Published by Calmann-Lévy.)

mostly 'charming, gracious, witty, well-educated'. 'Some of them are really remarkable: in company with a few foreign visitors of both sexes, these are the bright particular stars of that circle to which we have the honour to belong.' (Gentz to Brickmann.) Impertinent and ever ready to make fun of those they considered intruders, when once admitted to their circle as an equal, one was received in a friendly, almost affectionate manner, completely devoid of anything affected or starchy. One cannot say as much for all the men: some of those displayed a really insufferable arrogance; others could talk of nothing but the theatre, hunting, shooting and racing.[1] But one also occasionally met some Mecaenas, an Esterhazy or a Lobkowitz, great amateurs of music; the Palffys, enlightened patrons of the theatre, or those Liechtensteins, Harrachs and Czernins, distinguished collectors—connoisseurs of pictures and other *objets d'art* whose galleries still call forth the enthusiastic admiration of visitors to Vienna today.

All these *grands seigneurs* cared nothing for politics as long as their privileges were safeguarded, their social precedence unquestioned; nothing else mattered. They were quite willing to delegate all matters of administration, law and finance to a host of second-rate officials, those 'counsellors' of Austrian ministerial departments who were never to be seen in the drawing-rooms of Society.[2] The nobility had always enjoyed the fruits of the established order and they saw no reason to suppose that things would not continue in the same vein for ever.

1. Mrs. Trollope has reported a characteristic incident related to a Court *cotillon* where the dancers were supposed to change partners. 'A débutante, admitted to the honour of dancing before the Empress but not to the esoteric glories of the *Crème*, in the innocence of her young heart approached a gentleman of the *Crème* and offered him her hand for the dance. He looked at her in dumbfounded surprise, kept his eyes on the floor and remained motionless as if turned to stone. The poor blushing child turned to another, but unfortunately she again had picked a ferocious isolationist, *crème-de-la-crème*. . . "Me?" he asked with a kind of convulsive snigger; and turning on his heel began to chat with a woman of his own set who happened to be standing near him. . .'

2. 'Thus we find in Austria', notes M. de Sainte-Aulaire, 'this singular and dangerous situation: all the principal agents of the sovereign authority were drawn from socially inferior classes. Power lay entirely in the hands of men whose *amour propre* was in danger of being wounded every day.' This was of course characteristic of all the old régimes; the same thing was to be found in Russia just before the 1917 revolution.

Prince Metternich now reigned over this aristocratic oligarchy as unquestioned dictator.

He had undertaken the most difficult task of his life when he attempted to sit Antoinette von Leykam 'among the princesses'! But for the lady who had succeeded her, the situation was somewhat different. For Mélanie, third Princess Metternich, assumed of her own right that most coveted position 'on the sofa' reserved for the elect. She was the daughter of Countess Molly von Zichy-Ferraris who for years had exercised unquestioned authority over the highest social circles in the Austrian capital. The mother, held in awe and considered a power by the *corps diplomatique*, was 'a very cultured great lady, true friend, loyal and discreet, a heart of gold, high-principled, sensitive and generous'. Always in Metternich's confidence, the old Countess had used her influence to advance the Chancellor's marriage with her daughter. The latter had inherited—from such ancestors as Turkish cavaliers and warlike Hungarian squires—a commanding presence, passionate nature and indomitable arrogance. Her head was classic in shape, slightly rounded, with magnificent eyes (perhaps a little prominent) of which one was green and the other blue. 'Princess Mélanie's hair is black as ebony,' said M. de Sainte-Aulaire, 'her expression bold, she is somewhat stout and moves brusquely. Pride and disdain often mingle on that handsome face, an expression perhaps more becoming to her than a smile. Animated in conversation, she gets carried away by an impetuosity which she is obviously unable to control, and having little desire to please, seems to enjoy snapping her fingers in the faces of all and sundry.' And Mrs Trollope gives much the same description: 'She is young and full of charm', notes the Englishwoman. 'Her humorous and animated expression is not entirely without a touch of disdain. But that one can readily pardon a pretty young woman, especially when she tempers it, as does this seductive creature, with a deliciously sweet smile that plays around her lips at the very moment of her most outrageous sallies.' 'A charming face', wrote Madame du Montet; 'she is unquestionably chaste, but her tempestuous nature is something of a trial to her husband, to all those with whom she lives and to

233

Q

herself. And yet she is certainly capable of kindness and has in many ways a good heart.'

The conversation of this young woman who had received 'the normal education of a Countess' (Dr Jäger) but certainly possessed a great deal of natural intelligence, was full of variety, original and assertive. 'It was more than a conversation', said Varnhagen, 'she put you through your paces, daring you to prove your point, forcing you to some confession. Frank and determined, she left you in no doubt as to her favour or disapproval, but either had to be accepted as a matter of luck; she was unpredictable.'

This spontaneity, this vivacity of language often assumed an assertiveness which came perilously near (if we may say so) to 'caddishness'. Delightful to her equals, she became, as was the custom of her set, insufferable in her dealings with those she was pleased to consider her inferiors.

During the Carnaval of 1835, the Viennese aristocracy had promised to attend a large public ball: Mélanie insisted that a square be roped off in the middle of the hall to separate the noble visitors from the *hoi-polloi*. 'And the bourgeois', says the chronicler, 'hadn't the moral courage to walk out.'

Invited to dine at the house of the banker, Baron Eskeles, she took part of her golden dinner service with her. Knives, spoons and forks were produced from the pocket of one of her attendant *beaux* and placed on the table before her; the financier was obliged to grin and bear this insult from the wife of the all-powerful Chancellor. But sometimes her impertinences brought caustic and well-deserved reproof. 'You must make a lot of money, Monsieur', she called out in her strident voice to Franz Liszt, who had just been playing, as only he could, in the Chancellor's drawing-room. 'No, Madame, I make music', replied the great musician with dignity. On another occasion, receiving Labus, a famous Milanese archæologist, at her house (the great man had permitted himself to come with bare hands), she instructed a footman to hand him a pair of white kid gloves on a silver salver. The old gentleman, reported Dr Jäger, witness of the scene, remained completely master of the situation, and calmly deposited on the tray three pieces of silver.

234

Such stories can be multiplied *ad infinitum*. On occasion her indiscretions came near to provoking something in the nature of diplomatic incidents, as, for instance, a remark she permitted herself to the French ambassador. Louis-Philippe's representative had admired her tiara: 'At least, it has not been stolen', she replied. This of course was an insult to the July monarchy: it might well have had certain repercussions in Franco-Austrian diplomatic relations. 'You must excuse me, Monsieur,' said Metternich to M. de Sainte-Aulaire, 'it was not I who brought up my wife!' But he allowed her a great many liberties: a real abuse, for instance, of the diplomatic bag for the transport of baubles bought in Paris; an absolute disregard of the demands of tradespeople whose bills she often refused to pay for years. He also tolerated her tyrannical treatment of servants; the same bullying methods applied to her household in general and even to her children.

Metternich had intended to make a marriage of convenience, but this union with a woman who was young, beautiful and very sensual, quickly turned into something much more intimate and vital. If we are to believe M. de Sainte-Aulaire, Mélanie from early youth had been attracted to the great statesman and her pride and heart had both been cruelly wounded when he had preferred the blonde Antoinette von Leykam. But now the rival was dead and the man of her choice at last belonged to her; to go to him, she had broken her engagement with the young Baron von Hügel, who had been her passionate admirer and from now on was to assume the role of *cavalier-servant*. . . .[1] Is this romantic story true or had it been concocted? We shall only know when the forty

---

1. Von Hügel had returned from a mission abroad full of ardour and impatience. It had even been said that he had brought from Paris jewels and other wedding presents. He found that in his absence Mélanie had become engaged to Prince Metternich. In despair but still faithful and submissive, he started off again on a long journey announcing that he would only return when he was cured of his love. Princess Mélanie remarked sadly but not without pride: 'then he will never come back'. (*Mémoires de Sainte-Aulaire*.) But we know that he did come back to become an intimate of the couple. Von Hügel went with the Metternichs on most of their journeys. 'Mélanie's eyes, generally so haughty', reports Count Greppe, 'became gentle whenever she turned them towards this man who was never far from her side.'

volumes of Princess Mélanie's diary, still jealously guarded in the secret archives of Plass, are made available to historians.

Long extracts from the diary already published (in *Mémoires et Documents*) do not admit of any final conclusion. The words 'that poor Clement' seem to occur too often to warrant our assuming any overwhelming passion. One detects rather a deep attachment and genuine solicitude. One feels that Mélanie had a profound and sincere admiration for her distinguished husband and that in spite of her independent nature her ideas gradually merged with his: the result was a completely harmonious association, 'that conjugal phenomenon more often encountered in novels than in life'. (Mrs. Trollope.)

But he, the man who was growing old and still remained passionate, what did he feel about this young, ardent and spirited woman at his side? Visitors not infrequently mistook her for his 'daughter-in-law' while they looked about in vain for the 'real Princess Metternich'. 'Make him happy, he deserves it', Francis I had said to Mélanie the day after her wedding. And the Imperial wish had been fulfilled. Metternich had indeed found perfect happiness with his beautiful Hungarian wife. 'I only met her very late in life,' he confided to Varnhagen von Ense in the course of a country walk, 'but now I could not do without her.' Their sex relationship was highly satisfactory,[1] and five children, (of whom only two survived), were born within a comparatively short period (1832-1837).

His third wife knew how to play up to the Chancellor's vanity: she reigned supremely conscious of her beauty and her power in the midst of the most haughty and exclusive society imaginable. She belonged to it from birth, as indeed did Eléonore Kaunitz. But first her youth and subsequently her frequent residence abroad had not allowed the first wife to consolidate her position. Mélanie, on the other hand, was Viennese to her fingertips, a typical great lady of Central Europe. Since an Imperial decree had established equality of rank between the old inde-

1. The Prince's devoted friend, Dr Jäger, became rather anxious about such conjugal excesses, to the extreme annoyance of the temperamental lady, who finally refused to speak to him at all.

pendent princely families and the new *non-mediatised* (the Metter-
nich-Winneburgs belonged to the latter), Mélanie took precedence of some sixty other peeresses. 'I have often seen Madame de
Metternich sitting alone in the middle of her drawing-room for
most of the evening', says M. de Sainte-Aulaire; other 'mere
mortals' were placed in armchairs too far removed to allow her
to talk to them. One day when her drawing-room was very full
and all the chairs occupied, a distinguished foreign lady (but not
a princess), seeing this large sofa empty, took advantage of the
fact and innocently sat down: this was the event of the evening.

Mélanie, especially gifted, had made a home both brilliant and
intimate for her husband; exactly what he wanted. 'You cannot
imagine how lovely my rooms are when the sun shines on them',
wrote the old statesman. 'I have a spacious ante-chamber, a large
salon in which people who want to see me can wait. It is really
a magnificent room, eighteen feet high and the walls covered
with books right up to the ceiling. There are 15,000 volumes
arranged in beautiful mahogany cases without glass.... Then
comes my study. This is a large room with three windows; there
are also three large chests, for I like to be able to move about. ...[1]
I don't like small rooms', he adds, true as usual to type; 'above
all, I hate to have to work in them. In too narrow a space, the
mind shrivels, thought is restricted, and even the heart begins to
wither.'

In the spring, about the tenth of May, the Metternichs left
the sumptuous apartments of the Kaunitz palace and moved into
their villa at the Rennweg (a suburb of Vienna) surrounded by
immense gardens filled with elaborate flower-beds of all shapes
and sizes. Metternich was even more pleased with this setting.
'I wouldn't exchange my pavilion of the Rennweg and its
present contents for all the treasures of the world.' (14.7.37.) He
loved to show his friends round the gardens and to admire with
them the brilliant colours of the spring flowers. (Princesse

---

1. We can still see one of these enormous chests at the Ballhausplatz Palace. It
is a curious piece of furniture in mahogany decorated with carved gilt mouldings;
it contains no less than sixty-two drawers. It might even be the one which had
belonged to the Duc de Choiseul and that Metternich bought from Madame de
Sagan. (Mélanie's Journal.)

Pauline von Metternich's memoirs.) [1] At the end of June, they went to drink the waters at Baden, not far from the capital, and from there went on to Koenigswart in Bohemia or to Johannisberg in the Rhenish valley, finding in each instance approximately the same palatial surroundings. Everywhere, enormous rooms filled with *objets d'art*, with pictures and bronzes, the same gardens, the same terraces with their profusion of flowers.

Princess Metternich's receptions were scarcely equalled and certainly never surpassed. All aristocratic Vienna and the *corps diplomatique* flocked incessantly to her salons. During the season, she gave a ball every Sunday, but formal dinner parties, several times a week, went on throughout the year. This social round had begun on the very day of her marriage. 'We had hardly got back to the house', she related in her diary, 'when all Vienna was upon us, the drawing-rooms filled to over-flowing.' (January 30th, 1831.) And five years later (December 1836) we find the same refrain: 'Tonight all Vienna was here: the same scenes as in former years at the Ballplatz: complete chaos—the salons crowded to suffocation and the staircase even worse.' And in December of the same year 'the party became so large towards the end of the evening that I could hardly push my way into my own drawing-room. I had made it known that I should not begin to entertain before January; but they forced my doors before the stipulated date. Years go by and nothing changes. 'Tonight', writes Mélanie, on November 22nd, 1841, 'we had a party; it is more tiring than anything one can think of, for in such circumstances all the rooms seem too small. All Vienna seems to have been here. . . .' And the same crowds, in holiday time, thronged the Prince's country seats: 'Johannisberg is like a hotel', wrote Mélanie; 'people come here and then go off again when they have slept and eaten.' (October 11th, 1839.) 'Koenigswart Castle is so full that we couldn't take another guest and there is no more linen.' The whole Court came to their big receptions—Arch-

1. 'My gardener', he wrote, 'already has a tremendous reputation among the botanical big-wigs, and I am absolutely amazed when I consider his immense knowledge in relation to his humble origin. If ever Mr Canning were to lay out a garden, I should certainly recommend him for the job. That would be the greatest triumph I could hope to enjoy as far as Canning is concerned.'

dukes, Archduchesses, the Emperor and Empress in person. They also received all the crowned heads of Europe: Tsar Nicholas, as soon as he arrived at Vienna, hurried to kiss the hand of Princess Metternich. His son, the Grand-Duke Alexander (who was eventually to free the serfs), a most distinguished youth with a pleasing and cheerful face (he had been promoted to the rank of honorary colonel of hussars by the Austrian Emperor), came to play at Mélanie's house 'first with a ball, then skipping, and finally at making war'; he also performed the Russian national anthem as a solo.

Another day, it would be the Crown Prince of Prussia or the King of Naples, 'a handsome man, very like Napoleon, but capable of standing a quarter of an hour in front of you without finding a word to say'. Plenipotentiaries extraordinary from several Oriental countries added their picturesque and brilliant colouring to the scene; for instance, that Persian envoy, magnificently robed, perfumed with essence of roses, who assured his hostess that 'even before he received his invitation he had considered her house as his own', a remark which in his own country was an indication of the highest form of courtesy. There was also a Turkish minister, accompanied by an Indian, 'a fakir who looks like a savage and really alarmed us'. In fact all Europe, and all Asia too, seemed to have agreed to meet at the Ballhausplatz!

When the Duc d'Orléans and his brother the Duc de Nemours, came to Vienna, Princess Metternich 'found it scandalous that the young princes had not immediately visited her and that she should be obliged to run after them to the French embassy'! She had difficulty in hiding her irritation, which was noticed by the whole diplomatic corps.[1] But the next day, she had the satisfaction of opening her ball on the arm of Louis-Philippe's young and charming son. 'It was most successful,' wrote Mélanie, 'the supper was magnificent; we danced, in spite of the fact that so many men were in uniform, until four in the morning.'

1. From M. de Sainte-Aulaire, the French ambassador: 'Princess Metternich was one of the first to arrive and all eyes were fixed upon her. She looked cold and depressed but remained extremely dignified, and the magnificence of her costume showed that even ill-humour had not entirely precluded the desire to be admired.' 'Princess Metternich', writes the Duchesse de Dino, 'deserved a lesson: the Duke only talked to her for five minutes. . . . and then about homœopathy!'

On days when Princess Mélanie was not overwhelmed by her duties as hostess, we find her radiant by her husband's side at Court functions (where she frequently filled a leading rôle) or at the dinners and balls of the other great nobility. For seventeen years on end, her written accounts of her life are much the same: 'magnificent ball given by Princess Liechtenstein, too lovely for a mere mortal'; a *'fête* given by Flore Wrbna, a masked ball by Marie Esterhazy ("I wore the costume of the Dresden *chacolatière*. Sandor, as the fool, was the most comic of all.... Clement went with me and enjoyed himself immensely").' At the crowning of the Empress ('I was magnificently dressed with all my diamonds in my hair. I wore my lovely white gown embroidered with gold and a long red train also embroidered with gold which had come from Paris, it had a really beautiful design'); at the Hero's banquet ('I wore a laurel wreath with diamonds on my head'); at a dinner given by Solomon Rothschild ('he showed us his safe, unquestionably the most important piece of furniture in the house; it contains twelve millions!'); a dinner given by Colloredo for a number of Court dignitaries; gala evening *chez* Tatitscheff, the Russian Ambassador, another *chez* Beauvale, the English Ambassador, or again, *chez* M. de Sainte-Aulaire or his successor, M. de Flahaut, at one time the lover of Queen Hortense. ('All his table appointments are excellent and in very good taste; the silver is superb; in short the *ensemble* is perfect, in every way worthy of a great nobleman.') And then, there was the theatre: sometimes they went to applaud Fanny Elssler, sometimes to enjoy the naïve fun of comedians at the *An-der-Wien* theatre, or the *bel canto* of those Italian singers who brought the 'most exquisite delight' to the 'heart and mind' of the Chancellor.

Happily, apart from all this time spent amidst official pomp and gala performances, there were serener hours which Metternich and his wife could devote to more intimate joys and family affections. Children's parties, picnics, excursions by carriage or in large wagonettes into the agreeable surroundings of Vienna brought a note of gaiety to their existence. Several decades later, Princess Pauline von Metternich was still to remember those delightful evenings when her grandfather lit an enormous and magnificent Christmas tree and the children with shrieks of joy threw themselves on the masses of lovely toys that filled the room.[1]

Varnhagen von Ense was to tell with sentimental relish in his memoirs of the delightful hours he spent with the Metternichs in their villa at Baden. 'At dinner, I was sitting between the Prince and his daughter Léontine; opposite me, the Princess *enceinte* and not at all well, was in a deep armchair. The Prince's second daughter and a few gentlemen completed the small circle. The Prince was most affable and particularly attentive to us foreigners. He questioned us about Berlin and told amusing anecdotes about the time when he was Austrian Ambassador there. He joked and made a variety of witty remarks; although less talkative than in the past, he still creates around him an atmosphere of ease, confidence and general well-being.' For, by the side of Mélanie 'who had brought a spirit of arrogance into the house' (Dr Jäger), the Prince remained what he had always been for his friends, 'a simple, sincere, good-natured man'.

It was a typical Austrian conversation to which Varnhagen was privileged to listen: 'aristocratic, casual, assured, spontaneous, not without coquetry, and sometimes quite daring'. Political matters were not even mentioned. And yet these now, as in the past, were the Chancellor's real and main preoccupation. His sedentary habits were in no wise changed by his marriage to the mettlesome Mélanie: the sounds of entertaining so often to be heard in his house were not allowed to interrupt his work and he could only occasionally find time for our hour *tête-à-tête* with his wife. For Vienna's *arbiter elegantiarum* was also the arbiter of the destinies of Europe . . . of that Europe which was fast disappearing . . .

> . . . *Laissant*
> *Ces musiques, ces fleurs et ces sorbets aux pêches,*
> *Travailler jusqu'a l'aube et dicter des dépêches.* . . .

In politics, as in every other field, he found Mélanie's help

1. 'The most magnificent of all these toys', said Princess Pauline, 'came from the old Baron Solomon Rothschild, who as a devoted friend of the Prince knew that he could give him no greater pleasure than to prepare such surprises for his grandchildren.'

invaluable. From the first day of their marriage, she had plunged with an almost childish ardour into the study of political documents.[1] Reading certain pages of her diary one is inclined to wonder whether these are the words of a young wife or some ambitious diplomat flattered by his chief's partiality. She identifies herself with the Chancellor, even with the Austrian Empire!: 'We are expecting a considerable loss of life.' 'We are tired of playing the discreditable role of police to the Vatican.' 'Tsar Nicholas is in complete agreement with us.' There were no secrets for Mélanie as far as the Chancellery was concerned: all reports would go through her hands and Jäger went so far as to claim that she listened-in, hidden behind curtains, pencil and note-book in hand, to interviews with the most important foreign plenipotentiaries.

Did she have any direct influence on the course of events? Mélanie herself denied it, but Metternich's enemies thought otherwise. 'Not being physically able entirely to satisfy this robust Hungarian, he had to fall back', wrote the poet Grillparzer, 'on other methods of making himself agreeable without too much difficulty. Presents? Wasn't she already surfeited with bracelets and tiaras? What remained? Why, to allow the Jesuits in, of course, as a birthday present, and to forbid mixed marriages (to please her) for the New Year.' These words, inspired by hate, exaggerated the facts: little more than a nuance from time to time was involved, a slightly better feeling towards the Church perhaps than in the past, more regard for legitimist principles, a stricter attention to aristocratic privilege. Mélanie reinforced Metternich's own old convictions, and more than anything else she created around him an atmosphere into which no new idea could possibly penetrate. From now on the Chancellery was separated from the rest of the world by a veritable Wall of China, from that real world where humanity toils, suffers and aspires

1. 'Clement has initiated me into his theories and projects and I have been amazed to discover the extent of my own ignorance. I want to learn to understand him at the slightest hint, to be able to help him on all occasions, to follow his discussions and to be able myself in turn, to discuss with him; in short I want to be more than just a loving wife (which is really too easy a function).' (17.2.1831.) 'I should like always to be leaning on and looking over his shoulder to see how he writes his despatches, for that is as interesting as it is curious.' (11.3.1831.)

to a better future. [1] But as in the past, Metternich's doors stayed open to scholars, to thinkers, to men of letters; foreigners were especially well received, for the couple were aware that it was not the apostles of revolution who would go to the expense or take the trouble to visit Vienna in order to pay their respects to the Prince-Chancellor. Among Frenchmen who came to visit him, one finds a wide variety of types—alternating with the Duc de Bordeaux, the Duc de Lévis, with M. de Montbel and the 'very agreeable' M. de Bacourt, came a certain M. Rubichon ('quite a learned man, a chatterbox, full of obsessions not far removed from twaddle; he claims that there are too many men in the world and not enough cattle, which of course is only too true'); a young editor of the *Journal des Débats*, rabid opponent of Metternich and his system; Simon, the erstwhile Jacobin, Metternich's tutor when he was at Strasbourg and who was now trying to convince his old pupil of the 'merits of his dictionary'; Michel Chevalier, old *Saint-Simonien* with whom Metternich 'was delighted'; Emile de Girardin ('an ambiguous type'); Berryer, in whom even Mélanie recognised 'wit, intelligence, sound and honest judgment, and an almost unbelievable gift of eloquence'; Madame Pleyell ('very beautiful, a really distinguished pianist; she becomes extremely animated when she plays and makes a tremendous impression on young masculine admirers'); finally, the most illustrious of all, Honoré de Balzac, in person.

Nothing could have been more romantic than this meeting between the greatest novelist and the greatest diplomat of the century. Balzac had come to Vienna in 1835 to join Madame Hanska, who immediately introduced him into the home of Countess Lulu Thurheim. There he had met all the most important members of Russo-Polish Society: the Razoumovskis, Lubomirskis, Lanckoronskis. From there was but a step to the Metternich palace. 'Sir', said the Chancellor, shaking the great man's hand for the first time, 'I have not read any of your works, but I know you, and it is clear that either you are mad or that you are amusing yourself at the expense of other madmen and

1. 'I have just been with Clement for a most unusual walk through the slums', she wrote on March 3rd, 1843. 'A world I had never seen before; this excursion much amused us.'

that you wish to cure them by means of an even greater folly than their own.' From that moment, the two men became fast friends. If we are to believe Mélanie, Balzac declared that 'his thought and his objectives were completely understood'. He struck the Princess 'as a simple and good man', apart from his garments, which she found 'fantastic'. 'He is small and stout', she notes, 'but his eyes and his expression betray considerable intelligence. . . . He says he is a fanatic royalist. . . . I have not been able to ignite the slightest poetic spark in him.' (Mélanie's diary, 20 and 25.5.1835.) The Chancellor, on his side, had been enchanted by 'the way Balzac looks at things'. In the course of a long conversation he had even furnished the novelist with a subject for a play called *L'école des ménages* (an excellent subject—Pirandello anticipating); and yet the work which Balzac wrote around it was finally neither performed nor published. Metternich a collaborator of Balzac! Who would believe it if the anecdote were not corroborated by authentic documents?[1]

But it was a far cry from this affability, this friendliness, as soon as there was any question of bringing German artists or writers into the Metternich household. These were first rigorously sorted out as to their political opinions and even those who had passed the test and were found 'pure among the pure' were made very conscious of the distance between their own very modest position and that of the master of the house.

It is not difficult to imagine the number of susceptibilities wounded by this high-and-mighty attitude of the hosts of the Kaunitz palace. 'In the home of the Metternichs', E. Bauernfeld, author of several famous comedies, wrote later 'little interest was shown in men of letters who happened to be poor. But famous writers were received with great amiability. They were allowed to expose their liberal views until their hosts had thoroughly grasped the lay of the land. If it was then decided that their liberalism was sincere, they received a final invitation to dinner, after which their relations with Brutus came to a sudden end.'[2] Grillparzer, from the bias of his permanent hate, went so

1. See A. Bettelheim: *Balzac's Begegnung mit Metternich*, Wien, 1912.
2. E. Bauernfeld: *Erinnerungen aus Alt-Wien*, re-issued in 1923.

far as to state that Metternich was surrounded by unmitigated scoundrels, renegades and deserters of all types, and that the Chancellor himself expressed the utmost contempt for 'those imbeciles' who remained faithful to their convictions.

And Count Auersperg, one of the poets of freedom who wrote under the pen-name of Anastasius Grün, made the Chancellor's *salon* the subject of verse which later became famous. He pictured the man at the wheel of the Steamer Austria, the man who directed many a Congress of Princes. Always affable and charming, expert under the light of chandeliers at plucking roses from the *décolletages* of beautiful ladies, only to scatter the petals as he destroys and disintegrates countries. In the meanwhile, at the doors of his palace, stands a poor petitioner, polite and modest in his shabby clothes, waiting patiently for some slight sign of favour. 'And that modest petitioner', continues the poet, 'is no other than the Austrian people who take the liberty of wishing to be free. . . .'

If only there had been some other influences in Metternich's immediate surroundings to offset that of the uncompromising Mélanie. But of these there was no sign. 'Metternich', says Varnhagen, 'was entirely surrounded by flatterers, sincere or hypocritical as the case might be. The language of flattery was the only one used in his presence, and even visitors, little accustomed to this sycophancy, soon acquired the habits of the place; they found it was the only way to get on at all.' 'With amazing efficiency, the Chancellor had known how to choose his instruments: a whole gallery of living Metternichians, men permanently committed to all his ideas.'

Among these creatures of Metternich, the famous Gentz had long been awarded first place.

It is usual to describe Gentz as a 'publicist', but that is not quite accurate: Gentz was rather the Chancellor's mouthpiece. He had in fact started as a journalist, but had then entered the service of the Viennesse Chancellery and had there, with the title of *Hofrat*, performed functions of some importance since 1813. He was a strange looking little man: his physical appearance rather gave away a non-Aryan origin. He used to push his bust forward like a pouter-pigeon and wore a red wig. He slithered into the salons of Vienna with a look of uncertainty and almost of terror, kept hidden behind dark glasses. Extremely nervous, he was susceptible to every sound, to raised voices and to laughter, and closed up like a clam as soon as he encountered an unknown face, especially if it happened to be adorned by some unfamiliar moustache. But surprisingly enough, this little mouse of a man was mad about social life, about gambling and women. Metternich's patronage had given him (plebeian recently ennobled) an entrée to the most exclusive circles. He received in his modest home (especially during the Congress of Vienna) bearers of some of the greatest names in Europe. ('I had dining with me tonight', he wrote on March 17th, 1815, 'the four Courlande Princesses, Metternich, Talleyrand, Maurice and Wenceslas Liechtenstein, the Palffys and the Rohans.') He had been Fanny Elssler's lover. His generosity was proverbial, his venality known and exploited by all the Chancelleries of Europe. This old bachelor was often irritable, jaundiced and vain but he had also considerable knowledge and intelligence. 'He was a scholar,' said Meyendorff, 'a man of some intellectual distinction who wrote a notably concise and distinguished German, with a real feeling for style but an even stronger predilection for a proper sequence of ideas and sound logic. He had managed to graft a rich European culture onto the background of a German education. . . . He was fond of discussion and conducted it agreeably, bringing to birth a wealth of ideas in the best Socratic manner. . . . In private life, he was gentle, generous, sensitive to flattery, childishly vain which he did not attempt to hide, being incapable of dissimulation. Sensual, a *gourmet*, a coward (at least as much as one can be without fearing death), he was a mixture of weaknesses which made men laugh and of a great deal they found to admire; to say nothing of more sterling qualities which earned their affection.'

He was a perfect arsenal of gossip, epigram and satire and displayed very remarkable gifts in the technique of diplomacy. A political thinker of no mean calibre, his convictions were probably even more conservative than those of his chief. 'He was convinced', said Treitschke, 'that the evolution of humanity could be arrested by a sign from the Hofburg.' The turbulence of the masses offended his sensibility; news of any uprising or political assassination put him beside himself with horror. Metternich made him turn pale when he jokingly announced 'some day we shall certainly both be hung'. Instinctively he found the *Teuto-maniacs* repulsive and never tired of sarcasms about the grotesque appearance of revolutionary propagandists or of liberal professors, in their 'filthy German clothes', with a pile of books under their arms: 'revolting to God and man'. ('Gentz doesn't like the Gothic', Metternich wrote maliciously, 'since all the Goths are dead.') His origin did not prevent him posing as an anti-Semite, imputing to the Jews 'all the misfortunes of the modern world' (Gentz to Brinckmann) and making fun of 'Prince' Solomon de Rothschild (Gentz to Lebzeltern, August 8th, 1823) 'and calling the other members of that family—to whom, however, he owed several millions—"vulgar and ignorant Jews but presentable as to their exterior".'

This was the man who was considered, and rightly, as the *alter ego*, the right arm of the Austrian Chancellor. Metternich knew his weaknesses: his continual need of money, his pedantry, his lack of practical common sense and lack of any ordinary knowledge of life—he only considered Gentz as an instrument. But in the course of a collaboration which lasted several years, he had learnt to appreciate his assistant's knowledge, his perseverance at work, and above all his remarkable dialectical abilities. He confided to him the daily reading of the Press and especially the wording of all urgent messages: the chief submitted to his underling those that he himself had written and docilely accepted all the erasures and corrections which the latter made. (Prokesch's memoirs.) Only once was there a real political disagreement between the two men: Gentz, a specialist in Eastern questions, had sided—no one exactly knew why—with the Greek insurgents. He became reconciled with his chief later, after the July revolution, and his death, which cut their relationship short in 1832, was considered by Metternich as an irreparable loss.[1]

1. 'A man of outstanding talent', wrote Metternich, 'a real genius. I shall miss him when confronted with any really important matter.' (A. Prokesch, 15.6.1832.)

The void left by Gentz's death was never filled. The men who in future were to be found at the Chancellor's table and in his office at the Chancellery: Jarcke ('a miniature Gentz'), Clement Hügel (Mélanie's admirer), Prokesch-Osten (one-time *confidante* of the Eaglet), Hubner, Count Merey, Baron Werner—were men of integrity, conscientious and zealous officials, but nothing more. They were all too young, too inexperienced, they had all been brought up by the Master: any idea of opposing the exaggerations of the system never entered their heads. The circle was now closed. . . .

And even outside the Chancellery walls, Metternich found himself in the same atmosphere of adulation, of toadyism. Vienna, which had once been for him 'a town like any other', 'a town which frightens me'; that Vienna which had so long considered him a foreigner, had finally taken him to her heart. Metternich might well have adapted Montesquieu's slogan to himself: 'One can only grow old gracefully at Vienna.'

To judge by outward appearances, the Chancellor's popularity was unequalled in the Austrian capital. Indeed, apart from Strauss and his orchestra, no subject of conversation could compete with his personality as a matter of interest to the Viennese—it was both varied and inexhaustible. 'Everywhere and on all occasions, and whatever the social class involved, conversation always got back to the Chancellor.'[1] (Varnhagen). The most prominent personalities in the Empire bowed before him and seemed willing to concede him precedence.[2] Even the Archdukes showed a boundless deference towards him.

'It was curious to see them', wrote Sainte-Aulaire, 'waiting in Metternich's ante-chambers, or to note their demeanour when they met him in the corridors of the Hofburg. On these occasions, they would line up against the wall, hats doffed, rather in the

---

1. In 1839 the Chancellor was taken ill and it was rumoured in the city that he had had an apoplectic fit. 'One must have known Vienna at that period to realise the effect of this news. For ten days, while the danger lasted, the diplomatic corps did little else but make enquiries, hour by hour, as to what was happening at the Rennweg.' (Sainte-Aulaire.)

2. By an eccentricity of the protocols of Vienna, the position of Chancellor conveyed no automatic rank at Court. Metternich was there received as the most intimate of the privy counsellors; ten others had in fact been created before him.

attitude of a corporal before his captain. Metternich acknowledged their greetings with a curt bow, stopping to exchange a few words at most.' And these were the brothers, the cousins of the Emperor, all men of considerable standing, men who had held high positions of state and in the army.

He was greeted by cannon salvos, like a crowned head, whenever he moved about; recognised as a superior, as a leader, by all the statesmen of Europe. He might well consider himself, as the Shah of Persia suggested: 'the supreme commander of events and guarantor of world affairs'. 'I have become the *confidante* of the most diverse collection of men and parties', Metternich wrote to his friend Ficquelmont; 'sometimes I play the role of confessor, sometimes that of family doctor. That is why I am perhaps more the King of Prussia's Minister than Count Bernstorff; that is how I manage to keep the King of Bavaria from the brink of calamity; why Casimir Périer opens his heart to me about the dangers of his present position, and why the Pope begs me to manage his affairs.'[1]

Can we then be surprised if Metternich no longer listened to those who questioned him, interrupting 'deliberately or as a matter of habit' anyone who permitted himself to express an opinion in his presence? Can we be surprised that he finally came to consider his person and the public weal as one: his own need of rest as that of humanity in general? 'What would you do, Prince, if you were no longer active?' asked an elderly diplomat, General Baron de Wacquant-Gerzelles; to which Metternich replied with a certain show of irritation: 'You are postulating, General, an obvious impossibility.' But however much Metternich might consider himself a 'progressive thinker', for him as for so many others, Vienna—capital of the beautiful blue Danube, light-hearted and indolent, insidious and dangerous—had become a 'Capua of the mind'.

1. April 11th, 1832 (Vienna, Secret Archives). This letter has been quoted by E. Molden in his excellent work: *Die Orient politik des Fürsten Metternichs*. . . .

R

# XII

# HIS STAR BEGINS
# TO WANE

*'Monarchies are lost when they begin to lose faith in
their own destiny.'*

FULL of years and glory, on March 1st, 1835, after a brief and
painful illness, the Emperor Francis I had passed to a better
world: no more Jacobins to fear or fight, no more Liberals to
keep an eye on!

Till his last breath, Francis had remained devoted to the
Minister responsible for most of the glamour of his reign: 'Continue towards Prince Metternich, my most faithful servant and
friend, the trust which I myself conferred on him for so many
years. Make no decision about affairs of state, no final judgment
as to persons before consulting him.' These words were written
on his death-bed to his son and successor, Ferdinand.

The principle of hereditary monarchy—corner-stone of Metternich's system—had been subject to a rude ordeal at the time
of Francis' death. Once more that old familiar problem arose (as
indeed in our time also) to trouble the loyal hearts of faithful
subjects: what to do should the heir to the throne appear unfit to
govern?

Francis' eldest son was weak-witted. He was not exactly an
imbecile; not sufficiently irresponsible to be shut up in an asylum.
Kind, gentle, friendly, Ferdinand was merely mentally sub-
normal; he was also subject to frequent epileptic fits.[1]

---

1. Ségur-Cabanac (Viktor, Graf): *Kaiser Ferdinand als Regent und Mensch*, 1912.

By a strange coincidence, he was born on 'all fools' day'! His appearance was completely insignificant: he was short, with a large head and expressionless face, pasty complexion, anxious and furtive eyes; he spoke very quickly, as if to cover his shyness. Sometimes he seemed 'almost normal', especially when he was talking French. On other occasions he was guilty of the most astonishing *faux pas*. When receiving the Belgian ambassador, he could think of nothing better than to express his affection for the House of Orange! When receiving Sainte-Aulaire, he went to the trouble of wearing his Order-of-the-Holy-Ghost (an order categorically suppressed by Louis-Philippe) and was quite surprised to find the French ambassador 'not thrilled by this delicate attention'. The most fantastic stories were current about him among his subjects, but his remarkable kindness called forth a certain compassion in return: the public remembered his generosity in pardoning a fanatic who had made an attempt on his life (in 1831); how he had held the man in his arms to protect him from the crowd; how he forbade any action to be taken against him and even bestowed a pension on his family. People were chiefly sorry for his wife (for this abnormal young man was married), the young and beautiful Marie-Anne-Caroline of Savoy, a woman of great piety, unparalleled dignity, who 'looked like a saint' when attending church ceremonies, and who went out of her way to cover her husband's deficiencies by means of witty and agreeable conversation.

The question of the succession had been debated for many years. In a memorandum sent to Paris by the Ambassador Otto, on June 24th, 1812, he said: 'The Archbishop of Vienna has several times talked to the Emperor and advised him either to allow his son some participation in the Government now or else to declare him once for all unfit to rule. The prelate advised his sovereign that, being mortal, he owed it to his subjects not to leave the reins of government in the hands of a prince who, if they continued to bring him up as they were now doing, would end by being *non compos mentis*. To this the Emperor always replied that 'he would see about it', but that whatever happened Ferdinand would inevitably reign because he was the eldest of his sons,[1] *a reductio ad absurdum* of legitimist principles.[2]

During Francis' life-time, Metternich—for reasons of tact, of prudence or ambition—had never opposed the succession of Ferdinand. He had even agreed to have him crowned King of Hungary. But with the disappearance of Francis, it seems there had been a moment of hesitation at the Court. A family council had been called to inquire into the matter, but the reading of the will—unquestionably inspired by Metternich himself—made further discussion useless. 'In the Chancellor's apartments, I was waiting, with feverish impatience, to hear the result', wrote Dr Jäger, a valuable witness. 'At last the Prince came out, in full uniform, cheeks flushed, eyes brilliant. "The Rubicon is crossed", he said, "Ferdinand is now Emperor." Had I before me, I wondered, a new Richelieu, a new *maire du palais* as we had known them in the days of the *Mérovingien* Kings?'

Alas, Metternich was incapable—or at least was no longer capable of playing that role. Anything in the nature of Nietzsche's will-to-power was singularly lacking. 'I never felt in myself the capacities of a Richelieu or even the desire to achieve them', he owned. For this man who had smilingly assured the world that he was 'born a minister', had taken the most important functions of state, the highest honours, in his stride, as something due to him from birth, by virtue of his family connections, his capacities, his natural talents. Great nobleman, he had never had to struggle for a position which chance bestowed and his sovereign's partiality guaranteed.[3] But the master gone, it was inevitable that rivalries should run riot.

The death of Francis I and the accession of Ferdinand marks the culmination of Prince Metternich's career, but it also heralds the approach of his decline. 'Never, at any time or in any country, was the passing from one reign to the next accomplished with

1. Archives of foreign affairs.
2. 'There could have been no worse indictment of the principle', wrote the minister Kubeck the day after Francis' death, 'than this crazy application; this determination to maintain it in spite of consequences.'
3. He wrote to Sainte-Aulaire: 'I could leave my ministerial portfolio as Chancellor, in any drawing-room of the city, leave it at the disposal of the first comer, and a week later I should be pretty sure to find it where I left it!'

less commotion', he wrote in a circular letter to his Ambassadors, dated March 12th, 1835.

'As everything had been predisposed during the last reign, as everything of importance had been set upon a solid basis— nothing forgotten—since the whole of the enormous machinery of government had been saturated with the spirit of a monarch who spent his whole life on the throne; and since that spirit is noticeably to be found in his successor, Austria today is still the same as yesterday and the same as she always will be.'

But as Metternich was writing these words, so full of confidence, the initial difficulties had already cropped up. There were discontents within the bosom of the Imperial family itself: the Archduchess Sophia, Ferdinand's sister-in-law, a woman of somewhat violent temperament who lived in a state of permanent agitation, had perhaps hoped that the sickly heir would retire in favour of her own husband, the Archduke Francis-Charles. From now on, she was to concentrate all her inordinate ambition on her son, a child of five years old and in fact the future Emperor Franz-Josef. But in the old Emperor's will Francis-Charles was not mentioned at all; only the Archduke Louis, brother of the late monarch, was nominated together with Metternich as counsellor 'in regard to important matters of domestic adminis- tration'. Swallowing her rancour, Sophia for the moment relapsed into silence. Others were not as tactful.

Count Kolowrat, formerly Grand Burgrave of Bohemia, had been in charge, since 1826, of home affairs. If we are to believe Kubeck, he was 'poorly educated, conspicuously lacking in scientific method, weak and capricious, vain and stingy, falling easily a victim to the most unworthy influences'. But there were not lacking partisans who thought highly of his simplicity of manner, of his dislike of ostentation, and even claimed his lofti- ness of purpose. Possessed of a considerable private fortune, he had refused all emoluments from the Imperial Treasury. An advocate of severe economy, enlightened and hard working administrator (although regrettably given to cheese-paring), in the past he had often vetoed measures designed solely with a view to national prestige. His good qualities as much as his faults made

him the antithesis of Metternich and for some years there had
been a tendency in Viennese administrative circles to play one
against the other. Kolowrat himself had entered into the game
with zest. In showing his dislike of the Jesuits, his sympathy with
the Poles and above all with his own Czech compatriots, he had
made friends among the opposition and earned for himself—
quite unjustifiably—a reputation as a liberal thinker. He also
made much of being a real Austrian noble, in contradistinction to
the intruder, the foreigner, that Rhenish Count whom chance
alone had promoted to be Chancellor for the Habsburgs. Metternich, completely unperturbed, allowed him to pursue these
methods to his heart's content. In 1829, the first serious disagreement between the two men arose, and Kolowrat, always abnor-
mally touchy, had put himself in the wrong. Thus an almost
unhoped-for opportunity was offered the Prince Chancellor to
get rid of an enemy. But Metternich did not consider him in that
light; he described him as 'a useful tool', 'a sick man who loses
heart too quickly, with a tendency to attack symptoms rather
than the root of an evil . . . and who should be given another
chance. . . .'[1] Francis I had followed this advice, and had continued to use Kolowrat, although keeping him in the background.

It was from this long-imposed obscurity that Count Kol̶o̶
was now emerging. He claimed a voice at least equal to ▮▮▮▮
Metternich in all affairs of state and had no intention of allowing
the latter to become dictator as to the destiny of Austria. He refused absolutely to accept a subordinate position which Metternich
had proposed to create for him in the new Council of State. He
feigned illness and retired to his country estates, only to reappear
a few days later in excellent health and primed for battle. Had
Metternich been younger and more daring, he might perhaps
finally have disposed of an objectionable rival, but the weight of
years and the somniferous effect of the Viennese atmosphere were
increasingly taking toll of his powers of decision. Apart from
this, domestic administration and finance had never been his
province; he no longer felt the strength to tackle them, if he

---

1. Secret reports from the Chancellor to the Emperor Francis I, dated October
29th, 1829, and January 19th, 1830 (Personalia, Metternich. Vienna, Secret Archives.)

didn't employ Kolowrat he would have to find somebody else to take his place.[1] 'Hate is not in my make-up', he once wrote to Princess Lieven, and to dispose of a rival one would have had to hate him. Accustomed to attaining his ends by means of putting off and compromise, the old diplomat once more chose his well-tried methods. It was impossible to get the better of Kolowrat without stirring up public opinion, and that the Chancellor would never consent to do. So the struggle between these two men, with an empire as stake in the game, developed into a matter of secret meetings, ministerial conferences behind padded doors at the Ballhausplatz or the Hofburg. 'In a final conversation which lasted for three hours between Metternich and the Archduke John (says Srbik), the future destiny of Austria was decided as by a throw of the dice': after telling Kolowrat some 'bitter home truths', after threatening him with his own resignation, Metternich settled down to sharing the power with his rival.[2]

A Council of State was to be created under the presidency of the Archduke Louis with Metternich, Kolowrat and Francis-Charles as permanent members. 'From now on, we are united, one for all and all for one', said Metternich. He prided himself on having avoided dictatorship: 'the mere existence of this Council will tranquillise the masses who have a tendency to trust representational deliberations'. (To Count Martinitz, 5.9.1836.) In reality, he was setting up in Austria a ministerial oligarchy of the worst description, he was creating a triumvirate in which his own influence would persistently be paralysed by that of Kolowrat under the aegis of 'a phlegmatic and somnolent Prince as umpire'. The monarchy without a monarch was rapidly becoming a monarchy without a government.

The late Emperor Francis had undertaken nothing without

---

1. 'If we had a more capable man than Kolowrat, I should prefer him to undertake the duties we have in mind. We cannot sack Kolowrat—he would only come back as a ghost.' (To Clam, 6.8.1838.)
2. 'Ought some one man, by the side of the Emperor, to hold all the power in his own hands? And where is such a man to be found? The Archduke Ludwig? He doesn't want it. Myself? I don't want it either. Count Kolowrat? He would not be capable. Baron Eichoff? Nobody would obey him. And so we must have a Council. However much we dislike such a solution, it remains the only one possible'; that is how Metternich himself explained his decision.

previously consulting his Chancellor, and it was thus that Metternich had managed to stamp every branch of the administration
with his own personality: he enjoyed the privileges of a Prime
Minister without being called upon to bear official responsibility.[1]

But with the advent of the triumvirate the system was completely changed. As member of the Council of State, the *Staats
conferenz*, Metternich would in future be obliged to divide all
responsibilities with his two co-regents; Louis and Kolowrat
would leave him a free hand in the matter of foreign policy but
were determined to keep him out of all domestic matters
(reserved to Kolowrat).[2] Austria might well be going to rack and
ruin, the Chancellor was not supposed to know anything about
it.... His would be the task of 'representing the Empire to
foreign nations and protecting her interests in the matter of
foreign policy only'.

Installed in absolute power at the Chancellery of the Ballhausplatz, Metternich still unquestionably had a wide scope of
activity. He was very far ahead of his colleagues in every way,
and had unique experience and natural breadth of view. For him
there was 'no insignificant matter in the political arena'. He knew
how to 'dig out symptoms' from seemingly inoffensive facts or
events. 'Untouched by normal political passion and prejudice,
during his long ministry', wrote the French ambassador, 'he has
learnt a great deal, he knows both the weaknesses and strength
of his contemporaries, he has studied world affairs from every
angle....' And indeed he was justified in considering himself
the best-informed statesman in Europe. 'Questions of diplomacy',
he said, 'are always indirectly influenced by considerations of

1. We have made extensive investigations in the Viennese archives by looking
through a dossier concerned with Metternich's reports to Francis I and picking
out one particular month at random, i.e. November 1830. Apart from a few
documents having special reference to the revolution in Italy and to the early
proceedings of King Louis-Philippe, the only affairs mentioned are of secondary
importance: appointments of Bishops, of embassy secretaries, of a Commissar at
Cracow, the bestowal of decorations, authorisation given to a director of mines
allowing him to accept a diploma of honorary membership in the Geological
Society of Paris—and all the rest of much the same nature. But it was in the course
of daily conversations that matters of real importance were decided.

2. E. von Wertheimer: *Fürst Metternich und die Staatskonferenz* (Oesterr., Rundschau 10 Bd.1907; A. Fournier: '*Graf Kolowrat und die Oesterreichische Staatskonferenz
von 1836*'. *Histor. Studien und Skizzen* (Reihe).

temperament, by the natural predilections and even the state of temper of individuals, all this steps in when they begin to act.' And in order to succeed in this field, to enable him to see his adversaries (or his partner's) hands, Metternich possessed a unique method: an instrument which he had developed to an amazing pitch of efficiency—that mysterious 'dark-room' which opened all Ambassadors' reports, opened the correspondence of the highest dignitaries, not excepting even that of the Imperial family itself, and of foreign Sovereigns. Metternich had always admired the methods of Napoleon's secret service; he himself had been one of its victims but he had subsequently taken it as a model and developed and improved it out of all recognition. He had gone out of his way, by means of internal conventions, to attract onto Austrian territory a maximum of European postal services and general transport—among other items the Indian mail and all correspondence for Southern Italy (which, of course, might equally have gone *via* Marseilles or Piedmont). No other European state could claim to have its postal services spread out so far beyond its frontiers as those of Austria. He had his agents in a number of foreign countries: important civil servants, Sardinian, Florentine, Swiss, German and French, kept him informed as to details of postal activities, while subordinates opened and copied certain letters of special interest to Vienna.[1]

He had also skilfully managed to get a number of the diplomatic bags of other countries into the hands of his own couriers for transport: thus Austria undertook throughout Central Europe the postal arrangements of England, France, Sardinia and Bavaria. As soon as letters got into the hands of Austrian postal employees or customs officials, all hope of secrecy was at an end. Highly efficient methods allowed for the opening of envelopes without damage or leaving any trace (even in the case of seals). Letters from Napoleon, from the Pope, the Tsar, Charles X, from the Kings of Bavaria and Naples were laid open before the Austrian Emperor and Metternich, to say nothing of those of their own

---

1. Among Frenchmen who collaborated with Metternich in this way, we find the *Directeur General des Postes*, the Marquis de Vaulchier et Maupertuis, Consul. General at Milan. The Duc Decazes, himself, had offered his services.

wives and close relations, those of innumerable dignitaries, generals, prominent women, writers, politicians, *et al*. All codes were deciphered at Vienna with a really diabolical ingenuity. Eichenfeld, the director of decipherment, claimed to have found the key to eighty-five foreign cypher-systems, developed in a wide variety of languages and extremely complex. Metternich was particularly proud that his department had been able to unravel the Roman system, a work which had taken four years to complete. Throughout the world, the code experts of Vienna enjoyed such a reputation that certain foreign states—Naples, Spain, Russia—applied to the Ballhausplatz to have new codes drawn up for them. It is scarcely necessary to add that a copy was always kept. And when the perspicacity of the cryptographic experts fell down, the police intervened with their more brutal methods. In 1833, the French cypher was stolen for the space of a few hours, having been taken from the bedroom of Sainte-Aulaire's own son with the probable complicity of the Embassy Chancellor.[1]

An elaborate spy system completed this colossal means of documentation; it was spread throughout Russia, Germany, France and Italy.[2]

When he had to receive foreign Ambassadors, Metternich invariably had already seen the original text of their instructions and knew the motive of their visit.[3] It amused him to see how they would set about it. For nothing of what was hatching between Rome and Berlin, between Constantinople and Paris, Turin and Saint Petersburg or Naples and London was ignored by him. In a very few instances he allowed himself the mischievous pleasure

1. Joseph Karl: *Metternich's Geheimer Briefdienst*, Wien, 1935. This book by the eminent Viennese curator is brimful of hitherto unknown information of enthralling interest.

2. Among Austrian agents working in France, J. K. Mayr names the Marquis Giamboni, the Chevalier von Kentzinger (future Mayor of Strassburg), Baron Eckstein (of the Foreign Office), Captain Saint-Genis, Klindworth, Moechetti (in charge of Italian emigration), and finally Puget de Savignon (who sent reports about French navigation from Marseilles). In Italy, among other collaborators, we find the Marquis Tassoni, Trouqui, and the Tuscan, Tito Manzi.

3. Most of the intercepted despatches have been destroyed. Only some sixty-two dossiers of such documents now remain in the secret archives of Vienna. In the dossier 'France, 1832', we found complete copies of all reports sent by the Maréchal Marmont to Paris and of all the instructions received by him from his chiefs, Sébastiani and de Broglie between March 27th and December 15th, in all 107

of taking his visitors into his confidence, showing them copies of letters which had been intercepted and which they might find interesting or useful. (He did this, for instance, in 1833 in relation to the Tsar.) But, in general, all those with whom he had to do were supposed to ignore the sources of his information.[1]

And what was all this leading to? What did the Chancellor propose to do by means of all this elaborate machinery? What use would be made of the power thus concentrated in his own hands? As in the past, his main object was the maintenance of European peace. But, as one of his contemporaries very justly remarked: 'Peace today is no longer the re-established harmony of an organism recently feverish and disturbed. It is now a kind of paralysis after convulsions which, curbed for a brief moment, are certain to break out into something much worse.'

History, between 1833 and 1848, shows few events of importance. The really important evolution was not taking place on the surface but in the minds and hearts of the people. But Metternich's foreign policy was only concerned with surface matters. For one thing, he was satisfied just to maintain the *bloc* of the three Nordic powers which had been negotiated at München-grätz and Teplitz and was intended from now on to replace the older alliance of Five. This was a continuation of policies inau-

documents. One could scarcely believe one's eyes; these might have been the archives of the Quai d'Orsay itself. Another dossier (Varia, France 1833/4, part 28) contains ten extracts of letters addressed from Paris to Maréchal Marmont, several reports from the Comte de Germiny, a memorandum of 254 pages concerned with the French Foreign Office and giving the characteristics in detail of all the officials on home territory and at the Embassies, some sixty-four letters intercepted and partly de-ciphered addressed by de Broglie and Rigny to Sainte-Aulaire, twenty-two extracts from private correspondence concerning the workers' riots at Lyons, twenty-six copies of letters exchanged between members of the Rothschild family, a 'concise exposition' of the nature of the French government in February 1834 (probably drawn up by Klindworth), a report on the *Société populaire allemande de Paris* 'created by Lafayette, a branch of the *Société des Droits de l'Homme*, blind instrument of the main committee for propaganda', finally offers of service by the Marquis de Favras ('I am not asking for any brilliant position, I need bread').

1. Having received at Koenigswart a despatch in code from the Prince of Wallachia, he put on an act for Gentz 'pretending that he was waiting with impatience for the message to be de-coded at Vienna'. All the time, the intercepted message was lying de-coded on his table. On this occasion for once he was not accompanied by the party of coding experts who invariably accompanied him wherever he went, disguised as servants.

gurated during the *Congressional era* but simplified: it now hinged entirely on the good understanding between Metternich, the King of Prussia and the Tsar.[1]

Strong in the knowledge of his Russo-Prussian backing, Metternich could afford to consider calmly the political evolution of the two 'liberal sea-powers', England and France, and even nursed the ambitious scheme of sowing dissension between them.[2]

France, with whom he had so often fought, always drew him like a magnet. 'Nobody can govern the French', he wrote. . . . 'It is political passion *per se* that seems to obsess them, to whichever party they happen to belong. They have an itch always to be protecting someone or something.' 'A country must be governed with strength and consistency. But both strength and consistency are impossible when licence reigns, as in the case of France.' (7.8.1836.) 'Read the French newspapers. They accuse the Chamber of Deputies of prostitution! The Clubs and the Saint-Simoniens, it seems, are the true representatives of the people.' (2.7.1833.) 'The great instrument in France is money. Men who are committed to philanthropy and who are obliged to buy off their critics must indeed need a lot. Bribes are paid out openly.' 'France as a country and Paris as a city are more prone than anywhere else in the world to illusions. Noticeable among these is their habit of underestimating the influence of the daily Press. The French are apt to think when someone does not happen to touch themselves that other people will also be impervious; they are wrong.' (30.4.1836.) 'Paris is entirely self-sufficient. Everything for and by means of France may sound well to exclusively French ears, but it stinks for the rest of Europe. To live and let live as a principle has gone out of fashion among the Gauls, with the result that no progress is being made in any field.' (7.8.1839.) 'Every time France sets out to be liberal she would like to make the whole world follow suit.' At moments, he launched into dark prophecies which even today have lost

1. See Schiemann: *Kaiser Nickolaus*; L. von Ranke: *Briefwechsel des Koenigs Friedrich Wilhelm III.*
2. See Commander Weil: *Metternich et l'Entente cordiale.*

none of their pertinence. He wrote, for instance (1.8.1836): 'Any great country governed as France is, must inevitably suffer some severe shocks. The days of these new-rich are numbered; all that surface industrial prosperity will be ploughed in, will disappear. Horrible disorders will be the outcome of all these honeyed words, and liberalism and all its works will evaporate like smoke in a high wind.'

But these were considerations of a general order. When it came to any specific application of his theories, Metternich had no alternative to offer to the July monarchy. The man whom he was pleased to call 'the barricade King', he now admitted to be the only man 'whose behaviour has been sane in the midst of lunatics': 'I used to think him a schemer but I now see that he is a real King'. He had met Louis-Philippe in 1795, during the French campaign and had seen him again at Paris in 1825. And having carefully studied the complex character of the bourgeois-monarch, Metternich even flattered himself that he might become his political mentor. Whether or not it was in fact impertinent, such advice as he had given the King of France through the intermediary of his Ambassador appeared to have fallen on good ground. France's adventurous period was over. 'Thank Heaven', said Sainte-Aulaire, 'neither the King nor his ministers today wish to turn the world upside down; only the pub-politicians are amusing themselves remaking the map of Europe.'

But anything in the nature of an *entente* between Austria and the July monarchy was by no means easy to accomplish.

Louis-Philippe, for instance, had been premature in attempting, through his Prime Minister Thiers, to arrange a marriage between his son the Duc d'Orléans and an Austrian Archduchess.[1] The young heir to the throne had hopefully set out for Vienna but had there received a cutting rebuff. The Archduke Charles (victorious general of Aspern) had refused his daughter Theresa's hand, pretexting the objections of the Emperor and of Prince Metternich. The girl herself had been appalled by any notion of such a marriage. For whereas she found the suitor 'very agree-

1. L. de Lanzac de Laborie: *Correspondances du Siècle dernier. Un projet de mariage du Duc d'Orléans*, 1836 (1918).

261

able', she would never, she said, dare to marry him since 'she would certainly die as soon as the first (inevitable) uprising occurred in France'. 'Nothing in the world would have changed the young princess' mind in view of the fear by which she was obsessed.' Metternich sent word to Apponyi. She might perhaps have given way, like Marie-Antoinette and Marie-Louise if reasons of State had been brought forward. But the old doctrine, *Tu felix Austria nube*, had had its day. According to Mélanie's journal, the whole Imperial family was opposed to a third marriage with a French Prince. And Metternich had no reason to espouse his cause when the young Prince came in person 'to ask his advice' and 'to beg him not to oppose his happiness'. (Mélanie's Diary, 5 and 7.6.1836.)

Metternich's experience with Marie-Louise had been enough: it would have been madness to take a chance with Louis-Philippe when one had failed with Napoleon. Furthermore, the Austrian hierarchy—now become a symbol of reaction—was less popular than ever in Paris. And an alliance with a descendant of the Habsburgs would not even have served the purpose of stabilising the new French dynasty. 'Don't expect to get anything by shock methods from Vienna, either the Cabinet's friendship or the hand of a Princess', said Metternich. 'Nobody would dream of questioning the illustrious status of the House of Orleans; it is the dynasty that started on August 7th which has dragged it down. As the Duc de Chartres this Prince would have been a more desirable match; but as Prince Royal of France he is not acceptable.' (To Apponyi, 30.7.1836.)[1]

But thanks to remarkable tact shown by the young Duc d'Orléans himself and his brother, the Duc de Nemours, all unpleasantness arising from this episode soon disappeared. Unfortunately soon after this, Prime Minister Thiers returned to power a second time and began to embark on a policy of

1. Information that reached Vienna from Paris at this time was by no means reassuring. On June 25th, Alibaud had made an attempt on the King's life, and Metternich remarked: 'What a lesson in relation to the marriage!' (To Apponyi, 5.7.1836.) In March 1837, Mélanie entered in her diary: 'News has just arrived from France which proves that the situation is very alarming. Louis-Philippe is daily in danger of assassination.'

political adventure which was inevitably to create friction between France and Metternich's Austria.

Anxious to revive the Napoleonic tradition and enhance the sorely damaged prestige of his country, Thiers had espoused the cause of Mahomet Ali, rebel Pasha of Egypt, not hesitating to provoke a conflict which would put France at loggerheads with all the great powers of Europe. He meant to defend the cause of his Egyptian protégé on the very banks of the Rhine. 'We must engender a taste for war and spending in France today', he declared to Sainte-Aulaire. 'The King doesn't want war, but I shall find a way to persuade him. Metternich's hair will turn white when he sees how we propose to mix up the map of Europe.'

And in the summer of 1840, France was in fact within sight of war with the German Confederation, presided by Austria. That it was avoided was entirely due to the calm and considered attitude of Metternich and of Louis-Philippe.[1] 'I have a Prime Minister who wishes to drag me into war', the King told the diplomatists, 'but rest assured I would turn him out before I would submit to any such notion.' Metternich, on his side, paid no attention to the wave of emotion sweeping over the whole of Germany, thereby once more laying himself open to an accusation of treachery against the national cause.

'I am persuaded', he wrote, 'that this moment of crisis will pass, like so many others, without starting a war for which there is not the slightest pretext.'[2] 'War for political reasons only, is not to be contemplated today. . . . A great nation, France, is beginning to get worked up and declare herself in danger. Where are the supposed enemies waiting to attack her? Whence would they come? Not a single soldier in any direction outside her frontiers

1. We are unable to accept Bibl's thesis when he suggests that Metternich at that moment had a leaning to war. All the evidence he brings forward proves little more than that Vienna was merely taking precautions proper to the occasion and keeping in constant touch with other Germanic powers. The King of Prussia, in any event, had spontaneously declared that he would consider any attack by France on the Austrian possessions in Italy as a matter that directly concerned him. (Metternich to M. de Munch, November 28th, 1840.)

2. Circular letter to the Imperial Embassies and Consulates in Germany and Italy, August 27th, 1840.

is on the march.' 'There is one thing conspicuously lacking to enable this civilian Napoleon to play the role of Caesar: he has no enemies; not a man in sight upon the battle-fields of Europe. For without a valid cause (and such a cause must be the outcome of sound policy) the nations really cannot pass from peace to war.'[1]

At the critical moment, Louis-Philippe disposed of Thiers and replaced him with Guizot. Metternich breathed a sigh of relief.

As conservative and doctrinaire one as the other, Metternich and Guizot spoke the same language. 'There is no essential difference in the way our minds work', wrote Metternich. 'We start from the foundation of the same principles and we have the same objective. Should any minor differences arise in the course of our journey, there should be no difficulty in coming to an understanding. Monsieur Guizot is no proselytiser, and I, on my side, am well able to look beyond the restricted area of any single idea. . . . I am quite willing to take established facts into account. Let M. Guizot rest assured that I shall always be prepared to meet him half-way.' (To Apponyi, 19.4.1844.)

The July monarchy was indeed settling into the lap of order and the problems which had tortured Metternich throughout his official life were approaching a solution. For the first time in his experience as a Minister, he noted in 1842: 'there was not a single item on the agenda'.

And yet it was at this very moment that those whose ears were nearer to the ground, who were more alert than the elderly statesman, were to hear the first distant rumblings of the coming storm. That storm was to shake the whole social order of Europe to its foundations, completely destroying the elaborate political edifice which the Prince-Chancellor had been at so much pains to build. For the slogan 'get rich', first launched by the July monarchy, had not only had its effect in France. The whole of Europe had taken advantage of these long years of peace at home and abroad to revive fortunes lost at the beginning of the century; to enlarge them out of all proportion to current expectations. Everything contributed towards this end: the universal use of

1. To Apponyi, August 4th and October 23rd, 1840.

264

steam-propelled machinery, the new railroad systems, the expansion of world commerce, scientific discoveries. A new society—the great middle-class society of the nineteenth century—was coming to life.

And a revival of national sentiment was the outcome of this economic revival. It was no longer merely a handful of young enthusiasts, as in the days of the *Carbonari*, who were waving the national flag: the people themselves, the serious, hard-working, the most enlightened elements among them, were becoming conscious of their historic destiny. In 1840 the agressive attitude of France had produced a veritable frenzy of counter patriotic fervour in Germany. And Prussia very astutely took advantage of the situation to develop that 'customs union' which turned out in fact to have been the first step towards political union. The wide diversity of nationals who composed the Austrian Empire also began to show restlessness—Kollar, Jungman, Palacky started a Czech renaissance; Gay was active in Croatia; the young journalist Louis Kossuth was making his first appeals to the people of Hungary and Mazzini was about to become the idol of 'Young Italy' in the Lombardo-Venetian provinces.

It was only in Italy, however, that the new movement bore the stamp of revolution. In German-speaking countries it was for the moment merely ideological, with no specific programme, no organisation of groups with a view to action. In Bohemia there was an attempt to revive the Czech language, to create a new national literature, and to make popular drama and music generally available, to modernise a superannuated constitution.

Such needs were comparatively easy to satisfy. Those who put them forward were no incendiaries, no Jacobins: they were later to become followers of a Bismarck, a Cavour and even of the bureaucratic ministers of the Emperor Franz-Josef. All disturbance could easily have been warded off by means of a few energetic reforms, adapted to the conditions of the moment, conceived in terms of a moderate liberalism and enforced with a firm hand.

Alas, among all the nations concerned, Austria was least able to embark upon any such task. For to the intrinsic difficulties of

S

her always disjointed Empire she now added the lack of a guiding hand: the complete absence of any directing power was becoming more and more apparent; there was no longer either policy or pilot.

Like all patriarchal authorities, the Viennese government was at some pains to cater for the peasantry; indeed, it went out of its way to entertain and distract the masses. But subordinate officials—such as the police or the censor's department—insufficiently controlled by the higher ranks, were often guilty of grave abuses; and a persecution as odious as it was silly precluded any reasonable freedom in the realm of thought.[1] Such methods of government seemed increasingly incompatible with the spirit of the age. 'It will not be possible for Austria to remain as she is now for another generation', wrote Baron Andrian. 'This conviction is shared by governors and governed alike.... Could one find a single man in Austria today, whether on the throne or in the humblest cot, who does not consider a complete change of system long over-due...?'

Ought one to exclude the Prince-Chancellor from this generalisation? Did he alone ignore what was going on around him? Wasn't he in a better position than anyone to know the deficiencies of a régime which still bore his name? For decades he had complained of the lack of organisation in Austrian affairs: from the very start of his career he had sought a remedy, but all his projects had proved abortive. He had tried to unify the various departments of government and to centralise administration in a Council of State possessed of full powers of enforcement. But all such plans lay buried in the drawers of the Emperor's desk.

---

1. The imbecility of the Austrian censorship seems to have exceeded all limits. Actors on the stage were forbidden to wear either military or ecclesiastical garments. The word 'paladin' (pundit) was taboo for fear of possible offence to the 'Palatin' of Hungary, and in Mozart's *Don Juan* the great chorus in praise of 'liberty' was changed into one in praise of 'gaiety'! A sentence from Schiller's play, *The Brigands*, which runs 'this scoundrel is called Francis', was cut out in deference to the august name of the Emperor. Any invocation of the Deity became 'Oh heavens!' The name of Tranquillus was substituted for that of Descartes (the French philosopher's works were forbidden in Austria). Prudery forbade an elderly suitor to refer to a 'beautiful breast'. In a school book which talked of 'Cossacks mounted on small horses' the word 'small' was cut out lest it be considered an affront to an allied army.

And now it was too late: it was certainly not from the Archduke Louis or from Kolowrat that he could expect helpful collaboration. Louis' favourite maxim was: 'If you leave a thing long enough, it will solve itself.' And Kolowrat allowed no one a finger in his pie. 'I haven't even the power to appoint a caretaker', Metternich told his suite. He was becoming more and more disgusted with 'the ingratitude, the folly and the weakness of men. . . .'

Moments of acute discouragement overtook this man who had once been so optimistic: completely knocked out, he collapsed weak, ill, in tears and had to be put to bed. In 1839 the Egyptian question induced a state of high nervous tension. 'For a moment', wrote Mélanie, 'I thought he had an apoplectic fit; I lived through hours of anguish, the worst in my whole life.' In November 1842, another attack. He recovered but came back with diminished strength. And although he refused to attend Court ceremonies and confined his own receptions to two a week, advancing age was increasingly taking toll of his strength. 'It is not moral courage he lacks', said Mélanie, 'that he will keep to the end of his life, but his physical energy is declining.' 'Metternich is slowly sinking', wrote the Comte de Sambuy, Sardinian chargé d'affaires, in 1845.

But on all those occasions when he was able to succeed without too great an effort, he showed a maximum of good-will. He intervened on behalf of Confalonieri, Silvio Pellico and other Italian conspirators and had them released from their dark dungeons of the Spielberg (at the time of the Emperor's journey to Milan). Never inclined to shrink from hard work (which often snowed him under for some fifteen hours a day), he helped to modify the results of the financial crisis of 1841 (bankruptcy of Geymuller), helped to develop the port of Trieste (creating the Austrian 'Lloyds', drawing up a commercial treaty with England). He favoured as early as 1843 a project for the Suez Canal and at the instigation of the Rothschilds became the principal promoter of Austrian railways.[1]

1. We find some amusing entries in Mélanie's diary about the early trials on the iron way of Austria: 'I went with mother and the children', she wrote, 8.5.1838,

He succeeded in 1846 in realising one of the dreams of his youth, that old project of Leibnitz and of Gottschied—the creation of an Academy of Science at Vienna (150 years late if compared with Berlin). But he shrank now before any obstacle arising out of Austrian bureaucratic red tape, any tiresome problems of administration.

Nothing could be more characteristic than his attitude towards the significant new customs-union in Germany. Metternich was well aware of the full importance of the *Zollverein* drawn up under the aegis of Prussia. 'Austria', he wrote to Kubeck on October 20th, 1841, 'is about to find herself excluded from the rest of Germany in an important matter of her material interests.... I have just been in Germany, at the very heart of German industrial activity ... and I was deeply conscious of that inferiority which is the outcome of our lack of any specifically Austrian commercial policy.' The remedy was simple: the rate of Austrian tariffs should have been reduced, and common cause have been made with the states of Southern Germany: a second *Zollverein* would not have been impossible to create. Metternich knew this as well as anyone, but the resistance of the great Austrian industrialists, of big land-owners and blind civil servants, set it back many years....

For a long time now, all those who were struggling in behalf of liberal-constitutional or national ideals in Europe had concentrated their hatred upon one man. That man was Metternich. 'From the Baltic to the Pyrenees, from the Turkish to the Dutch frontier', said Sealsfeld, 'only one reaction is ever roused by mention of his name: and that is execration!' And if we follow Parisian polemics or listen to the Austro-German poets—to Odilon-

---

'to have a look at the engine.' Clement had been riding in the train with the Empress-mother, the Archduchess Sophie, several Archdukes among whom was the young Archduke Francis (the future Emperor Franz-Joseph) and Count Kolowrat. On another occasion, she wrote: 'At nine o'clock, Puckler came and wished to take us to see the arrival of 180 bullocks which had come by train. The weather was superb and we were able to view the unusual sight in comfort. The first impression was indeed strange: one could only see an engine drawing what appeared to be an interminable white line, and one could not distinguish a single detail. The train was composed of forty-eight carriages and was bringing pigs and bullocks. . . .'

Barrot, Ledru-Rollin, Victor Cousin, on the one hand; to Anastasius Grün and Grillparzer on the other—Metternich was the 'Don Quixote of legitimist dynasties' and must be considered responsible for the sufferings of all oppressed peoples. Poisoned pens described him as 'the crucifier of genius', 'an enemy of humanity', 'a Talleyrand in reverse' (one had been guilty of clericalism at the outset of his career, the other at the end), and as 'a tyrant who, having deceived the whole world by his lies, is now the only man alive who believes them. . . .'

Thus the anger of millions of misinformed men concentrated on the head of an elderly gentleman, now hard of hearing, disillusioned, sceptical, who spent his days perusing (and making marginal notes on) voluminous reports, in proffering wise counsel to Louis-Philippe, reading treatises on diplomacy and contemporary history to the young Archduke Franz, walking amidst the flower-beds of his garden, blowing soap-bubbles for his grandchildren, playing whist with members of the diplomatic corps, and in moments of leisure, in the dim-lit intimate atmosphere around his own hearth, listening to some member of the family read *Lettres Parisiennes* by the revolutionary Boerne, or the Satires of M. de Voltaire.

Toward 1846 Metternich began to build a large house on his land at the Rennweg, not far from his famous villa. It had been Mélanie's suggestion. 'The house is designed to receive the family when he who is our whole *raison d'être* has been taken from us.' And the old Chancellor took an active interest in the plans of this new home, the main door of which bore this pseudo-modest inscription: *Parva domus, magna quies*—'the house is small but great calm reigns there'. Passers-by sniggered: this Metternichian palace had little in common with the humble cottage suggested, and if one thing was conspicuously absent, that was calm.

As the years went by, portents of the gathering storm became more frequent and disagreement grew daily between the Chancellor, incarnation of the principle of stability, and the peoples of Europe increasingly in the grip of revolutionary frenzy.

In 1846 the peace of Europe was troubled by a rising in

Cracow and the small republic was annexed to Austria by Russia's imperious injunctions.[1]

After Poland, it was the turn of Switzerland which became, in 1847, the arena of a sanguinary conflict between federalized democracies and the Catholic *Sonderbund*, the latter supported by Austria.[2]

And after Switzerland, Germany. . . . On the eighth of February, 1847, King Frederick William IV decided to put a long-hatched plan into effect: convocation of the *States General*, or rather the united States of the eight Prussian provinces—an obvious concession to the parliamentary principle according to current theory.

And in the meanwhile, the great national movement broke out in Italy after the election of a liberal Pope, Mastaï-Ferreti (Pius IX). This movement assumed unprecedented proportions and quickly spread over the whole peninsula, breaking out in the most unexpected forms.

Patriotic banquets were arranged and manifestations in the Opera House, Austrian excise duties were subject to boycott, Italians refused to associate with officers of the Imperial army, Calabrian hats were worn ostentatiously, also Phrygian bonnets and white coifs (in the style of Hernani) trimmed with the Papal colours; walls were covered with posters and written inscriptions (*Morte ai Tedeschi, Il Tedesco alla porta*): the Diets of Milan and Venice decided to break their traditional silence and began to indulge in political proclamations. 'We feel the domination of Austria as the prod of iron in a wound', said the patriot writer Maniu, in December 1847.

And once more Metternich's attitude was calculated to exasperate public opinion. He persisted in his old conviction that 'Italian unity is nothing but an empty phrase, incompatible with existing rivalries in the peninsula: rivalries between families, between cities and between states'. (6.8.1847.) He sneered at the 'progressive Pope' who had, he said, succeeded the 'reforming

---

1. See M.Szarota: *Die letzten Tage der Republik Krakau*; Dr Wieslawa Knapowska: *La politique de Metternich avant l'annexion de la République de Cracovie*, 1933.
2. Guizot: *Mémoires*, Vol. VIII, page 421; W. Marlin: *Histoire de la Suisse, Essai sur la formation d'une confédération d'Etats*, 1926.

Virgin', patroness of the *Carbonari* in 1820. For him, a liberal Pope was a contradiction in terms.

He had increased the strength of Radetzky's army (camped in the Lombardo-Venetian provinces) up to the figure of 83,000 men and he was studying a possible military intervention in the affairs of the Peninsula, although well aware that chances of success were slight. 'Material force can do nothing against chimera, and that is what we are called upon to combat today.' (To Radetzky, 22.8.1847.)

At the same time, the 'hereditary provinces' of the crown of Austria, 'always behindhand, by one idea, one year and one battalion', were beginning to shake themselves out of a long sleep. The lazy submission of Czechs and Hungarians was at an end; even the proverbial indolence of Vienna was a thing of the past. In Hungary, the new Diet of 1847 was dominated by Kossuth and the radicals; the middle classes in the towns had been won over to the nationalist movement; an association formed with a view to boycotting Austrian importations in favour of Hungarian home products soon achieved the phenomenal membership of more than one hundred thousand, divided up among one hundred and thirty-eight branches.[1]

In Croatia, patriots started a nationalist movement against enforced teaching of the Hungarian language. 'The Magyars', said Gay, 'are but a tiny island in the Slavonic ocean; sooner or later, this island will be swamped.'

In Bohemia, nationalist propaganda reached the countryside, democratic societies were formed about 1846 at Prague, for political discussions behind closed doors. The Diet demanded that

1. In 1836 Metternich had written about Hungary: 'The country itself, its laws, its customs, its way of life, are several centuries behind the rest of Europe. A few madmen want to apply ideas which are the outcome of an advanced civilisation to a body politic which is not yet fit to receive them.' 'In 1844 he noted the rise of the urban middle classes 'who are having an overwhelming influence on the country's destiny'. 'Hungary', he said 'is like some great swamp. If men desire to transform it into a meadow or into agricultural lands, they must first drain off the stagnant waters.' But he energetically refused all aspirations to independence. 'What would happen to the country once separated from Austrian tutelage, with its weak degree of culture, its inferior industrial capacity, and taking into consideration the effort required to achieve a complete separation? What would the position of the country be in relation to her stronger neighbours?' ('Maxims in relation to Hungary.')

271

the Emperor should take up residence in Bohemia and claimed effective control of the bulk of the national revenue. Finally, even at Vienna, groups of writer, lawyers and University professors began to agitate and protest against the exaggerations of the censorship and submitted peritions to ministers and Archdukes. [1] And every night at the theatre the public madly applauded Edward Bauernfeld's comedy, *How to grow up*, a thinly-veiled skit on Metternich and his political system. [2]

In Mélanie's own drawing-room, Liszt was not afraid to say: 'You must choose, dear Princess, a constitution for Austria or I shall not play another note'. [3] As a final blow, a bad harvest produced unemployment and destitution: ten thousand workers were sacked in the course of the winter of 1846-1847. Exasperated proletarians one day surrounded the Emperor's carriage, others stoned the Pavilion of Mirrors which was an annex of the Hofburg. Threatening letters became more frequent. At one moment the Polish committee of Paris announced Metternich's imminent assassination, then a letter was received addressed to 'the Emperor of Austria, brigand chief', and demanding: 'Metternich to the gallows!' [4]

Towards the second half of 1847, Metternich began to understand: 'It is now clear to me', he said, 'that we are about to see great changes.' 'The present phase in the history of Europe is the most dangerous she has been called upon to face in the course of the last sixty years.' 'I am no prophet, but I am an experienced

---

1. A deputation had asked to be received by Metternich. 'I will receive each of these gentlemen separately, with pleasure', he replied, 'but I do not recognise anything in the nature of a "Committee" in Austria.'

2. The chief character of the play, Blase, the young man's guardian was a fellow with a swollen head. 'If I were to leave', he says, 'all would go to rack and ruin, nobody would know what to do. I do more work than anyone. I have just signed my name for the twentieth time.' When his ward suggests that a roof might be mended, Blase becomes indignant: 'Don't talk about reforms to me! The system on which the whole world rests is conservative. God himself is conservative. The firmament is a model of stability; are not the planets fixed in their courses?' How had the rigorous severity of the Viennese censorship come to pass this play? It would indeed be surprising had not everyone in Vienna known that Count Kolowrat had taken the author under his protection and was indirectly having a crack at Metternich. Bureaucratic rivalries—which can lose an Empire!

3. E. Bauernfeld, *Erinnerungen aus Altwien*.

4. See H. Schlitter: *Aus Oesterreichs Vormaerz*; Graf Hartig: *Die Genesis der Revolution in Oesterreich*; O. Rommel: *Der oesterreichische Vormaerz*, 1930.

old doctor. I know how to distinguish between a passing *malaise* and a mortal illness. It is the latter we are concerned with today. We shall hold out as long as we can but I begin to despair of the issue.'[1] 'If I am not greatly mistaken, the year 1848 will bring to light quite a number of things which last year were hidden under a cloud.'[2] Our 'old doctor' was not mistaken. The revolution of the mind was now accomplished; its protagonists were passing on to action.

1. Von Usedom: *Politische Briefe*, Berlin 1899.
2. To the King of Prussia, January 1st, 1848.

## XIII

# THE MASSES AWAKE
# TO SPRING

*Men, in the mass, are ungrateful, disloyal, untruth-*
*ful, cowardly, self-interested. . . . and the Prince*
*who stakes his throne upon their word—with no*
*other guarantee—is lost.* MACHIAVELLI

*'It is not when a river has already burst its banks*
*that men can hope to stop its head-long course.*
*Energetic methods must be brought into play at*
*the opportune moment to prevent the overflow.'*

SOME strange correlation seems often to have been apparent as
between the phenomena of nature and historic upheavals
among men. Who can forget the 'stormy' atmosphere—to use
the word in its accustomed sense—that existed in July 1914? And
at the beginning of that other fateful year of 1848, one might also
discover in atmospheric conditions some presage of the storm
about to burst on the political horizon. It was as if the natural
course of the seasons had been reversed. The inhabitants of
Vienna, accustomed since they could remember to long and hard
winters, noted to their surprise, in early February, the first spring
buds upon the branches. Thus nature herself, in a premature
rejuvenescence, was announcing the *Völkerfrühling*, that spring-
time awakening of the peoples, roused from their long sleep by
the call to freedom.

But nothing changed in the daily round of the Ballhausplatz.
On February 25th the young attaché Hubner, a frequent and

favoured guest, was writing: 'What surprises me is the cheerful indifference that reigns in Princess Mélanie's drawing-room in spite of the approaching storm which we all feel in the air. One notes this particularly in the course of those "intimate evenings" designed for the elect: a few diplomatic pundits and some local notabilities with the *jeunesse dorée* grouped around Princess Herminie presiding at her tea-table. We have enjoyed fine weather for so long in Austria that we can no longer conceive a tempest. The inclement conditions of the beginning of the century are now forgotten. The younger generation has only known blue skies, and if the clouds appeared to gather for a moment in 1830, they soon passed over, almost unnoticed.'[1]

Increasingly alarming despatches piled up on the Chancellor's desk. At the beginning of January, the revolution was successful at Naples and the King of the Two Sicilies proclaimed a Constitution without regard to the protests of Austria, Prussia and Russia. On the seventh of February, his example was followed by Charles-Albert of Sardinia, and shortly after that by the Grand Duke of Tuscany. Disorder broke out in Rome and Pius XI was obliged to dismiss all his ecclesiastical ministers and to declare a general amnesty. At Munich, the people demonstrated against Lola Montez, the royal favourite, and against all ministers supposed to have been sponsored by her. In the Lombardo-Venetian territories, the situation was growing daily worse: Austrians were now called *porchi tedeschi*[2] in the streets.

Metternich, having now reached the age of seventy-six, no longer displayed his former mental agility, the resourcefulness that was once his outstanding characteristic. If we are to believe Vizthum, who had always recognised in him a man of parts, he was now no more than 'a shadow of his former self'.[3] Well aware

---

1. Hadn't Sealsfeld, no friend of Metternich, written a few years before: 'Austria is nearer to a crisis than any other monarchy in Europe. But we shall not see there the customary concerted uprising, outcome of a well-conceived plan, that is not the manner in which the Austrian people will claim their rights. The provinces are too carefully watched; they do not hang together and their interests are often incompatible. At a pinch, Bohemians would not hesitate to march against Hungarians, Poles against Italians, the Austrians against them all.'
2. 'German pigs.'—TRANS.
3. Berlin-Dahlem, Archives.

that Europe was heading for some appalling catastrophe, he seemed quite unable to suggest a remedy.

'Everything suggests something ought to be done', 'but this is no moment to start any major reforms. All we can do is to haul in our sails and direct our course as circumstances may dictate.' If only he stayed at the helm, there might still be some hope. 'My resignation would amount to revolution. If they get rid of me, the whole structure will collapse.' The Chancellor was still convinced that half-measures would meet the case: we shall declare a state of siege in Lombardo-Venetia and then, at our leisure and in a proper state of calm, we can consider certain reforms of an administrative nature.

'The point at issue is whether to revive that Italian Chancellery which was suppressed in 1817; to do this would help to meet the grievances of the Central Diet of Milan', the Prussian Minister, Arnim, informed his government on January 17th: 'But for twenty years they have been talking about the need of an Italian Chancellery since the present administration is in the hands of men totally ignorant of Italian conditions and the aulic Counsellors do not even understand the language . . . what could better prove the irresponsibility and vacillation of the present government? But what else could one expect when those at the head of affairs are all old men, worn out by work, men who only desire to rest and who regard with horror any form of change?'[1]

'Metternich's imperturbability alarms me', wrote the young Hübner. 'I wonder what they would do should the worst happen? Metternich stands alone and he seems paralysed and powerless.' And he added: 'the more I examine the situation in Italy, the more convinced I am that the game is up. The government no longer disposes of the means to win. One doesn't arrest a revolution by means of diplomatic notes or leaders in the Press that no one reads. It's like trying to stop a steam-engine with a walking-stick.'[2]

Such was the state of mind in Vienna on the eve of those great events which were about to put an end to the July monarchy in

1. Archives, Berlin-Dahlem.
2. A. von Hübner: *Ein Jahr meines Lebens.*

France. Late in the afternoon of February 28th, a visitor was announced to Metternich: it was Anselm de Rothschild. Once more, as in 1830, a member of that family of great financiers was bringing bad news. Learning that the Republic had been declared in Paris, Metternich, half-fainting, collapsed into his armchair. 'Well, my friend, it's all up now!' he said in a tone of complete discouragement when Fonton, Russian chargé d'affaires, came to confirm the disaster. 'The judgments of God are terrible', cried Mélanie in turn. At the end of the day, after a session of the Cabinet which lasted for several hours, the *corps diplomatique* met as usual in the Chancellor's drawing-room. All the Ambassadors were there; all talked at once in the grip of obvious emotion. Metternich, however, had pulled himself together and was by then displaying an Olympian calm; 'I never lived through such an evening', Hübner concluded.[1]

The next day, the capital was in an uproar. At dawn, a poster appeared on the city walls: 'Before a month, Metternich will have fallen. All hail to the Austrian Constitution!' Government stock fell twenty points on the exchange; there was a rush on the National Bank and also to withdraw savings from the *sparkasse*. The masses were talking of 'state bankruptcy'; restaurant-keepers, butchers and bakers refused all bank-notes. 'Revolutions spread quickly', remarked Metternich, sententious as usual.

On the tenth of March, an Imperial edict informed the population that the change of government in France only concerned the French: any inclination to rebellion in Austria would be firmly and promptly quashed. 'Crushed, disgusted and much changed', according to the Prussian Minister, Metternich stuck to his guns. 'In the last analysis, I prefer the worst to the merely bad; it is

1. Herr von Arnim, the Prussian Minister, gave this account of the gathering: 'Last night there were a great many people in Prince Metternich's drawing-room, chiefly diplomatists. The. . . . impression produced here by the recent events in Paris is formidable. Everybody is thinking of the probable repercussions in Italy . . . this is openly discussed: there is bitter criticism of the Viceroy and of the inadequacy of measures taken in this respect. . . . Concessions have been suggested but the moment would seem ill-chosen, the government would appear to be afraid. And so nothing at all will be done. But certain provisos which had been the cause of justifiable complaints will be modified. Thus a new law is to be passed in connection with a special stamp for the Lombardo-Venetian kingdom.' (Berlin-Dahlem, Secret Archives.)

more clear-cut', he wrote to Kaunitz, in the midst of the fray. 'I feel calmer than before the struggle began. I am standing firm. Nothing can baffle me.' He succeeded in dissolving the Hungarian Diet where Kossuth was noisily demanding a responsible government. The arrival of Radowitz, envoy extraordinary from the King of Prussia, revived old hopes. 'I shall now create between Berlin, Vienna and Saint Petersburg a nucleus for thought and action': that old alliance of the three nordic powers which he was about to revive.[1] And joking statrted again in the *salons* of the Chancellery: Mélanie greeted Count Szechenyi with the words 'Welcome, citizen!' to which came the prompt retort, 'Thank you, enchanting *sans culottes*!'

But were they not taking the indolence and loyalty of the capital too much for granted? For the fire still smouldered. Impromptu meetings were being held all over the place: bourgeois and intellectuals were hectically preparing the convocation of the Provincial Diet of Lower Austria. At the instigation of the well-known writer, Bauernfeld, a petition to the Emperor was drawn up which called for the immediate convocation of a parliament, the formation of a national guard and an edict to proclaim the liberty of the Press. Students carried this document round into all the cafés of the city; the Archduke Francis-Charles undertook to present it to the Emperor.

Little by little an indefinable foreboding was spreading in the highest government circles. 'We are all very anxious at the Court', Princess Mélanie entered in her diary. 'Today, they all look to my poor Clement for help; they also wish to make him responsible for the errors of others in past years.' And those very Archdukes who used so modestly to stand with their backs against the wall as the Chancellor passed down the corridors of the Hofburg, were now asking themselves for the first time whether Metternich's system was really the way of salvation. Old antagonisms were awakening on the one hand, a natural inclination to more liberal views was drawing others. After all, who was this Prince Metternich? Once a great statesman, now

1. See also: Fritz Rheinöhl: *Aus dem Tagebuch der Erzherzogin Sophie* (Historische Blätter, Wien, 1931).

old and deaf, a Rhenish noble, called to take power at Austria's zero hour, who had rendered great service to the dynasty but who had been well repaid by the unique favour and honours conferred upon him. 'An employee', in short, admittedly more competent, in higher standing than the rest. But neither his person nor his system could be said to have merit except in so far as it contributed to the House of Austria. If Metternich were to become a nuisance, they must turn him out. That was how minds were working at the Hofburg, chiefly in the apartments of the Archduchess Sophia, an ambitious and scheming woman with a watchful eye on the dynastic succession, on that throne upon which her young son Franz-Josef would one day sit.

And so a Court *camarilla* was formed which the Chancellor's chief rival, Kolowrat, joined with alacrity. Gradually, Metternich was more and more deserted until he stood virtually alone. During the morning of the 10th of March, an official, Baron Sieber, paid a visit to Princess Mélanie to suggest that she deposit her diamonds at the house of friends since they were no longer safe at the Ballhausplatz. After this, even Madame de Metternich changed her tune. 'The calmest minds among us are profoundly shaken. All we women of the family now get together to pray fervently that God will grant us consolation, will assist and save us in our great distress.' Only the police affected optimism, maintained complete sang-froid. 'Nothing at all will happen', proclaimed the Prefect Sedlnitzki; and added: 'I am taking special precautions to protect the Chancellery'. On March 12th there was a gala reception and the Metternich *salons* were full to overflowing, as usual. But the atmosphere was strained; nervous tension was extreme. 'Is it true that you will be leaving tomorrow?' This question to her hostess came from Princess Félicie Esterhazy, a silly woman who often spoke out of turn. And she continued naïvely: 'It seems we are on the eve of some important event; we were told to buy candles for an illumination'.

'The great Viennese Revolution', of March 13th, 1848, differed materially from all previous mass uprisings. It was a 'kid-glove' affair, a revolution staged by university students and good peaceful burghers. And in spite of a few sanguinary skirmishes and acts of violence committed in the poorer districts by an exasperated populace, it was to keep to the end its initial and essential character of *gemüthligkeit* and loyalty. It started with respectful petitions to the supreme power and was to close the following day with enthusiastic cheering in honour of the feeble-minded Emperor, Ferdinand. Metternich and the traditional Austria were to be its only real victims.

The sky was grey on that historic morning, but the air was warm and balmy; it was spring. Already at eight o'clock, lecture-rooms at the University and at the Polytechnic were crowded. Professors were trying to calm the students by giving an account of their overtures to the Court on the previous day. 'The Emperor', they said, 'had deigned to accept their petition: there was now nothing to do but to wait for his reply.' But on all sides arose the cry 'we will wait no longer! We shall now make known our wishes to the people's representatives. To the Diet . . . march!' For on that same day the States General of Lower Austria was to hold its first session. In a long procession, the students advanced towards the centre of the city; on all sides, heads popped out of windows: 'They're coming, they're coming!' 'By 9 a.m.', relates M. de Gabriac, 'students of the Faculties of Philosophy, Theology, Law and Medicine were congregated in the Herren-gasse in front of the building where the "States" were to meet . . . they had attracted a considerable number of bourgeois sym-pathisers, together with an even larger number of onlookers. Some ten to fifteen thousand persons were already congregated in the Herrengasse and adjacent streets. The States-deputies arrived about ten o'clock and were followed by the students right into the conference hall where the demonstrators began to in-dulge in very violent language and to break up some of the furniture.'[1] 'Hail Austria and her glorious future! Long live freedom!' cried the youthful agitators. Impromptu speakers demanded a Constitution, a responsible ministry, freedom of the Press, freedom of religious opinion and . . . the Anschluss

1. Gabriac to Lamartine, March 14th, 1848. (Foreign Office archives.)

with Germany (!).[1] Count Montecuccoli, Earl-Marshal of the Austrian nobility, tried to calm them. 'The *States* agree with you', he said. And immediately it was decided to petition the Crown to form an advisory body composed of representatives from all the provincial Diets.

But whereas negotiations in the hall itself were going forward with comparative calm, agitation in the courtyard was reaching fever-pitch. A student read the incendiary discourse pronounced the day before by Kossuth in the Hungarian Diet. There were cries of 'We want a Constitution: down with Metternich!' Nobody was interested in the resolutions just accepted by the Diet. Very soon a frenzied crowd had again filled the conference chamber, while other demonstrators were moving on to the Ballhausplatz, cursing the Chancellor and simultaneously cheering the Emperor. Shortly, the large square of the Ballhausplatz, normally deserted, was invaded by an immense crowd.

The Metternich family was at the windows. 'Now we shall see how the Viennese conduct their little revolution', said Princess Mélanie, smiling and disdainful. 'They only need a large cart full of sausages with plenty of horseradish, and all would be to their heart's desire.'[2] Little Princess Pauline's eyes were glued to a handsome grenadier in a bearskin busby, one of twelve or fifteen responsible for the safety of the Chancellery. The crowd were shouting savage abuse; he turned pale but stood like a statue. . . . Metternich himself, in the meanwhile, was trying to hear snatches of a revolutionary speech with which a young medical student, carried shoulder-high, was haranguing the crowd: 'France, England, the United States, all the rest of Germany', shouted the orator, 'have pointed the way. The road to liberty is open; we have only to follow them. If Austria still hangs back, she owes it more than anything to a faulty system of education. But it is not the paternal heart of His Majesty the Emperor we have to blame; we all know the Emperor, we are all devoted to him; I am now speaking only of that unpopular Minister who is at the

1. That Anschluss was to come about on another March 13th, ninety years later, to the day.
2. Dr Jäger's *Mémoires*.

T

head of the government: of Prince Metternich! But Nature will help us; his days are numbered, and when Nature has run her course, we shall be free.'[1] 'Take down all he is saying', ordered Metternich, turning to Pilat, his secretary. Then, banging his fist on the table: 'The sickness has come to the surface at last!'

While all this was going on, the session of the Diet had ended in tumult and disorder. 'We surrender to brute force', cried the deputies. 'To the Hofburg!' And a procession formed: applauded by members of the middle classes, followed by street-urchins and smart women with their footmen in livery, the deputies walked four-by-four towards the Imperial Palace. The doors of the Hofburg flew open before them. Pell-mell they piled into the palace, followed by a few mere sightseers.

It was almost twelve noon, and so far no serious clash had occurred. 'The crowd seems inoffensive', concluded the Prussian Minister in a report he sent off post-haste to Berlin. 'The troops have been called up and all possible precautions taken . . . to an Austrian, such demonstrations appear dangerous but they are really very mild: there have been cries of "Long live the Emperor!" "Long live the freedom of the Press!" But the people of Vienna are not naturally seditious and I think it will all pass off quietly.'[2]

And if proper measures of precaution had indeed been taken, the day would have gone by without further incident. 'It is obvious that with some 11,000 well-trained troops on foot and with proper planning, order could well have been maintained', wrote this same diplomat the following day. 'The topography of Vienna itself would have contributed toward that end. All government offices were concentrated within a very small area at the centre. One only had to cross a garden to go from the Hofburg to the Chancellery. The Palace which housed the Diet of Lower Austria was only 200 metres away and grouped all around were the houses of all the great families and the important Ministries. The character of all these buildings has not changed at all since 1848, and when one visits the place as a tourist, one is

1. Gabriac to Lamartine, Archives of Foreign Affaires.
2. Berlin-Dahlem, Secret Archives.

amazed by the restricted compass within which the events of the 13th of March, 1848, took place. Nothing would have been easier than to cut off the disaffected area by means of a thin cordon of troops. But the authorities had shown a complete lack of decision, inexcusable weakness. And yet a committee presided by Kolowrat had been sitting for several days to insure the public safety. Metternich had been kept out. Who is to say that the Minister of the Interior was not viewing with a certain satisfaction the rising tide of popular fury against his rival? All such suppositions are admissible.

The fact remains that, having posted a few battalions on the bastions and glacis the crowds had been given a free hand in the centre of the city where the narrowness of the streets made any kind of crowding conducive to appalling disorder. And it was only early in the afternoon, when circulation had already become impossible, that the first small detachments of soldiers arrived upon the scene: the masses opened their ranks to let them through and formed up again behind them. The Archduke Albert, military governor of Lower Austria, who came on horseback at the head of a troop of Pioneers together with his brother the Archduke William, was greeted with cheers.

It was just at this moment that an unforeseen incident occurred: Someone in the crowd threw a large piece of wood into the air, probably a mere sign of enthusiasm. The Archduke Albert's horse took fright and shied. A commotion ensued. Believing the prince in danger, his Pioneers charged at the bayonet. Shrieks arose and the pacific sentiments of the crowd suddenly turned to anger. The people threw themselves on the soldiers, cursing them, trying to seize their rifles. At this, their commander gave the order to fire.[1] A salvo rang out. Some twenty dead and wounded were stretched out on the ground; the crowd fled in all directions crying: 'They have fired upon the citizens! To arms! Ring the tocsin!'

Thereupon, some rushed to the belfry of St Stephen's, others tried to seize the arsenal. A volley of bricks and stones were hurled at the Grenadiers and the Pioneer corps advancing at the

1. Gabriac to Lamartine.

charge. A detachment of cavalry called to the rescue were obliged to take refuge in the courtyard of the Diet building: the crowd followed them and pulled the cavalrymen off their horses; a wounded member of the crowd was hoisted onto a saddle and promenaded through the streets. Sanguinary clashes occurred on all sides between sections of the troops and bands of citizens. After the first shot, the authorities closed the gates of the city in order to prevent any further influx from outlying suburbs. Infantry and artillery detachments were reinforced on the Place Saint-Michel, at the doors of the Castle. On tubs, and facing the big guns, stump orators were haranguing the people. At last it had come to anarchy, to revolution![1]

And what in the meanwhile was taking place inside the Imperial Palace? An eye-witness, the poet Bauernfeld, has given us an account.[2]

After drawing up a short statement about the situation (which nobody had asked him to do!), he had decided to go to Court! For many days, his state of mental exaltation had prevented him from sleeping, to say nothing of shaving. His shoes were dirty, he was dressed in an old grey shirt, wore a proletarian hat and carried a heavy stick in his hand. In spite of this distinctly irregular 'court-dress', through the good offices of a friend, who was an official of the Chancellery, he gained admittance to the antechamber of the *Staatskonferenz* and demanded an audience of the Archduke Francis-Charles. There, surrounded by a crowd of courtiers, chamberlains, princes and generals, Bauernfeld handed out his *exposé* and launched into an impassioned speech about liberty and the rights of man. The assistants shook him warmly by the hand. A general opined that: 'Sedlnitzki and his police-force ought to be hung for having neglected to warn us of what was brewing among the masses'. The Archduke Francis-Charles appeared in the doorway and listened mildly to a new harangue by his strange visitor. 'We will immediately grant freedom of the Press and a constitution', he said, always benevolent and placid. 'We are about to call a council of Ministers and a Family Council.

1. A. Helfert: *Geschichte der oesterreichische Revolution*, 1907.
2. Bauernfeld: *Erinnerungen aus Alt-Vien.*

You must wait until the Archduke Louis has finished his breakfast.' Which last remark brought from Bauernfeld the indignant retort: 'How can one think of breakfast at such a moment?' 'Anyone', says Grillparzer, who also assisted at this amazing interview, 'anyone could then force his way into the palace, bang on the table with his fists, and insult the Archdukes.'

It was in the midst of this incredible uproar that Prince Metternich, about 1 p.m., made his first appearance. The old man once described by Canning as 'the Grand Inquisitor of Europe' had lost none of his impressive bearing; that wrinkled face with hollows at the temples, whose distinguishing feature was still the aquiline nose, wore a look of icy contempt. Thin, elegant, wearing a green tail-coat with light grey trousers, neck swathed in the familiar black silk jabot, with a gold-knobbed stick in hand, he passed through the ante-chambers casting a look of supreme disgust on the agitated crowd: nobody dared to speak a word. . . .

About what happened, in the hours that followed, behind closed doors in the Archducal apartments, we have only the scrappiest of information. 'When I think of all the imbecilities I heard in the course of that famous thirteenth of March', said Metternich later, 'I often ask myself whether those people were mad or merely drunk. They were all talking in the air; not one of those self-styled reformers could see farther than the end of his own nose.'[1] 'There has been a lot of talk about what ought to be done', wrote the Prussian Minister, 'and at last it has been decided to form a committee with a view to looking into the matter of concessions to be made.'[2] But it seems that these 'concessions' were to be confined, in fact, to the granting of freedom to the Press. Metternich had categorically opposed any dundamental changes affecting the existing order of society. He thought to by-pass immediate events, as he described it, to 'rise above them'.

According to him, the uproar in the streets was no criterion. 'Vienna', he subsequently wrote, 'is not Paris: Vienna is not a city that absorbs the life of the whole Empire and can thus dictate its policies according to her own whims. Vienna is only

1. Metternich to Hartig, April 2nd, 1848.
2. Berlin-Dahlem, Secret Archives.

285

the capital in so far as the Emperor himself resides there.' What did he care for the clamour in that 'country town' of Lower Austria? It was Europe that mattered; the international advance of republicanism must be arrested. Hadn't Louis-Philippe lost his throne by adopting the method of appeasement? And for the Austrian Empire such concessions would be all the more dangerous in that she rested on no other basis than the monarch himself, on those purely personal ties which united the dynasty with the several provinces. It was essential to respect both the letter and the spirit of the late Emperor Francis' will. Order must be restored in the streets, the Diet building must be cleaned and repaired, and the 'States General' must be allowed to continue in absolute calm, discussions already begun. But the Chancellor was preaching to deaf ears; nobody would take responsibility for energetic measures of repression; the Cabinet was completely paralysed. Metternich left the Palace in despair.

The gravity of the situation increased materially during the next few hours. On the *place du Palais*, gas was escaping from overthrown lamp-posts; rifle-shots were heard on all sides; a sinister light appeared on the horizon: the workers had risen in the suburbs, had set fire to police-stations, to factories, to the toll-houses, to Metternich's own villa. A few of them had managed to hammer in the *Schottentor* (one of the main city gates) and had joined up with the rioters at the centre. A bourgeois militia began to be organised. Inside the Hofburg, which by now resembled a besieged fortress, confusion had reached a climax. Deputations followed one after the other; students obtained permission to carry arms. Towards 6 p.m. it was decided again to call for Metternich. He was taking the air in his garden, surrounded by his wife and children and a few faithful friends.

It was time to act. What was to be done? Ought they to give full powers of martial law to General Prince Windischgraetz who was striding up and down the conference hall, restraining himself as best he could, glowering, with arms crossed, a 'little Duke of Alba'? Should they ask for the help of the bourgeois militia? After some further consultation with Metternich it was decided to declare a state of siege, and Windischgraetz went off

to exchange civilian clothes for his uniform. But in the ante-
chambers the crowd was furiously insistent. Scherzer, by trade a
wine merchant and now an officer of the new bourgeois guard,
declared emphatically that only Metternich's resignation could
put an end to the riots. 'Until that is done', he said, 'the middle
classes will not give their assistance to the army.'

Then suddenly the resistance of those in power began to give
way. Why not sacrifice to the people this man who was the
main object of their hate? The monarchy would still be sitting
pretty if only it got rid of this inconvenient old man and his
wandering, hazy speeches. Hadn't they been listening to hints for
some days now, hints by the ambitious Archduchess Sophia and
by the Empress Maria-Anna herself? A storm of reproaches immediately rose against Metternich: they began to see in him the
author of all their woes. The Archduke John asserted that, after
talking for an hour and a half, Metternich had said exactly
nothing. Kolowrat went one better: 'it has always been like that,
for the past twenty years', and the Archduke Louis, who had
been conferring with Scherzer, suddenly and categorically demanded the Prince's resignation. Had Metternich expected this
result? He who considered himself 'the main pillar of the building', could he conceive that they might do without him? Would
a monarchy that had survived six centuries give way to some
five-score hysterical undergraduates and a few drunken bourgeois? And all those reproaches from members of that Imperial
family who owed most of their greatness to him must have
seemed an inexplicable aberration, monstrous ingratitude. But
they would not have to tell him twice. If he was to be described as
the 'only obstacle to the maintenance of public order', he would
hand in his resignation without delay. He made only one stipu-
lation: it must be submitted to the Emperor in person.

During the tragic hours his capital had just lived through,
Ferdinand had scarcely realised what was happening around him.
He wandered about the palace like a ghost, wagging his head and
repeating mechanically: 'I'll consent to everything. I won't have
them fire on my dear people.' In seeking an endorsement from
this travesty of a monarch, Metternich then was accomplishing

287

a purely symbolic act. 'I submit', he said in his letter of resignation, 'to a power superior to that of the sovereign himself.'

When, after half an hour's delay, Prince Windischgraetz in his tight-fitting Hussar's uniform returned to the palace, everything had already been arranged. There was no more question of dictatorial powers under martial law: the revolutionaries had won. Calm, dignified, leaning on his gold-handled walking-stick, Metternich had left the Hofburg, contemptuously waving aside the effusions of Archdukes, Ministers and delegates who thanked him for his generous gesture. 'I am making no sacrifice, merely doing my duty. . . .' 'I shall not be taking the monarchy with me. No one has broad enough shoulders to do that. Monarchies disappear when they lose confidence in themselves.'

Her eyes black-rimmed with fever, an arrogant smile on her lips, Princess Mélanie stood waiting for him in the doorway: 'Well,' she said, 'have we all been murdered?' 'Yes, my dear,' he answered gravely, 'we have all been murdered.' That was the last word.

'Clement was resigned, calm, almost happy', Mélanie entered in her diary. 'I thank God', he said, 'I have been allowed to remain detached from current events; the overthrow of the existing social order is now inevitable. I could not have avoided concessions which will inevitably lead to chaos. As things are, I am saved the shame of signing them.'

Late that night he made a final visit to the Hofburg to take leave of the Empress Maria-Anna and beg her to postpone the abdication, which had now become inevitable, until the impending coming-of-age of the young Archduke Franz-Josef. Next morning, when Dr Jäger arrived to take his pulse, the Prince remarked as he opened his eyes: 'it is the pulse of Austria that should concern you'.

True enough, the revolutionary fever was only in its early stages. In the evening of March 13th, when an officer, carrying a flag appeared in the streets and above the shouting of the crowd announced the Prince's resignation, the formation of a *garde bourgeoise* and of a committee for assistance to the bereaved,[1]

1. Gabriac to Lamartine (Foreign Office Archives).

the city had lit up in a spontaneous outburst of rejoicing. Félite Esterhazy's candles were now put to good use; windows were broken at the house of the Prussian Minister, Arnim, who refused to follow suit. Thousands of people of all nations, Germans, Hungarians, Italians, and Poles, fraternised in the streets. They cheered the sovereign and shouted patriotic songs, thus putting the final touches to a Royal and Imperial revolution.

But the next morning, disorder broke out again. 'Today', wrote Arnim, 'bands of young students whose rifles are too heavy for them, together with detachments of the *garde bourgeoise*, are patrolling the streets followed by shouting urchins.' These minor disorders, however, were unfailingly loyal in character. 'Towards five o'clock in the afternoon', wrote M. de Gabriac, 'deputations were allowed into the courtyard of the Castle, and the Emperor, appearing on the balcony, was received with enthusiasm. . . . The Archduchess Sophia, whose recent opinions have made her very popular, also appeared between her two sons. She received a welcome hard to describe. . . .[1] I have just seen the Archduke Palatin, newly arrived from Pressburg, borne through the streets in a carriage drawn by the people: he was bringing an address from the Hungarian parliament, voted yesterday by an enormous majority. The Emperor has gone for a drive in an open carriage with the Archduke Francis-Charles and is greeted wherever he goes by deafening cheers.'[2]

In other quarters of the city, activities were less innocent: incendiaries were pursuing their sinister work. 'Business is entirely held up and it will be impossible to avert a disastrous commercial slump', wrote Gabriac. In the city itself, the movement is entirely political, but in the suburbs it is taking on a character of mob violence which is most alarming. Some members of the national Guard are saying that they will never be able to get control except

1. Was this woman, who had contributed more than anyone to the Chancellor's downfall, already repenting? Her diary, recently published, suggests it: 'A terrible, disastrous day', she wrote on March 13th-15th, 'days which have left a pain in the heart, a sickening memory which will never be wiped out; a shame and scandal for our beautiful Vienna become the theatre of systematically-organised revolution. . . overwhelming. . . humiliating. Monday night, our good old Metternich resigned.' (F. Reinohl, *op. cit.*)
2. Gabriac to Lamartine, March 15th, 1848. (Archives of Foreign Affairs.)

by using cannon.' The authorities had thought to appease the people by Metternich's resignation, by suppression of the censorship, by vague promises of constitutional reform, but this, it seemed, was no longer enough. The Chancellor's mere presence was a cause of irritation. Some forty soldiers had been quartered in his house, and Mélanie was amusing herself serving them with priceless Johannisberger wine in silver goblets. But towards the end of the afternoon, the Archduke Louis was obliged to inform the ex-Chancellor that he could no longer guarantee his safety. It became obvious that Metternich would have to leave Vienna. Irresponsible as usual, with regard to financial matters, he had no available money: Solomon de Rothschild, without even being asked, saved the situation by sending his benefactor a thousand ducats.

Later, at the darkest hour of night, the man so recently all-powerful left the capital, sneaking out incognito like a criminal. He had been obliged to seek refuge, during his last hours there, in the houses of friends: with Count Taaffe and with Prince Liechtenstein. For the Viennese, he had become once more the foreigner, a soldier of fortune. Almost universally abandoned, he was still surrounded by a very few faithful friends. His wife, who was making up by her courage and devotion for a host of past errors, took her place in the hired cab which was carrying them to an uncertain future. Charles von Hügel[1] got up on the box; he sacrificed his lovely villa of the Schoenbrunn in order to conduct their journey.[2] Rechberg, who made himself responsible for the children, took them by train. 'Clement was sitting next to me', wrote Mélanie. 'This man whose habits, whose comforts had been our daily preoccupation, for whom only yesterday I had tried to avoid all draughts, any chance of a chill, this man of seventy-five was without a roof to his head and had no notion what might become of him on the morrow.... In twenty-four hours, he had seen the collapse of a life-time of hard work.'

Metternich had expected to stop at Feldsberg, an estate be-

1. Charles von Hügel was the brother of Mélanie's admirer, Clement.
2. A son of Charles von Hügel published a detailed account of their flight in the *National Review* of June 1881.

longing to the Liechtensteins, 'to take a rest', he said, 'which since
the downfall of the Bastille I have everywhere failed to enjoy'.
But this plan was frustrated: the local municipality refused to
allow him to stay there. The Archbishop of Olmutz then forbade
him to enter the town towards which he was next headed. An
angry crowd insulted him at the station. There was no room
now for Metternich in Austria, or anywhere else on the continent
of Europe. It was to England, the only country where order and
freedom went hand in hand, that he looked for refuge, having
crossed through Germany at the gallop. 'There certainly goes a
fugitive king', cried a postmaster who saw him pass. Yes, kings
were indeed on the run; the Metternichian era was closed.

# EPILOGUE

PRINCE Metternich outlived by eleven years that political system which bears his name. He only drew his last breath in June 1859, the day after the battle of Magenta. For eleven years he had watched the European pageant as a passive witness; examined, as through a lorgnette from his private box, the unfolding of a new social order.

Endowed with astonishing vitality, he had recovered from his fall and found his normal equilibrium with a disconcerting rapidity. The very day after his resignation, he wrote to Pilat to suggest launching a new conservative daily newspaper in connection with which he would figure as a shareholder only. Having fought the Press for forty years, he now proposed to make use of it for the promulgation of his ideas. Not for one moment was he prepared to admit that he might have been wrong. 'Either I'm a fool or the world is mad', he said. 'It is not my business to solve that particular conundrum now, but I am confident as to the verdict posterity will give about the relative wisdom or folly of nineteenth-century theories and events, and no less confident about the place they will assign me in the struggle between good and evil.'

Deprived of his high State functions, driven out into exile, he only admitted 'unhappiness in so far as the world itself was sad'. 'Placed as I now am, from an observatory with a world-wide horizon, I have no reason to complain of my personal fate. It is the world I pity.' (March 28th, 1848.) He seemed indifferent to the financial difficulties into which the revolution had plunged him. 'Prince Metternich has been harshly treated', the Prussian Minister wrote to Vienna, on March 19th, 1848. 'He has not been given a pension. The States of Nassau wish to take away Johannisberg which they insist was given to him without proper legal sanction and which they claim as State property. Even if they do not seize the estate, he will probably be made to pay taxes back as far as 1815 (a considerable sum!), since he used to enjoy it tax-free.'[1]

The ex-Chancellor's financial difficulties did not end there. Deputies of the Austrian Diet openly accused him of lying and malversation. All his goods and property in Vienna and in Bohemia were sequestered pending an inquiry which was fully to exonerate him several years later. Luckily, he was allowed to keep the income from Johannisberg which, added to a generous allowance from the Tsar, insured him a reasonable if not luxurious existence. Metternich remained, as he had always been, a spoilt child of fortune.

After staying for a time at Mirvat's Hotel (now Claridges), the Metternichs took a house 'only a few steps removed from the Hyde and Green Parks'. It looked out over a space 'as large as two thirds of the city of Vienna' (presumably, Constitution Hill). Immediately, all London society flocked to their doors, showing absolute contempt for the Chartist demonstrations then taking place in the London streets. The Aberdeens came, and the Binghams, the Duke of Devonshire and the Duke of Beaufort, the Aylesburys, the Beauvales, the Greys. Finally, Palmerston himself, the great adversary of former years. The Londonderrys invited Metternich and his wife to a large fancy-dress ball, where Mélanie shuddered at the sight of cardboard crowns, of imitation sceptres and ermine cloaks with which the guests impersonated historic Kings and Queens of England and France. (For visitors arriving from the continent of Europe, such trappings awakened poignant memories in 1848!)

Another important victim of the revolution, Prince William of Prussia (the future Emperor), came to pay his respects to his father's and brother's erstwhile *confidante*. And if the Queen and Prince Albert, for political reasons, showed a certain coldness to the Metternichs (whom they had never liked), Queen Adelaide—

1. Berlin-Dahlem, Secret Archives.

devoted heart and soul to Austria—showered marks of attention and friendship upon them.[1]

Wellington used to come every morning and spend several hours with them. 'If I still had responsibilities of State', wrote Metternich, 'I could scarcely do justice to their performance in view of the great number of friends, old and new, who now visit our small drawing-room. People have offered to lend me whole castles and other country estates. I was well advised to keep my chin up when I came here.' Even in the streets, he found himself recognised, surrounded, complimented by public speakers. 'We could not have been better received in London, had I been John Bull in person.'

Metternich would probably have stayed on had he been able to afford it. It gave him great pleasure to study this city which he had not seen for forty eight years and which had developed out of all recognition during the half-century. The old man now found heavily populated working-class neighbourhoods where he had once known fields and meadows. He admired the phlegmatic English temperament and English political acumen. 'The skies are different here from those of Vienna or Berlin. The storm, of course, might also descend on London, but there are lightning-conductors. And where can one find "conductors" on the Continent?' In the English form of liberty, he found 'a diametrical opposite of that type of liberalism which so weighs on the rest of Europe'. 'I should like the incompetents who now hold power at Vienna to be here', he said, 'to learn by what methods, in this country where liberty reigns supreme, they also know how to check that licence which is liberty's negation.'

Pecuniary requirements made it imperative for him to seek less expensive surroundings. He went first to Richmond (the Metternichs lived in the old Palace where Queen Elizabeth died); then to Brighton, and finally to Brussels. In the Belgian capital he rented the house of the musician Bériot, Boulevard de l'Observa-

---

1. Metternich's first encounter with Queen Victoria dates to 1845. The Queen, then travelling on the Rhine, had found the Chancellor 'very amiable, older than she expected, theorising a great deal and speaking very slowly'. Metternich, on his side, wrote: 'She is not English, just plain Coburg', and was indignant at the Queen's 'childishness'.

toire, and later a mansion belonging to the family of Prince d'Arenberg, at the Sablons. The last move gave rise to rumours of a marriage between one of Metternich's daughters and a member of that illustrious Belgian family. But in spite of the friendship with which he was honoured by King Leopold, Metternich felt the call of his own country. And after three years in exile, he returned to Johannisberg in June 1851. 'The Rhine runs in my veins', he said, 'and the sight of it enchants me.'

The revolutionary fever in Germany had subsided. King Frederick-William of Prussia asked Metternich's permission to come and visit him, and then several times assured his host that he had now definitely given up his former 'liberal illusions'. He went so far as to show irritation at the sight of a tapestry in white, black and gold (the 'national' colours) in Mélanie's drawing-room. Decidedly the wind had changed. Metternich would soon be able to think about returning to Vienna, for he suffered, in spite of everything, from the absence of a real home. 'This is something which few men feel as strongly as I do, and which alone would be enough to give me a horror of communism.' Already in 1849 he had written: 'Time will heal the breach created between me and a country turned upside down by revolution; but this consummation must be left to that strongest of all dynamics—the force of circumstance.' Two years later, in the summer of 1851, the Austrian government made it known that there would be no opposition to his reappearance on the banks of the Danube.

Between the years of 1848-1851, Austria had passed through all the normal stages of revolution: rapture at first, followed by a growth of mob violence, the inability of the authorities to cope with the situation, civil war, and finally use of the armed forces to restore order. Kolowrat, who had stepped into the shoes of his illustrious rival, had only stayed in power for a single month. After fleeing the capital which had so spontaneously cheered him on March 14th, 1848, Ferdinand II had abdicated on December 2nd of that same year. It was the young Emperor Franz-Josef, Metternich's pupil, who abolished the much discussed Constitution almost as soon as it had been put into effect. He also took back Hungary with the help of the Russians and quelled the Viennese riots by means of Windischgraetz' big guns. This method of repression had caused considerable damage to the city: the Kolowrat palace burnt down, a room in the Ballhausplatz where Metternich worked for so many years completely destroyed. The revolutionary Bauernfeld, spouter of so much incendiary haranguing at the Hofburg, was now quite mad; Szechenyi, chief protagonist of the liberal creed in Hungary, had also passed beyond the boundary line of sanity. In his rare moments of lucidity, the latter could be heard to say: 'What Metternich told me twenty-five years ago is still ringing in my ears: If you take out a single stone, the whole edifice will topple.'

In Italy, Marshal Radetzki had crushed the opposition at Custozza and Novara. Order had been restored throughout the Austrian monarchy; but it was a new kind of order. Of the old Austria prior to 1848, nothing remained with the sole exception of the dynastic principle and a few illusions in the minds of Viennese officials. The realm had entered a period of dangerous experiment: 'Austria is in a state of transformation,' said Metternich during his visit to London, 'but she has taken the wrong turning.' The traditional and patriarchal type of authority had been replaced by a strong and highly centralised form of tyranny. The country was being ridden on a tight rein; non-German elements were bullied and so a foundation was being laid for their eventual defection.

There was little for Metternich to do in this new Vienna. The élite of Viennese Society had certainly given him a warm welcome. 'In the first days, after our arrival', wrote Mélanie, 'we were so swamped with callers, it would be impossible to count them. The whole Cabinet came to visit us as well as all the Archdukes then in residence.' And yet the appearance of the Prince and his wife at a large ball given by Schwarzenberg, new President of the Council, at the Chancellery, was interpreted as a gesture of defiance. Everyone was surprised to see the Metternichs, heads high, as if nothing had happened, showing off in these same salons where for so many years they had been the dictators of Viennese society. 'Why Mélanie, how unexpected;

you really are admirable', exclaimed the Archduchess Sophia. But the arrogant wife of the fallen statesman was receiving all this homage from 'the right people' as the most natural thing in the world. 'It is Austria should sink her eyes before me; I have done nothing to blush for.' She was already criticising the guests at the reception: 'They had invited all the wrong people, those we used to consider "the second society", circles whose leading ladies are much too flamboyantly smart. One saw no sign of mixing with the cream. . . .'(!)

Although back in his old surroundings, Metternich found himself debarred from any effective participation in political life. The many letters in which he had given advice to Franz-Josef and to Schwarzenberg during his exile had received evasive replies: and 'they' seemed no more disposed to listen now that he was back in Vienna. Meyendorff also went to see the ex-Chancellor and found him 'surprisingly calm and healthy, but more prosy than ever'. 'His judgment is still sound, but by no means as infallible as he would like to think', was the Russian diplomatist's conclusion: 'I don't know whether he will make any impression on his young sovereign who might well not see the practical import of opinions based on such very ancient history'. One is continually tempted to that classic injunction: 'Please, Mr Counsel, let's get on to the flood'![1]

Meyendorff was right; Metternich and Franz-Josef no longer spoke the same language. Methodical and tireless worker, the young monarch inclined to positive, not to say prosaic methods. He liked to be able to call upon specialised ability, to simplify problems and eliminate from his own mind everything that did not lend itself to a unified and centralised control. Metternich, on the other hand, had inherited (together with other traditions of the German Empire) a love of complexity, of the organic, the fluid, of improvisation. It was within such an order of ideas that he had once been able to exploit his personal charm, his knowledge of men, all the rich resources of a subtle mind. But the present vaguely 'constitutional' Austria, bureaucratic, militarised,

1. Meyendorff to Nesselrode, October 1st, 1851. (Reference is to Racine's *Les Plaideurs*.—TRANS.)

U

dominated by middle-class sentiment, could well dispense with such qualities—and did.

It was in matters of foreign policy that the rift between the two temperaments was most apparent. Schwarzenberg, supported by the Emperor, had begun to substitute for the old Prusso-Austrian dyarchy the notion of a general Austrian hegemony in Central Europe. Metternich heartily disapproved of such megalomaniac inclinations. Particularly, he deplored the humiliation inflicted upon Prussia at the congress of Olmutz which was indeed to result in terrible reprisals at Sadowa in 1866. And after the premature death of Schwarzenberg, Franz-Josef had committed even more fatal errors: he had broken with Russia and, during the Crimea, had ranged himself on the side of that Napoleonic France which was to fight him in Italy a few years later.

Metternich had always frowned upon any active policy, for Austria, in the Balkans.

'To push Austria eastwards, is to push her out of the West', he said. 'Don't talk to me about shipping on the Danube', retorted the old man, 'when the safety of the world is at stake.'[1] He wrote to Count Buol, the new Secretary of State for Foreign Affairs: 'It is not a question of Russian or Turkish interests, but of the peace of Europe'.[2] He categorically disliked the imprudent foreign policy of Nicholas I. The Continent was still suffering from the revolution of 1848; a new war might well provoke new social upheavals, and who had better cause to fear them than the Russian autocrat? But if nobody dared tell the truth to the Tsar, he—the old servant of the Habsburgs—was there to enlighten Franz-Josef.

For didn't the position of Austria in 1854 bear a striking resemblance to that of 1811 and 1812? Now, as at the time of the great clash between Napoleon and Alexander, the Empire's strength lay 'in freedom of movement and not in commitments tending to stimulate the appetites of Eastern powers'. And if Austria was unable to arrest the war, her main desideratum was

---

1. Meyendorff to Nesselrode, June 13th, 1854.
2. Metternich to Buol, June 18th and July 15th, 1852.

certainly to bring about peace as soon as possible.[1] But he was crying in the wilderness.

Were all the warnings of the ex-Chancellor, then, to remain sterile? No prophet in his own country, it was beyond the Austrian frontiers that Metternich was to find his spiritual heirs.

During his years of exile, two men, both young and conspicuously able, both cut out for a great future, had sat at the old master's feet, imbibing his wisdom: Disraeli,[2] who was to cement the British Empire, and Bismarck, founder of the second German Reich. So the ex-Chancellor who had been 'Europe's coachman' until 1848, would continue to influence world destiny through these two disciples, the two greatest statesmen of the second half of the nineteenth century.

It was during his stay in London that Metternich got to know the future Lord Beaconsfield, whom he completely captivated. 'What a different man he really was to what those fancied him, who formed their judgment in the glitter of Vienna', Disraeli wrote after their first meetings. 'A profound head and an affectionate heart. What divine conversation! I never heard the like. He sketched for me, with incomparable mastery, the present state of Europe . . . his enlightened thought shone through those smiling eyes; he was really brilliant.' And shortly after this, he announced a new visit to Metternich in the following terms: 'I shall come and see you, not merely because you are the only philosophic statesman I ever encountered, not merely because I catch wisdom from your lips and inspiration from your example, but because I feel for you the most tender and respectful affection, which could not be more profound if . . .'

And later, when a long correspondence had been established between them, Disraeli found Metternich's letters 'so full of ideas that they will never grow old'. 'Had he not been a Prince and Prime Minister', the young politician concluded, 'he would have been a great professor.'

The first meetings between Metternich and Bismarck took

1. Metternich to Buol, November 18th, 1853, January 17th and May 25th, 1854.
2. Moneypenny and Buckle: *Life of Disraeli*.

299

place on August 6th and 7th, 1851. Forty years later, having himself experienced the ingratitude of sovereigns and the uncertainties of fortune, the retired Iron Chancellor of the Reich still remembered all the details.

Bismarck had found the fallen statesman in the best possible frame of mind: amiable and gay. . . .' 'I am glad', he had said, 'to be out of harness. I used to be on the stage; now I watch from the stalls.' 'Without a break he discussed the history of political events from 1788 to 1848. He also talked of viticulture and of literature while we sampled some of the best wines of his famous vintage.'[1] Other meetings followed in 1852 and 1857. Metternich had aged considerably but never tired of reviving memories of the past (especially of the Napoleonic era) in honour of his Prussian visitor. He would also give his own political diagnosis of current events and problems.

Such sketchy information hardly gives us a comprehensive picture of the nature of Metternich's discussions with his young admirers. But, by the light of his own writings, it should not be over-hard to reconstruct one.

What did the old Chancellor talk about? Of those immutable laws which govern human societies, of the revolutionary illusion, of the lessons to be learnt from history. His mind perennially wrestled 'with tomorrow'. To be a successful man of the future, he taught, one must have been a man of the past, for without a past, there is no future. He was never able 'to shake free of the system called by his name'. 'To preserve is to act', he said; 'that maxim has always guided me. . . .' 'Revolution is a monstrous illusion; a fallacious palliative. . . . For revolutions, as indeed all other dangerous expedients, always come to a bad end; there is always a day of reckoning. Accounts must finally be made to balance; and the State must make good the deficit which it can only do at the expense of the taxpayers. That is the story of all revolutions; it is old as the world itself, but fools do not realise it any better for that. . . . Can the people govern? And who is to obey if the masses themselves call the tune?'

He opposed revolutionary with Christian doctrine 'which

1. Bismarck: *Briefwechsel mit seiner Frau.*

admits no *right* without its corresponding duty'. And that is why, he asserted, 'the decadence of empires always goes hand in hand with the growth of unbelief'. Having lost its immutable creed, the modern world is a prey to permanent anxiety; and, like the wandering Jew, finds no peace. Prophetically, he foretold the ills of the future. 'For the world to experience the golden age, we need only to replace all our sovereigns with usurpers—as happy as they are wise', he remarked ironically. He could well distinguish the danger and its causes: exaggerated nationalism, on the one hand; on the other the theory of the all-powerful state with its inevitable sequence—a complete loss of individual liberty. For liberty, in the last analysis, must be sacrificed to the collectivity: 'All the world's ills can be summed up in the single term "social revolution".' [1] And there was only one way to avoid it, to maintain political peace at all cost.

He was especially worried about the developments in Germany. 'What goes by the name of the German question, today is a contract between Prussia and Teutomania, a contract based on mutual savagery.' (January 6th, 1850.)

But France remained his chief interest. 'That country', he said, 'now resembles a nursery with toys and weapons littered all over the place. That great country knows neither how to live nor how to die; it is in full pursuit of experiment.... For whereas philosophy in Germany is losing itself in pantheism, in France, it has become communistic.' [2] 'In France there is nothing that could properly be called political procedure, they just play at politics.'

Sometimes, he was even more categorical: 'France, which is at the bottom of all our troubles on the Continent, France always several steps ahead of the rest of Europe has now reached the inevitable climax of her aberrations, mere movement *in vacuo*, absolute negation'.

'Popular feeling in France categorically wants peace; the various parties, taken separately, also want peace, but by each

1. To Buol, June 2nd, 1858.
2. To Monsignor Viale-Prelà, December 14th, 1849. Metternich had just read Proudhon's book: 'The author is mad,' he notes, 'unquestionably mad, but he has genius.' Shortly before that Metternich had been visited by Louis Blanc and had had a long discussion with him, to Mélanie's intense indignation. She described the famous socialist as an 'insolent scoundrel'. (Pauline Metternich's *Mémoires*.)

advancing a different method according to their individual interests—they create confusion worse confounded.'[1] 'France is at sixes and sevens, afraid of herself. . . . The model country now trembles before what she once with pride described as "progress" and which all the world—walking in her footsteps—hurried to receive as such. . . . France has now reached her eighth or tenth revolution and is waiting for the ninth or eleventh. . . . The body politic in France has been decapitated and is now in search of a new head.'

Could that idol of the moment, Louis-Napoleon, become the saviour of his country? Metternich was not convinced. Napoleon I had been a great soldier; Louis-Napoleon was merely 'the nephew of a great soldier', 'a clever opportunist', or perhaps 'a phlegmatic madman with every appearance of sanity'. And so the future looked dark. 'France will end by involving her neighbours in dangers they will only be able to control by force of arms.'[2] (This was to foretell 1870.)

Metternich's forecast of the future of the Habsburg Empire was profoundly pessimistic. He had given forty-seven years of his life to the thankless task of 'restraining his countrymen's advance to the edge of the precipice'. And now the old building had disintegrated: only the foundations remained, and some of the original materials. Would men have the courage to rebuild without 'contravening the laws of nature'? Was the break-up of what had been known as Austria, now perhaps inevitable? But he still hoped in spite of everything that this last remaining citadel of order and tradition might be preserved. 'Since the whole world admittedly suffered from the present evils there might still be some hope of mitigating their effect on the Empire'.[3] After all, right must win in the long run. That, too, was a law of nature. And didn't those two young men, who listened so respectfully to all he had to say—that Disraeli and that Bismarck—didn't they hate all those disturbers of the peace as much as he did? Perhaps they would be able to pick up the sword now falling from his senile hands. . . .

1. To Hartig, February 14th, 1851.  2. To Hartig, February 14th, 1851.
3. To Hartig, April 2nd, 1848.

Metternich had arrived at an age when serenity automatically sets in, when one grows reconciled to necessary evils, finding new joys in meditation, in a sense of regeneration and a vision *sub specie aeternitatis*. 'He no longer either felt bitterness or any desire for vengeance', says Duke Ernest of Coburg. From then on he was bathed in an aura of calm: even men of our generation who had grown up in the fear rather than the love of Metternich could not long remain insensitive to this new harmony.[1]

But shadows cast up from time to time against this halo in the gloaming, shadows of a distant past. Faces of women he had once loved rose up before him. It seemed as if the heroines of his life's drama were taking leave of him one by one, before the curtain fell: a certain Countess von Eltz, ninety-one years old, with whom as a child he had danced a minuet at the Court of the Elector of Mainz—then Princess Lieven, then the Sagan, the Bagration!

Time had not spared these ladies—once so lovely, so graceful, so much admired. When Metternich saw Princess Lieven on his last visit to London, she looked like some hoary ancestress stepped down from her frame in the family portrait gallery. Invariably dressed in black, she wore an immense hat with a green veil and always carried a gigantic fan. 'Solemn and impressive', wrote Princess Pauline Metternich, 'she would pass without deigning to look on us poor worms.' Always obsessed with politics, she kept well-informed as to what was going on in Paris and was 'in process of being won over to Napoleon'! A belated jealousy was all that remained of their former love: the Princess who had spared no sarcasm in relation to the Chancellor's second wife was equally lacking in indulgence towards the third whom she described as 'fat and vulgar'. And when it came to Metternich himself, Madame de Lieven, always sprightly, found him 'fatuous, very slow, very heavy, very dull; obscure and boring when his subject was himself and his infallibility'. 'But she fell victim again to her former lover's charm as soon as he began to talk of the past and above all of Napoleon.'[2]

The Duchesse de Sagan—*femme fatale* of the Congress of

1. Herzog Ernst II von Koburg: *Aus meinen Leben.*
2. *Mémoires of the Baron de Barante*, Vol. VII, page 421.

Vienna, was also to be seen at Richmond and later in Vienna, looking like a venerable ghost. But she was well-preserved and dressed in a manner suitable to her age—was, in fact, still supremely elegant. She had a lovely voice and spoke German with a classic perfection. The famous adventuress had certainly gained poise. Young Princess Pauline found her 'outstandingly distinguished'.

Princess Bagration looked like a slightly lunatic scarecrow. She still saw herself as in the golden days of her portrait by Isabey: crowned with roses, swathed in all the seven veils, in a setting of billowy clouds. But clouds and beauty had alike disappeared; only the veils and the roses now remained. Of her famous ringlets, some five or six faded and meagre yellow strands remained to mock; her skin was lemon, her body a skeleton—no less. This, however, did not deter the dear Princess from dressing in a garment of diaphanous batiste, tied with pink or light blue bows; her tiny head overshadowed by a hat that some 'eighteen-year-old *bergère* would have hesitated to put on'. But she made up for this fantastic exterior by a genuine and touching devotion to the friend of her youth. She displayed towards Metternich 'a variety of blandishment', she leant against him and looked up at him, 'her poor faded blue eyes in a haze of dreamy and devoted ecstasy'. The younger witnesses of these antics (merciless youth invariably is) had some difficulty in keeping their faces as they watched the great statesman, always dignified and distinguished, walking with this 'mincing mummy' on his arm.[1] Mélanie did no more than enter this understatement in her diary: 'The costumes and carriages of Princess Bagration are of a unique originality'.

But one after another they stepped down into the tomb: Princess Lieven, at Paris, in January 1857; Princess Bagration, in Austria, on May 21st of the same year. She had come especially to Vienna (scene of her youthful successes) to die. When at last she succumbed, Prince Metternich's intimates did not dare convey the news to him for three days. 'Really! I am surprised that she lasted so long', was all the old man found to say.

He was beginning to come to terms with death—death inexor-

1. Princess Metternich: *Souvenirs d'enfance et de jeunesse.*

ably feeling all his contemporaries: Wellington, Nicholas I,
Radetzki, Kubeck, Apponyi, his sister Pauline, Clement von
Hügel, and finally Raymond, the old French valet who had
served him for forty-six years. But only one loss, the cruellest of
all, profoundly shook him. In March 1854, Princess Mélanie
succumbed to a serious illness—she had never really recovered
from the shock of 1848.

She had been the most faithful and devoted of companions.
She had managed to keep up his courage during the years of exile
and had made a new and comfortable home after their return to
Vienna. Bossy and jealous she had indeed remained to the end:
she never cared to leave her Clement *tête-à-tête* with his old
admirers. But fate had reserved her an untroubled death. 'Her
last moments might be compared', wrote her husband, 'with a
light slowly going out, with a child falling gently to sleep; a
quiet setting forth to her eternal home.'

And now he was alone, an old oak with withered branches; a
'had-been', 'a celebrated figure of times past now relegated to the
attics of history'. But all his mental faculties were still active. 'I am
dead', he wrote to Buol, on May 12th, 1856, 'but I belong to that
category of corpses in which the nerves are still vibrating and
who can still be galvanised by issues affecting principle.' His life
was now planned with such regularity, so well-ordered, he had
no time to be bored. He devoted no less than eight hours a day
to reading and to correspondence. He regularly received from
Paris a variety of publications including *Charivari* and the *Revue
des Deux Mondes*: drawings by the caricaturist Cham, in the first
of these, made him laugh immoderately. Always an early riser,
in the afternoon he would take a walk in his private park and
there—true to the best traditions of German sentimentality—
admire the beauties of nature. On Sundays, after Mass, he would
devoutly read the Epistles of St Paul.

The last months of his life were saddened by Austria's war
with Piedmont and France. He had approved the Viennese
Cabinet's resistance to the aggressive disposition of the Court of
Turin. But when he suddenly saw France rise up and take her
place by the side of the Sardinian kingdom, he was reminded of

the epic struggles of his own youth and declared: 'How I regret not to be able to face Napoleon III as I once faced his uncle'. But whereas he consistently preached a firm stand, he was categorically opposed to a war in which Austria would have to tackle a Franco-Italian coalition alone—seeing that, on account of a bungling foreign policy, neither the help of Prussia nor of Russia would now be available.

Distressed by the turn events had taken, the Emperor Franz-Josef often came to see him, asked the old statesman's advice, but continued to follow his own inclinations. 'Above all, for the love of Heaven, no ultimatum to Italy!' cried Metternich. But, alas, the ultimatum, drawn up in much the same style as that of the famous tinder of 1914, had been despatched the previous evening. Metternich got caught up in the general agitation, he argued interminably, wrote more than ever, and drew up a series of memoralia which remained abortive.

It was in this state that Baron Hübner last saw him, in May, 1859. 'We took a little walk in the garden', he relates, 'Metternich leaning on my arm—I was surprised to find the burden so light. After which I followed him into his study where the conversation became more urgent and lively. As I was leaving, he repeated several times with some emphasis: "I was a rock of order". I had already closed the door, but I opened it again to take one last look at the great statesman. He was still sitting at his desk, pen in hand, thoughtful, a far-away look in his eyes; upright, calm, proud and majestic, he sat there looking as I had so often seen him at the Chancellery at the peak of his prosperity and power. He saw me through the partly-opened door, gave me a long and piercing look and murmured under his breath: "A rock of order!" '

Towards mid-day, on June 11th, 1859, at the age of eighty-six, Metternich passed quietly away (with no noticeable death-pangs), surrounded by his family and a few close friends. As he went, the knoll was also tolling on the battlefields of Italy—tolling for what once had been the power and glory of the Austrian Empire.

The body of the great Austrian Chancellor now lies in a strange land, in what was once his estate of Plass (now 'Plazy') in Czechoslovakia. The house where he was born at Coblenz has become an inn. His palace of the Rennweg was occupied, until recently, by His Italian Majesty's Embassy. New states have risen from the ashes of that old Austria of which he was once the mainstay. But of the Empire of the Habsburgs which stood for 'a thousand years of struggle in Europe, a thousand years of trusteeship in Europe, a thousand years of European faith' [1] not a single trace survives. 'All that remains of me will have been destroyed by worms with the exception of what will come to light fifty years after my death', Metternich had declared. 'But then my great-nephews, if I am privileged to leave any such behind me, then, I say, the members of my family will learn that they possessed in me an ancestor who thought, who saw, who had the will to act.' [2]

A perspicacious writer who is also well known as an historian recently asked: 'Wouldn't he have a great deal to teach us, if the Chancellor came back now?' In a Europe torn from its axis, given over to democracy, obedient to the clamour of the proletariat; a Europe in the grip of differing creeds, of bloody discord, men have once more folded up their tents and, impelled by relentless forces, have set out towards an unknown future.

Will the nations of the earth ever listen to the voice of reason? 'Science', a great English physicist recently remarked, 'only knows one form of change: everything grows old. It only knows one form of progress: each moment brings us nearer to the tomb. We are forced to admit the inexorable nature of such laws. This world is disappearing like a dream, returning to the void, disappearing like a tale that is told and which shallow human reasoning will never fathom. . . .'

1. Hugo von Hofmannsthal: *Die Idee Europas*, 1912.
2  From Troppau, November 29th, 1820.

# BIBLIOGRAPHY

PRINCE METTERNICH'S OWN CORRESPONDENCE

*Mémoires, documents et écrits divers laissés par le prince de Metternich, Chancelier de Cour et d'Etat, publiés par son fils*, le prince Richard de Metternich, classés et réunis par M. A. de Klinkowstroem. Vol. I to VIII, Plon, 1883. (An English translation exists of this work, that is to say of Vols. I to VIII only.)

J. Hanoteau: *Lettres du prince de Metternich à la princesse de Lieven.*

Prokesch-Osten: *Aus den Papieren.*

Metternich und Kubeck: *Ein Briefwechsel.*

Graf Hartig: *Fuerst Metternich und F. de Paula, Graf Hartig.* Vienna, 1923.

Von Bibl: *Metternich in neuer Beleuchtung. Sein geheimer Briefwechsel mit dem bayrischen Staatsminister Fuersten von Wrede,* 1928.

C. J. Burckardt: *Briefe des Staatskanzlers Fuersten Metternich-Winneburg.*

*Archivalien zur neueren Geschichte Oesterreichs.* Bund I. (Inventar des Fuerstlich Metternichschen Archivs von Plass.)

Grand-duke Nicolas Michailovitch: *Les rapports diplomatiques de Lebzeltern, ministre d'Autriche à la Cour de Russie.* Saint-Petersburg, 1913.

Charles von Duerm: *Correspondance du Cardinal Hercule Consalvi avec le Prince de Metternich.* Louvain, 1899.

C. de Grunwald: *Mémoires inédits de M. de Metternich, ambassadeur à Paris (Revue de Paris,* August 1st, 1936; October 1st and 15th, 1937).

*Correspondance du Prince de Metternich avec le Cardinal Viale-Prelà.*

## Biographical Works Concerned With Prince Metternich

Srbik (Heinrich, Ritter von): *Metternich*, Vols. I and II. 1925.

Bibl (Victor): *Metternich*. Paris, 1935.

Mazade (Charles): *Un Chancelier d'ancien régime. Le règne diplomatique du Prince de Metternich.*

A. Sorel: *Metternich* ('Essais d'histoire et de critique').

M. Paléologue: *Diplomates romantiques: Talleyrand, Metternich, Chateaubriand.*

Robert (André): *Metternich* (In the collection 'Hommes d'Etat', Vol. III), 1937.

Capefigue: *Diplomates européens*, 1843.

Loménie (L. de): *Galerie des contemporains illustres par un homme de rein*, 1842.

W. C. Binder: *Fürst Metternich und sein Zeitalter*, 1836.

A. J. Gross-Hoffinger: *Fürst Metternich und das oesterr. Staatssystem*, 1846.

Hormayr: *Kaiser Franz und Metternich. Ein nachgelassenes Fragment.* Leipzig, 1848.

Strobl von Ravensberg: *Metternich.*

A. O. Meyer: *Fürst Metternich*, 1824.

E. Schmidt-Weissenfels: *Fürst Metternich, Geschichte seines Lebens und seiner Zeit*, 1860.

A. Beer: *Metternich* ('Neuer Plutarch', vol. V), 1877.

I. A. Pilat: *Kurzer Abriss der Lebensgeschichte des Fuersten von Metternich*, 1825.
*Auszuege aus den Geheimen Memoiren des Fuersten von Metternich.*
Mitgeteilt von seinem Privatsekretaer E. L., 1849.

Haeusser: *Furst von Metternich.* (Historische Zeitschrift), 1860.

J. W. Wacherlik: *Der oesterreichische Staatskanzler Fuerst von Metternich*, 1872.

Springer: *Metternich.* (Preussische Jahrbuecher, Bund IV).

O. Lorenz: *Staatsmaenner und Geschichtsschreiber des 19. Jahrhunderts.* (Studies of Metternich and his political procedure), 1896.

F. B. Schaefer: *Metternich*, 1933.

# Bibliography

H. Schnee: *Metternich und seine Zeit*, 1933.

Th. von Heigel: *Metternich* (Charakterbilder aus der neueren Geschichte).

W. Tritsche: *Metternich Glanz und Versagen*. Berlin, 1935.

G. A. C. Sandeman: *Metternich*.

Algernon Cecil: *Metternich*.

Du Coudray: *Metternich*, 1935 (Jonathan Cape), London.

B. G. Malleson: *Life of Prince Metternich* (Statesman Series), 1888.

## A FEW WORKS CONSULTED BY THE AUTHOR:

### GENERAL HISTORY

Lavisse et Rambaud: *Histoire universelle*.

Treitschke: *Deutsche Geschichte*.

A. Sorel: *L'Europe et la Révolution française*.

*Cambridge Modern History*, 1907.

L. von Ranke: *Deutsche Geschichte*.

Edmond Vermeil: *L'Allemagne du Congrès de Vienne à la révolution hitlérienne*.

H. von Srbik: *Deutsche Einheilt*.

Seignobos (Ch.): *Histoire de l'Europe*.

### HISTORY OF CIVILIZATION IN AUSTRIA

B. Bibl: *Der Zerfall Osterreichs. Kaiser Franz und sein Erbe*.

A. Stern: *Geschichte Europas von Wiener Vertrag zum Frankfurter Frieden*, 1915.

E. Wertheimer: *Geschichte Oesterreichs und Ungarns im ersten Jahrzehnt des 19 Jahrhunderts*.

*Cambridge Modern History*: (Britain's Foreign Policy, vol. 10).

Springer: *Geschichte Oesterreichs seit dem Wiener Frieden*. 1809, two vols. 1863.

F. Palacky: *Die oesterreichische Staatsidee*. Prague, 1866.

R. Sieger: *Der oesterr. Staatsgedanke und seine geograph. Grundlagen*, 1908.

# Bibliography

J. Nadler und H. R. von Srbik: *Oesterreichs Erbe und Sendung im deutschen Raum*. (Particularly the articles by Otto Brunner, H. Kretschmayer, Paul Muller and H. R. von Srbik).

André Tibal: *Essais sur la formation d'une individualité nationale*, 1936.

Count A. Polzer-Hoditz: *L'Empéreur Charles et la missions historique de l'Autriche*.

F. Saltern: *Das oesterreichische Antlitz*.

Karl Tschuppik: *Maria Theresa*.

Von Bibl: *Francis II. Father-in-law of Napoleon*, 1936.

Oscar A. H. Schmitz: *Der oesterreichische Mensch*

H. J. Biedermann: *Geschichte der oesterreichischen Gesamtstaatsidee*, 1867-69.

E. Gunglia: *Maria Theresa. Ihr Leben und ihre Regierung*, 1917.

S. Whitman: *Austria*, 1899.

Schluessler: *Oesterreich und das Schicksal*, 1925.

A. Winkler: *Oesterreichs Weg*, 1936.

H. Sassmann: *Kulturgeschichte Oesterreichs. Vom Urzustand zur Gegenwart*, 1935.

E. Stranik: *Oesterreichs deutsche Leistung*, 1936.

H. Springer: *Grundlagen und Endziele der oesterreichisch-ungarischen Monarchie*, 1906.

W. Meynert: *Kaiser Franz I*. Vienna, 1822.

# INDEX

## A

Abrantes, Duchesse de, *see also* Madame Junot, 161, 162.
Adams, John Quincey, 198.
Adelaide, Queen, enthusiastic reception of exiled Metternichs in London, 293.
Adriatic sea, M. wants port on, 80.
Aiglon, l', see Reichstadt, Duc de.
Aix-la-Chapelle, Congress of (England, Austria, Russia, Prussia), 163, 164, 184, 191; results: Coalition troops to evacuate French territory, France to be admitted Quadruple Alliance.
Albani, Cardinal, 194.
Alexander, Tsar of Russia (1801-1825), Potsdam alliance, 26, 29; occasionally inspired, 59; sister's proposed marriage, 65, 69, 70, 79; Mme. Bagration spies for, 86; faced with Napoleonic invasion, 87; after victory, 88, 89; 'Napoleon or I', 96; his war indemnity claims, 97; alliance with Frederick Wm. III, 99; first steps to Coalition, 100, 101; potential liberator of Slavs, 108, 109; pursues invasion of France despite M., 111; at Congress of Vienna, 119, 121, 122, 124, 130, 131, 133, 134, 135; relations with M. improve, 136, 156; hears of Napoleon's escape and takes action, 137, 138; and women, 159, 162; initiator of Holy Alliance, 174, 175, 178; 'revolutionary with crown on his head', 180, 183, 184; at Laibach and Verona, 192; political change of heart, 194, 195; dies, 198, 210, 299.

Alexander III, Tsar, father of Nicholas II, 185.
Ali, *see* Mahomet.
Alliances, *see* Potsdam, 26; *see* Paris, Treaty of, 129, 130, 140, 184; Triple (Austria, Russia, Prussia) after Teplitz, 216; Quadruple (2nd Peace of Paris, 1815) Austria, England, Prussia, Russia (to which Bourbon France soon added), 191; informal, whereby Austria to supply Napoleon with 30,000 men, 87.
Alsace, retained by France, 141.
Andreossy, (note 1) 43.
Andrian, 48, 266.
Anglo-Austrian relations change after death of Castlereagh, 198 *et seq.*
Anglo-Russian entente disbelieved by Napoleon, 97; Wellington's Protocol, 200.
Anne, Grand-duchess, sister of Tsar, proposed marriage to Napoleon, 63 *et seq.*, special references 69-71, 73, 76.
Anonymous Tract written by M. against French Revolution, 16.
Anschluss, 280.
Anstedt, Russian delegate to Prague, 107, 125.
Anti-clericalism, 176.
Apocalypse, 'Beast of', name given to Napoleon, 88.
Apponyi, Count, 179, 183, 214, 219, 220; reports plot in Paris murder Duc de Reichstadt, 224, 262, 264, 305.
Aquinas, Saint Thomas, 180.
Archives (many released since last war, 34), *see* Vienna, Secret

312

Archives; *see* Dahlem (Berlin-Dahlem) for Prussian Secret; *see* Quai d'Orsay; Austrian Foreign affairs, 93, 95, 99, 252, 259; English F.O., 210.

Aristocracy, Austrian at first haughty to Metternichs, 18; comparison French, German, English with Austrian, 58; Bohemian nobles dispossessed 54; European throngs Congress of Vienna, 120; M. and Talleyrand, 132; M. deplores aesthetic indifference of Viennese, 150; M. married three women of Austria, 167; Viennese attitude to Antoinette von Leykam, 171; errors of *ancien régime*, 182; M., rigid aristocrat, had horror of middle classes, 182; all Vienna at M.'s reception, 238; Kolowrat genuine Austrian product, 254.

Artois, Comte de, brother of Louis XVI and of Louis XVIII, himself later King of France (1824-1830) as Charles X; as *émigré*, held Court at Mainz, 13.

Auersperg, Gabrielle de, 120.

Augereau, Pierre-François-Charles, *maréchal et pair de France*, Duc de Castiglione, responsible for *coup d'état* of 18th Fructidor; military triumphs on behalf republic and Empire, 40.

Augustus of Saxony, 22.

Aurore von Koenigsmark, 22.

Austerlitz, weddings at, 17, 18; result of battle of, 27, and M.'s position in Berlin after, 28.

Austria, 3, 8, 14, 17, 18, 26; Napoleon soft-pedalling with, 29; menacing, 30, 33; limits concessions, 34; history of, 48-62; a 'German League of nations', 53; rehabilitation after Wagram, 63; relations with France, 64; Marie-Louise of, 63 *et seq.*, special refs., 66, 67, 74, 75, 78, 79; relations with France resumed, 69; checkmated by Napoleon, 77; M. and, 80, 82, 83, 87; attitude to Napoleonic campaigns, 88, 93, 94, 95; plotting in by anti-French party, 95; M. no desire to fight France and fears Russia, 96, 97; free to join Coalition, 98, 99, 100, 102; and Coalition, 105, 106, 107, 109; M. does not wish to dethrone but curb Napoleon, 110; recovers lost provinces by first Treaty of Paris (1814), 115; triumphs, 116, 122; M. see Prussia as valuable asset to, 136; same size as Prussia but greater prestige, 137; benefits from Congress of Vienna, 140; but loses Rhenish territories, 141; as long as A. and Russia pursued same policy, all well between M. and Princess Lieven, 166; needed stability the 'System' offered, 186, 187; relation to German nationalism, 189; dominated Italy and Germany since Congress of Vienna, 193; prestige of, at Paris under Louis XVIII, 197; Treitschke accuses of having bullied Germany, 211; gives asylum to exiled Charles X, after July Revolution, 217; reactionaries want war against Louis-Philippe, 218; neutrality towards Belgium and Poland, 218; worries connected with Duke of Reichstadt, 220-224; plays Duke against Louis-Philippe, 225, 226, 228; Accession of Ferdinand, 250; Triumvirate (*Staatskonferenz*), 255, 256; symbol of reaction, 262; war with France threatened, 263; weak under triumvirate, 265-6; preparing to drop pilot M., 278; no room now for M., 291; M.'s forecast pessimistic, 302; death of M. and passing of Empire, 306.

Austrian, Empire, fall of, that colossus, 3; power of, 24; Chancellor would have agreed with Maurras, 3; attitude of mind, 54; character and ideology, 55, 56; M. *not* Austrian, 62; Court completely bankrupt, (note 2) 84; Chancellery optimistic about invasion of Russia, 87, 118; Chancellery criticises M. and conduct of Congress of Vienna, 126; Cabinet, long opposed by Sealsfeld, 143.

Avars, 49.

V

# B

Babenbergs, original Austrian dynasty, 49.

Baer, A., '*Zur Sendung Metternichs nach Paris*', 83 (note 1).

Bagration, Princess Katherine, *née* Countess Skavoronski, 22; mother of M.'s daughter Clementine, 23; supposed spy for Tsar, 86, 111, 121, 134, 159, 160, 162, 167, 303, 304.

Balance of Power, M'.s main preoccupation, 2; endangered by Napoleon's unruly appetites; 'stability of Europe', 57; M. nicknamed '*comte de la balance*', 86; Habsburg-Napoleonic marriage and, 86, 88; 'general stabilisation', 96, 100, 105; threatened by Alexander, 134; Prussia and, 136; 'European equilibrium', 140; after fall of Napoleon, 178; under French Restoration, 196; M. insists on general not partial federation, 201; Austria watches anxiously under Louis-Philippe, 218; chiefly concerned with, M., hostile to claims of Reichstadt, 224.

Balbi, Comtesse de, favourite of Comte de Provence (later Louis XVIII), 8.

Balkanisation of Central Europe, 5.

Balkans, 88, 109; M. always deprecated active policy in, 298.

Ballhausplatz, M.'s famous mansion inherited from Kaunitz becomes chief centre of Congress of Vienna, 119, 143, 161, 237, 238, 255, 256, 274, 280, 296.

Balzac, 243; collaborated with M., 244.

Barras, Paul, Vicomte de, ex-*conventionnel* and member of *Directoire*; former lover of Empress Josephine, 78.

Basle, Treaty of, 112.

Bassano, Duc de (formerly Maret), 69, 87, 88, 89, 97, 99, 104, 106, 111.

Bauernfeld, E., German patriotic man of letters, 244, 272; demands convocation of Parliament and freedom of Press, 278, 284, 296.

Bautzen, battle of, 99, 100.

Bavaria, 100, 109, 126 (note 2), 129, 140; Prussia and B. get Rhenish territories from Austria thanks to Congress of Vienna, 141; Bavarian Concordat, 146, 159.

Bavaria, Maximilian, Prince Elector, later King of, *see also* Zwei-Brücke, 12, 194.

Bavaria, Ludwig I, King of (1825-48), son of Maximilian above, 249; popular uprisings against his mistress Lola Montez, 275 (in revolutionary year of 1848, resigned in favour of his own son, Maximilian II).

Beau Brummel, 18.

Beauharnais, Eugène de, Duc de Leuchtenberg, son of Empress Josephine by former marriage; Viceroy of Italy; significance of his role in marriage of Marie-Louise, 68, 74, 75 (note 1), 132; his son rejected by M. and Francis I as King of Belgians, 219.

Beauvale, English Ambassador at Vienna, 240; Beauvales in London, 293.

Becker, A. (Napoleon's second marriage), 73 (note 2).

Beer, 'Orientpolitik Oesterreichs seit 1774', 200.

Beethoven, 150.

Beilstein, M.'s family estate in Bohemia, 10; Count Franz-Georg von Winneburg zu Beilstein, full name of M.'s father, 11; Baroness Antionette von Leykam created Countess B. on eve of marriage to M., 171.

Belgium, invaded by *sans culottes* army, 15; Franz-Georg's unsuccessful mission to, 18; revolutionary upheavals ignored by Austria, 218.

Belvedere, 56.

Beresina Pass, 92.

Berlin-Dahlem, see Dahlem.

Berlin, character of inhabitants, 25; M. ambassador to, 25; M. and Tsar win Frederick Wm III to Grand Alliance at, 26; M.'s last effort to enlist Prussian army against Napoleon, 27; M. leaves after Austerlitz, 28; 94, Court of, 163 (note 2); M.'s anecdotes, 241.

Bernadotte, 111.

Bernstorff, Gräfin, at Congress of Vienna, 121 (*Erinerrungen*), 124.

Bernstorff, Graf, 249.

Berry, Duc de, second son of Charles X, assassinated, 213.

Berry, Duchesse de, widow of above, daughter of Francis I of Naples had roused La Vendée to revolt against Louis-Philippe in 1832, imprisoned, meets M., 197.

Berthier, Louis-Alexandre, Maréchal de France, Prince de Wagram, Prince de Neuchatel, major-general of *Grande Armée*; admired by Napoleon, nevertheless signed abdication warrant, 40, 79, 105.

Bertrande, Abbé, M.'s Catholic tutor, 13.

Bibl, Professor von, 4, 61, 223; bibliography, 263.

Bignon, Baron Edouard, diplomatist and historian (1771-1841), 84, 192.

Bismarck, 67, 265, 299, 300, 302.

Blanc, Louis, French socialist; contributed to fall of July monarchy, member of *gouvernement provisoire* in 1848, exiled, returned 1870, sat extreme left *assemblée nationale* (1871), 182, 301.

Bohemia, 7, 99, 107, 120.

Boigne, Madame de, *see under* Memoirs.

Bonaparte, *see* Napoleon; *see* Jerome.

Borodino, (battle at, 1812), Prince Bagration, future hero of, 22, 92.

Bosnia, 32.

Bossuet, 178, 180.

Bouillé, Marquis de (*see also* 'Memoirs'), 9, 10.

Bouillé, General Marquis de, famous royalist, said 'to have preserved French army in period of chaos', father of above; organised abortive flight Louis XVI to Montmédy which was arrested at Varennes; played important part last days of monarchy.

Bourbons, 52, 112; governing France during Congress of Vienna, 130; Naples and Sicily returned to Italian branch of, 131, 132; French branch supports M., 135; B. of Naples, 140; restoration of, 153, 207; overthrown, 215.

Bourgeoisie, 17th and 18th Century, in Austria, 58, 182; 'middle classes', 183; under Canning, in England, 198; bourgeois-monarch, 261.

Bourgoin, Baron de, 'Le Cœur de Marie-Louise', 79, 226; see also under 'Memoirs'.

Boutiagine, young Russian diplomatist, 75, 88.

Bray, Comte de, 7, 10, (note 3) 11, (note 1) 14; *see also under* 'Memoirs'.

Brighton, Princess Lieven at, 165.

Brussels, overflowed by Jacobin lava, 15; M. meets Princess Lieven at, 164.

Bubna, General, 68, 92, 95, 97, 98, 101, 110; wiped out Carbonari in Piedmont, 211.

Buckland, (note 1) 86.

Buda, 49, 56.

Bulgaria, 32.

Burke, Edmund, welcomed young M. to England, 18.

*Burschenschaften*, German secret society, 208, 211.

Byron, Lord, 149.

**C**

Campo Formio, results of, 61.

Canning, 163, 170; succeeds Castlereagh and reverses English foreign policy, 198; disappearance of, 200, 201, 238, 285.

Capefigue, 35, 81, 114, 158.

Capo d'Istria, 19; envenomed criticism of M., 124; described by M. as 'arrant fool', 194.

Capua, 229.

Capuchin Chapel, tombs of the Habsburgs, 56, 226.

Carbonari, 230 *et seq.*, plots organised in France at Saumur, Belfort and La Rochelle, 207; finally disposed of by M., 211; M. considers movement sustained by France, 220, 226, 265, 271.

Carignano, Prince Charles Albert (of Savoy), 207 (had strong democratic sympathies, as Regent of Sardinia had granted constitution to be revoked by Charles Felix at Modena . . . has been called 'the Italian Hamlet').

Carlsbad Decrees, emergency congress of German statesmen called to combat revolution, 210, 211.

Carlsbad, 'scrap of paper', 216.

Casimir Périer, 249.

Castlereagh, at Congress of Vienna, 129; disliked by English Liberals, 129, 133, 146, 148, 165, 189, 190, 191, 195; opposed wholesale intervention, 199, 210; recriminations of, about Duke of Reichstadt, 223.

Castlereagh, Lady, 120, 121, 124.

Catalani, Madame, Italian *prima donna*, 150, 191.

Catholic, Habsburgs were, 50; *Sonderbund*, 270.

Catholic Church, Princess Mélanie pushes claims of, M. faithful son of, favours renewal Concordat, revision marriage laws, 176; M.'s correspondence with Cardinal Consalvi, (note 1) 194.

Catholicism in Austria, had lapsed after Reformation, 55.

Caulaincourt, A. A. L., Duc de Vicenza, French ambassador at Saint-Petersburg, 69, 74, 87, 107, 110, 113; warns Napoleon that Austria is on point of repudiating him, 114.

Caumont-la-Force, Duchesse de, *née* Marie Constance de Lamoignon, 8, 9, 13, 17, 35, 167.

Cavour, 265.

Censorship, M. develops important service and tampers with foreign diplomatic bags, 257, 259; imbecility of, 266.

Centralisation, early attempt at, 57; 'a unified procedure', 181.

Chabonas, *see* de la Garde.

Champ de Mars, scene of 'Oath of the Federation', 15.

Champagny, replaces Talleyrand, 31; demands Austrian rupture with England, 32, 44, 46, 61, 69, 85.

Charlemagne, 10, 49, 50, 54.

Charles, Archduke, 5, 46, 261.

Charles X, King of France, 1824–1830, previously Comte d'Artois (*see also* Artois), 13, 196; exiled, received by Austria, 217.

Charles V of Austria, 51.

Charles Albert of Savoy, *see* Carignano.

Charles Felix, King of Sardinia, triumphant entry into Turin, 211 (revoked Charles Albert's Constitution at Modena).

Chartist demonstrations, 293.

Chartres, Duc de, 262.

Chateaubriand, Vicomte de, 155; represented France at Congress of Verona, was manœuvring for French armed intervention in Spain, 192, 196; disliked by M., 197, 198, 210.

Chatillon, *pourparlers* at, 111, 112, 114.

Chaumont, Treaty of, 128; clause added to by M. on behalf of Joachim Murat, 132, 184. Treachery by Coalition of, revealed by Napoleon after escape from Elba, 135; quoted by Tsar as outmoded, 201.

China, 40.

Choisel, Duc de, Maréchal de France under Louis XIII and XIV, 237.

Christian Ethic, no place for international politics, 176.

Clam-Martiniz, Count, M.'s letter (5.9.1836), 255.

Clementine, M.'s daughter by Princess Bagration, 23, 160, 169.

Clergy, loyal, 57.

Coalition (fourth), 109; minister of, 110; M. disagrees with, about dethroning Bonaparte, 111; dissension about purpose of, 112; Allies alarmed by M.'s invidious position on account Habsburg-Napoleonic marriage, 113; majority desire annihilate Napoleon, 113; negotiations of, Paris and London, 128; wars of, 132; revived, 138, 184; deposed Napoleon and refused Marie-Louise as Regent, 223.

Cobden, Metternich's remark to, about Italy, 188.

Cobenzl, Louis, 'egged Francis on to war', 60.

Coblenz, family home of Metternichs, 10; invaded by French revolutionaries, 15, 306.

Coburg, 294 (note 1).

# Index

Coding system, Metternich's world-renowned, 258, 259.
Colloredo, 17, 25, 26, 240.
Colloredo, Princess, 120.
Communism, present anti-Communist campaign compared with Metternich's anti-revolutionary crusade, 185, 199, 295.
Compiègne, 79, 103.
Concert of Europe, virtually inaugurated by second Treaty (or Peace) of Paris, November 1815, 'foundations of a peace', 141.
Concordat, 176.
Confalonieri, Italian patriot, arrival at Vienna, 203, 205, 212, 213, 267.
Confederation of the Rhine, 31, 95, 96, 263.
Congress of Vienna, see Vienna.
Congressional era, 190, 191, 192; see Aix-la-Chapelle; Troppau; Laibach; Verona.
Consalvi, Cardinal, 126, 194.
Conservatism, M.'s, 182; M. considers only hope for Europe, 216, 242, 244, 245, 272 (note 2).
Constant, Benjamin, 13; friend of the Carbonari, 207.
Constantinople, 201.
Continental System, Napoleon's, Switzerland induced to revolt against, 110.
Cook, James, 13.
Council of Five, see 'Five'.
'Countries, the', hereditary possessions of Austrian imperial crown; revolt of crushed, 54; right revived, 56; attitude of, to political freedom, 57.
Courlande, 193; see Sagan, Duchesse de.
Courlandes chez Gentz, 246.
Cracow, annexation of, 256, 269-70 (note 1), 270.
Czartoryski, 134; influence lives on, see Alexander's speech to Polish Diet, 194.
Czech, renaissance, see also Palacky, 48; aspirations crushed by German element, 54; culture destroyed by Jesuits, 55; race-consciousness, 57; Kolowrat's sympathy with his compatriots, 254, 265, 271.
Czerniczeff, 79 (note 1).

**D**

Dahlem (Berlin-Dahlem), secret archives of Prussia, 4, 6, 67, 68, 72, 77, 79, 85, 112, 113, 145, 275, 276, 277, 285, 293.
Dalmatia, recovered by Austria after Treaty of Paris, 115.
Danube, 32, 51, 93, 128, 249, 295, 298.
Danubian basin, 5, 49; D. principalities, Austrian Emperor not indifferent to lot of, 109; D. countries, M.'s name not now popular in, 185.
Dauphin, Dauphine, 197.
Dauphin, eldest son of Louis-Philippe, see Orléans.
Davoust (or Davout), Duc d'Auerstadt, Prince d'Eckmuhl, Maréchal de France, one of Napoleon's best generals, 40.
Débats, Journal des, 197, 211, 243.
Debry, Jean, 11, 103.
Decembrist uprising, 213.
Demelitsch, on M.'s foreign policy, 87.
Democracy, 'illusion of', 185.
Disraeli, 299, 302.
Dolgorouki, Princess, wife of Tsar's aide-de-camp, 25.
Dresden, M. appointed (1801) to Court of Frederick Augustus at, 21, 24, 87, 91, 100, 101, 103, 106, 116, 130, 168.
Duerm, Charles van, 'correspondence of M. with Cardinal Consalvi', 194.
Duff-Cooper's 'Talleyrand', (note 3) 132.
Dufour du Pradt, Le Congrès de Karlsbad, (note 4) 210.
Duhamel, Georges, 174, 186.
Dutch bankers and Austrian loan (1810), 84.

**E**

Eastern Question, Capo d'Istria and, 194; M. and, 200; Gentz and, 247.
Eckmuhl, battle of, 46.
Egyptian question, 267.
Eichoff, Baron, as potential dictator, (note 2) 255.

317

Eight, Committee of, formed, 129; final decree of Congress of Vienna issued by, July 8th, 1815, 139.

Elba, Napoleon escapes from, 135.

Elliott, eccentric English Minister, 22.

Ellsler, Fanny, Viennese *comédienne*, falsely accused of relations with Duke of Reichstadt, 223; one of chief attractions of Vienna, 240; had been Gentz' mistress, 246.

Empress-mother of Russia, hatred of Napoleon, opposes marriage of Grand-duchess Anne, 70.

Enghien, Duc de, son of Prince de Condé, shot at Château de Vincennes by order of Napoleon after discovery of royalist plot, crime shocked Europe, 45.

England, M.'s first visit, 18; M. unsuccessful with Cabinet, 83; M. makes vague promises to, 86; Napoleon disbelieved possible Anglo-Russian *entente*, 97; English terms to Napoleon stiffer than M.'s, 97; M. negotiating with, prior to formation of Coalition, 100; English suspicious of M.'s Francophile policy, 113; Castlereagh, E.'s representative at Congress of Vienna, 129; English Liberals dislike Castlereagh, 130; now supporting M., 135; M. considers Cabinet 'tricky', 158; new Cabinet, 159; *Magna Carta*, 181; political evolution of Central Europe not to be compared with that of, 185; British Commonwealth, 186; Cabinet of Saint James and Russia, 198; foreign policy under Canning, 198; against large scale intervention, 199; Wellington's Protocol (1826) allies her with Russia, 200; foreign policy remains same after Canning, 200; Louis XVIII and Talleyrand upheld by E. in depriving Reichstadt of Duchy of Parma, 222; M. admires E. temperament and political acumen, 294.

Enlightenment, philosophy of M. and, 13; Joseph II and, 56.

Ense, Varnhagen von, author of *Denkwurdigkeiten*, *Gallerie von Bildnissen*, 144, 147, 157, 176, 236, 241, 245, 248.

Erfurt, 40, 43.

Eskeles, Viennese banker, 153; *haute finance* had own social coterie, 231; Princess Mélanie's insolence to, 234.

Esterhazy, Count, 7.

Esterhazy, Prince (was messenger to Caulaincourt), 113; Austrian ambassador to London, 190, 195.

Esterhazy, Countess Marie, daughter of Metternich, dies, 169, 240.

Europe, Balance of Power in, 2, 5, 16, 29, 30, 33, 34, 77; interests of, 82; destiny of, 83; attitude towards Napoleon's Russian campaign, 87; Alexander sees himself as liberator of, 88; Napoleon's marriage with Marie-Louise had changed face of, 89; general pacification needed for, 93; Napoleon could be master of, in pacific sense, 95; Napoleon's task to consolidate, 96, 99, 101, 104, 108, 115; just emerged from appalling test of endurance, 119; most famous names of, at Congress of Vienna, 122; diplomacy not representational in 1815, 127; Five Powers virtually govern, 129; all Powers of invited Congress of Vienna, 128; Napoleon declared ostracised by, 129; new order in, after Napoleon sent to Elba, 130; on *qui vive* for Talleyrand's latest *bon mot*, 132, 155; evolution of, 159; and Holy Alliance, 174, 177, 179, 184; sick of constant upheaval, 186; M. imposes 'System' on, 192; M. convinced E. wrong, events confirmed his opinion, 202; Carbonarism and, 203; conservative outlook, M.'s panacea, 216; M. opines 'beginning of end', 217; Cabinets of, harass M. about Duke of Reichstadt, 222; Louis-Philippe chief trouble-maker of, 225; all statesmen of, acknowledge M. as leader, 249; M. best-informed statesman of, 256; storm threatening, 264; peace troubled by rising in Cracow, 269, 270; climax, 272, 276; international advance of republicanism, 286, 298, 307, also note 1, 307.

Evangelisti, Abbé, secretary to Cardinal Consalvi, at Congress of Vienna, 126.

Eylau, victory of, 41.

**F**

Fain, Baron, account of meeting at Marcolini Palace, 104.

Federation, ceremony of, 15.

Ferdinand, Archduke, eldest son of Francis I, succeeded him as Emperor (1835-48), accession of, 250, 252; character of, 251; receives letter demanding death of M., 272; cheered by revolutionaries, 280; attitude to revolution, 287, 289; abdication Dec. 1848, 295.

Ferdinand, King of Naples, revolutionaries had seized power from, 192.

Ficquelmont, 249; formerly had been King of the Two Sicilies, 207.

Finckenstein, Count, Prussian Diplomatist, 67, 68, 76, 79.

Five, Committee of, became *de facto* Congress of Vienna; had originally been Committee of Four (England, Austria, Prussia, Russia) to which through Talleyrand, France was added, 128, 129; after Napoleon's defeat, reduced again to Four, signing treaties *in re* Poland and Saxony, 139; M. considers them 'national arbiters of European destiny', 201; replaced by outcome of Teplitz, 259.

Flanders, 140.

Floret, Counsellor, young French diplomatist, 69, 71, 77, 88, 92, 94, 156.

Follen, leader of French *Carbonari*, 208.

Fontainebleau, Treaty of, 32; Marie-Louise and, 78 (note).

Force, Duc de la, *see* article written 1936 about Duchesse de Caumont-la-Force (note 1), 35.

Fouché, Joseph, *Conventionnel montagnard*, known as *le Mitrailleur de Lyons*, also opprobriously as 'Fouché de Nantes'. Minister of Police (virtually Home Secretary) under Napoleon; created Duc

d'Otrante; after *Cent-Jours*, maintained his position under Restoration, betrayed successively: the Revolution, Napoleon, the Bourbons, 38, 40, 42, 75, 182.

Four, Committee of, 184, *see also above under* Five.

Fournier, 73, 256.

Fox, 18.

France, Marie-Antionette, 7; last days Louis XVI monarchy, 13, 14, 15; crusade against, 14; activities of revolutionary armies, 15; Metternich's anonymous tract against Revolution, 16; old Franco-Austrian alliance, 18; at Rastadt, 20; *Le Publiciste* and Metternich, 20; results of Revolution, 24; Haugwitz sold to, 25; Triple Alliance against, 26; Haugwitz and, 27; after Austerlitz, 27; Napoleon and Metternich, 29; bellicose activities, 31-34; Society in, 42, 44; Austrian attitude to, 64; possible influence of Marie-Louise, 66, 80; fear of Russian marriage project,67, 69; dossier 'Reports-France' in Viennese archives, 75; Metternich, Napoleon's dupe, 83; Napoleon back from Moscow, 88; concerning new dynasty, 86, 89; Metternich's Francophile policy, 87, 88; new dynasty bond between Napoleon and Francis I, 93; Metternich makes general pacification condition of further military support, 94; Metternich making last efforts negotiate, 96, 100; economic barrier against, 110; Alsace retained by, 141; French territory to be evacuated by coalition troops; France readmitted to Quadruple Alliance, 191; M.'s good relations with Restoration monarchy, 195; endorses Wellington's Protocol, 200; French *Carbonari*, 207; Andryane, emissary of secret societies, arrested, 212; M. indicts (1828), 213; 'very sick', 214; report on, by M., (note 1) 214; Charles X's Cabinet's grave blunder in issuing *Ordonnances Royales*, 216; M. accuses French of instigating insurrection in Italy, 219; feeling towards M. and Austria,

## Index

hostile, 219; 'had refused Marie-Louise as Regent', 223; Reichstadt considered M. sole obstacle between him and throne of France, 224; M. threatens Louis-Philippe's government with opposition by Reichstadt, 225; Cabinet divided as to war or peace with Austria, 227; negotiations about Italy, 228; M. believes 'no one can govern the French', 260; F. and Austria at loggerheads, 263; remains M.'s chief interest, 301.

Francis, Emperor of Holy Roman Empire and known as Francis II, forced by Napoleon surrender that title (note 1, p. 61), became Francis I of Austria only (1804), 7, 11, 14, 15, 21, 27, 43, 44, 47; 'the Emperor', 42; 'august master', 58; character of, 59, 60; as Francis I starts to restore Austria, 63; his part in marriage of Marie-Louise, 68, 69, 72, 74, 75, 77 (note), 78, 80, 83; Metternich's enemies try to undermine him with, 83; meets Napoleon at Dresden, 1812, 87; attitude to Napoleonic dynasty, 89; loyal to son-in-law, 92, 93; danger of assassination by anti-French forces in Austria, 95; letters from Napoleon to, 97, 106; temperamentally opposed to war, 99; hurriedly leaves capital, 100; prepared use influence on behalf Napoleon, 110; his principles, stated by Metternich to Coalition, 112; accused by Napoleon of not caring for his daughter, 113; confers title of Prince on Metternich and descendants, 116; supports Metternich, 135; refuses Imperial Crown of Germany, 36; hears of Napoleon's escape, 137, 138; resumed historic role as first German sovereign in Europe, 140; 149, 150; granted mortgages to Metternich, 152, 155, 156, 157; confers title on Metternich's second wife, 171; Alexander suggests Holy Alliance to, 174; refuses sign without Metternich's approval, 175, 179, 180; report to, from Metternich concerning Lombardo-Venetian state, 188; H.I.M., 190;

confers supreme title on M., 192, 193; described by George IV as 'our Emperor', 195; letter from M. about Restoration France, 197; M.'s report concerning Confalonieri, 204; appoints commission to enquire into activities of *Carbonarism*, 207; noted accession of Louis-Philippe without enthusiasm, 218; claims jurisdiction over Marie-Louise, 223, 226; death of, 250, 252; secret reports to, from M. about Kolowrat, 254, 255, 256, 286.

Francis Charles, Archduke, husband of Archduchess Sophia and father of the future Emperor Franz-Josef, 85, 253, 278, 284, 289.

Frankfort (Frankfurt), Coronation at, 7, 10, 14, 15, 16, 19, 110, 112, 133, 155, 209, 211; message sent via by Rothschilds, 215.

Franz-Josef, Emperor of Austria (1848-1916), 8, 253, 265, 269, 279, 288; succeeds Ferdinand, 295; adopts new policy of government, 296, 298, 306; M. advises against ultimatum to Italy, 306.

Frederick II, 'the Great', 25, 56, 177.

Frederick William III, King of Prussia, 14; obsessed with fear of Napoleon (after catastrophe of Ulm), 25, 26, 59; alliance with Alexander, 99, 108, 121, 137, 138, 160; Alexander suggests Holy Alliance to, 174, 192, 194; and Teplitz, 216, 260, 263, 295.

Frederick William IV, Convocation of States General, 270.

French empire, adherents of Napoleonic party confide in M., 225.

French newspapers, M. disapproves of, 260.

French revolution, 205; echoes of, 214; described as 'grandmother' of Duke of Reichstadt, 226.

French, tradition and/or influence: Duchesse de Caumont-la-Force's lasting influence on Metternich, 8, 10; at first, Vienna found him 'too French', 18.

French society, 42; F. friends forbidden for Duke of Reichstadt, 224; Bonapartist circles considered

M. grand inquisitor of Duke of Reichstadt.

Fribourg (misprint, read Freiburg), III, II2.

Frimont, Austrian general who finally subdued risings in Italy, 211, 219.

Frontiers, M. nicknamed 'god of boundaries', 1; of Austria diminished, 32; Austrian Empire without rigid national, 56; 'if France would remain within her proper geographical limits', 96; German, 97; M.'s tricky appeal promising France 'natural' frontiers, 110; Napoleon says, 'I will never leave France smaller than I found her', 113; French frontiers fixed by Treaty of Paris, 130.

**G**

Gabriac, M. de, writes to Lamartine about Viennese revolution, 280, 282, 283, 288, 289.

Gagern, Freiherr von, *Nein Anteil an der Politik*, 126.

Galicia threatened by project reconstruction of Poland, 134; Jesuits admitted with severe restrictions, 176.

Garde, de la, (note) 23, 121, 123, 137, 143, 159, 230.

Gentz, Friedrich von, outraged at time wasted by M. with Duchesse de Sagan, 126, 134, 136; severely criticises Congress of Vienna, 139, 148, 155, 175, 191, 194, 197, 204; shocked that M. did not take more advantage of Duke of Reichstadt, 224, 232; biography of, 245-8, (note 1) 259.

George IV, formerly Prince of Wales and Regent, 'first gentleman in Europe', received M. as young visitor to England, 18; visits Hanover, 164; considers M. 'leading statesman of Europe', 195.

Germany, was M. traitor to?, 2, 44, 66, 94, 120, 155, 185; M. wants federation under Austrian aegis, 189, 190; entirely dominated by Austria since Congress of Vienna, 193; G. Empire, Baron von Stein

and, 106; M.'s attitude to, after Napoleon's downfall, 189, 190; Carbonari no following in, 208; secret societies in, 209; murder of Kotzebue excuse for M.'s intervention in, 210; Congress of Carlsbad, 210.

German, 49, 50, 53, 54, 55, 58, 59, 62; Germanophiles, 92; boundaries, 97; patriots' hatred of M., 98; flower of G. manhood perished, 99; M. reminds Napoleon that he is German, 104; nationalism, 108; patriots let down by Congress of Vienna, 141; M., though racially German, more French by education, 146; Diet, 146; M.'s use of language heavy, 157; M. claims to be 'best of all Germans', 190; reactionary Austro-German wanted war against Louis-Philippe, 218; G. princes indicted by M., 218; G. 'people' quiet and cheerful, 230; G. artists and writers *non-grata* in M.'s household, 244; M. again accused of treachery by G. patriots, 263.

Germans (Pan), 3, 48.

Geymuller, Austrian banker, 231, 267.

Gitschin, Francis and M. go to, before negotiating with Tsar against Napoleon, 100, 101.

Gneisenau, 96.

Goethe, 115, 149, 151, 152, 189.

Gordon (to Castlereagh), 189, 210.

Grand Alliance, *see* Potsdam.

*Grande Armée*, 41, 46, 88.

Great War, 120.

Greek Question, Alexander, now won over to M.'s 'System', refuses intervene, 195; rebellion, 199; new Tsar, Nicholas I and, 198; Greece's fate under Wellington Protocol; England and Russia line up with rebels; Independence declared at London (1829), 200; G. rebellion seriously challenges the 'System', 199; further clamour in Greece (1828), 213.

Gregory XVI (1831-1846), Pope, 249.

Grillparzer, German patriot, 149, 242, 244, 269.

Grosjean, *Politique extérieure de la Restauration et l'Allemagne*, 196.

Grossmann, Carl, M.'s plan for Italian League, 140.

Grun, Anastasius, pen-name of Count Auersperg, lampoon of M. became famous, 245, 269.

Grunwald, C. de, *Le mariage de Napoleon et de Marie-Louise*, 74, 285.

Guizot, historian, Prime Minister under Louis-Philippe, replaces Thiers (often blamed for revolution of 1848), exiled to England, 156, 178; M. speaks same language as, 264; *Mémoires*, 270 (*see also under* 'Memoirs'); (later had *liaison* with Princess Lieven).

## H

Habichtsberg, Habsburg short for, 50.

Habsburg, House of, 2, 5, 15, 48, 49, 50–58, 60, 61, 62, 65, 66, 69, 70; blood of, 86, 103, 108, 113, 115, 118, 140, 179, 186; their Chancellor now Mentor of Continent, 192; 193, 220; 'Eagle has many eaglets', see Reichstadt, 221, 254, 262, 298, 302, 307.

Hanotaux, Jean, author of *Lettres du prince de Metternich à la princesse de Lieven*, 161, 166, 172.

Hanover, visited by George IV, 164.

Hardenberg, Prince von, 86, 100, 108, 136, 145.

Haugwitz, Graf von, treachery of, 25, 26, 27, 101.

Heigel, K. T. von, quoted (of M.) 'to talk like Plato and act like Philip of Macedonia', 140.

Heine, Heinrich, 149.

Helfert, author *Marie-Louise*, etc., 79, (note 1) 284.

Hofburg, 18, 56, 60, 118, 121, 127, 230, 247, 248, 255, 279, 281, 288, 296.

Holland, Queen of, 73.

Holy Roman Empire: Francis last 'German' Emperor of, 8; dissolution of, 50 (*see also* note 1, 61), 136, 140, 189, 191.

Holy Alliance (1815), 174–176; M.'s readjustment of, 184, 201, 204.

Hope, Baron, 126.

Hormayr, Baron, Counsellor of State Department, involved in Tyrolean plot, 95.

Hübner, Baron, fears approaching storm, 274–5, 276, 277, 306.

Hudelist, A., 115, 126.

Hügel, Charles von, helped Metternich's escape from Vienna revolution, 290.

Hügel, Baron Clement von, 235, 236.

Humboldt, William von, 46; Prussian delegate to Prague, 107, 108, 126, 148.

Hungarians, 48, 49, 56.

Hungary, Latin spoken in, 57; Archduke Joseph, Palatin of, joined anti-Metternich faction, 85; requisitions in, 99; at Congress of Vienna, 120; Diet, 201, 271.

## I

Illyria, M. doing propaganda for Napoleon in, 88; Napoleon's vague promises relinquish Austria's Illyrian provinces, 97; to be evacuated, among M.'s terms to Napoleon, 100, 107; Austria recovers, 115.

Intervention, M.'s notions of, 179; application of, 192; Tory minister Canning opposed to, 199; two different principles of, advanced by democratic France and reactionary Austria, 220; after Münchengraetz, 'three sovereigns no longer prepared to accept doctrine of non-intervention', 228.

Isabey, portrait of Caroline Murat by, 35.

Isonzo river, 32.

Italians to be distinguished from Germans in governing Empire, 188.

Italian influence in arts in Austria, 55; M.'s enthusiasm for *bel canto*, 150.

Italy, 44; Napoleon to relinquish conquered territories in, 100; Napoleon refuses, 102; Austria extending dominion over whole of, 140; the Bourbons of Naples, 140; Italian League, 140; after Congress of Vienna, Austria becomes increasingly Italianate, 141, 156, 185; described by M. as 'mere geographical notion', 187; M. makes sporadic efforts at reform but maintains contempt, 188, 189; federation of Italian princes under Austria, 189; under European mandate, Austrian armies restore absolutist régimes throughout, 192; entirely dominated by Austria, 193; centre of *Carbonarisme*, 205, 207; M. prepares for struggle with, 218; insurrections quickly crushed by Austria, 219; Duke of Reichstadt considered as King of, 226; Austrian troops enter Bologna and Ancona (March 17th, 1831), and French ambassador asks for his *visa*, 227; Prussia supports Austria's action in, against France (note 1), 263; national movement reaches climax, 270, 275; Italian demands under discussion, 276; repercussion of fall of July Government, 277.

then 'General' Bonaparte; became Empress of the French in 1804; Napoleon divorced in 1809; (had also been mistress of Barras), 37, 65, 69, 72, 78.

July monarchy, insulted by Princess Mélanie, 235; settling down, 264; about to collapse, 276.

July revolution, 216.

Junot (Andoche), later Duc d'Abrantes, Napoleon's aide-de-camp during first Italian campaign; took part in expedition to Egypt, and took Lisbon in 1807, went mad and committed suicide, 36, 37, 81, 82; sent to Spain, (note 1) 82.

Junot, Madame Laure (later Duchesse d'Abrantes), wife of above; account of affair with Metternich in her Memoirs, 38, 81, 82 (see note also), 161, 162, 167.


## J

Jacobins, 11, 13, 15; Napoleon heir of, 60; last of their influence, 86, 103, 115, 176, 177, 178; Jacobinism, 197, 243, 250, 265.

Jäger, Dr, 148, 155, 176, 178, 215, 216, 234, 236, 241, 242, 252, 281, 288.

Jahn, eccentric German patriot, 208.

Jerome Bonaparte, Napoleon's brother, King of Westphalia (1807-1813), 36, 43.

Jesuits, 55, 58, 59; admitted by Metternich to Silesia but with severe restrictions, 176, 242, 254.

Johannisberg, Abbey of, 152, 211, 238, 292, 293, 295.

John, Archduke, brother of Francis I, involved in plot against him, 95 (note 2), 255, 287.

Joseph, Archduke, sided with anti-M. faction, 85.

Joseph II, Emperor of Austria, son of Maria-Theresa, 56, 57, 60; was responsible for starting strained relations with Vatican, 176.

Josephine, *née* Tascher de la Pagerie, first married Vicomte de Beauharnais (victim of Revolution),


## K

Kagenegg, Countess Beatrix von, *see* Metternich (wife of Count Franz-Georg).

Kant, Emmanuel, 177.

Kaunitz, Prince Chancellor von, 17, 18, 19, 21, 27, 52, 65, 66, 86; Kaunitz tradition, 96, 119; Kaunitz Palace in Ballhausplatz, inherited from, becomes centre of Congress of Vienna, 132; Palace, sumptuous apartments of, 237.

Kaunitz, Eléonore von, *see* Metternich (first wife of).

Kaunitz, *née* Oettingen-Spielberg, mother of Princess Eléonore, 18.

Kiev, 88.

Klinkowstroem, A. de, edited M.'s Memoirs, 3, 100.

Koch, M.'s professor, also taught Benjamin-Constant and Talleyrand, 13.

Koenigswart, Schloss, M.'s property in Bohemia, 10, 151, 152, 184, 219, 238, 259.

Kolowrat, Count, 253, 254; beginning of serious dissention with M., 254, 255, 256, 267; joins *camarilla* against M., 279, 283, 287, 295.

Kossuth, 265, 271, 278, 281.
Kotzebue, murder of, 208, 210.
Kourakine, Prince, 70.
Kruft, Baron, 126.

**L**

Laborde, Comte de, and marriage of Marie-Louise, 64, 65, 68, 71, 73, 74.
Laclos, Choderlos de, *see Liaisons dangereuses*, 9.
Lafayette, friend of *Carbonari*, 207, 214, 217, 218, 227, 259.
Laffite, friend of *Carbonari*, 207.
La Force, Duchesse de, *see* Caumont-la-Force.
La Force, Duc de, wrote article in 1936 about ancestress, 35.
Laforest, French ambassador, 27.
Laforgue, Jules, reader to Empress Augusta, wife of Wm. I of Prussia, 163.
La Harpe, Tsar Alexander's famous Swiss tutor 'to whom he owed everything', criticises M. at Congress of Vienna, 125.
Laibach (in Carniola), Congress of, 1821, 180; King of Two Sicilies was added to great Five at; intervention in Italy decided; resulted in March Austrian armies restored absolutist régimes throughout Italy, 192, 195.
Lamark, General, 207.
Lamartine, 171, 280, 282, 283, 288, 289.
Lamoignon, Garde des Sceaux, 8.
Langres, Congress at, 111, 113.
Lanner, 229, 231.
Latin, universal medium, 53, 57.
Lauriston, 88.
Lawrence, Thomas, 142, 143, 146, 156, 172.
Lebzeltern, diplomatic mission to Vatican, 84, 98, 194, 195, 197, 209, 247.
Leghorn, message from, announcing Napoleon's escape, 138.
Leibnitz, 57, 58, 185, 268.
Leipzig, battle of, 70, 110, 123, 132.
Leo XII, Pope, offers M. a Cardinal's Hat, i.e. to become member of Sacred College, 194.

Leopold II, Emperor of Austria, father of Francis, 17, 56.
Lévy, Arthur, historian, authority on Bonaparte family, 36, 37, 132.
Leykam, Antoinette von, *see* second Princess Metternich.
*Liaisons dangereuses, see also* Laclos, 9.
Liberalism, L.'s enraged by new marriage laws, 176; M. says 'dogs of war unleashed', 179; Alexander and, 194; 'Liberal Pope', 271; L. circles, 204; Liberal views *non-grata*, 244; Gentz and, 247, 250; Kolowrat's reputation for, unjustified, 254; M. calls England and France 'two liberal sea-powers', 260; France too L. for M.'s taste, 260, 265.
Liebig, 148.
Liechtenstein, Prince John of, had been bad negotiator when he signed peace of Schönbrunn; M. now takes stand against, 85.
Liechtenstein, Princess, aunt of Princess Eléonore M., 17, 120.
Liechtenstein, Princess, at Congress of Vienna, 120, 240.
Lieven, Countess Dorothea (*née* Benckendorff), later Princess, 142, 143, 147, 149, 156, 160–166; *liaison* with M. ends, 167, 172, 174, 191, 193, 201, 255, 303, 304.
Lieven, Count, later created Prince and Serene Highness (Ambassador to London), 162.
Ligne, Prince de, author of famous 'le Congrès ne marche pas, il danse', 120, 133.
Liszt, Franz, 150, 234, 272.
Littoral, M. wanted commercial highway along, for Austria, 80.
Liverpool Cabinet, 130.
Liverpool, Lord, 130, 154.
Lola Montez, King Ludwig of Bavaria's favourite, popular uprising in Munich against Ministers said to be sponsored by her, 275.
Lombardo-Venetian territories, 115.
London, Coalition's negotiations at, 128; attaches importance M.'s movements, 170; M.'s last visit to, 293, 294, 299.
Londonderry, *see* Castlereagh; *see* Stewart.
Lorraine, 7, 52, 102.

Louis, Archduke, later Regent of Austria, 253, 255 (note 2), 256, 267, 284, 287, 290.

Louis XIV, 95.

Louis XVI of France, flight to Montmedy intercepted at Varennes (note 1) 10; last days of monarchy, 14, 15; old alliance with Austria through marriage to Marie-Antoinette, 52; Napoleon as 'successor of', 110.

Louis XVIII, formerly Comte de Provence (*see* Provence), King of France 1814-1824, 13, 133, 153 (note 4), 196; decorates M., 197, 222.

Louis-Philippe, son of Philippe Égalité, King of France, 1830-48; succeeded after three days' revolution known as '*Les Trois Glorieuses*', his reign also known as 'July Monarchy', 217; General Béliard, emissary from, snubbed by M. at Vienna, 218; M.'s attitude to hostile, 218, 219; 'unorthodox Bourbon' accused by M. as patron of world-revolution, 225; finally threatened by M. with opposition, 225, 226; claims of Duke of Reichstadt to French throne, 226; bows before Bonapartist menace, 227; decides abandon Italian insurgents, 227 (also note 2), 235, 239, 256; M.'s final estimation of, is better, 261, 262; doesn't want war, 263; dismisses Thiers and replaces him with Guizot, 264, 269; had lost throne through appeasement, 286.

Louise of Mecklenburg, Queen of Prussia (*see also* Prussia), 8, 10, 16, 25.

Low Countries, 10.

Lunéville, results of battle of, 61.

Lutzen, battle of, 99.

**M**

Madrid, 53.

Magenta, battle of (1859), 292.

Mahomet (or Mohammed), Ali, rebel Pasha of Egypt, 263.

Mainz, 8, 10, 12-15, 81, 191.

Maltzahn, Herr von, Prussian ambassador to Vienna, advised government that Austria might use Duke of Reichstadt against Louis-Philippe, 225.

Marat, 13.

Marcolini Palace, 91 *et seq.*, special references, 98, 101, 106, 114.

Maret, Duc de Bassano (*see also* Bassano), 69, 104, 106.

Marie-Anne-Caroline of Savoy, wife of Ferdinand, Emperor of Austria, 251, 287, 288.

Marie-Antoinette, 7, 15, 262.

Marie-Louise, Archduchess, daughter of Francis I, later Empress of the French, 63, 66, 68, 71, 73-79, 80, 83, 85, 90; Napoleon regrets marriage, 102, 113, 110; acquires Duchy of Parma, 140, 220; mother of Duc de Reichstadt, 221, 222, 226, 262.

Maria-Ludovica, Empress, third wife of Francis I, 43, 85.

Maria-Theresa, Empress of Austria until 1780, grandmother of Francis I, 7, 11, 17, 18, 52, 55, 56, 59, 78, 220.

Marmont, Maréchal, 142, 145, 148, 151, 153, 156, 187, 214, 258.

Mars, Champ de, *see* Federation, fête of.

Massema, typographical error, *see* Masséna.

Masséna (wrongly printed 'Massema' p. 40), André, Duc de Rivoli, Prince d'Essling, Maréchal de France, called by Napoleon '*l'enfant cheri de la victoire*', distinguished at Rivoli, Zurich, Siege of Genoa, Wagram, 40.

Masson, 75.

Maurras, Charles, 3.

Mayence, *see* Mainz.

Mayr, J. K., 148, 152, 258.

Mazade, Charles de, 4, 34.

Mazzini, 265.

Mecklenburg, Prince von, 139.

Mecklenburg, Princess Louise von, *see* Louise von Mecklenburg, Queen of Prussia.

Memoirs: Avrillon, Mademoiselle, 81, 181; Barnate, Baron de,

'Souvenirs', 221, 303; Boigne, Madame de, 23; Bouillé, Marquis de, 10; Bourgoing, Baron de, 79, 221, 226; Bray, Comte de, 11, 14; Edling, Princess, 75; Fitzthum-Eckstaedt, Graf, 46; Falloux,Comte de, *Mem. d'un Royaliste*, 173; Gabriac (letters to Lamartine), 280, 282, 283, 288, 289; Garde, de la, 23; Guizot, 178; Jäger, Dr., 148, 150, 155, 176, 178, 215, 216, 234, 236, 241, 242, 252, 281, 288; Mélanie, *Journal de la Princesse*, 38, 236, 237, 244, 262, 267; Metternich, Prince Clement von, *Mémoires et documents*, 13, 25, 26, 29, 72, 73, 74, 84, 101, 104, 135, 138, 185; Metternich, Pauline von, 238, 301; Montet, baronne de, 132, 133, 158, 168, 231, 233; Nesselrode, 22, 25, 82, 168; Pasquier, 132; Ragusa, Duke of, 148; Remusat, Madame de, 38; Talleyrand, 27, 154; Thurheim, Countess Lulu, 124, 134; Sainte-Aulaire, 'Souvenirs', 231.

Mendelssohn-Bartholdy, M.'s *Orient politik*, 200.

Mercy d'Argenteau, 66.

Metternich, Princess Antoinette, *née* von Leykam, becomes Chancellor's second wife, 171; dies in childbirth, 172 (mother of Prince Richard), 233, 235.

Metternich, Countess, later Princess Eléonore, *née* von Kaunitz, Chancellor's first wife, had several children, most of whom died of consumption, 17-20, 23, 27, 62, 72, 73, 76, 81, 82, 123, 167, 168; dies, 169, 170, 236.

Metternich, Count Franz-Georg von Winneburg zu Beilstein, the Chancellor's father, 10, 11, 15, 16, 18.

Metternich, Countess Beatrice von, *née* von Kagenegg, wife of above, the Chancellor's mother, 11, 12, 18.

Metternich, Princess Mélanie, *née* von Zichy-Ferraris, Chancellor's third wife, had five children of whom only two survived, wrote diary, 38, 173, 216, 233; snobbery of, 234, 237, 245; character of, 235; highly satisfactory marriage, 236;

receives 'all Vienna', 238; 'arrogant', 241; M. kept no political secrets from, 242; and Balzac, 244; uncompromisingly reactionary, 245; fears for husband's health, 267, 269; and Liszt, 272, 275, 277, 278, 279, 281, 288, 290, 297, 301; dies, 305.

Metternich, Princess Pauline, granddaughter of Chancellor (later famous at Court of Napoleon III), 114, 149, 155, 172, 238, 240, 281, 304.

Metternich, Prince Richard, assembled and published his father's Memoirs, son of second wife, husband of Princess Pauline, later shone as Austria's Ambassador at Court of Napoleon III, 3, 172.

Metternich, Prince Victor, son of Metternich by first wife, 168; dies in 1829 of consumption, 169, 188, 201.

Metternich System, 16, 108, 174 *et seq.*; Chancellor's credo, 178; threatened collapse of, 200, 300.

Metternich, village of, 15.

Metternichians, impervious to new ideas, 245.

Mexican independence, 199.

Meyendorff, Baron Peter von, Russian diplomatist, 143, 154, 155, 158, 159, 297, 298.

Mikhailowitch, Grand-duke Nicholas, Russian historian, 2.

Mockern, battle of, 'flower of German manhood perished', 99.

Moden, Ernst, book about Congress of Aix-la-Chapelle, 191; *Orient politik*, 249.

*Mondes, Revue des Deux*, 35, 81, 305.

Montaigne, 149.

Montez, Lola, favourite of King Ludwig of Bavaria, popular uprising against ministers sponsored by, 275.

Montherlant, 182.

Montmartre, 97, 114.

Moreau, Alexander's candidate for Commander-in-Chief, 109.

Moscow, retreat from, 88, 91, 99.

Mosloy, Count Otto de (often quoted as 'Otto'), French ambassador to Vienna, 78, 87, 88, 89,

92, 93, 94; superseded by Narbonne, 95, 97, 99, 251.

Münchengraetz, Treaty of, Francis I (Tsar and King of Prussia), gave *coup-de-grâce* to *Carbonari*, 228, 259.

Munich, Narbonne appointed ambassador to, 75.

Munster, 86.

Murat, Joachim, brother-in-law of Napoleon, Maréchal de France, later King of Naples 1808-1815, 36; deposed, although treaty of Naples had guaranteed his rights, 131, 132.

Murat, Princess Caroline, Napoleon's ambitious sister, wife of above, later Queen of Naples, 35-38, 81; deposed by order of Congress of Vienna, 131, 132, 161, 162, 167.

**N**

Naples, Kingdom of, Joachim Murat deposed by Congress of Vienna, 131; Treaty of (Jan. 11th, 1814), 132; presents from King to Metternich, 152; affairs of, discussed at Troppau, 191; new King's servile attitude to Coalition, 193; Wellington advises punitive expedition against rebels of, 195; important centre of *Carbonrrism*, 206, 239; revolution successful at, 275.

Napoleon Bonaparte, Emperor of the French, 1, 2, 13, 20, 22, 25, 27, 29, 30, 31, 32, 37, 42, 44-46, 59, 61, 62-80, 82-87; Russian retreat, 88; warned by M. against a second campaign, 89; character of, 91; deluded, 92, 94; M. urges self-preservation, 93; M. urges for go dream of world-domination, 96; personal ascendancy of, over M., 97; adamant, 101; M. attempts convert him, 102, 103, 104; 'Your Majesty is lost', 105; Stein and M'.s different methods with, 106; 'raving like Lear', before abdication, 107, 109, 110; M. tries save Napoleonic dynasty, 111, 113; warned by Caulaincourt, 114;

M.'s memories of, (note 1) 114; escapes from Elba, 135, 137, 138; Napoleonic Empire destroyed, 140; said of M., 'nothing but a big liar', 154; abrupt, peremptory, 155, 156, 158, 168, 177; his methods of government influenced M., 180; considered liberty of Press insuperable danger, 181, 182, 185, 188, 220; M. no reason to hate Napoleon's son since had never hated the father, 222; secret service, 257, 298.

Napoleon II, *see* Duc de Reichstadt; M. claims extreme tact in not pushing claims of, 225.

Napoleon III (Louis-Napoleon), 6, 172, 228, 302, 303, 306.

Napoleonic restoration, M. hostile to and declared Bonapartes finally excluded from all thrones, 224.

Nationalism, M.'s attitude to, 57; M. failed to understand, and was hostile to, 186; wars of liberation left M. cold, 189, 190; frenzy of, 265.

Narbonne, Comte de, 75, 92, 95, 96, 100, 106, 107.

Nations, the, component parts of Austrian Empire, general revolt of, 271.

Navarin Bay, battle of, 171; Egyptian and Ottoman fleets destroyed at, 200.

Neipperg, second husband of Marie-Louise, 221, 222.

Nemours, Duc de, Louis-Philippe's second son, 239, 262.

Nesselrode, Count, Russian Chancellor, 22, 25, 75, 82, 153, 156, 158, 165, 168, 191, 297, 298.

Neufchatel, Duc de, *see* Berthier, sent to fetch Archduchess Marie-Louise, 79.

Neva, 69.

Nicholas, Grand-duke, brother of Alexander, succeeded him as Nicholas I, 162; accession of, 'a bellicose despot', 198; Tsar and son visit Princess Mélanie, 239, 242, (note 1) 260; gives M. generous allowance, 293, 298.

Nicholas II, son of Alexander III, Tsar in 1894, murdered by Bolsheviks (1918), 185.

# Index

Niebelungengau, 49.
Niemen, 95.
Nobles, nobility, *see* Aristocracy.
Notre Dame de Paris, 79, 98; Jacobins install 'goddess of reason', 177.
Novarra, Marshal Radetski, triumphs over Italians at, 296; (Novara typographical error, 296).

## O

Oesterreich, *see* Ostmark.
Oettingen-Spielberg, H.S.H. Princess von, 6.
Oettingen-Spielberg, Princes von, later Kaunitz, mother of Princess Éleonore Metternich, 18.
Olmutz, Congress of, 298.
Oncken, W., (note 1) 86.
*Ordonnances Royales*, Polignac's fatal reactionary measures which brought about fall of elder branch of Bourbons (1830), 215.
Orléans, House of, 262, *see also* Louis-Philippe.
Orléans, Duc de, Louis-Philippe's eldest son, 239, 261 (also note 1), 262.
Ostmark, origin of name 'Oesterreich' for Austria, 49.
Otto, *see* de Mosloy, Count Otto de.
Otrante, Duc de, *see also* Fouché, (note 1) 132.
Owen, Robert, 182.

## P

Palacky, *see also* Czech renaissance, 48, 265.
Pallfy, 17, 116.
Palmerston, 189, 293.
Pan-Germans, 31, 136 (*see also* Germans).
Papal States, discontent in, prisons full, 212, 219, 270; Sebastiani objects to Austria sending troops into, 220.
Paris, 14, 29, 34, 45, 71, 72, 74; Marie-Louise looking forward to, 78, 80; M. fêted at, 82; propaganda by M. in, 110; Coalition negotiated at, 128, 164, 169, 170; welcomes M. under Restoration, 197; revolutionary centre of *Carbonarism*, 213; important letter describing July revolution, 215; Louis-Philippe, 217; visitors from, *non grata* in Austria after July revolution, 217, 227, 235; under July monarchy, 260; reactionary Austria unpopular in, 262; Polish committee of, threaten to assassinate M., 272.
Paris, Treaty of (known also as first and second 'Peace of Paris' 1814-1815), 129, 130, 140, 184.
Parisian scene, 70; society, 81, 82; opinion, 112.
Parma, Duchy of, Duke of Reichstadt deprived of, 222; given to Marie-Louise, 140.
Pascal, 149.
Patriarchal spirit in Austria, 57, 175, 266; type of authority changed under Franz-Josef, 296.
Pauline, Princess, *see* Metternich.
Peasants, position of, in Austria, 58; 'the people', 182.
Pellico, Silvio, 212, 267.
Périgord, Countess Edmond de, *née* Courlande, sister of Duchesse de Sagan, Talleyrand's confidante and ex-mistress, 121, 133.
Périgord, old district of France now absorbed into Dordogne and part of Lot-et-Garonne, birthplace of Talleyrand, 133.
Persia, 239; Shah of, considers M.'the guarantor of world affairs', 249.
Petersburg, Saint, 4, 45, 69, 70, 87, 88, 109, 166; Wellington's Protocol, signed in 1826, 200.
Peuschwitz, armistice arranged at, 101.
Peyronnet's Press Laws, *see* 'Ordonnances Royales'.
Pichler, C., (note 2) 95.
Picquot, Prussian chargé d'affaires at Vienna, 72.
Piedmont, 207, 257; became allied with France, Austria's fatal war with, saddened Chancellor's last days, 305; 'the knell tolling on Italian battlefields', 306.

Pitt, 17; Castlereagh shared his suspicion of Russia, 130.

Pius VII (Pope) (1800-23), signed Concordat, crowned Napoleon at Notre Dame, 83, 84, 145; issued Bull *'Ecclesiam'* against *Carbonari*, September 13th, 1821, 212.

Pius IX, Pope (1846-78), 'progressive' Pope, sneered at by M., 270; M. considers 'liberal' Pope a contradiction in terms, 271; was obliged dismiss all his ecclesiastical Ministers and declare a general amnesty, 275.

Plass, monastic domain acquired by M., 152; now known as Plazy (and in Czechoslovakia), M. is buried there, 306.

Pleyell, Madame, Berlioz's former faithless fiancée, 243.

Poland, destiny of, (note 1) 78; partitions and Russian campaign, 87, 134-7; Alexander alleges devotion to liberal institutions before Polish Diet, 194; secret societies in, 209; revolutionary upheavals ignored by Austria, 218; Reichstadt suggested as King of, 224; Kolowrat's sympathy with, 254, 270, 272.

Police, reports on Congress of Vienna, 125, 127; reports on Countess Julie Zichy, 127; intervened in 1833 when French coding cypher stolen, 258; H.Q. at Vienna, 203; crush *Carbonarism*, 212; measures in Austria after July revolution, 217; Prefect of Lyons and refugees, 227; optimistic on eve of Vienna revolution, 279; 'Sedlnitzki and his police force ought to be hung for not warning us', 284; general inefficiency of, during revolution, 284.

Polignac, 196, 202.

Pope, the: there were five tenants of the Holy See during the period of M.'s life-time covered by this book: Pius VII (1800-23), Leo XII (1823-29), Pius VIII (1829-30), Gregory XVI (1831-46), Pius IX, Mastäi Ferreti (1846-78). For references, 83, 84, 145 and 212 *see*

Pius VII; for ref. 194, *see* Leo XII; 249 (presumably Gregory XVI); 270 refers to Pius IX, as also 275.

Posterity, M.'s appeal to, 1; his standing with, 5, 307.

Potsdam, Treaty of (known also as 'Grand Alliance') between Russia and Prussia, Austria immediately became a third party, 26.

Power, balance of, 2, 25; 'stability of Europe', 57; M. nicknamed 'comte de la balance', 86; effect on, of Habsburg-Napoleonic marriage, 86, 88; 'general stabilisation', 96, 100, 105; threatened by Alexander, 134; Prussia and, 136; 'European equilibrium', 140; situation after fall of Napoleon, 178; under French Restoration, 196; M. insists on general not partial federation, 201; M.'s mission 'to keep peace in Europe', 218; M. chiefly concerned with, 224.

Pozzo di Borgo, 103, 227.

Pragmatic Sanctions (1713), 53.

Prague, Napoleon and Coalition's plenipotentiaries at, 105, 106, 107 (note 2), 153.

Press censorship, *see* Censorship.

*Privilegium majus*, 51.

Progress, 'stupid 19th C. believed in', 2; M. considered himself progressive thinker, 249; 'eternal pursuit of in human societies', 187; 'one form of p.', 307.

Prokesch-Osten, 187, 189, 223, 226, 247, 248.

Prophecies, M.'s, (note 2) 34.

Protestantism, sternly suppressed by Jesuits, 55.

Proudhon, 182, 301.

Proust, Marcel, 15.

Provence, Comte de, brother of Louis XVI, King of France as Louis XVIII (1814-24), succeeded by his brother Charles X, 8, 13, 114.

Prussia, 8, 14, 24-26, 28 (note 1), 29; rigid ideology, 41, 56, 60, 67, 72, 76, 86; population rose, 92; Scharnhorst, Gneisenau, Stein, 96; claims against Napoleon, 97; M. and, 99; uprising in Eastern, 99; M.'s negotiation with, 100, 102,

W

106, 130, 131, 133, 136, 137; gets
Rhenish territories from Austria,
141; King of, and M., 156, 249;
Empress Augusta of, 163; German
nationalism and, 189; urge to
expansion, 189; M. ruthless opponent of aggressive Prussianism,
190; Crown Prince of, 239.
Prussians ill disposed to M. at
Congress of Vienna, 125.
*Publiciste, le,* and M., 20.
Puckler Muskau, Prince (famous
*inter alia* as patron of Beethoven),
145.

## Q

Quadruple Alliance, 'a European
Directoire', 184; 'this small group
who held monopoly of power in
Europe', 90, 91.
Quai d'Orsay (French F.O.), archives
of, (note 1) 94; (note 2) 196, 202,
259.
Quennell, Peter, edited *The Private
Letters of Princess Lieven to
Prince Metternich,* (note 2) 161.

## R

Races, comprising Austrian Empire,
48, 49, 53, 54, 57; variety of, 186.
Radetzky, General, 99; victor at
Novara, 296, 305.
Rastadt, Congress at, 10, 11, 19, 20,
21, 103.
Ratisbonne, 46.
Ravelsberg, Strobl von, reports that
Princess Eléonore was unfaithful,
168; (bibliography), 309.
Rayneval, French ambassador to
Vienna, 201, 202.
Razoumovski, 86, 243.
Récamier, M. found her 'beautiful
but dull', 191.
Reform, Joseph II, 'his reforming
zeal', 56; 'all M.'s plans lay buried
in the drawers of the Emperor's
desk', 266, 267.
Reformation, the, in early days of,
only about 20% Austrian nobility
and bourgeoisie had remained
Catholic, 55.

Reichenbach, Russian, Prussian and
Austrian delegates meet at, 101,
106.
Reichstadt, Duc de (l'Aiglon), son of
Napoleon and Marie-Louise, ref.
E. Wertheimer's *Der Herzog von
Reichstadt,* (note 1) 68, 220, 221,
222; presence Napoleon's son on
Austrian soil threatens international
complications, 223; R. considers
M. sole obstacle to throne of
France, 224; dies and is buried in
Capuchin Crypt, 226, 227.
Reinohl, 278, 289.
Rémusat, Madame de, 36, 38 (*see
also* 'Memoirs').
Rennweg, M.'s villa at, 123, 237,
269, 307.
Restoration of Bourbons, 195, 196;
F. government well-intentioned
but weak, 197, 213 (note 1), 215;
M. accused of accepting bribes in
connection with, 153.
Retz, Cardinal de, 52.
Revolution (and minor revolutions),
1, 2; revolutionary France, 11, 15,
16; 'the very words of', 1793, 33;
Francis fought, 59, 192; Castlereagh savage enemy of, 129; M.
discusses with Restoration monarchy, 196; Confalonieri, 204;
revolutionary aspirations in Germany, 208; world-wide, 210 (note
2), 220; in Italy, quickly 'blown
away', 227; Gentz and, 247;
'1848', 273; brewing in Austria,
277; Viennese at its height, 283-4;
'a monstrous illusion', 300.
Rhenish, 13, 62; territory, 136;
Prussia and Bavaria get R. territories from Austria as result
Congress of Vienna, 141; R.
country still loyal to Francis in
1818, 191.
Rhine, 16, 94, 100, 110; 'incalculable
consequences of installing Prussia
on', 141, 146; political evolution of
populations beyond, 185; 'frontier
river' now become Prussian, 191.
Rhine, Confederation of, 31, 96, 107,
137, 140.
Richelieu, Cardinal, 154, 252.
Richelieu, Duc de, 191, 196; recriminations of, about Duke of
Reichstadt, 223.

Risorgimento, 'Italia reggenerata', 207.
Roberjot, 103.
Robert, A. *L'idée nationale autrichienne*, (note 2) 95.
Robespierre, 33, 177.
Roman Empire, *see* 'Holy'.
Romanoffs, 70, 108, 162.
Romantic movement, significance of, 190, 229.
Rome, *see* 'Vatican' especially, 176; Princess Lieven in, 166; King of, 221.
Rossini, 150.
Rothschilds, the, 153, 210, 215, 227, 240, 241, 247, 267; Anselm brings bad news, 277; Solomon sends M. 1,000 ducats for his escape from Vienna, 290.
Roumainzoff, 44, 70, 147.
Rousseau, 13.
Russia, 24, 40, 41, 44, 49, 65, 100; R. marriage project, 67 *et seq.*; M. foresees collapse of, as result Napoleon's invasion, 87; R.morale during Napoleonic campaign, 88; objects prolongation armistice, 106; M. fears hegemony of, in Central Europe, 108; Russians suspicious of M., 113, 120; opposed by Triple Alliance, 131; 'dynamic pressure of young Moscovy', 133; presents from Tsars to M., 152-3; R. Cabinet gives financial aid to M., 153; led by Austria at Laibach, 195; 'will never dare oppose England', 198; allied with England by Wellington's Protocol (1826), 200; secret societies in, 209; M. accuses of instigating secret societies at Turin, 212; officers of Imperial Guard incite troops to revolt, 213.
Russian, emigré, author's position as, 8; R. *cabala* directed against Napoleon, M.'s tact with, 106, 107; R. generals, 93; Napoleon refused believe Russo-English *entente* possible, 97; army badly organised, 99.

**S**

Sadowa, 298.
Sagan, Duchesse de, Wilhelmine de

Biran de Courlande, 115, 120, 121 (note 2), 126; spiteful criticism of M. by, 127, 159, 160, 162, 167, 237, 303, 304.
Saint Aignan, 110.
Saint Aulaire, 154; his 'Talleyrand', (note 3) 132, 231, 232, 233; as Louis-Philippe's representative is insulted by Princess Mélanie, 235, 237, 239, 240; notes deferential treatment of M. by Archdukes, 248, 252, 258, 259, 261, 263.
Saint Helena, 114.
Saint Julien, Comte de, 69, 87.
Saint Petersburg, *see* Petersburg.
Saint Pierre, Abbé, 174, 179.
Saint Simon, 182, 183, 243.
Salm Prince, 11.
Salvotti, Judge Antonio, 204, 207.
Salzburg, Archbishops of, initiated first German Opera House, 55, 140, 141.
*Sans-culottes* invade Mainz, 15, 278.
Santerre, Commander Garde Nationale 1793, M.'s tutor, Simon, helped him prepare attack on Tuileries, 13.
Sardinia, King of, servile attitude to M., 193; proclaims constitution, 275.
Savary, General, 70.
Savoy, Prince Eugène of, 62; *see also under* Charles Albert and Charles Felix, 211.
Saxony, attitude of King Friedrich Augustus's delegate to Congress of Vienna, 129.
Saxony, and Congress of Vienna, issues raised by Talleyrand, 131, 136; a diminished buffer state between Russia and Austria, 137.
Scharnhorst, General von, 96.
Schönbrunn, Palace of, 56.
Schönbrunn, Peace of, *see* Liechtenstein, Prince John.
Schwartzenberg, Prince von, Ambassador at Saint Petersburg, 45; later at Paris, 69, 70, 71, 73-77, 79, 80; family, 84, 85, 100, 105; becomes Coalition's Commander-in-Chief, 109, 111, 138, 148, 222; family, 231, 296, 297, 298.
Science, M. and, 19, 148 (note 1).
Sealsfeld, 1, 144, 151, 193, 231, 268, 275.

Sébastiani, hostile to M., 219, 227, 259.

Secret Societies, 203 *et seq.*, histories of, (note 1) 206; in Germany, Russia, Poland, 209.

Seven Years, war of, 24.

Sheridan, 18.

Sicily, Murat's rights over, 132; Sicilies, Kingdom of Two; a centre of *Carbonarism*, 207; proclaims Constitution despite Austria, Russia, Prussia, 275.

Silesia, battlefields of, 100; frontier of, 107.

Simon, John Frederick, M.'s Protestant-Rousseauist tutor, later disciple of Marat and active revolutionary; compiled a dictionary, 13, 243.

Six, Committee of, known as the Big Six, 128.

Social order, M. 'a rock of', 306.

Socialism, then emerging, M. realised significance of, 182.

Sophia, Archduchess, 253, 278, 279, 287; enthusiastically welcomed by Vienna mob, 289, 297.

Sorel, Albert, French historian, 2, 4, 103, 104, 107, 110, 151.

Spain, Napoleon's usurpation, 33; Francis, son of an Infanta of, 60; Janot sent to, 82, 128; Chateaubriand at Congress of Verona was manœuvring French armed intervention in, 192, 222.

Spy system, M.'s elaborate, throughout Europe, 258.

Srbik, Heinrich, Ritter von, author monumental biography of M., 3, 5, 6, 41, 149, 177, 189, 255.

Staatskonferenz consisting: Metternich, Kolowrat, Archduke Francis Charles, under Archduke Louis, 255, 256, 284.

Stackelberg; Russian ambassador at Austrian Court, (note 1) 147.

Stadion, 30 (note 1), 31, 33, 34, 36, 39, 44, 45; resignation after Wagram, 47, 60, 62, 63; conspires against Metternich, 85, 100, 107, 113, 126; says, 'Austria no longer a German Power', 141.

Staël, Madame de, M.'s disapproval of, 25.

Stein, Baron von, German reformer-patriot, 29 (note 1), 88, 96, 98, 99; indignant, 106; his methods compared with Metternich's, 106, 135; disappointed, 137; prophesies Austria will become progressively Italianate, 141, 154.

Stein, Freiherr von, Book about Vienna Congress, 126.

Stendhal, 1, 154.

Stern, *Geschichte Europas*, 310.

Stewart, Lord Charles William (Vane), half-brother of Castlereagh whom he succeeded as 3rd Marquess of Londonderry; at one time Ambassador to Vienna; represented England at Congresses of Troppau, Laibach and Verona, 146.

Strachey, Lytton, Portrait of Princess Lieven in Miniatures, 162.

Strasbourg, capital of Alsace, 12, 194.

Strauss, Johann, 229, 231, 248.

Students, M.'s fellow, 13; in Germany (*Burschenschaften*), 208; and Viennese revolution, 280, 281; 'hysterical undergraduates', 287; 289; obtained permission to carry arms, 286.

Sweden, destiny of, 78 (note 1), 100; Crown Prince approached by M., 111.

Swiss neutrality violated, 109.

Swiss Federation and Catholic Sonderbund, 270.

Switzerland, 110; leading secret society known as Migraim, 209, 270.

Syria, 159.

System, *see* Metternich System.


**T**

Taafe, 290.

Talleyrand, Prince de, formerly Bishop of Autun, 11, 13, 31, 32, 36, 38; resignation as Foreign Secretary, 39, 44; at Congress of Vienna, 121, 128-132; 'out and out opportunist', 133, 135, 139, 153, 154; influence on M., 158, 162, 187, 222, 269.

Tarnopol returned by Russia to Austria (1809), 135.

Teplitz, 216; Austria-Russia-Prussia

*bloc* replaces old Committee of Five, 259.

Teutomania, Pan-German activities, 3, 136, 190, 208, 247, 301.

Thiers, Prime Minister, 261; embarks on policy of aggression for France, 262-3; dismissed, succeeded by Guizot, 264.

Three Emperors, League of, *see* Holy Alliance.

Thugut, 'war baron', 60, 157.

Thurheim, Countess Lulu, 124, 144, 145, 243.

Thurn-und-Taxis, Princess, sister of Queen Louise of Prussia, 121, 191.

Thurn-und-Taxis, Prince, 171.

Tibal, André, book on 'Austrian character', 55 (note 1).

Tilsit, Peace of, 34.

Traz, Robert de, 179.

Treilhard, *conventionnel*, 10, 11, 20, 103.

Treitschke, 158, 159, 208, 246.

Triple Alliance, England, France and Austria against Russia and Prussia, Jan. 3rd, 1815, 131; about to be revived, 278.

Trollope, Mrs, 144, 149, 155, 158, 177, 231, 232, 233, 236.

Troppau (erroneously spelt Troppeau, p. 183), letter from M. to Alexander from, 183.

Troppau (in Silesia), Congress of, in 1820, same group as at Aix; Naples discussed, 191, 192; *see also* Bignon's work, 192 (note 1); sealed Alexander's political conversion, 194.

Troyes, 111.

Tsar, *see* Alexander; *see* Nicholas.

Tschuppik, historian, 21.

Tuileries, under Louis XVI and Revolution, 13, 15; under Napoleon, 35, 41, 45, 135; Marie-Louise at, 78, 79.

Turcoing, battle of, 60.

Turkey, Turks in 1529; destiny of, 78, 88; Turkish hegemony over Greece established by Wellington's Protocol; T. defeated, battle of Navarin Bay, 200.

Tyrol, plot concerning, 95, 100, 115.

## U

Uniformity, attempt by Joseph II to enforce, 56.

Usedom, von, 273.

Ussel, d', reasons why Napoleon could not afford lay down his arms, 98, 100.

Utrecht, Treaty of, 52.

## V

Varennes, Louis XVI, flying from Versailles to join General Marquis de Bouillé at Montmédy, was recognised at Varennes, arrested and taken back to Paris; note on page 10 should read 'to' not 'from' Varennes; 'the General and his son', not 'and his own father'.

Vatican, 83, 84; claims lost territories at Congress of Vienna, 126; territories seized from, 132; 'Papal Nuncio', 146; M.'s attitude to, 176; M.'s correspondence with Cardinal Consalvi, (note 1) 194, 242.

Verona, Congress of, 164; Italian princelings added to original group of Aix; Chateaubriand represented France, 192.

Versailles, 14, 55.

Victoria, Queen of England, 293, 294.

Vienna, 18, 23, 24, 41, 42, 43, 45, 49, 51, 52, 53, 55, 61-63; archives of Quai d'Orsay at, 65; Viennese Cabinet, 65; Chancellery, 68; diplomatic relations with Saint Petersburg resumed, 69, 71; Cabinet checkmated by Napoleon, 77, 80, 82; M. goes home to, 83; policy of Cabinet towards Napoleon in 1811, 86; hears of Napoleon's defeat in Russia, 88; anxiety about next move, 89, 94, 102, 109; M.'s triumphal return to, 116, 117; and Restoration in France, 196; best professors of, instructed Eaglet, 222; 'Capua of the Mind', 229 *et seq.*; 'Old Vienna', 230, 244; appalled by news of M.'s illness, 248; Protocols of, did not allow Chancellor automatic rank at Court, 248;

Archbishop of, takes Francis to task about Ferdinand, 251; the Great Revolution, 279 *et seq.*; Prussian Minister reports revolution, 282; revolution at its climax, 283-4; M. calls it 'a county town of lower Austria', 285; Metternichs back in, 296, 304.

Vienna Congress of: 118 *et seq.*; M. prime mover, 119; spirit of careless gaiety, 120; report of, by Secret Police, 121, 125, 127; festivities of, 122-124; grievances and hostility to M. on all sides, 124-125, 126; procedure of, compared with our own time, 127, 146, 163, 171, 188; followed by 'Congressional era', 190, 192, 193.

Vienna Secret Archives, 3, 4, 6, 30, 31, 33, 36, 37, 39, 41, 44, 45, 69, 71; Viennese archives reticent, 75, 75-78, 80, 82, 83, 145 (note 1), 204, 213, 214, 217, 218; Report of Cabinet deliberations concerning insurrection in Italy, 219, 220, 227, 228, 249, 254, 258.

Viennese, society turned against M., 85; public critical of Congress extravagance, 127; composition of, 231-3; bankers, 231.

Vienna, Treaty of, 84, 85.

Villèle, 197.

Vincennes, Château de, Duc d'Enghien shot there in 1804, by order of Napoleon, hence the reference, 45.

Vincent, official of Austrian Embassy at Paris, 29.

Vistula, 87, 94.

Vitrolles, delegate of French royalists to Chatillon, 112.

Vogt, Nicholas, official historian German Empire, M. attended his lectures, 13.

Voltaire, 149, 269.

**W**

Wagram, battle of, 46, 61, 63, 130.

Wales, Prince of, *see* George IV.

Wallachia, Hospodar of, 146, 25  '6

Wallis, Austrian Minister of Finance opposes M., 84, 85, 126.

Warsaw, Duchy of, Napoleon refuses relinquish, 97, 100, 107, 134.

Waterloo, 138.

Webster, C. K., 128; 'Foreign policy of Castlereagh', 195.

Weill, author of *Les dessous du Congress de Vienne*, 75, 111, 125, 260.

Weimar, pamphleteers, 146.

Weishaupt's illuminist doctrines, 209.

Wellesley, Sir H., English ambassador at Vienna (1823), 199.

Wellington, Duke of, 137, 195; signed Protocol at St Petersburg (1826), 200.

Wertheimer, E., 68, 75, 83.

Wessenberg, sent to England to negotiate, 98, 113.

Westphalia, 8, 19, 36.

Wiener-Neustadt, revolt of 'hereditary countries' crushed at, 54.

William I of Prussia, 8, 163.

William II of Prussia, 108.

Windischgraetz, 126, 286, 288, 296.

Winneburg, 10; Winneburg zu Beilstein, 11.

Wrbna Count, Lord High Chamberlain to Emperor Francis, 126.

**Y**

Yorck, General, 99.

**Z**

Zichy, Count, 139; member of anti-Metternich faction, 85.

Zichy, Countess Charles, *née* Julie Festetics, 120, 121, 160.

Zichy-Ferraris, Mélanie, Chancellor's third wife, *see* M.

Zichy-Ferraris, Countess Molly von, mother of above, 233.

Zollverein, 265, 267, 268.

Zwei-Brücke, Prince Maximilian von, later first King of Bavaria, 12; *see* Bavaria, King of.